Regulation of Infrastructure Markets

Davide Maresca

Regulation of Infrastructure Markets

Legal Cases and Materials on Seaports, Railways and Airports

Springer

Davide Maresca
Dottore di ricerca, Università degli Studi di Genova
Genova
Italy

ISBN 978-3-642-33819-9 ISBN 978-3-642-33820-5 (eBook)
DOI 10.1007/978-3-642-33820-5
Springer Heidelberg New York Dordrecht London

Library of Congress Control Number: 2012949813

Printed on acid-free paper

Springer is part of Springer Science+Business Media (www.springer.com)

To Simona

Preface

The writing and publication of a book is often a composition of different factors that give its author the motivation to start a work that, in its early stages, has an uncertain final form. In my case, I had three strong motivations.

The first motivation for this book derived from my research method. During my still short experience as a lecturer and researcher, I have always concentrated my efforts on the interpretation of the living law in order to understand the real implications of the law in the life of the people it affects. In fact, I think that before entering into the study of academic doctrines, it is necessary to understand the "reality of law". By this I mean that although scholars can discuss theories and academic contrasts as long as they like, in the end, the most import goal of a researcher should always be a "product" directly applicable to concrete situations.

For this reason, during my studies, I have always appreciated every source that could provide me with concrete examples of the application of the law, as close to reality as possible, and preferably through the direct reading of cases. One such source is the fantastic casebook of Berman, Goebel, Davey, and Fox, *Cases and Materials on European Union Law* (2011), where it is possible to read and gain a deeper understanding of every single relevant case concerning European Union law. Only through the direct reading of the judgments it is possible to understand the true grounds for judicial decisions. Judicial opinions offer the most reliable way to grasp a law's effects as applied to real life, and consequently, provide the most reliable indicia for determining best behaviors according to the law. In fact, the underlying goal of legal certainty is tightly bound to the comprehension of judicial decisions, which create the real behavioral parameters for people and companies.

The second motivation is set in my desire to carry out a new academic challenge. I have focused my years of research activity on the regulation of infrastructures from two distinct, yet related, perspectives: access to relevant markets and the law of competition. Yet despite the ample scholarship on infrastructure regulation, I never found a complete reference of cases related to transport infrastructures. During my studies, I reflected on how much I would have appreciated a casebook through which I could have directly compared scholars' theories to judicial decisions. I soon realized how much simpler my research would be had I direct access to the most important cases on this issue. Moreover, such a book has the potential to both support researchers' and professors' activities and, in my opinion, stimulate academic discussion on the laws as they are actually applied by the most important courts, rather confining such discussion to topics emerging from academic conferences or workshops.

The third reason for writing this book is set in my lectureship purpose. I often prepare lectures for graduate and post-graduate programs on European Transport Law. I have always preferred an empirical approach to teaching effected through the explanation of cases and the direct study of the opinions of courts. The point is that I could never suggest to my students a text to use as a reference of cases. This is one of the most important reasons leading me to put together this compendium of all the most important cases I discussed with students and the most important materials on which I based my research. The result should be a casebook where scholars and students can appreciate the different approaches to the regulation of different infrastructure markets: seaports, railways, and airports.

The research method of this book is based on the direct reading of cases. However, before entering into the discussion on the single facilities, I thought it was necessary to introduce the most important applicable rules of European Union law. Indeed, it is now clear that the European model of regulation has gone beyond its initial purposes and is already competent to regulate the situations internally located within a member State, as the concrete effects of the public or private restraint of competition can potentially interest people and companies from other member States.

Consequently, the boundaries of the application of European Union law have expanded beyond traditional geographical borders. In order to understand whether a concrete situation falls within the scope of European Union law, it is necessary to find a specific norm emanating from the treaties that set the field of application for European rules. It is, therefore, possible to state that some matters are entirely covered by European Union law even if the actual effects of measures and behaviors are internally located within a particular member State. If only one other European subject can have a potential interest in that situation, it will be regulated by European Union law.

In the infrastructures market, the potential interest of operators from different member States is always present thanks to the globalized dimension of transport services companies. Indeed, maritime services and air services have become liberalized and every single company from Europe has the right to access every facility under the same conditions as domestic operators. This framework has enjoyed many years of application and is leading to the liberalization of transport infrastructures, even if national practices continue to create some breaches of European Union law. The case of railways is a little different. There, the liberalization of services is not yet a concrete reality, although there are some tendencies to let European carriers enter into national markets. For this reason, the discussion of cases on regulation in the railway sector in this book takes into consideration the experience of the United States of America, where we can see cases of rail de-regulation over the past two hundred years. Importantly, the same principles applied by the Supreme Court were introduced in the rail liberalization directives and are now being applied by the European Court of Justice and by the European Commission.

The result is that European Union law created a common legal framework that defines a real uniform law applicable to the regulation of transport infrastructures. The aim of this book is to provide the main principles and reasoning that are behind this uniform law.

As with any project that takes a lot of time, this book benefited from the important help of many people that I thank but I cannot list all of them. First of all, I should thank my father, for the education and inspiration of my research activity, and Professor Sergio Carbone who trained me in the study of this difficult field. I also thank Justin Kesselman who gave me detailed, page by page, comments and an important concrete help. Last but not least, I thank Simona, who helped me in the research and always supported me, and my mother, who continuously encouraged me.

Davide Maresca

Table of Contents

Table of Cases

Chapter 1 European Union Law: Main Principles and the Regulation of Public Infrastructures

Chapter 2 The infrastructures management as a Service of General Interest

Chapter 3 Seaports

Chapter 4 Railways

Chapter 5 Airports

Chapter 1 European Union Law: Main Principles and the Regulation of Public Infrastructures

1.1 European Union Law's Fundamental Principles and Scientific Method

There are three main sources of European Union law: primary law, secondary law, and soft law[1]. Primary law is comprised of the Treaty on European Union, the Treaty on the Functioning of the European Union, and general principles of the European Union[2]. Secondary law is comprised of directives[3] (legislative acts providing States with obligations to be met through instruments supplied by national laws), regulations (legislative acts directly and generally applicable to all Member States and to all European citizens), and decisions (legislative acts directly applicable only to those States or citizens to whom they expressly refer). Soft laws are non-legislative acts (such as Communications, Green Papers, and White Papers) that provide a correct interpretation of the Primary and Secondary laws[4].

Market regulation[5] of public utility services, as well as the standard and emergency public procurement awarding of works and services, fall within the field of European Union law as matters of "competition law" and "internal market law." These three issues (market regulation, standard procurements, and emergency procurements) will be discussed from two points of view. First, they will be discussed

---

1 See De Búrca G. - Weiler J.H.H., *The worlds of European constitutionalism*. Cambridge, 2012 and Twomey P. - O'Keeffe D., *Legal Issues of the Amsterdam Treaty*, Oxford, 1999 p. 185 ff.

2 The most important principle regulating the relationship between the European Union and the member States is the subsidiarity principle: Strozzi G., *Le principe de subsidiarité dans la perspective de l'intégration européenne: une énigme et baucoup d'attentes*, in *Révue trimestrielle de droit européen*, 1994, pp. 373 ff. and Maresca M., *Il riparto delle competenze legislative nell'ordinamento italiano con riguardo alla materia dei trasporti e dei. L'incidenza dei principi fondamentali e degli obblighi internazionali, in Dir. comm. internaz., 2002, p. 273 ff.*

3 See Fuchs M., *From legislators to the end-user: practical difficulties of implementing European directives*. Wiesbaden, 2011.

4 See the complete work of Tesauro G., *Diritto dell'Unione europea*, Padova, 2010.

5 According to Breyer S., *Regulation and its reform*, Cambridge, 1982, the European regulation of markets needs a structural reform towards a more effective balance of powers.

substantively: this means listing and explaining the rules applicable to each sector in order to define the scope of the legislature (in this case of the European Union) in the adoption of applicable bills of law (Secondary law). Second, they will be approached from a procedural perspective: this means describing and analyzing the different procedures that have emerged from the substantive legislation. In other words, the goal is to discern the correct behaviors for a public body in order to ensure both cogency with European legislation and respect for stakeholders' rights.

1.2 European Legal Principles Applicable to Infrastructures Regulation

1.2.1 The Internal Market

Before commencing the procedural examination, it is necessary to take a panoramic view of the different market regulations that, according to European law, will be applied in a standard administrative procedure for market regulation.

The internal market[6] is one of the pillars of the European Union. Completed in 1992, the single market is an area without internal frontiers, wherein persons, goods, services, and capital can move freely in accordance with the Treaty on the Functioning of European Union. The internal market is essential for prosperity, growth, and employment in the EU, contributing to the achievement of its objectives under the Lisbon strategy[7]. As an integrated, open, and competitive area, it promotes mobility, competitiveness, and innovation, interacting in particular with EU policies[8]. To ensure that everyone, whether citizen or business, can make the most of the advantages of the single market, the EU concentrates on dismantling barriers still impeding its operation. It seeks to harmonize legislation in order to improve its response to the challenges of globalization and to adapt to advances such as new technologies.

At its core, this means that every person or company aiming to carry out an economic activity has the right to begin an enterprise under the same conditions as any other person or company residing in any other member state. Consequently, in the roads and highways sector, every interested company has the right to participate in the construction and maintenance of roads without unreasonable national

---

[6] A paraphrase of intermal market principles is clearly explained in Micossi S., *Regulation and Deregulation of industrial products in the Internal Market of the European Union: finding the right balance*, in *The Forum for Us-Ec legal-economic affairs*, The Mentor Group, 20-23 September 1995.

[7] See Kaczorowska A., *European Union law*. Abingdon, 2011.

[8] See the interesting explanation of European legal system of Foster N., *Foster on EU law*, Oxford, 2011

restrictions[9]. A recent decision of the European Court of Justice (case 1) ECJ, 12 July 2012, Case C-176/11, in Rep. 2012, HIT hoteli, igralnice, turizem dd Nova Gorica and HIT LARIX, prirejanje posebnih iger na srečo in turizem dd v Bundesminister für Finanzen) clearly explained the concepts of restriction and proportionality:

(...)

16 Article 56 TFEU requires the abolition of all restrictions on the freedom to provide services, even if those restrictions apply without distinction to national providers of services and to those from other Member States, when they are liable to prohibit, impede or render less advantageous the activities of a service provider established in another Member State where it lawfully provides similar services. Moreover, the freedom to provide services is for the benefit of both providers and recipients of services (see, inter alia, Joined Cases C-403/08 and C-429/08 *Football Association Premier League and Others* [2011] ECR I-0000, paragraph 85 and the case-law cited).

17 More specifically, in the area of advertising for games of chance, the Court has held that national legislation whose effect is to prohibit the promotion in a Member State of gambling organised legally in other Member States constitutes a restriction on the freedom to provide services (see, to this effect, Joined Cases C-447/08 and C-448/08 *Sjöberg and Gerdin* [2010] ECR I-6921, paragraphs 33 and 34).

18 Likewise, national legislation such as that at issue in the main proceedings constitutes a restriction on the freedom to provide services since it impedes the access of consumers resident in Austria to the services offered in casinos located in another Member State, by making the promotion in Austria of those activities subject to an authorisation scheme which requires, in particular, that the operator of the casino concerned prove that the legal provisions for the protection of gamblers adopted in the Member State where that casino is operated at least correspond to the relevant Austrian legal provisions ('the contested condition').

19 Consequently, it must be held that national legislation such as that at issue in the main proceedings constitutes a restriction on the freedom to provide services that is guaranteed by Article 56 TFEU.

Justification of the restriction on the freedom to provide services

20 It is necessary to consider to what extent the restriction at issue in the main proceedings may be allowed as a derogation expressly provided for by Articles 51 TFEU and 52 TFEU, applicable in this area by virtue of Article 62 TFEU, or justified, in accordance with the case-law of the Court, by overriding reasons in the public interest.

21 It is clear from the Court's case-law that restrictions on gaming activities may be justified by overriding reasons in the public interest, such as consumer protection and the prevention of both fraud and incitement to squander money on gambling (see, to this effect, Case C-46/08 *Carmen Media Group* [2010] ECR I-8149, paragraph 55 and the case-law cited).

---

[9] See also the reasonings of Farrell, S., *Financing European Transport Infrastructure*, London, 1999, concerning the admissible financing techniques under European law framework.

22 However, the restrictions imposed by the Member States must satisfy the conditions laid down in the case-law of the Court as regards their proportionality, that is to say, be suitable for ensuring attainment of the objective pursued and not go beyond what is necessary in order to achieve that objective. It should also be recalled in this connection that national legislation is appropriate for ensuring attainment of the objective relied on only if it genuinely reflects a concern to attain it in a consistent and systematic manner. In any event, the restrictions must be applied without discrimination (see, to this effect, Case C-42/07 *Liga Portuguesa de Futebol Profissional and Bwin International* [2009] ECR I-7633, paragraphs 59 to 61 and the case-law cited).

23 In the case in point, it is not in dispute that the national legislation at issue and, in particular, the contested condition pursue the objective of protecting consumers against the risks connected with games of chance, which, as is clear from paragraph 21 of the present judgment, is capable of constituting an overriding reason in the public interest such as to justify restrictions on the freedom to provide services.

24 In this connection, the Court has repeatedly held that legislation on games of chance is one of the areas in which there are significant moral, religious and cultural differences between the Member States. In the absence of harmonisation in the field, it is for each Member State to determine in those areas, in accordance with its own scale of values, what is required to protect the interests in question (*Liga Portuguesa de Futebol Profissional and Bwin International*, paragraph 57 and the case-law cited).

25 Thus, the mere fact that a Member State has opted for a system of protection which differs from that adopted by another Member State cannot affect the assessment of the proportionality of the provisions enacted to that end. Those provisions must be assessed solely by reference to the objectives pursued by the competent authorities of the Member State concerned and the level of protection which they seek to ensure (*Liga Portuguesa de Futebol Profissional and Bwin International*, paragraph 58 and the case-law cited).

26 Here, the Austrian Government takes the view that the restriction on the freedom to provide services at issue in the main proceedings is not disproportionate in relation to the objectives pursued. It states that the number of casinos is limited in Austria to a maximum of 15 and casino operators are required to observe strict rules concerning the protection of gamblers, such as the duty to retain details of their identity for at least five years or the duty of the casino's management to observe a gambler's conduct in order to determine whether the frequency and intensity of his participation in gaming jeopardize the minimum income required for his subsistence.

27 According to the Austrian Government, in practice the application of those preventive rules has resulted in a significant reduction in the number of gamblers, as more than 80 000 persons were subject in 2011 to restrictions or bars on entering Austrian casinos. Therefore, in the absence of the contested condition, gamblers would be further encouraged to cross the border and to incur greater risks in casinos located in other Member States where similar regulatory guarantees of protection in some cases do not exist.

28 In that regard, it is apparent from the contested condition that, in order for a permit to carry out advertising in Austria for casinos established abroad to be granted, the levels of protection for gamblers that exist in the various legal systems concerned must first be compared.

29 Such an authorization scheme is in principle capable of fulfilling the condition of proportionality if it is limited to making authorization to carry out advertising for gaming establishments established in another Member State conditional upon the legislation of the

latter providing guarantees that are in essence equivalent to those of the national legislation with regard to the legitimate aim of protecting its residents against the risks connected with games of chance.

30 Such a condition does not appear to constitute an excessive burden for operators given the objective, recognized by the Court as an overriding reason in the public interest, of protecting the population against the risks inherent in games of chance.

31 Since the Member States are free to set the objectives of their policy on games of chance and to define in detail the level of protection sought (see *Liga Portuguesa de Futebol Profissional and Bwin International*, paragraph 59 and the case-law cited), it must be held that legislation such as that at issue in the main proceedings does not go beyond what is necessary provided that it merely requires, in order for authorization to carry out advertising to be granted, that it be established that, in the other Member State, the applicable legislation ensures protection against the risks of gaming that is in essence of a level equivalent to that which it guarantees itself.

32 The position would, however, be different, and the legislation would have to be regarded as disproportionate, if it required the rules in the other Member State to be identical or if it imposed rules not directly related to protection against the risks of gaming.

33 In the procedure referred to in Article 267 TFEU, a provision which is based on a clear separation of functions between the national courts and the Court of Justice, any assessment of the facts is a matter for the national court (see Joined Cases C-316/07, C-358/07 to C-360/07, C-409/07 and C-410/07 *Stoß and Others* [2010] ECR I-8069, paragraph 46 and the case-law cited).

34 Thus, it is for the referring court to satisfy itself that the contested condition is limited to making authorization to carry out advertising for gaming establishments established in another Member State conditional upon the legislation of the latter providing guarantees that are in essence equivalent to those of the national legislation with regard to the legitimate aim of protecting individuals against the risks connected with games of chance.

35 The referring court will, in particular, be able to consider whether Paragraph 56(2)(1) of the GSpG, by the reference which it makes to Paragraph 21 in its entirety, imposes conditions that go beyond consumer protection.

36 In light of the foregoing, the answer to the question referred is that Article 56 TFEU must be interpreted as not precluding legislation of a Member State which permits the advertising in that State of casinos located in another Member State only where the legal provisions for the protection of gamblers adopted in that other Member State provide guarantees that are in essence equivalent to those of the corresponding legal provisions in force in the first Member State.

1.2.2 The Direct Effects of European Union Law and Member States Liability

This principle is made concrete by the particular effects of EU law, according to which every European citizen has the right to assert European laws upon national jurisdictions[10]. According to the European Court of Justice (Van Gend en Loos of February 5th 1963, case 26/62) "*EU law . . . as it imposes duties on single citizens, gives them subjective rights which national judges have a duty to protect.*" In fact, the Court has pointed out that the EC Treaty (now TFEU) did not only create reciprocal obligations among Member States, but also intended to enact "*a juridical system of new kind in the field of international law, applying to States which have given up, even if in limited sectors, to their sovereign power, law system which recognizes as subjects not only member States but also their citizens.*" Furthermore, there are some features that risk causing a violation of the Treaty on the Functioning of the European Union, mainly of the principle of separation between public administration and business activities[11]. As a result, member States could face liability for damages caused by breach of EU dispositions concerning such rights (case 2) ECJ, 19 November 1991, Joined cases C-6/90 and C-9/90, Francovich, in Rep., Page I-05357):

(…)

3. The full effectiveness of Community rules would be impaired and the protection of the rights which they grant would be weakened if individuals were unable to obtain reparation when their rights are infringed by a breach of Community law for which a Member State can be held responsible. Such a possibility of reparation by the Member State is particularly indispensable where the full effectiveness of Community rules is subject to prior action on the part of the State and where, consequently, in the absence of such action, individuals cannot enforce before the national courts the rights conferred upon them by Community law.

It follows that the principle whereby a State must be liable for loss and damage caused to individuals by breaches of Community law for which the State can be held responsible is inherent in the system of the Treaty.

A further basis for the obligation of Member States to make good such loss and damage is to be found in Article 5 of the Treaty, under which they are required to take all appropriate measures, whether general or particular, to ensure the implementation of Community law, and consequently to nullify the unlawful consequences of a breach of Community law.

4. Although the liability of the Member State to make good loss and damage caused to individuals by breaches of Community law for which it can be held responsible is required by Community law, the conditions under which there is a right to reparation depend on the na-

---

10 Nehl H. P., *Legal protection in the field of EU funds*, in *European state aid law quarterly*, 2011, p. 629 ff.

11 Rittberger B., Phelan W. (eds), *Why do the EU Member States accept the supremacy of European law? Explaining supremacy as an alternative to bilateral reciprocity*, in *Journal of European Public Policy*, 2011, p. 766 ff.

ture of the breach of Community law giving rise to the loss and damage which have been caused.

In the case of a Member State which fails to fulfil its obligation under the third paragraph of Article 189 of the Treaty to take all the measures necessary to achieve the result prescribed by a directive the full effectiveness of that rule of Community law requires that there should be a right to reparation where three conditions are met, that is to say, first, that the result prescribed by the directive should entail the grant of rights to individuals; secondly, that it should be possible to identify the content of those rights on the basis of the provisions of the directive; and thirdly, that there should be a causal link between the breach of the State' s obligation and the loss and damage suffered by the injured parties.

In the absence of any Community legislation, it is in accordance with the rules of national law on liability that the State must make reparation for the consequences of the loss and damage caused. Nevertheless, the relevant substantive and procedural conditions laid down by the national law of the Member States must not be less favourable than those relating to similar domestic claims and must not be so framed as to make it virtually impossible or excessively difficult to obtain reparation.

The same principle was applied by the European Court of Justice in recognizing the right to obtain temporary measures from national courts on grounds of European Union law[12] (case 3) ECJ, 5 March 1996, Joined cases C-46/93 and C-48/93, Brasserie du Pêcheur SA v Bundesrepublik Deutschland and The Queen v Secretary of State for Transport, ex parte: Factortame Ltd, in Rep., p. I-01029):

(…)

1. The application of the principle that Member States are obliged to make good loss and damage caused to individuals by breaches of Community law for which they can be held responsible cannot be discarded where the breach relates to a provision of directly applicable Community law. The right of individuals to rely on directly effective provisions before national courts is only a minimum guarantee and is not sufficient in itself to ensure the full and complete implementation of Community law. That right, whose purpose is to ensure that provisions of Community law prevail over national provisions, cannot, in every case, secure for individuals the benefit of the rights conferred on them by Community law and, in particular, avoid their sustaining damage as a result of a breach of Community law attributable to a Member State.

2. Since the Treaty contains no provision expressly and specifically governing the consequences of breaches of Community law by Member States, it is for the Court, in pursuance of the task conferred on it by Article 164 of the Treaty of ensuring that in the interpretation and application of the Treaty the law is observed, to rule on such a question in accordance with generally accepted methods of interpretation, in particular by reference to the fundamental principles of the Community legal system and, where necessary, general principles common to the legal systems of the Member States.

3. The principle that Member States are obliged to make good loss or damage caused to individuals by breaches of Community law for which they can be held responsible is applicable where the national legislature was responsible for the breaches. That principle, which is inherent in the system of the Treaty, holds good for any case in which a Member State

12 See Bermann G.A.– Goebel R.J.– Davey W.J.– Fox E.M., *Cases and Materials on European Union Law*, New York, 2010.

breaches Community law, whatever be the organ of the State whose act or omission was responsible for the breach, and, in view of the fundamental requirement of the Community legal order that Community law be uniformly applied, the obligation to make good damage enshrined in that principle cannot depend on domestic rules as to the division of powers between constitutional authorities.

4. In order to define the conditions under which a Member State may incur liability for damage caused to individuals by a breach of Community law, account should first be taken of the principles inherent in the Community legal order which form the basis for State liability, namely, the full effectiveness of Community rules and the effective protection of the rights which they confer and the obligation to cooperate imposed on Member States by Article 5 of the Treaty. Reference should also be made to the rules which have been defined on non-contractual liability on the part of the Community, in so far as, under the second paragraph of Article 215 of the Treaty, they were constructed on the basis of the general principles common to the laws of the Member States and it is not appropriate, in the absence of particular justification, to have different rules governing the liability of the Community and the liability of Member States in like circumstances, since the protection of the rights which individuals derive from Community law cannot vary depending on whether a national authority or a Community authority is responsible for the damage. Accordingly, where a breach of Community law by a Member State is attributable to the national legislature acting in a field in which it has a wide discretion to make legislative choices, individuals suffering loss or injury thereby are entitled to reparation where the rule of Community law breached is intended to confer rights upon them, the breach is sufficiently serious and there is a direct causal link between the breach and the damage sustained by the individuals. Subject to that reservation, the State must make good the consequences of the loss or damage caused by the breach of Community law attributable to it, in accordance with its national law on liability. However, the conditions laid down by the applicable national laws must not be less favourable than those relating to similar domestic claims or framed in such a way as in practice to make it impossible or excessively difficult to obtain reparation. In particular, pursuant to the national legislation which it applies, the national court cannot make reparation of loss or damage conditional upon fault (intentional or negligent) on the part of the organ of the State responsible for the breach, going beyond that of a sufficiently serious breach of Community law. The decisive test for finding that a breach of Community law is sufficiently serious is whether the Member State concerned manifestly and gravely disregarded the limits on its discretion.The factors which the competent court may take into consideration include the clarity and precision of the rule breached, the measure of discretion left by that rule to the national or Community authorities, whether the infringement and the damage caused was intentional or involuntary, whether any error of law was excusable or inexcusable, the fact that the position taken by a Community institution may have contributed towards the omission, and the adoption or retention of national measures or practices contrary to Community law.On any view, a breach of Community law will be sufficiently serious if it has persisted despite a judgment finding the infringement in question to be established, or a preliminary ruling or settled case-law of the Court on the matter from which it is clear that the conduct in question constituted an infringement.

5. Reparation from Member States for loss or damage caused to individuals as a result of breaches of Community law must be commensurate with the loss or damage sustained. In the absence of relevant Community provisions, it is for the domestic legal system of each Member State to set the criteria for determining the extent of reparation. However, those criteria must not be less favourable than those applying to similar claims based on domestic law and must not be such as in practice to make it impossible or excessively difficult to ob-

tain reparation. National legislation which generally limits the damage for which reparation may be granted to damage done to certain, specifically protected individual interests not including loss of profit by individuals is not compatible with Community law. Moreover, it must be possible to award specific damages, such as the exemplary damages provided for by English law, pursuant to claims or actions founded on Community law, if such damages may be awarded pursuant to similar claims or actions founded on domestic law.

6. The obligation for Member States to make good loss or damage caused to individuals by breaches of Community law attributable to the State cannot be limited to damage sustained after the delivery of a judgment of the Court finding the infringement in question. Since the right to reparation under Community law exists where the requisite conditions are satisfied, to allow the obligation of the Member State concerned to make reparation to be confined to loss or damage sustained after delivery of a judgment of the Court finding the infringement in question would amount to calling in question the right to reparation conferred by the Community legal order. In addition, to make the reparation of loss or damage conditional upon the requirement that there must have been a prior finding by the Court of an infringement of Community law attributable to the Member State concerned would be contrary to the principle of the effectiveness of Community law, since it would preclude any right to reparation so long as the presumed infringement had not been the subject of an action brought by the Commission under Article 169 of the Treaty and of a finding of an infringement by the Court. Rights arising for individuals out of Community provisions having direct effect in the domestic legal systems of the Member States cannot depend on the Commission's assessment of the expediency of taking action against a Member State pursuant to Article 169 of the Treaty or on the delivery by the Court of any judgment finding an infringement.

The principle of effective judicial protection of European Union legal rights brought the European Court of Justice to hold that member States have the obligation to provide interim measures for the suspension of the effects of national laws that risk breaching European Union law[13] (case 4) 13 March 2007, Case C-432/05, Unibet (London) Ltd and Unibet (International) Ltd v Justitiekanslern, in Rep., I-02271):

(…)

36 By its first question, the Högsta domstolen asks, in essence, whether the principle of effective judicial protection of an individual's rights under Community law must be interpreted as requiring it to be possible in the legal order of a Member State to bring a free-standing action for an examination as to whether national provisions are compatible with Article 49 EC if other legal remedies permit the question of compatibility to be determined as a preliminary issue.

37 It is to be noted at the outset that, according to settled case-law, the principle of effective judicial protection is a general principle of Community law stemming from the constitutional traditions common to the Member States, which has been enshrined in Articles 6 and 13 of the European Convention for the Protection of Human Rights and Fundamental Freedoms (Case 222/84 Johnston [1986] ECR 1651, paragraphs 18 and 19; Case 222/86

---

[13] See Shelton D. (ed.), *International law and domestic legal systems: incorporation, transformation and persuasion*. Oxford, 2011.

Heylens and Others [1987] ECR 4097, paragraph 14; Case C-424/99 Commission v Austria [2001] ECR I-9285, paragraph 45; Case C-50/00 P Unión de Pequeños Agricultores v Council [2002] ECR I-6677, paragraph 39; and Case C-467/01 Eribrand [2003] ECR I-6471, paragraph 61) and which has also been reaffirmed by Article 47 of the Charter of fundamental rights of the European Union, proclaimed on 7 December 2000 in Nice (OJ 2000 C 364, p. 1).

38 Under the principle of cooperation laid down in Article 10 EC, it is for the Member States to ensure judicial protection of an individual's rights under Community law (see, to that effect, Case 33/76 Rewe, [1976] ECR 1989, paragraph 5; Case 45/76 Comet [1976] ECR 2043, paragraph 12; Case 106/77 Simmenthal [1978] ECR 629, paragraphs 21 and 22; Case C-213/89 Factortame and Others [1990] ECR I-2433, paragraph 19; and Case C-312/93 Peterbroeck [1995] ECR I-4599, paragraph 12).

39 It is also to be noted that, in the absence of Community rules governing the matter, it is for the domestic legal system of each Member State to designate the courts and tribunals having jurisdiction and to lay down the detailed procedural rules governing actions for safeguarding rights which individuals derive from Community law (see, inter alia, Rewe, paragraph 5; Comet, paragraph 13; Peterbroeck, paragraph 12; Case C-453/99 Courage and Crehan [2001] ECR I-6297, paragraph 29; and Case C-13/01 Safalero [2003] ECR I-8679, paragraph 49).

40 Although the EC Treaty has made it possible in a number of instances for private persons to bring a direct action, where appropriate, before the Community Court, it was not intended to create new remedies in the national courts to ensure the observance of Community law other than those already laid down by national law (Case 158/80 Rewe [1981] ECR 1805, paragraph 44).

41 It would be otherwise only if it were apparent from the overall scheme of the national legal system in question that no legal remedy existed which made it possible to ensure, even indirectly, respect for an individual's rights under Community law (see, to that effect, Case 33/76 Rewe, paragraph 5; Comet, paragraph 16; and Factortame, paragraphs 19 to 23).

42 Thus, while it is, in principle, for national law to determine an individual's standing and legal interest in bringing proceedings, Community law nevertheless requires that the national legislation does not undermine the right to effective judicial protection (see, inter alia, Joined Cases C-87/90 to C-89/90 Verholen and Others [1991] ECR I-3757, paragraph 24, and Safalero, paragraph 50). It is for the Member States to establish a system of legal remedies and procedures which ensure respect for that right (Unión de Pequeños Agricultores v Council, paragraph 41).

43 In that regard, the detailed procedural rules governing actions for safeguarding an individual's rights under Community law must be no less favourable than those governing similar domestic actions (principle of equivalence) and must not render practically impossible or excessively difficult the exercise of rights conferred by Community law (principle of effectiveness) (see, inter alia, Case 33/76 Rewe, paragraph 5; Comet, paragraphs 13 to 16; Peterbroeck, paragraph 12; Courage and Crehan, paragraph 29; Eribrand, paragraph 62; and Safalero, paragraph 49).

44 Moreover, it is for the national courts to interpret the procedural rules governing actions brought before them, such as the requirement for there to be a specific legal relationship between the applicant and the State, in such a way as to enable those rules, wherever

possible, to be implemented in such a manner as to contribute to the attainment of the objective, referred to at paragraph 37 above, of ensuring effective judicial protection of an individual's rights under Community law.

45 It is in the light of those considerations that the answer must be given to the first question referred by the Högsta domstolen.

46 According to that court, Swedish law does not provide for a self-standing action which seeks primarily to dispute the compatibility of a national provision with higher-ranking legal rules.

47 In that regard, it is to be noted, as is apparent from the case-law referred to at paragraph 40 above and has been argued by all the governments which have submitted observations to the Court and by the Commission of the European Communities, that the principle of effective judicial protection does not require it to be possible, as such, to bring a free-standing action which seeks primarily to dispute the compatibility of national provisions with Community law, provided that the principles of equivalence and effectiveness are observed in the domestic system of judicial remedies.

48 Firstly, it is apparent from the order for reference that Swedish law does not provide for such a free-standing action, regardless of whether the higher-ranking legal rule to be complied with is a national rule or a Community rule.

49 However, with regard to those two categories of legal rules, Swedish law permits individuals to obtain an examination of that question of compatibility in proceedings before the ordinary courts or before the administrative courts by way of a preliminary issue.

50 It is also apparent from the order for reference that the court which is to determine that question is required to disapply the contested provision if it considers that it conflicts with a higher-ranking legal rule, regardless of whether it is a national or a Community rule.

51 In that examination, it is only where a provision adopted by the Swedish Parliament or Government is manifestly in conflict with a higher-ranking legal rule that such a provision is to be disapplied. As is apparent from paragraph 3 above, that condition does not apply, on the other hand, where the higher-ranking rule in question is a rule of Community law.

52 Therefore, as was observed by all the governments which submitted observations and by the Commission, it is clear that the detailed procedural rules governing actions brought under Swedish law for safeguarding an individual's rights under Community law are no less favourable than the rules governing actions for safeguarding an individual's rights under national provisions.

53 It is necessary, secondly, to establish whether the effect of the indirect legal remedies provided for by Swedish law for disputing the compatibility of a national provision with Community law is to render practically impossible or excessively difficult the exercise of rights conferred by Community law.

54 In that regard, each case which raises the question whether a national procedural provision renders the application of Community law impossible or excessively difficult must be analysed by reference to the role of that provision in the procedure, its progress and its special features, viewed as a whole, before the various national instances (Peterbroeck, paragraph 14).

55 It is apparent from the order for reference that Swedish law does not prevent a person, such as Unibet, from disputing the compatibility of national legislation, such as the Law on Lotteries, with Community law but that, on the contrary, there exist various indirect legal remedies for that purpose.

56 Thus, firstly, the Högsta domstolen states that Unibet may obtain an examination of whether the Law on Lotteries is compatible with Community law in the context of a claim for damages before the ordinary courts.

57 It is also clear from the order for reference that Unibet brought such a claim and that the Högsta domstolen found it to be admissible.

58 Consequently, where an examination of the compatibility of the Law on Lotteries with Community law takes place in the context of the determination of a claim for damages, that action constitutes a remedy which enables Unibet to ensure effective protection of the rights conferred on it by Community law.

59 It is for the Högsta domstolen to ensure that the examination of the compatibility of that law with Community law takes place irrespective of the assessment of the merits of the case with regard to the requirements for damage and a causal link in the claim for damages.

60 Secondly, the Högsta domstolen adds that, if Unibet applied to the Swedish Government for an exception to the prohibition on the promotion of its services in Sweden, any decision rejecting that application could be the subject of judicial review proceedings before the Regeringsrätten, in which Unibet would be able to argue that the provisions of the Law on Lotteries are incompatible with Community law. Where appropriate, the competent court would be required to disapply the provisions of that law that were considered to be in conflict with Community law.

61 It is to be noted that such judicial review proceedings, which would enable Unibet to obtain a judicial decision that those provisions are incompatible with Community law, constitute a legal remedy securing effective judicial protection of its rights under Community law (see, to that effect, Heylens, paragraph 14, and Case C-340/89 Vlassopoulou [1991] ECR I-2357, paragraph 22).

62 Moreover, the Högsta domstolen states that if Unibet disregarded the provisions of the Law on Lotteries and administrative action or criminal proceedings were brought against it by the competent national authorities, it would have the opportunity, in proceedings brought before the administrative court or an ordinary court, to dispute the compatibility of those provisions with Community law. Where appropriate, the competent court would be required to disapply the provisions of that law that were considered to be in conflict with Community law.

63 In addition to the remedies referred to at paragraphs 56 and 60 above, it would therefore be possible for Unibet to claim in court proceedings against the administration or in criminal proceedings that measures taken or required to be taken against it were incompatible with Community law on account of the fact that it had not been permitted by the competent national authorities to promote its services in Sweden.

64 In any event, it is clear from paragraphs 56 to 61 above that Unibet must be regarded as having available to it legal remedies which ensure effective judicial protection of its rights under Community law. If, on the contrary, as mentioned at paragraph 62 above, it was forced to be subject to administrative or criminal proceedings and to any penalties that may result as the sole form of legal remedy for disputing the compatibility of the national

provision at issue with Community law, that would not be sufficient to secure for it such effective judicial protection.

65 Accordingly, the answer to the first question must be that the principle of effective judicial protection of an individual's rights under Community law must be interpreted as meaning that it does not require the national legal order of a Member State to provide for a free-standing action for an examination of whether national provisions are compatible with Article 49 EC, provided that other effective legal remedies, which are no less favourable than those governing similar domestic actions, make it possible for such a question of compatibility to be determined as a preliminary issue, which is a matter for the national court to establish.

Question 2

66 By its second question, the Högsta domstolen essentially asks whether the principle of effective judicial protection of an individual's rights under Community law requires it to be possible in the legal order of a Member State to obtain interim relief suspending the application of national measures until the competent court has given a ruling on whether those measures are compatible with Community law.

67 As a preliminary point, it must be pointed out that a court seised of a dispute governed by Community law must be in a position to grant interim relief in order to ensure the full effectiveness of the judgment to be given on the existence of the rights claimed under Community law (Factortame, paragraph 21, and Case C-226/99 Siples [2001] ECR I-277, paragraph 19).

68 Under the national law set out in the order for reference, the purpose of applications for such relief can only be to provide interim protection of the rights the applicant asserts in the substantive action, as is apparent from paragraph 9 above.

69 In the action in the main proceedings, it is not disputed that Unibet made two applications for interim relief, the first in connection with an application for a declaration, and the second in connection with a claim for damages.

70 With regard to the first of those applications for interim relief, it is apparent from the order for reference that the application for a declaration was considered to be inadmissible, under national law, at first instance and on appeal. Whilst upholding that interpretation of national law, the Högsta domstolen none the less has doubts concerning the requirements of Community law in that regard, which led it to ask the first question referred for a preliminary ruling (see paragraphs 36 to 65 above).

71 According to the answer to the first question, the principle of effective judicial protection of an individual's rights under Community law does not require the national legal order of a Member State to provide for a free-standing action for an examination of whether national provisions are compatible with Community law, provided that other legal remedies make it possible for such an issue of compatibility to be determined as a preliminary issue, which is a matter for the national court to establish.

72 Where it is uncertain under national law, applied in accordance with the requirements of Community law, whether an action to safeguard respect for an individual's rights under Community law is admissible, the principle of effective judicial protection requires the national court to be able, none the less, at that stage, to grant the interim relief necessary to ensure those rights are respected.

73 However, the principle of effective judicial protection of an individual's rights under Community law does not require it to be possible in the legal order of a Member State to obtain interim relief from the competent national court in the context of an application that is inadmissible under the law of that Member State, provided that Community law, as interpreted in accordance with paragraph 71 above, does not call into question that inadmissibility.

74 With regard to the application for interim relief made in connection with the claim for damages, it is apparent from the order for reference and from other documents in the case-file that that claim was considered to be admissible.

75 As the Advocate General stated at point 74 of her Opinion and as was noted at paragraph 67 above, the national court seised of a dispute governed by Community law must be able to grant interim relief in order to ensure the full effectiveness of the judgment to be given on the existence of the rights claimed under Community law.

76 Consequently, where the competent national court examines, in the context of the claim for damages, whether the Law on Lotteries is compatible with Community law, it must be able to grant the interim relief sought, provided that such relief is necessary, which it is a matter for the national court to determine, in order to ensure the full effectiveness of the judgment to be given on the existence of the rights claimed under Community law.

77 It follows from the foregoing that the answer to the second question must be that the principle of effective judicial protection of an individual's rights under Community law must be interpreted as requiring it to be possible in the legal order of a Member State for interim relief to be granted until the competent court has given a ruling on whether national provisions are compatible with Community law, where the grant of such relief is necessary to ensure the full effectiveness of the judgment to be given on the existence of such rights.

Question 3

78 By its third question, the Högsta domstolen asks essentially whether, having regard to the principle of effective judicial protection of an individual's rights under Community law, and where the compatibility of national provisions with Community law is being challenged, the grant of interim relief to suspend the application of such provisions, until the competent court has given a ruling on whether those provisions are compatible with Community law, is governed by the criteria laid down by the national law applicable before the competent court or by Community criteria.

79 It is clear from established case-law that the suspension of enforcement of a national provision based on a Community regulation in proceedings pending before a national court, whilst it is governed by national procedural law, is in all Member States subject to conditions which are uniform and analagous with the conditions for an application for interim relief brought before the Community Court (Joined Cases C-143/88 and C-92/89 Zuckerfabrik SüderdithmarschenandZuckerfabrik Soest [1991] ECR I-415, paragraphs 26 and 27; Case C-465/93 Atlanta Fruchthandelsgesellschaft [1995] ECR I-3761, paragraph 39; and Joined Cases C-453/03, C-11/04, C-12/04 and C-194/04 ABNA and Others [2005] ECR I-10423, paragraph 104). However, the case in the main proceedings is different from those giving rise to those judgments in that Unibet's application for interim relief does not seek to suspend the effects of a national provision adopted in accordance with a Community regulation where the legality of that regulation is contested, but rather the effects of national legislation where the compatibility of that legislation with Community law is contested.

80 Therefore, in the absence of Community rules governing the matter, it is for the domestic legal system of each Member State to determine the conditions under which interim relief is to be granted for safeguarding an individual's rights under Community law.

81 Accordingly, the grant of interim relief to suspend the application of national provisions until the competent court has given a ruling on whether those provisions are compatible with Community law is governed by the criteria laid down by the national law applicable before that court.

82 However, those criteria cannot be less favourable than those applying to similar domestic actions (principle of equivalence) and must not render practically impossible or excessively difficult the interim judicial protection of rights conferred by Community law (principle of effectiveness).

83 The answer to the third question must therefore be that the principle of effective judicial protection of an individual's rights under Community law must be interpreted as meaning that, where the compatibility of national provisions with Community law is being challenged, the grant of any interim relief to suspend the application of such provisions until the competent court has given a ruling on whether those provisions are compatible with Community law is governed by the criteria laid down by the national law applicable before that court, provided that those criteria are no less favourable than those applying to similar domestic actions and do not render practically impossible or excessively difficult the interim judicial protection of those rights.

1.2.3 Competition Law

Free competition is the key feature of a European common market based on an open economy[14]. It encourages economic performance and offers consumers a wider choice of better-quality products and services at lower prices. European Union competition policies prevent competition from being distorted in the internal market by ensuring that similar rules apply to all the companies[15] operating within it.

The Treaty on the Functioning of the European Union provides the basis for the European rules on competition. The competition rules applicable to firms regulate two avoided behaviors that have the effect of distorting competition: (a) agreements; (b) abuses of dominant positions. The European Union has therefore put in place regulations to both prosecute firms and also prevent them from engaging in anti-competitive behaviors.

[14] See Waelbroeck M., *Le traitè CEE est il neutre à l'égard des politiques économiques des Etats membres?*, in *Hacia un nuoevo orden internacional y europeo, Estudios en homenaye a Diez de Velasco*, Madrid, 1993, p. 1297 ff.

[15] The notion of undertaking can be understood through the reading of Bonelli F., *La nozione di impresa nelle regole di concorrenza del Trattato C.E.E.*, in Verrucoli P. (a cura di), *La nozione d'impresa nell'ordinamento comunitario*, Milano, 1977, p. 37 ff.

1.2.3.1 Agreements

There are two kinds of avoided agreements under EU law: horizontal agreements and vertical agreements.

A horizontal agreement is a cooperative or concerted practice entered into between actual or potential competitors, while a vertical agreement is a cooperative arrangement for the sale and purchase of goods or services entered into between companies operating at different levels of the production or distribution chain.

These two kinds of agreements[16] are avoided if their effect is to restrict competition in the relevant market, which is identified according to two profiles: goods and territory. The *relevant market of goods* means a market of all those goods and/or services which are regarded as interchangeable or substitutable by the consumer, by reason of their characteristics, their prices, and their intended use. We can affirm that infrastructures are not interchangeable for the consumer, so that in this sector, the relevant market must refer to the specific facility taken into consideration. The *relevant territorial or geographic market* means a market in the area in which the undertakings concerned are involved in the supply and demand of goods and/or services, in which the conditions for competition are sufficiently homogenous, and which are distinguishable from neighboring areas insofar as the conditions for competition are considerably different in those areas.

The relevant market within which to assess a given competition issue is therefore established by the combination of the product and geographic markets (case 5) ECJ, 9 November 1983, Case 322/81, Michelin, in Rep., p. 03461):

(…)

22 by a first set of submissions concerning the content of the decision at issue the applicant denies that it holds a dominant position on the market in new replacement tyres for heavy vehicles in the Netherlands . in substance it contends that the commission ' s assessment of its market position is vitiated by error first because the commission confined its analysis to the Netherlands market alone and relied on an incorrect definition of the relevant product market and secondly because in finding the existence of a dominant position it took account of immaterial factors and disregarded criteria excluding the existence of such a position.

(1) The substantial part of the common market at issue

23 The applicant ' s first submission under this head challenges the commission ' s finding that the substantial part of the common market on which it holds a dominant position is the Netherlands . Michelin nv maintains that this geographical definition of the market is too narrow . it is contradicted by the fact that the commission itself based its decision on factors concerning the Michelin group as a whole , such as its technological lead and financial strength which , in the applicant ' s view , relate to a much wider market or even the world market . the activities of Michelin nv ' s main competitors are world-wide too.

---

[16] The notion of agreement goes beyond the concept of contract. See Miller L., *The emergence of EU contract law: exploring europeanization*, Oxford, 2011 and Tizzano R. (ed.), *Il diritto privato dell'Unione europea*, Torino, 2006, p. 1668 ff.

24 The commission maintains that this objection concerns less the definition of the market than the criteria used to establish the existence of a dominant position . since tyre manufacturers have on the whole chosen to sell their products on the various national markets through the intermediary of national subsidiaries , the competition faced by Michelin nv is on the Netherlands market.

28 The point to be made in this regard is that the commission addressed its decision not to the Michelin group as a whole but only to its Netherlands subsidiary whose activities are concentrated on the Netherlands market . it has not been disputed that Michelin nv ' s main competitors also carry on their activities in the Netherlands through Netherlands subsidiaries of their respective groups.

26 The commission ' s allegation concerns Michelin nv ' s conduct towards tyre dealers and more particularly its discount policy . in this regard the commercial policy of the various subsidiaries of the groups competing at the european or even the world level is generally adapted to the specific conditions existing on each market. in practice dealers established in the Netherlands obtain their supplies only from suppliers operating in the Netherlands . the commission was therefore right to take the view that the competition facing Michelin nv is mainly on the Netherlands market and that it is at that level that the objective conditions of competition are alike for traders.

27 This finding is not related to the question whether in such circumstances factors relating to the position of the Michelin group and its competitors as a whole and to a much wider market may enter into consideration in the adoption of a decision as to whether a dominant position exists on the relevant product market.

28 Hence the relevant substantial part of the common market in this case is the Netherlands and it is at the level of the Netherlands market that Michelin nv ' s position must be assessed.

(2) assessment of Michelin nv's position in relation to its competitors

29 Before the submissions and arguments regarding the assessment of Michelin nv ' s position in relation to its competitors are examined more closely it should be recalled , as the court has repeatedly held , most recently in its judgment of 13 february 1979 in case 85/76 hoffmann-la roche v commission (1979) ecr 461 , that article 86 of the treaty is an application of the general aim of the activities of the community laid down by article 3 (f) of the treaty , namely the institution of a system ensuring that competition in the common market is not distorted.

30 Consequently article 86 prohibits any abuse by an undertaking of a dominant position on the common market or a substantial part thereof in so far as it may affect trade between member states , that is to say in so far as it prohibits any abuse of a position of economic strength enjoyed by an undertaking which enables it to hinder the maintenance of effective competition on the relevant market by allowing it to behave to an appreciable extent independently of its competitors and customers and ultimately of consumers.

31 The various criteria and evidence relied upon by the parties regarding the existence of a dominant position must be examined in that light . they concern first Michelin nv ' s share of the relevant product market and secondly the other factors which must be taken into consideration in the assessment of Michelin nv ' s position in relation to its competitors , customers and consumers.

(a) Michelin nv ' s share of the relevant product market

32 The applicant first of all denies that it possesses the market share from which the commission deduced the existence of a dominant position and contends that the commission based its decision on an artificial and arbitrary definition of the relevant product market.

33 In its decision the commission relied upon the fact that from 1975 to 1980 Michelin nv ' s share of the market in new replacement tyres for lorries , buses and similar vehicles in the Netherlands was 57 to 65% whereas the market shares of its main competitors were only 4 to 8% .

34 Michelin nv does not dispute those figures but maintains that the commission failed to take account of the relationships between competing products by excluding in particular car and van tyres as well as retreads : if retreads for heavy vehicles are taken into consideration for example , Michelin nv ' s market share is only some 37% , which is not such as to establish a dominant position.

(aa) the market in replacement tyres for heavy vehicles

35 The applicant claims that the definition of the relevant market on which the commission based its decision is too wide , inasmuch as in the eyes of the consumer different types and sizes of tyres for heavy vehicles are not interchangeable , and at the same time too narrow inasmuch as car and van tyres are excluded from it although they occupy similar positions on the market . it further argues that the commission ' s reasoning in its decision is contradictory in so far as it puts itself alternately in the shoes of the ultimate consumer and in those of the dealer . however , at the level of dealers ' total sales , the average proportion of sales of Michelin heavy-vehicle tyres represents only 12 to 18% , which rules out the existence of any dominant position.

36 The commission defends the definition of the relevant product market used in its decision by pointing out that with a technically homogeneous product it is not possible to distinguish different markets depending on the dimensions , size or specific types of products : in that connection the elasticity of supply between different types and dimensions of tyre must be taken into account . on the other hand the criteria of interchangeability and elasticity of demand allow a distinction to be drawn between the market in tyres for heavy vehicles and the market in car tyres owing to the particular structure of demand , which , in the case of tyres for heavy vehicles , is characterized by the presence above all of experienced trade buyers.

37 As the court has repeatedly emphasized , most recently in its judgment of 11 december 1980 in case 31/80 nv l ' oreal and sa l ' oreal v pvba de nieuwe amck (1980) ecr 3775 , for the purposes of investigating the possibly dominant position of an undertaking on a given market , the possibilities of competition must be judged in the context of the market comprising the totality of the products which , with respect to their characteristics , are particularly suitable for satisfying constant needs and are only to a limited extent interchangeable with other products . however , it must be noted that the determination of the relevant market is useful in assessing whether the undertaking concerned is in a position to prevent effective competition from being maintained and behave to an appreciable extent independently of its competitors and customers and consumers . for this purpose , therefore , an examination limited to the objective characteristics only of the relevant products cannot be sufficient: the competitive conditions and the structure of supply and demand on the market must also be taken into consideration.

38 Moreover , it was for that reason that the commission and Michelin nv agreed that new , original-equipment tyres should not be taken into consideration in the assessment of market shares . owing to the particular structure of demand for such tyres characterized by direct orders from car manufacturers , competition in this sphere is in fact governed by completely different factors and rules.

39 As far as replacement tyres are concerned , the first point which must be made is that at the user level there is no interchangeability between car and van tyres on the one hand and heavy-vehicle tyres on the other . car and van tyres therefore have no influence at all on competition on the market in heavy-vehicle tyres.

40 Furthermore , the structure of demand for each of those groups of products is different . most buyers of heavy-vehicle tyres are trade users , particularly haulage undertakings, for whom , as the commission explained , the purchase of replacement tyres represents an item of considerable expenditure and who constantly ask their tyre dealers for advice and long-term specialized services adapted to their specific needs . on the other hand , for the average buyer of car or van tyres the purchase of tyres is an occasional event and even if the buyer operates a business he does not expect such specialized advice and service adapted to specific needs . hence the sale of heavy-vehicle tyres requires a particularly specialized distribution network which is not the case with the distribution of car and van tyres.

41 The final point which must be made is that there is no elasticity of supply between tyres for heavy vehicles and car tyres owing to significant differences in production techniques and in the plant and tools needed for their manufacture . the fact that time and considerable investment are required in order to modify production plant for the manufacture of light-vehicle tyres instead of heavy-vehicle tyres or vice versa means that there is no discernible relationship between the two categories of tyre enabling production to be adapted to demand on the market . moreover , that was why in 1977 , when the supply of tyres for heavy vehicles was insufficient , Michelin nv decided to grant an extra bonus instead of using surplus production capacity for car tyres to meet demand.

42 The commission rightly examined the structure of the market and demand primarily at the level of dealers to whom Michelin nv applied the practice in question . Michelin nv has itself stated , although in another context , that it was compelled to change its discount system to take account of the tendency towards specialization amongst its dealers , some of whom , such as garage owners , no longer sold tyres for heavy vehicles and vans . this confirms the differences existing in the structure of demand between different groups of dealers . nor has Michelin nv disputed that the distinction drawn between tyres for heavy vehicles , vans and cars is also applied by all its competitors , especially as regards discount terms , even if in the case of certain types of tyre the distinctions drawn by different manufacturers may vary in detail.

43 Nevertheless , it cannot be deduced from the fact that the conduct to which exception is taken in this case affects dealers that Michelin nv ' s position ought to be assessed on the basis of the proportion of Michelin heavy-vehicle tyres in the dealers ' total turnover . since it is a question of investigating whether Michelin nv holds a dominant position in the case of certain products , it is unimportant that the dealers also deal in other products if there is no competition between those products and the products in question.

44 On the other hand , in deciding whether a dominant position exists , neither the absence of elasticity of supply between different types and dimensions of tyres for heavy vehicles , which is due to differences in the conditions of production , nor the absence of interchangeability and elasticity of demand between those types and dimensions of tyre from

the point of view of the specific needs of the user allow a number of smaller markets , reflecting those types and dimensions , to be distinguished , as Michelin nv suggests . those differences between different types and dimensions of tyre are not vitally important for dealers , who must meet demand from customers for the whole range of heavy-vehicle tyres . furthermore , in the absence of any specialization on the part of the undertakings concerned , such differences in the type and dimensions of a product are not a crucial factor in the assessment of an undertaking' s market position because in view of their similarity and the manner in which they complement one another at the technical level , the conditions of competition on the market are the same for all the types and dimensions of the product.

45 In establishing that Michelin nv has a dominant position the commission was therefore right to assess its market share with reference to replacement tyres for lorries, buses and similar vehicles and to exclude consideration of car and van tyres.

1.2.3.2 Abuse of Dominant Position

A dominant position exists where an undertaking or group of undertakings would be in a position to behave to an appreciable extent independently of its competitors, customers, and ultimately of its consumers. Such a position would usually arise when an undertaking or group of undertakings has a large share of the market as a potential seller or buyer of specific goods or services (in this case as a constructor or maintenance enterprise of roads and highways), provided that other factors analyzed in the assessment point in the same direction (other factors can be, for example, possibilities for entry (entry barriers), financial power, access to the sources of supply for the market, capability to dictate the market conditions, etc.).

Public Authorities have the duty to verify the concrete effects of the abuse or agreement and will apply European law only if it will affect the market among member States[17]. However, this does not mean that conduct entirely located in one member State will exclude the application of European Union law, as it is sufficient that they are capable of having such effects (see Michelin case):

(…)

101 In its decision the commission stated that other manufacturers , whose chances of penetrating the Netherlands market were reduced owing to the fact that dealers ' freedom to purchase was restricted , mostly had their production plant in other member states and that 25 to 28% of heavy-vehicle tyres competing with Michelin tyres on the Netherlands market came from other member states of the community.

---

[17] The public intervention into the economy is the key issue of a well regulated economy. However, it is not simple to understand the boundaries of public powers: see Tesauro G., *Intervento pubblico nell'economia e art. 90, n. 2, del Trattato CE*, in *Dir. Un Eur.*, 1996, p. 719 ff., Radaelli C.M., *Governing European Regulation: The challenges Ahead*, The Robert Schuman Centre - European University Institute, Policy Paper n. 3, 1998 and Mc Craw T.K., *Prophets of regulation*, Cambridge, 1984.

102 Michelin nv , supported by the French government , contended that conduct confined to the territory of one member state cannot affect trade between member states . in its view the commission ' s arguments amount to a presumption that trade is affected and are based on a purely abstract and theoretical analysis ; the commission has not specifically established that the applicant's conduct affects competition and seals off the Netherlands market.

103 In this connection it must be stated that when the holder of a dominant position obstructs access to the market by competitors it makes no difference whether such conduct is confined to a single member state as long as it is capable of affecting patterns of trade and competition on the common market.

104 It has not been denied in this case that important patterns of trade exist as a result of the establishment of competitors of significant size in other member states . the effects of the discount system on the chances of Michelin nv ' s competitors of obtaining access to the Netherlands market have already been examined in the context of the examination of the abusive nature of Michelin nv ' s conduct . it must also be remembered that article 86 does not require it to be proved that the abusive conduct has in fact appreciably affected trade between member states but that it is capable of having that effect.

The same approach must be followed by national Public Authorities, in strict cooperation with the Commission in the application of competition law to undertakings that enjoy a single or collective dominant position[18].

According to European law, Public Authorities are authorized to adopt a decision by which to determine the existence and abuse of a particular dominant position. Yet it has to be emphasized that both abuse of dominant position and avoided agreements must be in reference to the relevant market (of goods and geographical) as previously described.

1.2.4 State Aid

Another important market regulation duty for Public Authorities, along with the duty to give notice to the European Commission[19], is monitoring the State aid benefits[20] from member States to the companies in charge of works of construction and maintenance of infrastructures.

---

[18] A clear application of these principles in the transport sector can be read in Munari F., *Il diritto comunitario dei trasporti*, Milano, 1996.

[19] For a description of the role and competences of the Europena Commission in the assessment of State aids, see Smith M.P., *Autonomy by the Rules: The European Commission and the Development of State Aid Policy*, in *Journal of Common Market Studies*, 1998, p. 55 ff.

[20] See Biondi A. - Eeckhout P. - Flynn J. (ed.), *The law of State Aid in the European Union*, Oxford, 2004, Keppenne J.P., *Guide des aides d'Etat en droit communautaire*, Bruxelles, 1999, Nicolaides P. - Kekelekis M. - Buyskes M., *State aid Policy in the European community*, The Hague, 2005 and Dony M. - Renard F. - Smits C., *Controle des aides d'Etat*, in Idot L. (a cura di), *Commentaire J. Égret, Droit Communautaire de la concurrence*, Bruxelles, 2007.

The objective of State aid control is, as established in the founding Treaties of the European Union, to ensure that government interventions do not distort competition and trade inside the EU. Indeed, State aid is defined as an advantage in any form that is conferred on a selective basis to undertakings by national public authorities. Therefore, subsidies granted to individuals or general measures open to all enterprises are not covered by Article 107 of the Treaty on the Functioning of the European Union (TFEU) and do not constitute State aid.

The Treaty on the Functioning of European Union pronounces the general prohibition of State aid. The founders, however, saw of course that in some circumstances, government interventions are necessary for a well-functioning and equitable economy. Therefore, the Treaty leaves room for a number of policy objectives for which State aid can be considered compatible.

We can see an example of the complex reasoning of the European Court of Justice in the air transport sector with a clear explanation of the private investor test (case 6) Court of First Instance,: 12 December 2000, case T-296/97, Alitalia - Linee aeree italiane SpA v Commission of the European Communities, in Rep., p. II-03871):

(...)

First part: the participation of private investors in the recapitalization

76 The applicant maintains that the participation of private investors in its recapitalization effort is sufficient to show that that recapitalization satisfies the private investor test. The Commission has clearly overlooked that point. The contested decision states that no private investor is taking part in the capital increase of ITL 2 750 billion (point VII, fifth paragraph).

77 First, the applicant observes that the company's employees, who are private investors, had agreed to subscribe to the increase in capital to an amount of ITL 310 billion, which represents approximately 20% of its capital. Second, it observes that the company is quoted on the Italian Stock Exchange and private shareholders already held 13.6% of its capital on 1 July 1996. It points out that, under Italian law, shares which existing shareholders have not exercised an option to purchase must be offered on the Stock Exchange. Since, apart from the advance of ITL 1 000 billion already paid on 1 July 1996, IRI merely stated that it was prepared to participate in the various phases of the applicant's recapitalization, it was only in the absence of any private participation that it would subscribe the entire increase in capital.

78 Furthermore, the Italian Government expressed its firm intention to privatise the applicant without delay once authorisation to increase its capital had been obtained (letter of 20 December 1996 from the President of the Italian Council of Ministers to the President of the Commission, annex 13 to the application), by repealing in 1996 the statutory provision that 51% of the company's capital must be held by the public sector.

79 The applicant then observes that IRI paid it ITL 2 000 billion (ITL 1 000 billion in June 1996 and ITL 1 000 billion in 1997). IRI then received the proceeds of the sale of 18.4% of the company's capital to private investors for approximately ITL 787 billion. A further capital increase, ITL 1 000 billion of which was subscribed by private investors, was decided upon in January 1998. The applicant therefore maintains that, even ignoring

the amount subscribed by its employees, IRI's total investment (ITL 1 213 billion) in its restructuring is less than the amount subscribed by private shareholders (ITL 1 787 billion). The applicant further states that, at the time it filed its reply, IRI held 53% of its capital and private shareholders held 47%. Last, the applicant maintains that the success of private participation in the increase of its capital was such that the second and third instalments payable by IRI (ITL 500 billion and ITL 250 billion respectively) and authorised in the contested decision were not paid. It refers again to the report of the Commission's consultants of 27 May 1998, in which they observe that the amount invested by IRI is lower and the profitability proportionately higher than the forecasts of the plan. The Commission therefore made a manifest error in assessing the restructuring plan, in so far as the plan, from its first version and in the light of the situation then existing and the developments foreseeable in the short term, was capable of satisfying the private investor test.

80 The Court observes that the test based on the conduct of a private investor operating in normal market-economy conditions ensues from the principle that the public and private sectors are to be treated equally, pursuant to which capital placed directly or indirectly at the disposal of an undertaking by the State in circumstances which correspond to normal market conditions cannot be regarded as State aid (Case C-303/88 Italy v Commission [1991] ECR I-1433, hereinafter ENI-Lanerossi judgment, paragraph 20; Case T-358/94 Air France v Commission [1996] ECR II-2109, paragraph 70).

81 A capital contribution from public funds must therefore be regarded as satisfying the private investor test and not constituting State aid if, inter alia, it was made at the same time as a significant capital contribution on the part of a private investor made in comparable circumstances (see, in that regard, Air France, cited in paragraph 80 above, paragraphs 148 and 149).

82 As regards, first, the employees' participation in the applicant's capital, it was reasonable for the Commission to decide that it cannot be taken into consideration since the conditions under which this works are very different from those applicable to IRI's contribution (contested decision, point VII, fifth paragraph).

83 In that regard, it should be observed that, under the agreement concluded on 19 June 1996, the applicant's employees consented to a change in salary. In return, they were to receive shares in Alitalia to the amount of ITL 310 billion, corresponding to the annual saving in labour costs.

84 In those circumstances, the employees' actual participation in the applicant's capital does not itself show that IRI's contribution satisfies the private investor test. It must be emphasised, in that regard, that the conduct of a private investor in a market economy is guided by prospects of profitability (Case C-305/89 Italy v Commission [1991] ECR I-1603, hereinafter Alfa Romeo, paragraph 20, Joined Cases C-278/92, C-279/92 and C-280/92 Spain v Commission [1994] ECR I-4103, paragraphs 20 to 22, and Joined Cases T-126/96 and T-127/96 BFM and EFIM v Commission [1998] ECR II-3437, paragraph 79). The employees' participation was motivated by the desire to keep their jobs and therefore, above all, by considerations pertaining to the applicant's viability and survival rather than by prospects of profitability.

85 As regards, next, the participation of private investors, the Commission stated in the contested decision that even [if] it is assumed that the ... share of Alitalia's capital held by private investors may be deemed to have real economic significance, no private investor is taking part in the capital increase of ITL 2 750 billion (point VII, fifth paragraph).

86 It should be observed that, in the context of an action for annulment under Article 173 of the Treaty, the legality of a Community measure must be assessed on the basis of the elements of fact and of law existing at the time when the measure was adopted. In particular, the complex assessments made by the Commission must be examined solely on the basis of the information available to the Commission at the time when those assessments were made (Case C-288/96 Germany v Commission [2000] ECR I-8237, paragraph 34; Joined Cases T-371/94 and T-394/94 British Airways and Others and British Midland Airways v Commission [1998] ECR II-2405, paragraph 81, and Salomon, cited in paragraph 61 above, paragraph 115).

87 Throughout the administrative procedure, the Italian authorities and the applicant proceeded, for the purpose of calculating the efficiency of the investment, on the assumption that IRI alone would subscribe to the planned increases in capital.

88 It should be noted, in that regard, that the initial plan envisaged a capital injection of ITL 3 000 billion by IRI and a participation in the capital by the applicant's employees of ITL 310 billion. Having regard to the share already held by minority shareholders, it was estimated that IRI's share of the capital at the end of the operation would be approximately 80%. That point was confirmed in the Italian authorities' reply of 6 September 1996 to a request for information from the Commission, in which it is stated:

In order to simplify the calculation, it was assumed that, at the end of the recapitalization process, existing minority shareholders will hold a very small share of the company's capital. The employees will receive shares in return for lower wages and increased productivity. In that context, it may be foreseen that the employees will hold approximately 20% of the shares and IRI the remaining 80%.

89 Furthermore, according to the applicant, an 80% participation in its capital by IRI at the end of the restructuring period was a minimum estimate. The applicant stated during a presentation which it made to the Directorate-General for Transport (DG VII) on 23 October 1996: [The] 80% assumption is a "worst case" scenario. During that presentation, it also stated: [E]xisting minority shareholders (currently approximately 10%) will be massively diluted, probably to less than 1% ... [and] employees will have some 20% of the ordinary equity but are expected to only have an effective equity share of 12% to 15%.

90 On the basis of the figures notified to the Commission, the latter's consultants observed in their report of 11 December 1996: [T]he plan assumes that the entire [ITL] 3 000 billion recapitalization will be subscribed only by IRI (Section IV C 2). They also stated: According to the Plan, the IRI share of equity capital was assumed to be 80% ... It appears more likely that IRI's equity interest in Alitalia will be higher than the forecasted 80% interest in 2000 (Section IV C 2).

91 Far from contradicting those assertions, the applicant acknowledged, in a document dated 19 December 1996 communicated to the Commission by the Italian authorities by letter of 20 December 1996, that the Commission's consultants' that IRI's share of Alitalia's capital at the end of the plan [would] probably be higher than forecast in the "submission" of July last. The applicant again informed the Commission, by letter of 15 April 1997, that IRI was going to subscribe the entire increase in capital, which at the time was fixed at ITL 2 800 billion. The letter states: IRI is forecast to pay ITL 2 800 billion with a planned timing of ITL 1 000 billion in July 1996, ITL 500 billion in July 1997 and the balance of ITL 1 300 billion in December 1997. No other public authority funding is being considered.

92 In those circumstances, the Commission was entitled to consider in the contested decision that ... no private investor is taking part in the capital increase of ITL 2 750 billion. Even if, according to the Italian Government, the prime objective of the restructuring plan [was] to establish the basis for the privatization of the company and that, for that purpose, it was considered possible that private investors might subscribe part of the second instalment of the recapitalization forecast (the restructuring plan of July 1996), that was a mere assumption which the applicant itself did not take into account in calculating the efficiency of IRI's investment.

93 Last, the fact that the restructuring plan was intended to establish conditions favourable to the applicant's privatization does not show that IRI's investment satisfies the private investor test. Even though the possibility of private-investor participation was envisaged in the restructuring plan and although, effectively, such participation in the applicant's capital did come about following the adoption of the contested decision, such circumstances, in the absence at the time when the contested decision was adopted of a formal commitment by a private investor to make a capital contribution of real economic significance, do not show, in the light of what was stated in paragraph 86 above, that IRI's conduct satisfied the private investor test.

By complementing the fundamental rules with a series of legislative acts that provide for a number of exemptions, the European Commission has established a unique worldwide system of rules[21] under which State aid is monitored and assessed in the European Union. This legal framework is regularly reviewed to improve its efficiency and to respond to the call of the European Councils for less, but better, targeted State aid in order to boost the European economy[22].

As we can see, the assessment of Public Authorities is different from the systems for controlling agreements and abuse of dominant positions. Nevertheless, the administrative procedure for releasing a decision is the same and is designed on standard procedure number one.

1.2.5 General Principles of European Union Law

One of the most important, and perhaps the most important, principle according to which the Public Authorities' activities must be performed, is that of legal certainty. It is a principle regulated through European law, as well as national laws that limit the regulation power of public bodies.. In other words, the applicable laws must make market controls (i.e., competition, access to the market, and state aids) predictable for citizens and companies.

---

21 A complete explanation of the European framwork on competition can be read in Idot L. (ed.), *Commentaire J. Égret, Droit Communautaire de la concurrence*, Bruxelles, 2007.

22 See Collins A.R., *Is the Regulation of State aid a necessary component o fan effective Competition Law frame work*, in *Eur. Business Law Rev.*, 2005, p. 379 ff.

1.2.5.1 Legal Certainty

Legal certainty is prescribed by national and international law[23] and holds that the law must provide those subject to it with the ability to regulate their conduct. Legal certainty is internationally recognized as a central requirement for the rule of law[24].

As such, a legal system should permit those subject to the law to regulate their conduct with certainty and to protect those subject to the law from the arbitrary use of state power. Legal certainty thus entails a requirement that decisions be made according to legal rules, i.e., being lawful. The concept of legal certainty may be strongly linked to that of individual autonomy in national jurisprudence. The degree to which the concept of legal certainty is incorporated into law varies depending on national jurisprudence. However, legal certainty frequently serves as the central principle for the development of legal methods by which law is made, interpreted, and applied.

Legal certainty is also an established legal concept both in the civil law and common law legal systems. In the civil law tradition, legal certainty is defined in terms of maximum predictability of officials' behavior. It is this concept that must inspire the Public Authorities' activity. Indeed, legal certainty is regarded as the grounding value for the legality of legislative and administrative measures taken by Public Authorities.

Legal certainty has acquired great importance as a general principle of European Union law, having been recognized as such by the European Court of Justice since the 1960s. It is also an important general principle of international law and public law, which predate European Union law. As a general principle of European Union law, it directs that the law be certain: that it be clear and precise, and its legal implications foreseeable, especially when applied to financial obligations. The adoption of laws that will have legal effect in the European Union must have a proper legal basis. Legislation in member states implementing European Union law must be worded so that it is clear and understandable to those who are subject to the law.

Under European Union law, the general principle of legal certainty prohibits ex post facto laws, i.e. laws that take effect before they are published. This general principle also requires that sufficient information be made public to enable parties to know what the law is so that they may comply with it. For example in Opel Austria v Council (case 7) Court of First Instance, 22 January 1997, Case T-115/94, Opel Austria v Council, in Rep., p. II-39) the European Court of Justice held that a European Council regulation did not come into effect until it had been

---

23 For a perspective of the general principles applied to international investments, see Bungenberg M. - Griebel J. - Hindelang S. (Ed.). *International investment law and EU law*, Berlin, 2011.

24 Ratio J., *The Principle of Legal Certainty in EC Law*, Berlin, 2003 analyzed the principle of legal certainty starting from its first application in the State aids policy through the recent cases involving different European institutions.

published. Opel had brought the action on the basis that the Regulation in question violated the principle of legal certainty, because it legally came into effect before the notice and publication of the regulation.

(...)

14 The principle of legal certainty requires Community legislation to be certain and its application foreseeable by individuals and that every Community measure having legal effects must be clear and precise and must be brought to the notice of the person concerned in such a way that he can ascertain exactly the time at which the measure comes into being and starts to have legal effects. That requirement must be observed all the more strictly in the case of a measure liable to have financial consequences in order that those concerned may know precisely the extent of the obligations which it imposes on them.

15 A regulation which creates a situation in which two contradictory rules of law co-exist as to the duties imposed on the importation of certain products into the Community cannot be regarded as Community legislation which is certain and its application foreseeable by those subject to it; accordingly, it infringes the principle of legal certainty.

16 Although there is a presumption that the date of publication of a Community measure is the date actually appearing on each issue of the Official Journal, should evidence to the contrary be produced, regard must be had to the date of actual publication.

In back-dating the issue of the Official Journal in which a Community measure was published, the Council infringes the principle of legal certainty, since, by acting in that way, it does not place the person concerned in a position to ascertain exactly the time at which the measure comes into being and starts to have legal effects.

The doctrine of legitimate expectation[25], which has its roots in the principles of legal certainty and good faith, is also a central element of the general principle of legal certainty in European Union law[26]. The legitimate expectation doctrine holds that "*those who act in good faith on the basis of law as it is, or seems to be, should not be frustrated in their expectations.*" This means that a public administration, once it has induced a party to take a particular course of action, must not renege on its earlier position if doing so would cause that party to suffer loss. The European Court of Justice has considered the legitimate expectation doctrine in numerous cases involving agricultural policy and European Council regulations where violations of the general principle of legal certainty were alleged, with the leading case being Mulder v Minister van Landbouw en Visserij (case 8) ECJ, 28 April 1988, Case 120/86, Mulder, in Rep., p. 2321):

Mr Mulder maintains that the legislation in question infringes general principles of community law and is therefore invalid . he claims in the first place that regulation no 857/84

---

[25] The legitimate expectation doctrine has its origins in the English legal system: Steele I., *Substantive Legitimate Expectations: Striking the Right Balance?*, in *Law Quarterly Review*, 2005, p. 300 ff.

[26] An exhaustive analysis of the legitimate expectation principle under European Unione law was carried out by Moldén K. - Jure A.B., *The protection of Legitimate Expectations in European community Law,* Stockholm, 1997.

infringes the principles of legal certainty and protection of legitimate expectations, since those persons who took advantage of the system introduced by regulation no 1078/77 were entitled to expect to be able to resume production upon the expiry of their non-marketing undertaking . he also claims that the legislation in question infringes the principle of proportionality and the prohibition of discrimination between producers, and amounts to de facto expropriation of his holding . finally, mr Mulder considers that the community legislature misused its powers by using a market-regulating instrument in order to adopt a measure of structural policy.

On the other hand, the Netherlands government, the council and the commission all contend that the legislation in question is valid . the council and the commission base their view mainly upon the argument that the member states have available to them several ways of granting quotas not subject to the additional levy to those producers who, during the reference year, received a premium under regulation no 1078/77 . the Netherlands government and the commission - in an alternative submission - analyse the scope of the general principles relied upon and conclude that they have been properly respected in this case . as regards more particularly the principles of legal certainty and protection of legitimate expectations, the Netherlands government and the commission contend that they have not been infringed because the producers concerned were not entitled to expect that, upon the expiry of their five-year undertaking, they would have an unlimited right to resume milk production.

It must be conceded, as the Netherlands government and the commission have correctly observed, that a producer who has voluntarily ceased production for a certain period cannot legitimately expect to be able to resume production under the same conditions as those which previously applied and not to be subject to any rules of market or structural policy adopted in the mean time.

The fact remains that where such a producer, as in the present case, has been encouraged by a community measure to suspend marketing for a limited period in the general interest and against payment of a premium he may legitimately expect not to be subject, upon the expiry of his undertaking, to restrictions which specifically affect him precisely because he availed himself of the possibilities offered by the community provisions.

However, the regulations on the additional levy on milk give rise to such restrictions for producers who, pursuant to an undertaking entered into under regulation no 1078/77, did not deliver milk during the reference year . as stated in the reply to the first question, those producers may in fact be denied a reference quantity under the new system precisely because of that undertaking if they do not fulfil the specific conditions laid down in regulation no 857/84 or if the member states have no reference quantities available.

Contrary to the commission' s contention, total and continuous exclusion of that kind for the entire period of application of the regulations on the additional levy, preventing the producers concerned from resuming the marketing of milk at the end of the five-year period, was not an occurrence which those producers could have foreseen when they entered into an undertaking, for a limited period, not to deliver milk . there is nothing in the provisions of regulation no 1078/77 or in its preamble to show that the non-marketing undertaking entered into under that regulation might, upon its expiry, entail a bar to resumption of the activity in question . such an effect therefore frustrates those producers' legitimate expectation that the effects of the system to which they had rendered themselves subject would be limited.

It follows that the regulations on the additional levy on milk were adopted in breach of the principle of protection of legitimate expectations . those regulations must therefore be declared invalid on that ground, and it is unnecessary to consider the other arguments as to their invalidity put forward in the course of the proceedings.

The misuse of power test is another significant element of the general principle of legal certainty in European Union law. It holds that a lawful power must not be exercised for any other purpose than that for which it was conferred. According to the misuse of power test, a decision by a European Union institution is only a misuse of power if "*it appears, on the basis of objective, relevant and consistent evidence, to have been adopted with the exclusive or main purpose of achieving any end other than those stated.*" A rare instance where the European Court of Justice has held that a European Union institution has misused its powers, and therefore violated the general principle of legal certainty, is Giuffrida v Commission (case 9) ECJ, 29 September 1976, Case 105/75, Giuffrida, in Rep, p. 1395). The general principle of legal certainty is particularly stringently applied when European Union law imposes financial burdens on private parties.

(...)

10 it is clear from the abovementioned note and from the foregoing statements that internal competition n. a/108 was organized by the appointing authority for the sole purpose of remedying the anomalous administrative status of a specific official and of appointing that same official to the post declared vacant.

11 the pursuit of such a specific objective is contrary to the aims of any recruitment procedure, including the internal competition procedure, and thus constitutes a misuse of powers.

12 the existence of misuse of powers in this instance is moreover confirmed by the fact that one of the conditions for admission to the competition was that the successful candidate must have held the secretariat for meetings of council working parties or committees on regional policy for at least four years.

The principle of legal certainty was also applied in the context of national legislation and practices, specifically with respect to their effect on the common market and the restrictions placed on the circulation of freights and services (case 10) ECJ, 28 January 2010, Case C-333/08, European Commission v French Republic, in Rep., p. I-00757):

(...)

111 During the pre-litigation procedure and before the Court, the Commission has argued that the adoption of the 2001 Decree, which only entered into force on 2 December 2006 following the publication of the ministerial order referred to in Article 2 thereof, the publication, in 2002, of the notice to undertakings, and the publication, in 2003, of guidelines for the constitution of a file concerning the use of a processing aid applicable to categories of processing aids listed in the annex to the 2001 Decree (the guidelines) have created a situation of legal uncertainty which itself constitutes an unjustified obstacle to Article 28 EC.

112 In that regard, it should be noted that the lapse of time between the adoption of the 2001 Decree and the publication, on 2 December 2006, of the ministerial order permitting the entry of that decree into force and the coexistence during that period of the said decree and the 1912 Decree have given rise to an ambiguous factual situation by maintaining, for economic operators, a state of uncertainty as regards the possibilities for marketing in France processing aids or foodstuffs in the preparation of which processing aids were used which are lawfully manufactured and/or marketed in other Member States.

113 That legal uncertainty has been reinforced, first, by the notice to undertakings which indicated to economic operators that there was no obstacle, as from the publication date of that notice, to the application of certain provisions of the 2001 Decree and, second, by the guidelines published by AFFSA on 2 July 2003 which were, in its own words, applicable to categories of processing aids listed in the annex to the 2001 Decree.

114 Even if those guidelines were in conformity with the requirements arising from the case-law of the Court concerning the existence of a simplified registration procedure, an economic operator would not have been able to constitute a file concerning the use of a processing aid and seeking to enter the latter on a positive list referred to in Article 2 of the 2001 Decree at a time when that list had not been established, the ministerial order intended to make provision for that list having not yet been either adopted or published.

115 In those circumstances, the Commission's second head of claim concerning the 2001 Decree must be regarded as well founded.

1.2.5.2 Separation

In order to guarantee the transparency of the public administration's activities, Public Authorities in charge of controlling private subject conduct must not engage in any kind of economic activity, as that would run the risk of violating article 102 TFEU, which imposes a separation of administrative powers from economic activities.

1.2.5.2.1 Horizontal Separation

Firstly, the separation between the manager of infrastructures and the service provider is an imperative European principle. The principle of horizontal separation requires that the manager of goods and networks be autonomous and independent from the service provider. To that end, the owner of the networks must approve access to every potential service provider in order to facilitate regular competition in the roads management and construction markets. It is useful to recall that, in fact, public enterprises are companies in all senses and thus subject to the competition discipline: as "*established by consolidated EU principles, for the competition discipline a company is "any entity exercising an economic activity independently from its juridical status and how it is financed*" (see chapter 2 case 14) ECJ, April 23rd 1991, case 41/90, Klaus Hoefner e Fritz Elser - Macrotron GmbH, see chapter 2).

Moreover the principle of separation between the owner of the network and the service provider are violated when some selected companies are *de facto* stopped from using public infrastructures in favor of other authorized companies. Such discrimination implies a violation of the general principle of non-discrimination as interpreted by the Court of Justice and by norms for freedom of access to the market, which must necessarily be given to every company established within the European Union independently from the public or private nature of the property of various subjects.

As more fully explained in the second chapter of the book, the jurisprudence of the European Court of Justice punishes "indistinctly applicable measures," which, in other words, do not have an explicit subjective field of application but nonetheless restrict the free circulation of economic activities (case11) ECJ, October 17th 2002, case C-79/01, Payroll, in Rep., p. I-08923):

26 It must also be borne in mind that Article 43 EC requires the elimination of restrictions on the freedom of establishment and that all measures which prohibit, impede or render less attractive the exercise of such freedom must be regarded as constituting such restrictions (see, for example, Case C-439/99 Commission v Italy [2002] ECR I-305, paragraph 22).

27 In this case, even if the prohibition whereby DPCs which are not established and staffed solely by employment consultants or persons of equivalent status are not permitted to provide services consisting in the calculation and printing of pay slips to undertakings with less than 250 employees is not directly discriminatory, it constitutes, for an economic operator established in a Member State other than the Italian Republic, an obstacle to the carrying-on of his business through an undertaking in the latter Member State, which constitutes a restriction within the meaning of Article 43 EC.

28 However, it is clear from settled case-law, that where such measures apply to any person or undertaking carrying on an activity in the territory of the host Member State, they may be justified where they serve overriding requirements relating to the public interest, are suitable for securing the attainment of the objective which they pursue and do not go beyond what is necessary in order to attain it (see Case C-19/92 Kraus [1993] ECR I-1663, paragraph 32; Gebhard, cited above, paragraph 37; Case C-212/97 Centros [1999] ECR I-1459, paragraph 34; Pfeiffer, cited above, paragraph 19; Case C-424/97 Haim [2000] ECR I-5123, paragraph 57; Mac Quen and Others, cited above, paragraph 26, and Commission v Italy, cited above, paragraph 23).

Indeed European jurisprudence has long provided that "*national acts limiting the exercise of fundamental freedoms guaranteed by the Treaty must satisfy four conditions: be applied in a non discriminatory manner, answer imperative reasons of public interest, be right for guaranteeing the reaching the aim and not go past what is necessary to attain it*" (see chapter 2 case 12) ECJ, November 30th 1995, case C-55/94, Gebhard, in Rep. p. I-4165).

1.2.5.2.2 Vertical Separation

Vertical separation means that the public administration cannot engage in any economic activity. This is another European Union principle. The necessary coherence with the principle of separation emerging from EU law, which we have already discussed at length, makes it advisable that competences of control and regulation be exercised by a pubic authority that is not an service provider in the same market (case 12) ECJ, 13 December 1991, Case C-18/88, Regie de Telegraphe, in Rep., p. I-05941).

(…)

14 The national court asks whether Articles 3(f), 90 and 86 of the EEC Treaty preclude a Member State from granting to the company operating the public telecommunications network the power to lay down the standards for telephone equipment and to check that economic operators meet those standards when it is competing with those operators on the market for terminals.

15 Under Belgian law, the RTT holds a monopoly for the establishment and operation of the public telecommunications network. Moreover, only equipment supplied by the RTT or approved by it can be connected to the network. The RTT thus has the power to grant or withhold authorization to connect telephone equipment to the network, the power to lay down the technical standards to be met by that equipment, and the power to check whether the equipment not produced by it is in conformity with the specifications that it has laid down.

16 At the present stage of development of the Community, that monopoly, which is intended to make a public telephone network available to users, constitutes a service of general economic interest within the meaning of Article 90(2) of the Treaty.

17 The Court has consistently held that an undertaking vested with a legal monopoly may be regarded as occupying a dominant position within the meaning of Article 86 of the Treaty and that the territory of a Member State to which that monopoly extends may constitute a substantial part of the common market (judgments in Case C-41/90 Hoefner [1991] ECR I-1979, paragraph 28, and in Case C-260/89 ERT [1991] ECR I-2925, paragraph 31).

18 The Court has also held that an abuse within the meaning of Article 86 is committed where, without any objective necessity, an undertaking holding a dominant position on a particular market reserves to itself an ancillary activity which might be carried out by another undertaking as part of its activities on a neighbouring but separate market, with the possibility of eliminating all competition from such undertaking (judgment in Case 311/84 CBEM [1985] ECR 3261).

19 Therefore the fact that an undertaking holding a monopoly in the market for the establishment and operation of the network, without any objective necessity, reserves to itself a neighbouring but separate market, in this case the market for the importation, marketing, connection, commissioning and maintenance of equipment for connection to the said network, thereby eliminating all competition from other undertakings, constitutes an infringement of Article 86 of the Treaty.

20 However, Article 86 applies only to anti-competitive conduct engaged in by undertakings on their own initiative (see judgment in Case C-202/88 France v Commission "Telecommunications terminals", [1991] ECR I-1223), not to measures adopted by States. As regards measures adopted by States, it is Article 90(1) that applies. Under that provision, Member States must not, by laws, regulations or administrative measures, put public undertakings and undertakings to which they grant special or exclusive rights in a position which the said undertakings could not themselves attain by their own conduct without infringing Article 86.

21 Accordingly, where the extension of the dominant position of a public undertaking or undertaking to which the State has granted special or exclusive rights results from a State measure, such a measure constitutes an infringement of Article 90 in conjunction with Article 86 of the Treaty.

The notion of enterprise encompasses any entity providing an economic activity. Regardless of its juridical status and modality of financing, economic activity includes any activity consisting of the offering of goods or services in a specific market[27] (see chapter 2, case 16) ECJ, June 18th 1998, Commission v. Italia, case C-35/96, in Rep. p. I-03851).

1.2.5.3 The "In-House Providing"

The Public Authorities' action must be consistent with the norms of the internal market[28] and the in-house providing in coherence with the descriptions in the Services of General Interest. It is thus necessary to provide a mechanism for choosing the manager of streets through a public call for tenders unless the requirements of analogous control and prevalent destination of the service are present (case 13) ECJ, 18 November 1999, case C-107/98, Teckal, in Rep., p. I-08121). It may be helpful to consider a decision of the Court of Justice to better understand the conditions that could legitimate a direct contract:

37 It is clear from the order for reference that the Municipality of Viano entrusted to AGAC, by a single measure, both the provision of certain services and the supply of certain products. It is also common ground that the value of those products is greater than that of the services.

38 It follows a contrario from Article 2 of Directive 92/50 that, if a public contract relates both to products within the meaning of Directive 93/36 and to services within the meaning of Directive 92/50, it will fall within the scope of Directive 93/36 if the value of the products covered by the contract exceeds that of the services.

39 In order to provide a satisfactory answer to the national court which has referred a question to it, the Court of Justice may deem it necessary to consider provisions of Community law to which the national court has not referred in its question (Case 35/85 Procureur de la République v Tissier [1986] ECR 1207, paragraph 9, and Case C-315/88 Bagli Pennacchiotti [1990] ECR I-1323, paragraph 10).

40 It follows that, in order to provide an interpretation of Community law which will be of assistance to the national court in this case, it is necessary to interpret the provisions of Directive 93/36, not Article 6 of Directive 92/50.

---

[27] See Bonelli F., *La nozione di impresa nelle regole di concorrenza del Trattato C.E.E.*, in Verrucoli P. (a cura di), *La nozione d'impresa nell'ordinamento comunitario*, Milano, 1977, p. 37 ff.

[28] See Pescatore P., *Public and Private Aspects of Community Law*, in *Annual Proceedings of the Fordham Corporate Law Institute*, 1986, p. 383 ff.

41 In order to determine whether the fact that a local authority entrusts the supply of products to a consortium in which it has a holding must give rise to a tendering procedure as provided for under Directive 93/36, it is necessary to consider whether the assignment of that task constitutes a public supply contract.

42 If that is the case, and if the estimated amount of the contract, without value added tax, is equal to or greater than ECU 200 000, Directive 93/36 will apply. Whether the supplier is or is not a contracting authority is not conclusive in this regard.

43 It should be pointed out that the only permitted exceptions to the application of Directive 93/36 are those which are exhaustively and expressly mentioned therein (see, with reference to Directive 77/62, Case C-71/92 Commission v Spain [1993] ECR I-5923, paragraph 10).

44 Directive 93/36 does not contain any provision comparable to Article 6 of Directive 92/50, which excludes from its scope public contracts awarded, under certain conditions, to contracting authorities.

45 It should also be noted that this finding does not affect the obligation on those contracting authorities to apply in turn the tendering procedures laid down in Directive 93/36.

46 In its capacity as a local authority, the Municipality of Viano is a contracting authority within the meaning of Article 1(b) of Directive 93/36. It is therefore a matter for the national court to ascertain whether the relationship between the Municipality of Viano and AGAC also meets the other conditions which Directive 93/36 lays down for a public supply contract.

47 That will, in accordance with Article 1(a) of Directive 93/36, be the case if the contract in question is a contract for pecuniary interest, concluded in writing, involving, inter alia, the purchase of products.

48 It is common ground in the present case that AGAC supplies products, namely fuel, to the Municipality of Viano in return for payment of a price.

49 As to whether there is a contract, the national court must determine whether there has been an agreement between two separate persons.

50 In that regard, in accordance with Article 1(a) of Directive 93/36, it is, in principle, sufficient if the contract was concluded between, on the one hand, a local authority and, on the other, a person legally distinct from that local authority. The position can be otherwise only in the case where the local authority exercises over the person concerned a control which is similar to that which it exercises over its own departments and, at the same time, that person carries out the essential part of its activities with the controlling local authority or authorities.

51 The answer to the question must therefore be that Directive 93/36 is applicable in the case where a contracting authority, such as a local authority, plans to conclude in writing, with an entity which is formally distinct from it and independent of it in regard to decision-making, a contract for pecuniary interest for the supply of products, whether or not that entity is itself a contracting authority.

1.2.6 Main Principles Pertaining to Concessions and Public Contracts

The Treaty on the Functioning of the European Union prohibits any discrimination on grounds of nationality and establishes rules for the free movement of goods, the freedom of establishment, and the freedom to provide services. Works and service concessions in particular are subject to common market rules that are based on the following principles[29]:

1.2.6.1 Equality of Treatment

This principle implies in particular that all potential concessionaires know the rules in advance and that they apply to everybody in the same way. The Court has stipulated that in order to permit an objective comparison between offers, these offers should all conform to the tender specifications. Further, if an awarding authority takes account of changes to a specific offer after the tenders are opened, the Court considers that the tenderer concerned has obtained an advantage. Provisions reserving public contracts only to companies of which the State or the public sector is a major or sole shareholder contravene the principle of equality of treatment.

II. Transparency. The principle of transparency can be honored by any appropriate means, including advertising, which contains the information necessary to enable potential concessionaires to decide whether they are interested in participating. In every member State, administrative rules or practices provide that the awarding authorities must make their intentions public before launching a concession. In its Telaustria judgment, the Court of Justice of the European Union reiterated the awarding authority's obligation to guarantee all potential tenderers a proper degree of advertising in awarding concessions. A clear example of the obligation of transparency can be read in a recent case (case 14) ECJ, 19 July 2012, Case C-470/11, SIA Garkalns v Rīgas dome, in Rep. 2012):

(...)

41 In those circumstances, it must be ascertained whether the restriction on the freedom to provide services imposed by the national legislation at issue in the main proceedings is appropriate for achieving the objective of protecting consumers against the risks linked to betting and gaming and whether it does not go beyond what is necessary to achieve that objective.

42 In addition, in order to be consistent with the principle of equal treatment and to meet the obligation of transparency which flows from that principle, an authorisation scheme for betting and gaming must be based on objective, non-discriminatory criteria known in advance, in such a way as to circumscribe the exercise by the authorities of their discretion so that it is not used arbitrarily (see, to that effect, *Sporting Exchange*, paragraph 50).

---

29 For a complete explanation, see Craig P. - De Búrca G., *EU law: text, cases and materials*. Oxford, 2011.

43 In order to enable the impartiality of the authorization procedures to be monitored, it is also necessary for the competent authorities to base each of their decisions on reasoning which is accessible to the public, stating precisely the reasons for which, as the case may be, authorization has been refused.

44 In that connection, the Court has held that it is for the national courts to ensure, in the light, in particular, of the actual rules for applying the restrictive legislation concerned, that that legislation genuinely meets the concern to reduce opportunities for gambling and to limit activities in that domain in a consistent and systematic manner (see, to that effect, *Carmen Media Group*, paragraph 65 and the case-law cited).

45 In the case under consideration, it cannot be denied that, as is apparent from the order for reference, in allowing authorization to open an amusement arcade to be refused on grounds of substantial impairment of the interests of the State and of the residents of the administrative area concerned, the national legislation at issue in the main proceedings confers a broad discretion on the administrative authorities, particularly for the purposes of assessing the interests which that legislation is intended to protect.

46 Discretion, such as that at issue in the main proceedings, could be justified if the national legislation itself were genuinely intended to meet the concern to reduce opportunities for gambling and to limit activities in that domain in a consistent and systematic manner, or to ensure that local residents can live in peace or even, generally, to preserve public order, by conferring on the local authorities, for that purpose, a certain discretion in applying the rules relating to the organization of betting and gaming.

47 In order to assess the proportionality of the national legislation at issue, it is therefore for the national court to verify, in particular, that the State strictly supervises the activities related to betting and gaming; that the refusal of the local authorities to authorize the opening of new establishments of that type genuinely pursues the declared objective of protecting consumers; and that the criterion of 'substantial impairment of the interests of the State and of the residents of the administrative area concerned' is applied without discrimination.

1.2.6.2 Proportionality

According to the principle of proportionality, any measure chosen should be both necessary and appropriate in light of the objectives sought. With regard to concessions, a member State may not impose technical, professional, or financial conditions that are excessive and disproportionate when selecting candidates. Nor should the duration of the concession be set in such a way that it limits open competition beyond what is required to ensure that the investment is paid off and there is a reasonable return on invested capital, whilst maintaining a risk inherent in the exploitation by the concessionaire. The principle of proportionality was recently applied by the European Court of Justice in the tax sector (case 15) ECJ, 19 July 2012, Case C-263/11, Ainārs Rēdlihs v Valsts ieņēmumu dienests, in Rep., 2012)

41 By its second question, the referring court asks, essentially, whether European Union law must be interpreted as meaning that a rule of national law allowing a fine to be imposed, fixed at the level of the VAT which would normally be applicable for the value of the goods supplied, on an individual who has failed to fulfill his obligation to register in the

register of taxable persons for VAT purposes, although that individual was not liable for that tax, is compatible with the principle of proportionality.

42 Article 213(1) of the VAT Directive provides that every taxable person is required to state when his activity as a taxable person commences, changes or ceases.

43 A national measure such as that provided for in Article 3(3) and (5) of the Law on VAT, according to which taxable persons who have carried out transactions in respect of which the total value of the supplies of goods and services subject to VAT has exceeded LVL 10 000 during the previous twelve months are required to register in the register of taxable persons for VAT purposes, gives specific effect to the obligations on taxable persons under Article 213(1) of the VAT Directive.

44 That directive does not expressly provide for a system of penalties in the event of infringement of the obligations in Article 213(1) thereof. It is settled case-law that, in the absence of harmonization of European Union legislation in the field of penalties applicable in cases where conditions laid down by arrangements under that legislation are not complied with, Member States are empowered to choose the penalties which seem to them to be appropriate. They must, however, exercise that power in accordance with European Union law and its general principles, and consequently with the principle of proportionality (see Case 68/88 *Commission* v *Greece* [1989] ECR 2965, paragraph 23; Case C-210/91 *Commission* v *Greece* [1992] ECR I-6735, paragraph 19; and Case C-36/94 *Siesse* [1995] ECR I-3573, paragraph 21).

45 It is therefore legitimate for the Member States, in order to ensure the correct levying and collection of the tax and to prevent fraud, to provide in their respective provisions of national law for appropriate penalties to sanction the failure to observe the obligation to register in the register of taxable persons for VAT purposes.

46 Such penalties must not, however, go further than is necessary to attain those objectives (see, to that effect, Joined Cases C-95/07 and C-96/07 *Ecotrade* [2008] ECR I-3457, paragraphs 65 to 67, and Case C-284/11 *EMS-Bulgaria Transport* [2012] ECR I-0000, paragraph 67).

47 In order to assess whether the penalty here at issue is consistent with the principle of proportionality, the nature and the degree of seriousness of the infringement which that penalty seeks to sanction must, inter alia, be taken into account, as must also the means of establishing the amount of that penalty.

48 As regards, first, the nature and seriousness of the infringement which the penalty at issue seeks to sanction, it is important to point out that that penalty is intended to sanction solely the failure to comply with the obligation to register in the register of taxable persons for VAT purposes. The Court has had the opportunity to state, in this regard, that the obligations set out in Article 213 of the VAT Directive, of which the obligation for the taxable person to declare the commencement of his activity as a taxable person is one, constitute only a formal requirement for the purposes of verification (see, to that effect, Case C-385/09 *Nidera Handelscompagnie* [2010] ECR I-10385, paragraph 50).

49 The penalty at issue is thus not designed to ensure recovery of the tax from the party liable for it. The competent authorities may proceed with such recovery, regardless of whether a penalty is imposed for failure to register.

50 With regard, secondly, to the means of establishing the amount of the penalty at issue, it is important to note that this constitutes a fixed percentage, set at a level equal to that of the tax payable on the supplies effected, even if the object of that penalty is not the recovery of the tax, as stated in the previous paragraph.

51 Moreover, it must be observed that, as is apparent from the written observations of the Latvian Government, the Latvian legislature has adopted new provisions which provide for a graduated scale of penalties for failure to register.

52 In the present case, it is possible that the procedure for establishing the amount of the penalty may go further than is necessary to attain the objectives set out in paragraph 45 of this judgment.

53 Such a penalty may therefore prove to be disproportionate.

54 It is for the national court to determine whether the amount of the penalty does not go further than is necessary to attain the objectives of ensuring the correct levying and collection of the tax and the prevention of fraud, having regard to the facts of the case and, inter alia, the sum actually imposed and the possible existence of fraud or circumvention of the applicable legislation attributable to the taxable person whose failure to register is being penalised.

55 The answer to the second question is therefore that European Union law must be interpreted as meaning that it is possible that a rule of national law allowing a fine to be imposed, fixed at the level of the rate of VAT normally applicable for the value of the goods transferred in the supplies made, on an individual who has failed to fulfil his obligation to register in the register of taxable persons for VAT purposes and who was not liable for that tax, may be contrary to the principle of proportionality. It is for the national court to determine whether the amount of the penalty does not go further than is necessary to attain the objectives of ensuring the correct levying and collection of the tax and preventing fraud, having regard to the facts of the case and, inter alia, the sum actually imposed and the possible existence of fraud or circumvention of the applicable legislation attributable to the taxable person whose failure to register is being penalized.

1.2.6.3 Mutual Recognition

According to the principle of mutual recognition, a member State must accept the products and services supplied by economic operators from another member State. It must also accept the technical specifications, checks, diplomas, certificates, and qualifications required in another member State if these are recognized as equivalent. A complete outline of the mutual recognition principle can be understood by reading a leading case concerning the recognition of academic titles (case 16) ECJ, 13 November 2003, Case C-313/01, Christine Morgenbesser v Consiglio dell'Ordine degli avvocati di Genova, in Rep., p. I-13467):

(...)

56 Having regard to the above, it needs to be examined whether Articles 39 EC and 43 EC apply in the circumstances of the case in the main proceedings. Only if those provisions do not apply will it be necessary to examine the other provisions of the Treaty mentioned by the referring court in its question.

57 According to the case-law the principles of which were set out in *Vlassopoulou* , the authorities of a Member State, when considering a request by a national of another Member State for authorisation to exercise a regulated profession, must take into consideration the professional qualification of the person concerned by making a comparison between the qualifications certified by his diplomas, certificates and other formal qualifications and by his relevant professional experience and the professional qualifications required by the national rules for the exercise of the profession in question (see, most recently, Case C-232/99 *Commission* v *Spain* [2002] ECR I-4235, paragraph 21).

58 That obligation extends to all diplomas, certificates and other evidence of formal qualifications as well as to the relevant experience of the person concerned, irrespective of whether they were acquired in a Member State or in a third country, and it does not cease to exist as a result of the adoption of directives on the mutual recognition of diplomas (Case C-238/98 *Hocsman* [2000] ECR I-6623, paragraphs 23 and 31; *Commission* v *Spain* , paragraph 22).

59 According to the Bar Council of Genoa, the activity of praticante is a training activity, to which the provisions of Articles 39 EC and 43 EC do not apply.

60 However, the period of practice at issue in the main proceedings comprises the pursuit of activities, normally remunerated by the client or by the firm for which the praticante works, with a view to access to a regulated profession to which Article 43 EC applies. In so far as the remuneration of the praticante takes the form of a salary, Article 39 EC may also apply.

61 Both Article 39 EC and Article 43 EC may therefore apply to a situation such as that in the main proceedings. However, the analysis does not differ according to whether it is freedom of movement for workers or the freedom of establishment which is relied upon in opposing the refusal, on the part of the Bar Council of Genoa acting in its capacity as the competent authority for enrolling praticanti on the register, to take the legal diploma obtained in another Member State and the professional experience acquired into account for the purposes of enrolment.

62 As the Court has already held, the exercise of the right of establishment is hindered if national rules fail to take account of learning, skills and qualifications already acquired by the person concerned in another Member State, so that the competent national authorities must measure whether such factors sufficiently demonstrate that missing learning and skills have been acquired (*Vlassopoulou* , paragraphs 15 and 20; *Fernández de Bobadilla* , paragraph 33).

63 In that context, contrary to what the Italian Government claims, a case such as that at issue in the main proceedings is not concerned with a simple question of recognising academic qualifications.

64 It is true that the recognition, for academic and civil purposes, of the equivalence of a diploma obtained in one Member State may be relevant, and even decisive, for enrolment with the bar of another Member State (Case 71/76 *Thieffry* [1977] ECR 765).

65 It does not follow, however, that, for the purposes of the comparative examination which the competent authority of the host Member State must undertake in circumstances such as those in the main proceedings, it is necessary to examine the academic equivalence of the diploma relied upon by the person concerned in relation to the diploma normally required of nationals of that State.

66 The taking into account of the diploma of the person concerned, such as the maîtrise en droit granted by a French university, must therefore be carried out in the context of the assessment of the whole of the training, academic and professional, which that person is able to demonstrate.

67 It is therefore the duty of the competent authority to examine, in accordance with the principles set out by the Court of Justice in*Vlassopoulou* and *Fernández de Bobadilla* , whether, and to what extent, the knowledge certified by the diploma granted in another Member State and the qualifications or professional experience obtained there, together with the experience obtained in the Member State in which the candidate seeks enrolment, must be regarded as satisfying, even partially, the conditions required for access to the activity concerned.

68 That examination procedure must enable the authorities of the host Member State to assure themselves, on an objective basis, that the foreign diploma certifies that its holder has knowledge and qualifications which are, if not identical, at least equivalent to those certified by the national diploma. That assessment of the equivalence of the foreign diploma must be carried out exclusively in the light of the level of knowledge and qualifications which its holder can be assumed to possess having regard to that diploma, having regard to the nature and duration of the studies and practical training to which the diploma relates (Case 222/86 *Heylens and Others*[1987] ECR 4097, paragraph 13; *Vlassopoulou* , paragraph 17).

69 In the course of that examination, a Member State may, however, take into consideration objective differences relating to both the legal framework of the profession in question in the Member State of origin and to its field of activity. In the case of the profession of lawyer, a Member State may therefore carry out a comparative examination of diplomas, taking account of the differences identified between the national legal systems concerned (*Vlassopoulou* , paragraph 18).

70 If that comparative examination of diplomas results in the finding that the knowledge and qualifications certified by the foreign diploma correspond to those required by the national provisions, the Member State must recognise that diploma as fulfilling the requirements laid down by its national provisions. If, on the other hand, the comparison reveals that the knowledge and qualifications certified by the foreign diploma and those required by the national provisions correspond only partially, the host Member State is entitled to require the person concerned to show that he has acquired the knowledge and qualifications which are lacking (*Vlassopoulou* , paragraph 19).

71 By the same token, the competent national authorities must measure whether the learning and skills acquired in the host Member State, either through a course of study or by way of practical experience, sufficiently demonstrate that the missing knowledge and qualifications have in the meantime been acquired (*Vlassopoulou,* paragraph 20).

72 In the light of the above, the answer to the referring court must be that Community law precludes the authorities of a Member State from refusing to enroll the holder of a legal diploma obtained in another Member State in the register of persons undertaking the necessary period of practice for admission to the bar solely on the ground that it is not a legal diploma issued, confirmed or recognised as equivalent by a university of the first State.

1.3 Procedures for Regulating the Infrastructures Market with Legal Certainty, Good Administration, and Sincere Cooperation

The first explanation of the applicable law will focus on the procedural issues, divided into three different models respectively referred to as:

1. A standard procedure for market regulation;
2. A standard procedure for public procurement of works and services[30]; and
3. Non-standard procedures for awarding public contracts.

In essence, we have designed three different hypotheses for procedures under European Union law. These three procedures have to be performed by Public Authorities in order to carry on the management, construction, reconstruction, maintenance, and protection of infrastructures and facilities.

Standard procedure model n. 1 is the perfect example of a European administrative procedure for market regulation that fulfills the legislative obligations of European member States under European Union law by allowing the Public Authorities to carry on all of these activities. Models n. 2 and 3 will be examined separately, after a brief explanation of the main principles of concessions and public procurement.

Indeed, infrastructure construction and maintenance are ruled by the special European discipline related to "*Services of General Interest.*" Under European Union legislation, article 14 of the Treaty on the Functioning of the European Union, services of general interests have to be exercised according to high standards of quality and quantity. In this context, the public roads are services of general interest, which means they are goods for general use and shall be used under conditions and in ways expressly specified by the public administration.

1.4 A Standard Procedure for Market Regulation in the Infrastructures Sector Guided by the Principle of Good Administration (Model n. 1)

The first procedure is the most used in European States for regulating the market of services of general interest. Let's begin with a quick explanation of how this procedure is structured.

The standard market regulation procedure is comprised the following eight steps: (1) Instance or complaint: the communication sent by a private person or by

[30] Malinconico C., *Codice degli appalti pubblici e privati: disciplina statale e comunitaria, lavori, forniture, servizi e settori esclusi*, Milan, 2004, explained a complete description of European procedures for the awarding of public contracts.

a company (generally speaking, a private party) to the public administration with the explicit request to start an administrative procedure in order to release an authorization or to adopt any other different decision with a direct effect on the instant person or company; (2) Logging: the activity of the public administration to give a number to the procedure; (3) Notice of proceedings initiation: the notice to the instant party of the receipt and logging; (4) Formal letter to interested subjects with an invitation to submit comments within a time limit: the contact of other interested parties; (5) Completion of the investigation/inquiry activities ex officio: the verification of facts and legal basis of the instance; (6) Notice of inquiry results and invitation to submit comments: notification of the results to interested parties; (7) Measure of closing the investigation: the adoption of the act/decision by the public administration; and (8) Notification of the measure of closing the investigation: the notice of the adoption to the interested parties.

The first step of the procedure is the Instance:

1. Interested parties: every citizen or company is allowed to submit a complaint. But it is necessary that the instant has a real and concrete interest in the activity of the ASR (for example, in competition procedures this might include a company damaged by agreements, conduct, or consumers)
2. The Authority: Public Authorities can start their procedures also ex officio on the basis of information acquired by their own instruments

In other words we can see that the first action of an administrative procedure can be acquired by a private entity or ex officio. This means that public authorities always have the obligation to take into consideration private instances and, if there is a concrete interest of the party, to carry on the procedure according to the following steps.

According to the second step, Public Authorities must give a protocol number to the complaint that will be used for the procedure. This may seem banal, but it is an international and European obligation according to the principle of good administration. As certainty of law, transparency, and good administration are general principles of the European Union, this implies that a violation of the principle is a breach of European Treaties and a civil liability for the State.

According to international practice, good administration by public bodies means:

1. *Getting it right* (legitimate expectation): All public bodies must comply with the law and have regard for the rights of those concerned. They should act according to their statutory powers and duties and any other rules governing the services they provide. They should follow their own policies and procedural guidance, whether published or internal. Public bodies must act in accordance with recognized quality standards, established good practices, or both (with clinical care for example).

2. *Being customer focused*: Public bodies should provide services that are easily accessible to their customers. Policies and procedures should be clear and there must be accurate, complete, and understandable information regarding the service. Public bodies should also aim to ensure that customers are clear about their entitlements, about what they can and cannot expect from the public body, and about their own responsibilities.
3. *Being open and accountable*: Public bodies should give people information and, if appropriate, advice that is clear, accurate, complete, relevant, and timely. Public bodies should be open and truthful when accounting for their decisions and actions. They should state their criteria for decision-making and give reasons for their decisions.
4. *Acting fairly and proportionately*: Public bodies should be prepared to listen to their customers and avoid being defensive when things go wrong. Public bodies should treat people equally and impartially. They should also understand and respect the diversity of their customers and ensure equal access to services and treatment regardless of background or circumstance.
5. *Putting things right*: When mistakes happen, public bodies should acknowledge them, apologize, explain what went wrong, and put things right quickly and effectively. Putting things right may include reviewing any decisions found to be incorrect, as well as reviewing and amending any policies and procedures found to be ineffective, unworkable, or unfair, and giving appropriate notice before changing the rules.
6. *Seeking continuous improvement*: Public bodies should review their policies and procedures regularly to ensure they are effective; actively seek and welcome all feedback, both compliments and complaints; use feedback to improve their public service delivery and performance; and capture and review lessons learned from complaints so that they contribute to developing services.

According to the principle of fair cooperation between public administrations, the market regulator has a duty to provide notification as to whether a procedure should involve more authorities.

The principle of "sincere cooperation" stems from Article 4 of the Treaty on European Union (TEU) in the context of relations between the European Union (EU) and member States, and Article 13 of the TEU in the context of relations between the EU institutions. Essentially, this Article states that the member States must take all appropriate measures to fulfill their obligations arising out of the Treaty and do nothing detrimental to the proper functioning of the European Union (case 17) ECJ, 29 March 2012, Case T-398/07, Kingdom of Spain v European Commission, in Rep. 2012):

(…)

39 By its first plea in law, the Kingdom of Spain claims that the Commission was in breach of its duty of sincere cooperation, laid down in Article 10 EC and Article 7(2) of the Framework Directive, with CMT during the administrative proceedings at issue.

40 It must be borne in mind that the obligation of sincere cooperation laid down in Article 10 EC is incumbent both on all authorities of the Member States acting within the scope of their powers and on the institutions of the European Union, which have a reciprocal obligation to afford such sincere cooperation to the Member States (order of July 1990 in Case C-2/88 Imm *Zwartveld and Others* [1990] ECR I-3365, paragraph 17; see Case C-94/00 *Roquette Frères* [2002] ECR I-9011, paragraph 31 and case-law cited). Where, as in the present case, European Union and national authorities are called upon to assist in the attainment of the objectives of the Treaty by the coordinated exercise of their respective powers, such cooperation is particularly crucial (*Roquette Frères*, paragraph 32).

41 As regards the admissibility of the part of this plea relating to the infringement of Article 7(2) of the Framework Directive, which is disputed by the Commission, the Court must join the Commission in observing that the Kingdom of Spain, within this plea, has merely asserted that the scope of the obligation of cooperation cannot be restricted to a mechanism for the notification of draft measures on the part of the national regulatory authorities ('the NRA') and subsequent comments on the part of the Commission, and has not presented any arguments to demonstrate that that provision has been infringed.

42 In response to questions at the hearing on the relevance, in this case, of that provision, the Kingdom of Spain declared that Article 7(2) was an application, within the regulatory framework relating to electronic communications, of the duty of sincere cooperation laid down in Article 10 EC.

43 It is clear from Article 21 of the Statute of the Court of Justice and Article 44(1)(c) of the Rules of Procedure of the General Court that every application initiating proceedings must state the subject-matter of the proceedings and contain a summary of the pleas in law on which it is based. That statement must be sufficiently clear and precise to enable the defendant to prepare its defence and the Court to rule on the action, if necessary, without any further information. In order to guarantee legal certainty and the sound administration of justice it is necessary, in order for an action to be admissible, that the basic legal and factual particulars relied on be indicated, at least in summary form, coherently and intelligibly in the application itself (see Case T-201/04 *Microsoft* v *Commission* [2007] ECR II-3601, paragraph 94 and case-law cited).

44 Further, a mere abstract statement of the grounds in the application does not alone satisfy the requirements of the Rules of Procedure and the application must specify the nature of the grounds on which the application is based (Joined Cases 19/60, 21/60, 2/61 and 3/61*Fives Lille Cail and Others* v *High Authority* [1961] ECR 281, at 295, and judgment of 18 December 2008 in Case T-455/05*Componenta* v *Commission*, not published in the ECR, paragraph 45).

45 It is clear that the Kingdom of Spain has not presented any sufficiently clear argument in support of the part of the plea relating to the infringement of Article 7(2) of the Framework Directive in the context of the administrative proceedings which led to the adoption of the contested decision. That part of the plea must therefore be declared to be inadmissible since it does not meet the requirements of the case-law cited in paragraphs 43 and 44 above.

46 As regards the substance of this plea in so far as it relates to an infringement of Article 10 EC, in the first place, the Kingdom of Spain's assertion that the Commission was in breach of its duty of sincere cooperation by not sufficiently involving CMT in the administrative proceedings must be rejected.

47 It should be emphasised, so far as concerns relationships formed in the context of proceedings conducted by the Commission pursuant to Articles 81 EC and 82 EC, that the rules for the operation of the duty of sincere cooperation which stems from Article 10 EC and which binds the Commission in its relationships with the Member States have been stated in, inter alia, Articles 11 to 16 of Regulation No 1/2003, in Chapter IV headed 'Cooperation'. Those provisions do not impose an obligation on the Commission to consult the NRA, nor do they provide for the Commission being able, as claimed by the Kingdom of Spain, to undertake 'joint action' with them in proceedings conducted by the Commission pursuant to Articles 81 EC and 82 EC.

48 Next, it is clear that CMT was in fact involved in the administrative proceedings in this case. First, as is clear from paragraphs 4 to 6 above, the Commission sent to CMT three requests for information, to which CMT replied. Second, the Commission sent to CMT, on 24 May 2006, a non-confidential version of the statement of objections. The Commission also informed CMT that it was open to it, if it chose, to send to the Commission written comments on the statement of objections or again to present observations or questions orally at the hearing. No written observations were presented by CMT. Third, the Kingdom of Spain does not dispute that several representatives of CMT were present at the hearing of 12 and 13 June 2006 and that CMT also intervened orally at that hearing. Fourth, on 26 June 2006 CMT also replied in writing to a number of questions put by the complainant during the hearing. Fifth, the Kingdom of Spain does not dispute the Commission's assertion that the members of the team responsible for the file met CMT on several occasions in order to discuss the investigation. Sixth, the Kingdom of Spain does not dispute the Commission's assertions that on 14 June 2007 several representatives of CMT met the Commission and presented observations on the wording of some recitals of the contested decision, which were taken into consideration for the second meeting of the advisory committee referred to in Article 14 of Regulation No 1/2003. CMT did not submit any additional comments in that regard. Moreover, a CMT expert took part in a meeting of that advisory committee, which took place on 15 June 2007. It must be held that the Kingdom of Spain fails to explain, in its action, why the participation of CMT, as described above, was insufficient in the present case.

49 In that regard, the arguments relied on by the Kingdom of Spain to demonstrate the significance of the failure by the Commission to comply with its duty of sincere cooperation can also not be accepted.

Cooperation between institutions in the application European law is essential to the proper functioning of the European Union. Indeed, the Court of Justice has recognized the duty of sincere cooperation as a general principle of Community law. While sincere cooperation is not explicitly mentioned in the Treaties, this does not affect its status as a requirement with which all member States and European institutions must comply. Specifically, inter-institutional cooperation takes place in various ways, including exchanges of letters between the Council and the Commission, inter-institutional agreements, and joint declarations of the institutions.

According to the fourth step of the standard procedure, Public Authorities have to submit a formal letter to all stakeholders with an invitation to submit comments within a time limit.

Public bodies should behave helpfully, dealing with people promptly, within reasonable timescales, and within any published time limits. They should tell people if things take longer than the public body has stated or than people can reasonably expect them to take.

Public bodies should communicate effectively, using clear language that people can understand and that is appropriate to them and their circumstances. On the other hand, private parties have to give notice to the public administration of any concrete information that can be useful to carry on a real and complete assessment of the facts constituting the basis of the adoption of the decision.

After the submission of comments by third parties, public authorities should complete the investigation/inquiry (step 5). The preliminary investigation and inquiry will be conducted entirely by the relevant office, which may require the cooperation of third parties or stakeholders. The investigation has to cover the different fields in the different market regulation sectors:

1. Free access to the market (free circulation of services and companies);
2. Competition (agreement, conduct, relevant market, impact/damage to competition);
3. State aids (origin, form of benefits, selectivity, concrete economic advantage, relevant market).

After the completion of the investigation phase, according to the step 6, the public administration should provide notice to all stakeholders in order to allow one last possibility to submit observations.

This requires public bodies to inform third parties that investigations are completed and communicate the deadline by which stakeholders may submit comments or observations (the date by which the parties must take action should not be so long as to conflict with the principle of good administration). It is, indeed, important to provide a last chance to obtain evidence of the competition damage (conduct, agreement).

After the term to submit last comments, the public administration (step 7) adopts the concrete measures to effect the market regulation (avoid abuses or agreements, invite to fulfill with law, etc. . . .). The measures are adopted through acts specifically governed by the different member States' national laws.

The public administration, after having adopted the measures, must give notice to all stakeholders (step 8). The content of the notice must specify the phases of the whole procedure, the reasons for the investigation, and a clear motivation. In other words, the closing decision has to provide a review of the whole procedure, both from a procedural point of view and from a substantive one.

1.5 Introduction to the Standard Procedures for Awarding of Works and Services (Design, Construction, and Maintenance)

Before we begin the description of model procedures n. 2 and 3, it is necessary to distinguish public contracts from concessions, because of the different treatment provided by the Directives and by the Court of Justice (We can make reference to the Communication of the European Commission of 2000).

1.5.1 Works Concessions

European Directives distinguish a works concession from a public works contract by the fact that the concessionaire is granted the right to exploit a construction as consideration for having built it. The existence of an exploitation risk related to the investment made is the determining factor. This right of exploitation may also be accompanied by payment.

The right of exploitation implies the transfer of the responsibilities of operation from the grantor to the concessionaire. These responsibilities cover the technical, financial, and managerial aspects of the construction. For example, the concessionaire is responsible for making the investments required in order to have a construction that is available to users under good conditions. He is responsible for paying off the construction and bears the risks inherent in the construction, management, and use of the facilities.

The right of exploitation allows the concessionaire to demand payment, over a certain period of time, from those who use the structure erected and/or other forms of remuneration from exploitation, such as tolls, fees, or "shadow tolls." The fact that the right of exploitation may be accompanied by payment does not change the risk repartition if the sum paid covers only a part of the cost of the construction. For example, it can happen that a State bears part of the costs of operating the concession in order to keep prices down for users. This partial remuneration can take the form of a flat rate amount or a sum paid on the basis of the number of users. This partial remuneration should not, however, have the effect of eliminating the risk inherent in exploitation that is borne by the concessionaire - otherwise it will be reclassified as a public works contract.

1.5.2 Service Concessions

The Directive 2004/18/EC defines service concessions as contracts of the same type as a public service contract except for the fact that the remuneration for the provision of services consists either solely in the right to exploit the service or in this right together with payment. Service concessions are, however, not subject to any detailed rules in the Directive.

Nonetheless, service concessions are subject to the principles and rules provided by the EU Treaties (primary law). A service concession exists when the operator bears the risks involved in establishing and exploiting the service. The operator obtains revenue from the user, particularly by charging fees. As is the case for works concessions, service concessions are characterized by a transfer of the responsibility of exploitation.

Sometimes it is difficult to distinguish a service concession from a public work concession. If the main subject matter of the contract concerns the building of a structure on behalf of the grantor, it should be considered a works concession. This is the case, for example, for a motorway or toll bridge. If the contract includes several elements that may be separated, the rules that apply to each should be applied separately. For example, motorway catering services may be the subject of a different service concession than those involving its construction or management.

Both works and services concessions are awarded by national Public Authorities through the four specific procedures provided by the Directives.

1.5.2.1 The Open Procedure

In an open procedure, any interested economic operator may submit a tender. The minimum time limit for the receipt of tenders is fifty-two days from the date on which the contract notice was published. If a prior information notice has been published, this time limit can be cut to thirty-six days. In no case may the time limit for the receipt of tenders be less than twenty-two days.

1.5.2.2 The Restricted Procedure

In the case of restricted procedures, any economic operator may request to participate and only candidates invited to do so may submit a tender.

The time limit for the receipt of requests to participate is thirty-seven days from the date of the contract notice. The contracting authority then, simultaneously and in writing, invites the selected candidates to submit their tenders. There should be a minimum of five candidates, except if there are not enough with the required capabilities. The minimum time limit for the receipt of tenders shall be forty days from the date on which the invitation is sent. If a prior information notice has been published, this may be shortened to thirty-six days. The minimum time limit for the receipt of tenders may not be less than twenty-two days. Exceptionally and when urgency requires, the contracting authority may set a minimum time limit of fifteen days (ten days if the notice is sent electronically) for requests to participate and of ten days for the receipt of tenders.

1.5.2.3 The Negotiated Procedure

In a negotiated procedure, the contracting authority consults the economic operators of its choice and negotiates the terms of the contract with them.

1.5.2.4 The Competitive Dialogue

A contracting authority may make use of the competitive dialogue for complex contracts if it is not able to define by itself the technical solutions to satisfy its needs or is not able to specify the legal and/or financial make-up of a project. Large infrastructure projects would seem to lend themselves to this type of dialogue.

The contracting authority publishes a contract notice that includes the award criteria. The minimum time limit for receipt of requests to participate is thirty-seven days. The contracting authority then, simultaneously and in writing, invites the selected candidates (a minimum of three) to conduct a dialogue. The discussion commences, may take place in stages and continues until the (technical and/or economic and legal) solutions have been defined. The contracting authority ensures equal treatment of all tenderers and protects the confidentiality of the information. At the end of the dialogue, the candidates submit their final tenders. These tenders may be specified, but without changing the basic features of the contract. The contracting authority awards the contract in accordance with the award criteria that are set during the dialogue and on the basis of the most economically advantageous tender.

These procedures are applicable only within the field of application of the Directives. The Directive 2004/18/EC applies to public works contracts, public supply contracts, and public service contracts having a value, excluding taxations, estimated to be no less than the pre-established thresholds. For those member States that have not adopted the single currency, the value of these thresholds is calculated and published by the European Commission in the Official Journal once the recalculated thresholds in Euros are published.

The following public contracts are excluded from the field of application of the directive: (1) contracts covered by the "special sectors" directive and contracts awarded with the purpose of providing or exploiting public telecommunications networks; (2) contracts that are declared to be secret or affect the essential interests of a Member State; (3) contracts concluded pursuant to international agreements; (4) contracts concerning the following services: the acquisition or rental of existing buildings; the acquisition, development, and (co)production of broadcasting programs; arbitration and conciliation services; the purchase, sale, or transfer of financial instruments; central bank services; and employment contracts; (5) RTD services which do not belong exclusively to the contracting authority or which are not wholly financed by it; (6) service contracts awarded on the basis of an exclusive right; (7) service concessions; and (8) certain public contracts awarded in the field of defense and security.

The Directive 2004/17/EC applies to all contracting authorities or public enterprises that pursue activities in one of the following fields: gas, electricity, water, transport services, postal services, the extraction of fuels, or the provision of ports or airports, as well as to all contracting entities which, when they are neither contracting authorities nor public undertakings, pursue one (or more) of the above activities and enjoy special or exclusive rights granted by a competent authority of a member State.

The directive 2004/17/EC applies to contracts in the following fields:

- the provision or operation of fixed networks intended to provide a service to the public in connection with the production, transport, or distribution of gas or electricity, or the supply of gas or electricity to such networks;
- the provision or operation of fixed networks intended to provide a service to the public in connection with the production, transport, or distribution of water, or the supply of water to such networks;
- where the contracting entity is active in the drinking water sector, contracts or design contests connected with irrigation, land drainage, or hydraulic engineering projects, or contracts connected with the disposal or treatment of sewage;
- the provision or operation of networks providing a service to the public in the field of transport by railway, automated systems, tramway, trolley-bus, bus, or cable.
  Bus transport services are excluded from the scope of the Directive where other entities are free to provide those services, either in general or in a particular geographical area, under the same conditions as the contracting entities;
- the provision of postal services, On condition that such services are provided by an entity that also provides postal services and the market is not yet open to competition: mail management services (e.g., mailroom management services), added-value services linked to and provided entirely by electronic means (e.g., the secure transmission of coded documents and address management services), direct mail bearing no address, financial services (e.g., postal money orders and postal transfers), philatelic services, and logistics services;
- the exploitation of a geographical area for the purpose of (1) exploring for or extracting oil, gas, coal, or other solid fuels; or (2) the provision of airports, maritime or inland ports, or other terminal facilities to carriers by air, sea, or inland waterway.

Contracts awarded in these sectors are no longer subject to the Directive if effective competition exists. Member States have had the possibility of asking the Commission to adopt a decision testifying to the existence of effective competition in a member State for a given sector in accordance with a specific procedure. This procedure is based on the characteristics of the goods and services under consideration, the existence of alternatives, prices, and the presence of several competitors. On its own initiative or at the request of the national contracting entities, when the national transposition of the Directive allows them to do so, the Commission may adopt a decision testifying to the existence of effective competition in a member State and for a given sector. If no decision of effective competition is made by the Commission within the set deadline, the exclusion becomes applicable.

Before going through the examination of models n. 2 and 3, it is also necessary to provide a brief explanation of subcontracting conditions. Public Authorities could oblige private parties to award parts of contracts to third parties in order to encourage the involvement of small and medium-sized undertakings in the public contracts procurement market.

If the subcontractor is a contracting Authority (or a public enterprise), it has to award subcontracts according to the procedures provided by the Directive. In any event, Public Authorities, according to the Directive, could: (a) require the concessionaire to award contracts representing a minimum of 30% of the total value of the work for which the concession contract is to be awarded, to third parties, at the same time providing the option for candidates to increase this percentage (the minimum percentage being specified in the concession contract), or (b) request the candidates for concession contracts to specify in their tenders the percentage, if any, of the total value of the work for which the concession contract is to be awarded that they intend to assign to third parties. When considering subcontracting and the notion of contracting authority, it is useful to read the Opinion of Advocate General Geelhoed (case 18) Opinion, 24 June 2004, Case C-126/03, Commission of the European Communities v Federal Republic of Germany, in Rep., p. I-11197):

(…)

29. As to the case-law relied on by the German Government, (6) this goes to the question of whether or not a given body is a public body. There are three conditions; all must be met. The body must have been established for the specific purpose of meeting needs in the general interest, not of an industrial or commercial character; it must have legal personality; and it must be closely dependent on the State, regional or local authorities or other bodies governed by public law. Unlike a regional or local authority, a 'body governed by public law' is thus not by definition a contracting authority. However, where a public body meets the cumulative criteria, then it too is by definition a contracting authority within the meaning of the Directive, and the procedural rules set out in that Directive must be fully observed, whether or not the contract awarded concerns tasks in the general interest, and whether or not these are carried out under normal market conditions

30. I think Mannesmann Anlagenbau Austria (7) may be helpful on that point – the Court explained there that Article 1(a) of the Directive makes no distinction between public works contracts awarded by a contracting authority for the purposes of fulfilling its task of meeting needs in the general interest, and those which are unrelated to that task – the reason for this being to avoid the risk of preference being given to national tenderers or applicants whenever a contract is awarded by the contracting authorities.

31. In the present case, therefore, it is immaterial that the activity in question may be unrelated to the body's task in the general interest, or may not involve any public funds. Where, under the terms of the Directive, a body ranks as a contracting authority, the Di-

rective requires it to conduct award procedures. Accordingly that rule applies even where the contracting authority itself is trading as a supplier on the market, and subcontracting certain parts of a contract to a third party. It is, after all, entirely possible that non-economic considerations might be involved in the selection of a subcontractor, just as it is possible that public funds might be used in the course of the operation.

32. Incidentally, I agree with the Commission's view that it was open to the City of Munich to set up a legally independent body if it wished to offer services to third parties under normal market conditions. If such an organisation aims to make a profit, bears the losses related to the exercise of its activities itself, and performs no public tasks, it is not a public body, and hence not a contracting authority within the meaning of the Directive; its activities will therefore not be subject to the provisions of the directives coordinating public procurement procedures. A body which aims to make a profit and bears the losses associated with the exercise of its activity will not normally become involved in an award procedure on conditions which are not economically justified. (8)

33. Germany has argued that European procurement law does not require 'tenders within tenders'. It cites Article 1(a)(ii) of Directive 92/50, which excludes certain tasks from the scope of the Directive, and refers in that connection to Article 7 of Directive 93/38, a directive dealing with a number of specific sectors; that provision, which excludes contracts awarded for purposes of resale or hire to third parties from the scope of the directive, is, it suggests, applicable to Directive 92/50 by virtue of the reference to it there, the reason for the exclusion being that the purchase of the goods occurs in principle in a context of free competition, and the ensuing commercial discipline prevents a contracting authority in the sector from favouring particular tenderers on non-economic grounds. It claims that is also the position in the present case.

34. I disagree. The purpose of Article 1(a)(ii) of Directive 92/50 is to exclude from the scope of that Directive any contracts relating to the specific areas covered by Directive 90/531 (since replaced by Directive 93/38), because they are covered by what is now Directive 93/38. The provision in question, as the Commission has observed, establishes a dividing-line between Directive 92/50 and Directive 93/38. Directives 93/36 (9) and 93/37 (10) both contain a similar dividing-line. It is only in areas where the sectoral directive applies that Article 7 of that directive has any part to play. However, it not Directive 93/38 which applies to the present case, but Directive 92/50. Article 7 of the former is therefore not applicable, nor may it be applied by analogy.

35. Similarly, there is no merit in the German Government's contention that it would not be possible to conduct an award procedure for services which had to be subcontracted within the context of an award procedure in which the City of Munich was itself a bidder, either prior to that procedure or after it. First, that is no reason to disregard European public procurement legislation. Moreover, it is apparent from documents in the case-file that neither in the notice nor the conditions of tender is there a requirement that the tenderer identify any subcontractor beforehand. The conditions expressly state that subcontracting was allowed. In such a case, any subcontracting had to occur under normal conditions of competition and the party awarded the contract was obliged, on request, to inform the principal subsequently of the identity of the subcontractor.

1.6 Standard Procedure for Public Procurement of Works and Services (Model n. 2)

The following outlines the basic steps of the awarding procedure for works and services provided by Directives 2004/18/EC and 2004/17/EC: (1) drafting of call for tenders with the predetermination of participation requirements and adjudication criteria; (2) publication of call for tenders with invitation to submit attendance proposal; (3) letter or invitation to submit attendance proposals (only in some kinds of procedures such as restricted and negotiated); (4) proposals examination; (5) awarding; and (6) awarding notice to all participants. These steps function to make everyone know which company was chosen and why.

The first step is very important because a violation of European laws can result when participation requirements and awarding criteria are drafted according to discriminatory criteria (citizenship, for example).

The criteria allowed by European Union law are either the lowest price only or, where the contract is awarded to the most economically advantageous tender, various criteria linked to the subject matter of the contract in question (quality, price, technical merit, aesthetic and functional characteristics, environmental characteristics, etc.). As a general rule, the contracting entity should specify the relative weighting it gives to each of the criteria.

In drafting contract notices, it is very important to define the technical specifications in order to make the awarding as transparent as possible. Technical specifications define the characteristics required of a material, supply, or service such that they fulfill the use for which they are intended. These characteristics include environmental performance, design, conformity assessment, performance, safety, dimensions, quality assurance, and production methods. For public works contracts, they also cover test, inspection, and acceptance conditions, as well as construction techniques.

When drawing up its technical specifications, a contracting entity refers to national standards transposing European standards, European technical approvals, and international standards. It can also determine performance and functional requirements, particularly in the environmental domain (e.g., European eco-labels). The tenderer's tender is valid if he/she manages to prove that it meets the requirements defined by the technical specifications in an equivalent fashion. An appropriate means may be the submission of a technical dossier or a test report from a recognized body (e.g., a laboratory or certification and inspection body).

In principle, technical specifications do not mention a specific make or process nor do they refer to trademarks, patents, or a specific production.

The publication of call for tenders (step 2) with invitation to submit attendance proposals has two objectives: (1) enable economic operators in all member States to be fully aware of the procurement guidelines throughout the community, and (2) increase the number of potential tenderers, thereby increasing the chances of getting the best service at the most competitive price. These two objectives are prescribed as crucial from the perspective of European law.

According to the directives, there are five kinds of these acts of procedure that need to be published. The first is the prior information notice (not compulsory). After having sent the notice of publication of a prior information notice, the contracting authority publishes this notice on its buyer profile itself or sends it to the Office for Official Publications of the European Communities (Publications Office). This publication is compulsory only when the contracting authority wishes to reduce the time limits for the receipt of tenders.

The second is the notice of publication of a prior information notice (not compulsory), if the prior information notice is only published on the website of the contracting authority.

The third is the contract notice or notice of a design contest (compulsory). The contracting authority may publish this notice itself nationally and should send it to the Publications Office. The notice is published in full in an official language of the Community, and a summary is translated into the other languages.

The fourth is the contract award notice and notice of the results of a design contest (compulsory). The notices sent by the contracting authorities to the Commission can be transmitted by traditional or electronic means. Standard forms and details on transmission procedures are accessible on the information system for public procurement.

Each contracting authority shall provide information, as soon as possible, on the decisions reached concerning the award of a contract, including grounds for not awarding it. It shall draw up a written report for all contracts.

The last kind of act that needs to be published is the decision, including decisions not to award a contract with the clear explanation to any unsuccessful candidate of the reasons for rejecting them, and to any tenderer who has made an admissible tender of the relative advantages of the tender selected, as well as the name of the economic operator chosen.

The exchange and storage of information involving the various parties to the contract ensure the integrity of the data and confidentiality. The contracting authority verifies the content of the tenders only after the time limit set for submitting them has expired. Use of electronic means is non-discriminatory and helps to speed up the procedures. Devices for the electronic receipt of tenders permit the use of electronic signatures, guarantee the authenticity, integrity, and confidentiality of the data, and are capable of detecting possible fraud.

After the publication of the call for tender, some procedures (that provide a prequalification process) require the submission of the letter of invitation to admitted subjects. In the negotiated procedures, the contracting authorities consult the economic operators of their choice and negotiate the terms of contract with one or more of them. In the restricted procedures, negotiated procedures with publication of a contract notice, and in the competitive dialogue procedures, the contracting authority may limit the number of suitable candidates they will invite to tender. The Public Authority, according to the complexity of the contract, could also negotiate or conduct a dialogue with candidates, provided a sufficient number of suitable candidates are available. Nevertheless, it has the obligation to indicate in the contract notice the objective and non-discriminatory criteria or rules they intend to apply, the minimum number of candidates they intend to invite, and where appropriate, the maximum number.

After the publication of the call and, eventually, the submission of letters of invitation, private parties will submit their own bid. At this stage, Public Authorities must carry out the examination of the proposals (step 4). Proposals have to be verified according to the awarding criteria provided in the contract notice that was published and have to refer to capability requirements, financial requirements, and technical requirements.

After the evaluation of the proposals, the contracting authority should adopt the awarding act (step 5). Without prejudice to national laws, regulations, or administrative provisions concerning the remuneration of certain services, the criteria on which the contracting authorities shall base the award of public contracts shall be either: (a) when the award is made to the tender most economically advantageous from the point of view of the contracting authority, or (b) the lowest price only.

The decision will have to be noticed to all participants (step 6). The contracting authority must notify all tenderers the final award of the contract according to the principles of transparency and good administration. The contracting authority shall make known to every participant the decision, referring to the requirements indicated in the call.

1.7 Non-Standard Procedures for Awarding Public Contracts (Model n. 3)

This issue is important because by their nature, infrastructures activities often need quick interventions of the Public Authorities to guarantee safety and traffic efficiency according to the standards required by the Services of General Interest rules (see next chapter). However, it is not possible to avoid a public tender procedure, because a minimum procedure is required even in emergency cases with very restricted terms.

For example, although below-threshold contracts are not ensnared by the Regulations, there is case law providing that where the contract is of certain interest to suppliers located in other EU member States, contracting authorities must still procure them in accordance with the general TFEU principles of non-discrimination, equal treatment, transparency, proportionality, and mutual recognition.

What these principles imply in practice is that the contract has to be adequately advertised and some form of fair competition held thereafter. The scope and nature of the advertisement will depend on the nature of the contract in question and who is or is not likely to be interested in it.

When contracts are over the thresholds but the concrete situation, because of emergencies or technical implications, don't consent to run for the standard procedure, the Directives provide two different procedures: the restricted procedure and the negotiated procedure.

In the restricted procedure, all stakeholders may express an interest in tendering for the contract but only those meeting the contracting authority's selection criteria will actually be invited to do so. So when responding to the Official Journal of the European Union (OJEU) notice, the first step is for candidates to submit any information required by the authority as part of its selection stage. Candidates who get through the selection stage will then submit a tender when invited to do so by the authority. While no negotiation with the tenderers is permitted, there are no restrictions under the Regulations as to when the procedure can be used.

There are two types of negotiated procedures. Under the negotiated procedure without prior advert, the contracting authority is not required to issue an OJEU notice and may negotiate directly with the supplier of its choice. Under the negotiated procedure with prior advert, however, an OJEU notice must be published.

All interested parties may express an interest in tendering for the contract, but only those meeting the contracting authority's selection criteria will actually be invited to do so.

Under the negotiated procedure with prior advert, tenderers are invited to negotiate the terms of the advertised contract with the contracting authority. The Regulations do not set out any rules to govern the conduct of negotiations, which means that the contracting authority can, within certain parameters, establish its own procedures for the negotiation and tender stage.

The negotiated procedure can only be used in the very limited circumstances described in the Regulations. These cases are different if we refer to the procedure with the prior publication of a contract notice and the procedure without the prior publication of the contract notice.

According to the directive, contracting authorities may award their public contracts by negotiated procedure, after publication of a contract notice, in the following cases: (a) in the event of irregular tenders or the submission of tenders which are unacceptable under national provisions compatible with Articles 4, 24, 25, 27 and Chapter VII, in response to an open or restricted procedure or a competitive dialogue insofar as the original terms of the contract are not substantially altered; (b) in exceptional cases, when the nature of the works, supplies, or services or the risks attaching thereto do not permit prior overall pricing; (c) in the case of intellectual services, such as services involving the design of works, insofar as the nature of the services to be provided is such that contract specifications cannot be established with sufficient precision to permit the award of the contract by selection of the best tender according to the rules governing open or restricted procedures; and (d) in public works contracts for works which are performed solely for purposes of research, testing, or development and not with the aim of ensuring profitability or recovering research and development costs. In these cases, contracting authorities shall negotiate with companies the tenders submitted by them in order to adapt them to the requirements they need.

During the negotiations, Public Authorities have the obligation to ensure the equal treatment of all tenderers. Indeed, they cannot provide information in a discriminatory manner that may give some tenderers an advantage over others. Contracting authorities may provide for the negotiated procedure to take place in successive stages in order to reduce the number of tenders to be negotiated by applying the award criteria in the contract notice or the specifications. The contract notice or the specifications will indicate whether recourse has been made to this option.

The negotiated procedure without prior publication of a contract notice in the following cases is allowed only in six cases strictly identified by the directive.

The first three cases concern public works contracts, public supply contracts, and public service contracts. These kind of contracts can be adjudicated through the negotiated procedure without prior notice only (a) when no tenders, no suitable tenders, or no applications have been submitted in response to an open procedure or a restricted procedure, provided that the initial conditions of contract are not substantially altered and on condition that a report is sent to the Commission if it so requests; (b) when, for technical or artistic reasons, or for reasons connected with the protection of exclusive rights, the contract may be awarded only to a particular economic operator; or (c) insofar as is strictly necessary when, for reasons of extreme urgency brought about by events unforeseeable by the contracting authorities in question, the time limit for the open, restricted, or negotiated procedures with publication of a contract notice as referred to in Article 30 cannot be complied with. The circumstances invoked to justify extreme urgency must not in any event be attributable to the contracting authority.

The fourth case concerns public service contracts, but the contract concerned must follow a design contest and must, under the applicable rules, be awarded to the successful candidate or to one of the successful candidates. In the latter case, all successful candidates must be invited to participate in the negotiations.

The fifth and sixth cases concern both public works contracts and public service contracts. First of all, the directive refers to those situations where there is a need for additional works or services not included in the project initially considered or in the original contract, but which have, through unforeseen circumstances, become necessary for the performance of the works or services described therein, on condition that the award is made to the economic operator performing such works or services. This procedure is admissible only (a) when such additional works or services cannot be technically or economically separated from the original contract without major inconvenience to the contracting authorities, or (b) when such works or services, although separable from the performance of the original contract, are strictly necessary for its completion. However, the aggregate value of contracts awarded for additional works or services may not exceed 50% of the amount of the original contract. The last case of negotiated procedure without prior notice is provided for new works or services consisting in the repetition of similar works or services entrusted to the economic operator to whom the same contracting authorities awarded an original contract, provided that such works or services are in conformity with a basic project for which the original contract was awarded according to the open or restricted procedure. This procedure may be used only during the three years following the conclusion of the original contract.

Bibliography

Bermann G.A.– Goebel R.J.– Davey W.J.– Fox E.M., *Cases and Materials on European Union Law*, New York, 2010.

Biondi A. - Eeckhout P. - Flynn J. (a cura di), *The law of State Aid in the European Union*, Oxford, 2004.

Bonelli F., *La nozione di impresa nelle regole di concorrenza del Trattato C.E.E.*, in Verrucoli P. (a cura di), *La nozione d'impresa nell'ordinamento comunitario*, Milano, 1977, p. 37 ff.

Breyer S., *Regulation and its reform*, Cambridge, 1982.

Bungenberg M. - Griebel J. - Hindelang S. (Ed.). *International investment law and EU law*, Berlin, 2011.

Collins A.R., *Is the Regulation of State aid a necessary component o fan effective Competition Law frame work*, in *Eur. Business Law Rev.*, 2005, p. 379 ff.

Craig P. - De Búrca G., *EU law: text, cases and materials*. Oxford, 2011.

De Búrca G. - Weiler J.H.H., *The worlds of European constitutionalism*. Cambridge, 2012.

Dony M. - Renard F. - Smits C., *Controle des aides d'Etat*, in Idot L. (a cura di), *Commentaire J. Égret, Droit Communautaire de la concurrence*, Bruxelles, 2007.

Farrell, S., *Financing European Transport Infrastructure*, Londra, 1999.

Foster N., *Foster on EU law*, Oxford, 2011.

Fuchs M., *From legislators to the end-user: practical difficulties of implementing European directives*. Wiesbaden, 2011.

Steele I., *Substantive Legitimate Expectations: Striking the Right Balance?*, in *Law Quarterly Review*, 2005, p. 300 ff.

Idot L. (a cura di), *Commentaire J. Égret, Droit Communautaire de la concurrence*, Bruxelles, 2007.

Kaczorowska A., *European Union law*. Abingdon, 2011.

Keppenne J.P., *Guide des aides d'Etat en droit communautaire*, Bruxelles, 1999.

Malinconico C., *Codice degli appalti pubblici e privati: disciplina statale e comunitaria, lavori, forniture, servizi e settori esclusi*, Milano, 2004.

Maresca M., *Il riparto delle competenze legislative nell'ordinamento italiano con riguardo alla materia dei trasporti e dei porti. L'incidenza dei principi fondamentali e degli obblighi internazionali*, in *Dir. comm. internaz.*, 2002, p. 273 ff.

Mc Craw T.K., *Prophets of regulation*, Cambridge, 1984.

Micossi S., *Regulation and Deregulation of industrial products in the Internal Market of the European Union: finding the right balance*, in *The Forum for Us-Ec legal-economic affairs*, The Mentor Group, 20-23 September 1995.

Miller L., *The emergence of EU contract law: exploring europeanization*, Oxford, 2011.

Moldén K. - Jure A.B., *The protection of Legitimate Expectations in European community Law,* Stockholm, 1997.

Munari F., *Il diritto comunitario dei trasporti*, Milano, 1996.

Nehl H. P., *Legal protection in the field of EU funds*, in *European state aid law quarterly*, 2011, p. 629 ff.

Nicolaides P. - Kekelekis M. - Buyskes M., *State aid Policy in the European community*, The Hague, 2005.

Pescatore P., *Public and Private Aspects of Community Law*, in *Annual Proceedings of the Fordham Corporate Law Institute*, 1986, p. 383.

Radaelli c.M., *Governing European Regulation: The challenges Ahead*, The Robert Schuman Centre - European University Institute, Policy Paper n. 3, 1998.

Ratio J., *The Principle of Legal Certainty in EC Law*, Berlin, 2003.

Rittberger B., Phelan W. (eds), *Why do the EU Member States accept the supremacy of European law? Explaining supremacy as an alternative to bilateral reciprocity*, in *Journal of European Public Policy*, 2011, p. 766 ff.

Shelton D. (ed.), *International law and domestic legal systems: incorporation, transformation and persuasion*. Oxford, 2011.

Smith M.P., *Autonomy by the Rules: The European Commission and the Development of State Aid Policy*, in *Journal of Common Market Studies*, 1998, p. 55 ff.

Strozzi G., *Le principe de subsidiarité dans la perspective de l'intégration européenne: une énigme et baucoup d'attentes*, in *Révue trimestrielle de droit européen*, 1994, pp. 373 ff.

Tesauro G., *Diritto dell'Unione europea*, Padova, 2010.

Tesauro G., *Intervento pubblico nell'economia e art. 90, n. 2, del Trattato CE*, in *Dir. Un Eur.*, 1996, p. 719 ff.

Tizzano R. (ed), *Il diritto privato dell'Unione europea*, Torino, 2006, p. 1668 ff.

Twomey P. - O'Keeffe D., *Legal Issues of the Amsterdam Treaty*, Oxford, 1999 p. 185 ff.

Waelbroeck M., *Le traitè CEE est il neutre à l'égard des politiques économiques des Etats membres?*, in *Hacia un nuoevo orden internacional y europeo, Estudios en homenaye a Diez de Velasco*, Madrid, 1993, p. 1297 ff.

Chapter 2 Infrastructures Management as a Service of General Interest

2.1 The Construction and Management of Infrastructures as a Service of General Interest

The maintenance, construction, and management of public infrastructures are considered services of general interests under European Union Law. Nevertheless, no legislation of the European Union offers a specific regulation, despite the detailed regulation framework contained in the general principles of the Treaty on the Functioning of the European Union (TFEU) and in the public procurement directives (Directives 2004/18/EC and 2004/17/EC). The difficult duty for the national courts in the application of European law to infrastructures is the evaluation of the compliance between the national laws and European principles concerning services of general interest and public enterprises. The main principle established at the European level is the separation between business activities and public administration. The objective is to guarantee free competition and, consequently, a high standard of services.

The concept of "Service of General Interest,"[1] as defined in the rules of the Treaty on the Functioning of the European Union (mainly in art. 14 TFEU, ex art. 16 TCE), has been at the center of a large discussion amongst European Union institutions regarding its strong influence in reducing limitations on free competition among entrepreneurial activities.

According to the European Commission in its Communication of 1996, Services of General Interest (SGI) are different from usual entrepreneurial activities because their objective is to satisfy a public need. Indeed, public authorities have the discretion to consider whether offering such services is necessary, even when the relative market is not profitable enough to guarantee qualifying services. The notion of SGI is, indeed, based on the need to guarantee in every place both a service of a minimum quality standard and a low price for everyone.

Such services contribute to the aims of solidarity and equal treatment, on which the European model of society is based. The most significant example of SGI is the obligation of universal service, i.e., the obligation to offer a certain service

---

1 In the European Union Law a general notion of service of general interest is absente but it is possible to define the concept through the applicable principles taken from the Treaty on Functioning of European Union: Karayigit T., *The Notion of Services of General Economic Interest Revisited*, in *European Public Law*, 2009, p. 575 ff.

throughout the country at accessible prices and at similar qualitative conditions, independently from the profitability of each operation. The definition of SGI doesn't pretend to be objective and qualified in relation to the nature of the service offered, but it refers to the concrete classification of activities included by the authorities of each member State.

Such a choice has a very clear logical base, justified on the ground that only member States are capable of deciding which services need to be offered to their citizens, given the economic and juridical traditions belonging to each country.

The importance of this concept is strongly connected to the liberalization of the relevant market. Indeed, the first relevant rule is article 106 of the Treaty on the Functioning of the European Union (TFEU), which admits special or exclusive rights for companies in charge of SGI, allowing limitation and even exclusion of competition in such markets, strictly for the pursuit of the assigned mission. Even though it could be thought that this article actually legitimated the existence of monopolies and exclusive rights, it actually set the first limits on the attribution of such kinds of advantages, which, until then, had been present with no such controls.

Indeed, until the innovations brought by the Amsterdam Treaty, SGI were a relevant subject only from the point of view of conditions limiting competition. Article 106 aims to exclude the support for State-owned companies, or for any other company offering SGI, according to certain conditions: the advantage is required to be proportionate to the implementation of a public mission and not surpass what is necessary to pursue it. In other words, art. 106 allows States to grant companies special or exclusive rights in the occurrence of market failure where alternative measures for protecting and promoting competition cannot be applied. Scholars and courts analyzed the field of application of art. 106 through the identification of those cases where the exclusion of competition is admitted thanks to specific public tenders:. this model is called "competition for the market."[2]

A clear position of the European Court of Justice on the application of art. 106 TFEU can be understood reading the case 1) ECJ, 19 May 1993, case C-320/91, Corbeau in Rep.,p. I-2533:

1 By judgment of 13 November 1991, received at the Court on 11 December 1991, the Tribunal Correctionnel de Liège (Criminal Court, Liège) referred to the Court for a preliminary ruling under Article 177 of the EEC Treaty four questions on the interpretation of Articles 86 and 90 of the Treaty in order to enable it to determine the compatibility with those articles of the Belgian rules on the postal monopoly.

---

[2] For a complete explanation see: Kovar R., *Droit Communautaire et service public: espritd'orthodoxie ou pensée laicisée*, in *Rev. trim. Doit eur.*, 1996, p. 493 ff., Tesauro G., *Diritto dell'Unione europea*, Padova, 2010, Henry G. – Matheu M., *Des nouvelles régulations pour les services publics en concurrence,* in C. Henry - Matheu M. - Jeunmaitre A., *Réguler les services publics en réseau: l'expérience européenne*, Paris, 2003, p. 7 ff.; Cassese S., *Lo spazio giuridico globale*, Roma-Bari, 2003, p. 39 ff.

2 The questions were raised in criminal proceedings before that court against Paul Corbeau, a businessman from Liège, charged with infringing the Belgian legislation on the postal monopoly.

3 In Belgium the Law of 26 December 1956 on the postal service (Moniteur Belge of 30-31 December 1956, p. 8619) and the Law of 6 July 1971 establishing the Régie des Postes (Moniteur Belge of 14 August 1971, p. 9510) confer on the Régie des Postes, a legal person under public law, an exclusive right to collect, carry and distribute throughout the Kingdom all correspondence of whatever nature, and lay down penalties for any infringement of that exclusive right.

4 It may be seen from the documents in the main proceedings which have been sent to the Court, from the written observations submitted and from the oral argument presented at the hearing, that Mr Corbeau provides, within the City of Liège and the surrounding areas, a service consisting in collecting mail from the address of the sender and distributing it by noon on the following day, provided that the addressee is located within the district concerned. As regards correspondence destined for addressees outside that district, Mr Corbeau collects it from the sender' s address and sends it by post.

5 Upon complaint from the Régie des Postes, the Tribunal Correctionnel de Liège decided, in view of its doubts with regard to the compatibility of the Belgian rules in question with Community law, to stay the proceedings and to refer the following questions to the Court of Justice for a preliminary ruling:

(a) To what extent is a postal monopoly, such as that organized under the Belgian Law of 26 December 1956 on the postal monopoly, in conformity, as Community law now stands, with the rules of the Treaty of Rome (and in particular with Articles 90, 85 and 86) and with the rules of derived law in force which are applicable in this area?

(b) To what extent, if at all, must such a monopoly be modified in order to comply with the Community obligations imposed on the Member States in this area, and in particular with Article 90(1), and with the rules of derived law applicable in this area?

(c) Is an undertaking in which a statutory monopoly is vested and which enjoys exclusive rights analogous to those described in the Belgian Law of 26 December 1956, subject to the rules of European competition law (and in particular to Articles 7 and 85 to 90 inclusive) by virtue of Article 90(2) of the EEC Treaty?

(d) Does such an undertaking hold a dominant position in a substantial part of the common market within the meaning of Article 86 of the Treaty of Rome, a position deriving either from a statutory monopoly or from the particular circumstances?

6 Reference is made to the Report for the Hearing for a fuller account of the facts, the procedure in the main proceedings and the written observations submitted to the Court, which are hereinafter mentioned or discussed only in so far as is necessary for the reasoning of the Court.

7 With regard to the facts in the main proceedings, the questions referred to the Court must be understood as meaning that the national court is substantially concerned with the question whether Article 90 of the Treaty must be interpreted as meaning that it is contrary to that article for the legislation of a Member State which confers on a body such as the Régie des Postes the exclusive right to collect, carry and distribute mail to prohibit an economic operator established in that State from offering, under threat of criminal penalties, certain specific services on that market.

8 To reply to that question, as thus reformulated, it should first be pointed out that a body such as the Régie des Postes, which has been granted exclusive rights as regards the collection, carriage and distribution of mail, must be regarded as an undertaking to which the Member State concerned has granted exclusive rights within the meaning of Article 90(1) of the Treaty.

9 Next it should be recalled that the Court has consistently held that an undertaking having a statutory monopoly over a substantial part of the common market may be regarded as having a dominant position within the meaning of Article 86 of the Treaty (see the judgments in Case C-179/90 Merci Convenzionali Porto di Genova [1991] ECR I-5889 at paragraph 14 and in Case C-18/88 RTT v GB-Inno-BM [1991] ECR I-5941 at paragraph 17).

10 However, Article 86 applies only to anti-competitive conduct engaged in by undertakings on their own initiative, not to measures adopted by States (see the RTT v GB-Inno-BM judgment, cited above, paragraph 20).

11 The Court has had occasion to state in this respect that although the mere fact that a Member State has created a dominant position by the grant of exclusive rights is not as such incompatible with Article 86, the Treaty none the less requires the Member States not to adopt or maintain in force any measure which might deprive those provisions of their effectiveness (see the judgment in Case C-260/89 ERT [1991] ECR I-2925, paragraph 35).

12 Thus Article 90(1) provides that in the case of public undertakings to which Member States grant special or exclusive rights, they are neither to enact nor to maintain in force any measure contrary to the rules contained in the Treaty with regard to competition.

13 That provision must be read in conjunction with Article 90(2) which provides that undertakings entrusted with the operation of services of general economic interest are to be subject to the rules on competition in so far as the application of such rules does not obstruct the performance, in law or in fact, of the particular tasks assigned to them.

14 That latter provision thus permits the Member States to confer on undertakings to which they entrust the operation of services of general economic interest, exclusive rights which may hinder the application of the rules of the Treaty on competition in so far as restrictions on competition, or even the exclusion of all competition, by other economic operators are necessary to ensure the performance of the particular tasks assigned to the undertakings possessed of the exclusive rights.

15 As regards the services at issue in the main proceedings, it cannot be disputed that the Régie des Postes is entrusted with a service of general economic interest consisting in the obligation to collect, carry and distribute mail on behalf of all users throughout the territory of the Member State concerned, at uniform tariffs and on similar quality conditions, irrespective of the specific situations or the degree of economic profitability of each individual operation.

16 The question which falls to be considered is therefore the extent to which a restriction on competition or even the exclusion of all competition from other economic operators is necessary in order to allow the holder of the exclusive right to perform its task of general interest and in particular to have the benefit of economically acceptable conditions.

17 The starting point of such an examination must be the premise that the obligation on the part of the undertaking entrusted with that task to perform its services in conditions of economic equilibrium presupposes that it will be possible to offset less profitable sectors

against the profitable sectors and hence justifies a restriction of competition from individual undertakings where the economically profitable sectors are concerned.

18 Indeed, to authorize individual undertakings to compete with the holder of the exclusive rights in the sectors of their choice corresponding to those rights would make it possible for them to concentrate on the economically profitable operations and to offer more advantageous tariffs than those adopted by the holders of the exclusive rights since, unlike the latter, they are not bound for economic reasons to offset losses in the unprofitable sectors against profits in the more profitable sectors.

19 However, the exclusion of competition is not justified as regards specific services dissociable from the service of general interest which meet special needs of economic operators and which call for certain additional services not offered by the traditional postal service, such as collection from the senders' address, greater speed or reliability of distribution or the possibility of changing the destination in the course of transit, in so far as such specific services, by their nature and the conditions in which they are offered, such as the geographical area in which they are provided, do not compromise the economic equilibrium of the service of general economic interest performed by the holder of the exclusive right.

20 It is for the national court to consider whether the services at issue in the dispute before it meet those criteria.

21 The answer to the questions referred to the Court by the Tribunal Correctionnel de Liège should therefore be that it is contrary to Article 90 of the EEC Treaty for legislation of a Member State which confers on a body such as the Régie des Postes the exclusive right to collect, carry and distribute mail, to prohibit, under threat of criminal penalties, an economic operator established in that State from offering certain specific services dissociable from the service of general interest which meet the special needs of economic operators and call for certain additional services not offered by the traditional postal service, in so far as those services do not compromise the economic equilibrium of the service of general economic interest performed by the holder of the exclusive right. It is for the national court to consider whether the services in question in the main proceedings meet those criteria.

After Amsterdam, an enforceable right is granted to consumers who benefit of another norm (article 14 TFEU) enabling them to expect, not only minimal levels of Services of General Interest, but also a performance which must aim at satisfying determinate quality standards[3]. Therefore, users of infrastructures have both the right to have connections on non profitable connections and the right to a quality service in terms of time, safety and efficiency.

In this context Member States were forced to liberalize Services of General Interest by allowing private companies to attend public call for tenders for providing services either in a situation of natural monopoly (competition for the market) and for free competition in the market (competition in the market), keeping however in

3 The nature of enforcable right is suggested by Maresca M., *L'accesso ai servizi di interesse generale, de-regolazione e ri-regolazione degli users' rights*, in *Dir. Un. Eur.* 2005, p. 441 ff., Ross M., *Article 16 EC and services of general interest: from derogation to obligation?*, in *European Law Review*, 2000, p. 22 ff. and Carbajo J.C. - Estache A. - Kennedy D., *Regulating the Quality of Privatized Transport Services*, The World Bank, Washington D.C., 1997.

mind that liberalization must not undermine the consumer's satisfaction which has, after Amsterdam, been raised to a real subjective right.

The most important decision on the regulation of Services General Interest that forced the liberalization was set in the Altmark[4] case, case 2) ECJ 24 July 2003, case C-280/00, Altmark, Rep., p. I-7747):

32 In the main proceedings, the grant of licences to Altmark Trans is challenged only to the extent that that company needed public subsidies to discharge the public service obligations deriving from those licences. The dispute thus relates essentially to the question whether the public subsidies thus received by Altmark Trans were lawfully granted.

33 Having found that the payment of subsidies to Altmark Trans for the commercial operation of the licences at issue in the main proceedings was not contrary to national law, the Bundesverwaltungsgericht considers the compatibility of those subsidies with Community law.

34 The main provisions of the Treaty governing public subsidies are those on State aid, namely Article 92 et seq. of the EC Treaty. Article 77 of the EC Treaty creates an exception in the field of transport to the general rules applicable to State aid, by providing that aids which meet the needs of coordination of transport or represent reimbursement for the discharge of certain obligations inherent in the concept of a public service are compatible with the Treaty.

35 Regulation No 1191/69 was adopted by the Council on the basis of Articles 75 of the EC Treaty (now, after amendment, Article 71 EC) and 94 of the EC Treaty (now Article 89 EC), that is, on the basis both of the Treaty provisions relating to the common transport policy and of those relating to State aid.

36 Regulation No 1191/69 establishes a system of Community rules applicable to public service obligations in the field of transport. However, under the second subparagraph of Article 1(1) of the regulation, Member States may exclude from its scope any undertakings whose activities are confined exclusively to the operation of urban, suburban or regional services.

37 In those circumstances, the first point to examine is whether Regulation No 1191/69 is applicable to the transport services at issue in the main proceedings. Only if that is not the case will the application of the general provisions of the Treaty on State aid to the subsidies at issue in the main proceedings have to be considered. The third part of the national court's question should therefore be answered first.

(…)

43 To answer this part of the question, it must first be determined whether Regulation No 1191/69 imposes binding rules which the Member States must comply with when they consider imposing public service obligations in the land transport sector.

44 It is clear both from the preamble and from the body of that regulation that it does indeed impose binding rules on the Member States.

[4] For an analysis of the juridical consequences of the Altmark judgment see Maddalon P., *Paquet Altmark: quelle securité juridique?*, in *Contracts, concurrence, consommation*, 2006, p. 18 ff.

45 According to the first recital in the preamble to Regulation No 1191/69, one of the objectives of the common transport policy is to eliminate disparities resulting from obligations inherent in the concept of a public service imposed on transport undertakings by Member States which are liable to cause substantial distortion to conditions of competition. The second recital states that it is therefore necessary to terminate the public service obligations defined in the regulation, although in certain cases it may be essential to maintain them in order to ensure the provision of adequate transport services.

46 Article 1(3) of Regulation No 1191/69 states that the competent authorities of the Member States are to terminate all obligations inherent in the concept of a public service, as defined in the regulation, imposed on transport by rail, road and inland waterway. Under Article 1(4), in order to ensure adequate transport services, taking into account in particular social and environmental factors and town and country planning, or with a view to offering particular fares to certain categories of passenger, those authorities may conclude public service contracts with a transport undertaking, in accordance with the conditions and details of operation laid down in Section V of the regulation. Article 1(5) then states, however, that the authorities may maintain or impose public service obligations for urban, suburban and regional passenger transport services, in accordance with the conditions and details of operation, including methods of compensation, laid down in Sections II to IV of the regulation.

47 Consequently, in so far as the licences at issue in the main proceedings impose public service obligations and are accompanied by subsidies to help finance the performance of those obligations, the grant of those licences and subsidies was subject in principle to the provisions of Regulation No 1191/69.

48 However, the second subparagraph of Article 1(1) of the regulation authorises Member States to exclude from the scope of the regulation any undertakings whose activities are confined exclusively to the operation of urban, suburban or regional transport services.

49 Originally, until 31 December 1995, the Federal Republic of Germany made use of the derogation in the second subparagraph of Article 1(1) of Regulation No 1191/69 by expressly excluding in national legislation the application of that regulation to urban, suburban and regional transport undertakings.

50 Since 1 January 1996, the German legislation no longer expressly provides for such a derogation. On the contrary, the regulation was declared applicable to the grant of licenses for bus transport in Germany operated in the public interest by the third sentence of Paragraph 8(4) and Paragraph 13a of the PBefG. However, the German legislation does not expressly determine whether the regulation also applies to the grant of licences for bus transport operated commercially.

51 It must be examined whether the fact that Regulation No 1191/69 does not apply to commercially operated services — assuming that to be the case — is contrary to that regulation.

52 Altmark Trans, the Regierungspräsidium and Nahverkehrsgesellschaft submit that, since the second subparagraph of Article 1(1) of Regulation No 1191/69 allows the application of that regulation to be excluded for an entire category of transport services, that provision must *a fortiori* allow a limited part of those services to be excluded from the application of the regulation.

53 It is to be remembered that, as explained in paragraphs 44 to 47 above, Regulation No 1191/69 establishes a system which the Member States must comply with when they consider imposing public service obligations on undertakings in the land transport sector.

54 However, Member States may, with respect to undertakings which operate urban, suburban or regional services, introduce a derogation from the provisions of Regulation No 1191/69, under the second paragraph of Article 1(1) of the regulation. The German legislature made general use of this derogation until 31 December 1995.

55 In those circumstances, it must be concluded that the amendment to the PBefG which took effect on 1 January 1996 contributes to the implementation of the objectives pursued by Regulation No 1191/69.

56 By that amendment, the German legislature introduced a distinction, as regards the grant of licences for passenger transport by bus, between commercial operation and operation in the public interest. By virtue of Paragraph 13a of the PBefG, Regulation No 1191/69 became applicable to the grant of licences for operation in the public interest. That amendment to the PBefG thus cut down the scope of the derogation provided for in the second subparagraph of Article 1(1) of the regulation. The German legislation thus came closer to the objectives pursued by that regulation.

57 It follows from those considerations that a Member State may legitimately, on the basis of the power to derogate provided for in the second subparagraph of Article 1(1) of Regulation No 1191/69, not only exclude urban, suburban or regional scheduled services completely from the scope of that regulation, but may also apply that derogation in a more limited way. In other words, that provision in principle allows the German legislature to provide that, for transport services provided on a commercial basis, public service obligations may be imposed and subsidies granted without complying with the conditions and details of operation laid down in that regulation.

58 The national legislation must, however, clearly delimit the use made of that option of derogation, so as to make it possible to determine the situations in which the derogation applies and those in which Regulation No 1191/69 applies.

59 As the Court has consistently held, it is particularly important, in order to satisfy the requirement of legal certainty, that individuals should have the benefit of a clear and precise legal situation enabling them to ascertain the full extent of their rights and, where appropriate, to rely on them before the national courts (see Case 29/84 *Commission* v *Germany* [1985] ECR 1661, paragraph 23; Case 363/85 *Commission* v *Italy* [1987] ECR 1733, paragraph 7; Case C-59/89 *Commission* v *Germany* [1991] ECR I-2607, paragraph 18; and Case C-236/95 *Commission* v *Greece* [1996] ECR I-4459, paragraph 13).

60 The order for reference contains a number of points which suggest that those requirements of clarity may not have been complied with in the present case.

61 Thus according to the order for reference, first, the commercial system of operation may apply also to undertakings which need public subsidies to operate licensed transport services. The national court stated, second, that this right to choose, which was conferred on the operator by the legislature, [is] removed in practice in the case of scheduled services in local public transport which are largely in deficit, the need for public subsidies automatically resulting in such services being classified as in the public interest.

62 It appears to follow from the above that licences for transport services which need public subsidies for their operation may be subject to either the commercial or the public interest rules. If that were indeed the case, the provisions of the national legislation concerned would not determine clearly and precisely the situations in which such licences fall within one or other category. In so far as Regulation No 1191/69 does not apply to com-

mercial operations, any uncertainty as to the dividing line between that and operations in the public interest would extend also to the scope of that regulation in Germany.

63 It is for the national court to ascertain whether the application by the German legislature of the derogation provided for in the second subparagraph of Article 1(1) of Regulation No 1191/69 satisfies the requirements of clarity and precision needed to comply with the principle of legal certainty.

64 The answer to the third part of the question referred for a preliminary ruling must therefore be that Regulation No 1191/69, and more particularly the second subparagraph of Article 1(1) thereof, must be interpreted as allowing a Member State not to apply the regulation to the operation of urban, suburban or regional scheduled transport services which necessarily depend on public subsidies, and to limit its application to cases where the provision of an adequate transport service is not otherwise possible, provided however that the principle of legal certainty is duly observed.

65 It must further be stated that, should the national court decide that the principle of legal certainty was not complied with in the main proceedings, it will have to consider that Regulation No 1191/69 is fully applicable in Germany, and thus applies also to commercial operations. In that event, it will have to be ascertained whether the licences at issue in the main proceedings were granted in conformity with that regulation and, if so, whether the subsidies at issue in the main proceedings were granted in conformity with it. Where those licences and subsidies do not satisfy the conditions laid down by the regulation, the national court will have to conclude that they are not compatible with Community law, without it being necessary to consider them from the point of view of the provisions of the Treaty.

66 Consequently, it is only to the extent that the national court concludes that Regulation No 1191/69 does not apply to commercial operations and that the use made by the German legislature of the option to derogate provided for by that regulation complies with the principle of legal certainty that it will have to consider whether the subsidies at issue in the main proceedings were granted in conformity with the provisions of the Treaty relating to State aid.

(…)

74 To answer the first part of the question, the various elements of the concept of State aid in Article 92(1) of the Treaty must be considered. It is settled case-law that classification as aid requires that all the conditions set out in that provision are fulfilled (see Case C-142/87 *Belgium* v *Commission* (*Tubemeuse*) [1990] ECR I-959, paragraph 25; Joined Cases C-278/92 to C-280/92 *Spain* v *Commission* [1994] ECR I-4103, paragraph 20; and Case C-482/99 *France* v *Commission* [2002] ECR I-4397, paragraph 68).

75 Article 92(1) of the Treaty lays down the following conditions. First, there must be an intervention by the State or through State resources. Second, the intervention must be liable to affect trade between Member States. Third, it must confer an advantage on the recipient. Fourth, it must distort or threaten to distort competition.

76 The national court's question concerns more particularly the second of those conditions.

77 In this respect, it must be observed, first, that it is not impossible that a public subsidy granted to an undertaking which provides only local or regional transport services and does not provide any transport services outside its State of origin may none the less have an effect on trade between Member States.

78 Where a Member State grants a public subsidy to an undertaking, the supply of transport services by that undertaking may for that reason be maintained or increased with the result that undertakings established in other Member States have less chance of providing their transport services in the market in that Member State (see, to that effect, Case 102/87 *France* v *Commission* [1988] ECR 4067, paragraph 19; Case C-305/89 *Italy* v *Commission* [1991] ECR I-1603, paragraph 26; and *Spain* v *Commission* , paragraph 40).

79 In the present case, that finding is not merely hypothetical, since, as appears in particular from the observations of the Commission, several Member States have since 1995 started to open certain transport markets to competition from undertakings established in other Member States, so that a number of undertakings are already offering their urban, suburban or regional transport services in Member States other than their State of origin.

80 Next, the Commission notice of 6 March 1996 on the *de minimis* rule for State aid (OJ 1996 C 68, p. 9), as its fourth paragraph states, does not concern transport. Similarly, Commission Regulation (EC) No 69/2001 of 12 January 2001 on the application of Articles 87 and 88 of the EC Treaty to *de minimis* aid (OJ 2001 L 10, p. 30), in accordance with the third recital in the preamble and Article 1(a), does not apply to that sector.

81 Finally, according to the Court's case-law, there is no threshold or percentage below which it may be considered that trade between Member States is not affected. The relatively small amount of aid or the relatively small size of the undertaking which receives it does not as such exclude the possibility that trade between Member States might be affected (see *Tubemeuse* , paragraph 43, and *Spain* v *Commission* , paragraph 42).

82 The second condition for the application of Article 92(1) of the Treaty, namely that the aid must be capable of affecting trade between Member States, does not therefore depend on the local or regional character of the transport services supplied or on the scale of the field of activity concerned.

83 However, for a State measure to be able to come under Article 92(1) of the Treaty, it must also, as stated in paragraph 75 above, be capable of being regarded as an advantage conferred on the recipient undertaking.

84 Measures which, whatever their form, are likely directly or indirectly to favour certain undertakings (Case 6/64 *Costa* [1964] ECR 585, at p. 595) or are to be regarded as an economic advantage which the recipient undertaking would not have obtained under normal market conditions (Case C-39/94 *SFEI and Others* [1996] ECR I-3547, paragraph 60, and Case C-342/96 *Spain* v *Commission* [1999] ECR I-2459, paragraph 41) are regarded as aid.

85 Mention should, however, be made of the Court's decision in a case concerning an indemnity provided for by Council Directive 75/439/EEC of 16 June 1975 on the disposal of waste oils (OJ 1975 L 194, p. 23). That indemnity was able to be granted to waste oil collection and/or disposal undertakings as compensation for the collection and/or disposal obligations imposed on them by the Member State, provided that it did not exceed the annual uncovered costs actually recorded by the undertakings taking into account a reasonable profit. The Court held that an indemnity of that type did not constitute aid within the meaning of Articles 92 et seq. of the Treaty, but rather consideration for the services performed by the collection or disposal undertakings (see Case 240/83 *ADBHU* [1985] ECR 531, paragraph 3, last sentence, and paragraph 18)

86 Similarly, the Court has held that, provided that a tax on direct sales imposed on pharmaceutical laboratories corresponds to the additional costs actually incurred by wholesale distributors in discharging their public service obligations, not assessing wholesale dis-

tributors to the tax may be regarded as compensation for the services they provide and hence not State aid within the meaning of Article 92 of the Treaty. The Court said that, provided there was the necessary equivalence between the exemption and the additional costs incurred, wholesale distributors would not be enjoying any real advantage for the purposes of Article 92(1) of the Treaty, because the only effect of the tax would be to put distributors and laboratories on an equal competitive footing (*Ferring* , paragraph 27).

87 It follows from those judgments that, where a State measure must be regarded as compensation for the services provided by the recipient undertakings in order to discharge public service obligations, so that those undertakings do not enjoy a real financial advantage and the measure thus does not have the effect of putting them in a more favourable competitive position than the undertakings competing with them, such a measure is not caught by Article 92(1) of the Treaty.

88 However, for such compensation to escape classification as State aid in a particular case, a number of conditions must be satisfied.

89 First, the recipient undertaking must actually have public service obligations to discharge, and the obligations must be clearly defined. In the main proceedings, the national court will therefore have to examine whether the public service obligations which were imposed on Altmark Trans are clear from the national legislation and/or the licences at issue in the main proceedings.

90 Second, the parameters on the basis of which the compensation is calculated must be established in advance in an objective and transparent manner, to avoid it conferring an economic advantage which may favour the recipient undertaking over competing undertakings.

91 Payment by a Member State of compensation for the loss incurred by an undertaking without the parameters of such compensation having been established beforehand, where it turns out after the event that the operation of certain services in connection with the discharge of public service obligations was not economically viable, therefore constitutes a financial measure which falls within the concept of State aid within the meaning of Article 92(1) of the Treaty.

92 Third, the compensation cannot exceed what is necessary to cover all or part of the costs incurred in the discharge of public service obligations, taking into account the relevant receipts and a reasonable profit for discharging those obligations. Compliance with such a condition is essential to ensure that the recipient undertaking is not given any advantage which distorts or threatens to distort competition by strengthening that undertaking's competitive position.

93 Fourth, where the undertaking which is to discharge public service obligations, in a specific case, is not chosen pursuant to a public procurement procedure which would allow for the selection of the tenderer capable of providing those services at the least cost to the community, the level of compensation needed must be determined on the basis of an analysis of the costs which a typical undertaking, well run and adequately provided with means of transport so as to be able to meet the necessary public service requirements, would have incurred in discharging those obligations, taking into account the relevant receipts and a reasonable profit for discharging the obligations.

94 It follows from the above considerations that, where public subsidies granted to undertakings expressly required to discharge public service obligations in order to compensate for the costs incurred in discharging those obligations comply with the conditions set out in

paragraphs 89 to 93 above, such subsidies do not fall within Article 92(1) of the Treaty. Conversely, a State measure which does not comply with one or more of those conditions must be regarded as State aid within the meaning of that provision.

95 The answer to the first part of the question referred for a preliminary ruling must therefore be that the condition for the application of Article 92(1) of the Treaty that the aid must be such as to affect trade between Member States does not depend on the local or regional character of the transport services supplied or on the scale of the field of activity concerned. However, public subsidies intended to enable the operation of urban, suburban or regional scheduled transport services are not caught by that provision where such subsidies are to be regarded as compensation for the services provided by the recipient undertakings in order to discharge public service obligations. For the purpose of applying that criterion, it is for the national court to ascertain that the following conditions are satisfied:

- first, the recipient undertaking is actually required to discharge public service obligations and those obligations have been clearly defined;
- second, the parameters on the basis of which the compensation is calculated have been established beforehand in an objective and transparent manner.
- third, the compensation does not exceed what is necessary to cover all or part of the costs incurred in discharging the public service obligations, taking into account the relevant receipts and a reasonable profit for discharging those obligations;
- fourth, where the undertaking which is to discharge public service obligations is not chosen in a public procurement procedure, the level of compensation needed has been determined on the basis of an analysis of the costs which a typical undertaking, well run and adequately provided with means of transport so as to be able to meet the necessary public service requirements, would have incurred in discharging those obligations, taking into account the relevant receipts and a reasonable profit for discharging the obligations.

96 By the second part of the question referred for a preliminary ruling, the national court essentially asks whether Article 77 of the Treaty may be applied to public subsidies which compensate for the additional costs incurred in discharging public service obligations without taking into account Regulation No 1191/69.

(…)

101 Article 77 of the EC Treaty provides that aids which meet the needs of coordination of transport or represent reimbursement for the discharge of certain obligations inherent in the concept of a public service are compatible with the Treaty.

102 In paragraph 37 above, it was stated that, if there were no regulation applicable to the case in the main proceedings, it would have to be examined whether the subsidies at issue in the main proceedings fell within the provisions of the Treaty concerning State aid.

103 It follows from paragraphs 65 and 66 above that Regulation No 1191/69 could be applicable to the case in the main proceedings to the extent that the German legislature has not excluded the application of that regulation to commercial operations or has not done so in compliance with the principle of legal certainty. If that proves to be the case, the provisions of that regulation will apply to the subsidies at issue in the main proceedings, and the national court will not have to consider whether they are consistent with the provisions of primary law.

104 If, however, Regulation No 1191/69 were not applicable to the case in the main proceedings, it follows from the answer to the first part of the question that, in so far as the subsidies at issue in the main proceedings are to be regarded as compensation for the transport services provided in order to discharge public service obligations and satisfy the conditions set out in paragraphs 89 to 93 above, those subsidies would not come under Article 92 of the Treaty, so that there would be no need to rely on the exception to that provision under Article 77 of the Treaty.

105 Consequently, the provisions of primary law concerning State aid and the common transport policy would be applicable to the subsidies at issue in the main proceedings only in so far as, first, those subsidies did not come under the provisions of Regulation No 1191/69 and, second, where they were granted to compensate for the additional costs incurred in discharging public service obligations, the conditions set out in paragraphs 89 to 93 above were not all satisfied.

106 However, even if the subsidies at issue in the main proceedings were to be tested against the Treaty provisions on State aid, the exception provided for in Article 77 could not be applied as such.

107 On 4 June 1970 the Council adopted Regulation (EEC) No 1107/70 on the granting of aids for transport by rail, road and inland waterway (OJ, English Special Edition 1970 (II), p. 360). Article 3 of that regulation provides that [w]ithout prejudice to the provisions of ... Regulation (EEC) No 1192/69 ... and of ... Regulation (EEC) No 1191/69 ... Member States shall neither take coordination measures nor impose obligations inherent in the concept of a public service which involve the granting of aids pursuant to Article 77 of the Treaty except in the following cases or circumstances. It follows that Member States are no longer authorised to rely on Article 77 of the Treaty outside the cases referred to in secondary Community legislation.

108 So, to the extent that Regulation No 1191/69 does not apply in the present case and the subsidies at issue in the main proceedings fall within Article 92(1) of the Treaty, Regulation No 1107/70 lists exhaustively the circumstances in which the authorities of the Member States may grant aids under Article 77 of the Treaty.

109 Accordingly, the answer to the second part of the question referred for a preliminary ruling must be that Article 77 of the Treaty cannot be applied to public subsidies which compensate for the additional costs incurred in discharging public service obligations without taking into account Regulation No 1191/69.

Liberalization of SGI envisions privatization as a first step, i.e., shares passing from the State to private subjects[5].

Praxis, especially the Italian one, has demonstrated situations where privatization was only formal, through a change of the juridical form of the company offering the services[6]. However, changing the service provider from a public body to a public company, held totally or primarily by public entities, has nothing to do with

---

5 A concrete example of privatization in a national market can be read in Thatcher M., *Institutions, Regulation and Change: New Regulatory Agencies in the British privatised utilities*, in *Britain in the 1990's*, 1998.

6 See Flynn L., *Competition policy and public services in EC Law after the Maastricht and Amsterdam Treaties*, in Twomey P. - O'Keeffe D., *Legal Issues of the Amsterdam Treaty*, Oxford, 1999 p. 185 ff.

a real liberalization[7], assuming that those activities, which according to the EU law concept of enterprise are in every sense entrepreneurial activities, actually remain on public property, thus keeping consumers from benefitting from liberalization. Doctrine has often spoken about deregulation, intended as a reduction of governmental restraints on operators' behavior, as a necessary condition for actual liberalization.

However, the concept of deregulation is not enough to obtain the result of protecting the consumer (towards whom liberalization must be aimed). Reforming regulation of SGI has therefore been enacted, using the so called "re-regulation," which consists of reformulating controls over the private sector, including its growth, to make regulation more transparent and economical. The instrument that seems to be the best is the independent administrative authority, which, through a regulatory management system, grants impartial control with no political interference.

2.2 Standards of Infrastructures Regulation with Respect to European Union Laws Concerning Quality, Safety and the Principle of Separation: The Direct Effect of European Union Law

A majority of member States' national legislation contain a specific act regulating infrastructures management. It is, in this work, impossible to describe the compliance with respect to every national law, so I tried to relate the EU law to the common principles of national laws in the infrastructures sector. The majority of national laws, for example, have clear definitions of the bodies providing construction and service, the object of the services, and the regulation duties attributed to public bodies.

From a careful analysis of dispositions contained in the laws, it is quite clear that most rules seem to comply with EU law, especially with the internal market articles (which protect free access to the market) and with the discipline of Services of General Economic Interest as it emerges from application of art. 106 of the Treaty on the Functioning of the European Union[8].

---

7 A deep examination of the European Union law of ownership was carried out by Verhoeven A., *Privatisation and EC Law: Is the European Commission "Neutral" with Respect to Public Versus Private Ownership of Companies?*, in *International and Comparative Law Quarterly* 1996, p. 861 ff. and by Kovar R., *Les prises de partecipation publiques et le regime communautaire des aides d'Etat*, in *Rev. Trim. dr. Comn.*, 1992, p. 110 ff.

8 See the reasoning of Svane L.P., *Public service compensation in practice: Commission package on State aid for services of general economic interest*, in *Comp. Policy newsletter*, 2005, p. 34 ff. concerning the concrete application of art. 106 TFEU and its compensation standards.

Each member States has chosen to provide supervision through many public authorities (Agency, Ministers of Transport and Communication, Inspectorate, etc. . . .), allowing the managing and construction of infrastructures to qualify as SGI according to national policies. The European Union leaves to its members the discretion of choosing those services having particular importance to each specific nation. Services of General Interest are classified mainly in relation to the object of their activity. This activity must satisfy a general and essential need of the members collectivity, i.e., a group of people among whom there are relations of equality and solidarity.

In evaluating the needs of the collective, great freedom is given to member States, so that they themselves define the objectives of national policies. The jurisprudence of the Court of Justice of the European Communities has acknowledged the safety, defense, protection, and/or social cohesion of the collective, *inter alia*, to be among such needs. Services of General Interest must answer needs such as instruction, health, communications, information, drinkable water, and transport, all of which improve social life and are essential for the protection of fundamental liberties. Socioeconomic activities are, on the other hand, usually not left only to the market forces, as there are other ways in which administrations act to regulate and control them.

The strong interest the Community has in such services, e.g., construction, management, and maintenance, is based on their relevant contributions to the general competitiveness of European industry and to economic, social, and territorial cohesion. Moreover the consumers of such services, European citizens, expect to receive high quality services at low prices. Consumers and their needs are consequently at the center of public action in this sector (see the Communication of European Commission on Services of General Interest 2001/C 17/04 and the Green Book on Services of General Interest COM/2003/0270).

Therefore, national infrastructures laws provide standards of quality and safety that can be considered coherent with aims and actions of the European Community (see the Casees: 1) ECJ, May 19th 1993 – penal trial against Paul Corbeau – trial c--320/91; and 5) ECJ, July 3rd 2003. - Chronopost SA, La Poste and French Republic vs Union française de l'express (Ufex), DHL International, Federal express international (France) e CRIE – reunited trials C-83/01 P, C-93/01 P e C-94/01 P):

(…)

31 By their first plea, the appellants allege that the Court of First Instance infringed Article 92(1) of the Treaty, by giving an incorrect interpretation of the concept of normal market conditions used in the *SFEI* judgment.

32 In that regard, the Court of First Instance stated, in paragraph 75 of the judgment under appeal, that the Commission should at least have checked that the payment received by La Poste was comparable to that demanded by a private holding company or a private group of undertakings not operating in a reserved sector.

33 That assessment, which fails to take account of the fact that an undertaking such as La Poste is in a situation which is very different from that of a private undertaking acting under normal market conditions, is flawed in law.

34 La Poste is entrusted with a service of general economic interest within the meaning of Article 90(2) of the EC Treaty (now Article 86(2) EC) (see Case C-320/91 *Corbeau* [1993] ECR I-2533, paragraph 15). Such a service essentially consists in the obligation to collect, carry and deliver mail for the benefit of all users throughout the territory of the Member State concerned, at uniform tariffs and on similar conditions as to quality.

35 To that end, La Poste had to acquire, or was afforded, substantial infrastructures and resources (the postal network), enabling it to provide the basic postal service to all users, even in sparsely populated areas where the tariffs did not cover the cost of providing the service in question.

36 Because of the characteristics of the service which the La Poste network must be able to ensure, the creation and maintenance of that network are not in line with a purely commercial approach. As was recalled in paragraph 22 above, Ufex and Others have indeed accepted that a network such as that available to SFMI-Chronopost is clearly not a market network. Therefore that network would never have been created by a private undertaking.

37 Moreover, the provision of logistical and commercial assistance is inseparably linked to the La Poste network, since it consists precisely in making available that network which has no equivalent on the market.

38 Accordingly, in the absence of any possibility of comparing the situation of La Poste with that of a private group of undertakings not operating in a reserved sector, normal market conditions, which are necessarily hypothetical, must be assessed by reference to the objective and verifiable elements which are available.

39 In the present case, the costs borne by La Poste in respect of the provision to its subsidiary of logistical and commercial assistance can constitute such objective and verifiable elements.

On that basis, there is no question of State aid to SFMI-Chronopost if, first, it is established that the price charged properly covers all the additional, variable costs incurred in providing the logistical and commercial assistance, an appropriate contribution to the fixed costs arising from use of the postal network and an adequate return on the capital investment in so far as it is used for SFMI-Chronopost's competitive activity and if, second, there is nothing to suggest that those elements have been underestimated or fixed in an arbitrary fashion.

41 In the light of all the foregoing considerations, the Court of First Instance erred in law in interpreting Article 92(1) of the Treaty as meaning that the Commission was not entitled to determine whether there was aid to SFMI-Chronopost by reference to the costs borne by La Poste but that it should have checked whether the payment received by La Poste was comparable to that demanded by a private holding company or a private group of undertakings not operating in a reserved sector, pursuing a structural policy — whether general or sectorial — and guided by long-term prospects.

42 The first plea must therefore be declared well founded and the judgment under appeal must accordingly be set aside.

Furthermore, there are some features that risk causing a violation of the Treaty on the Functioning of the European Union, mainly of the principle of separation between public administration and business activities[9]. This could cause member States to face liability for damages caused by breach of EU dispositions concerning such rights. Indeed, EU laws have direct effect and, as such, directly give individual citizens and companies subjective rights which can be asserted in the courts. Direct effect is now considered a basic principle of EU law. Each citizen must abide by obligations imposed by EU law, but at the same has rights that can be asserted before national and EU judges.

Thanks to the direct effect of EU law, individual citizens can use EU norms independently from the existence of national laws recognizing them. As said before, this principle was introduced by the Court of Justice of the European Community with the ruling Van Gend en Loos of February 5th 1963, case 26/62 (Case 4). In this ruling the Court established that

> EU law (…) as it imposes duties on single citizens, gives them subjective rights which national judges have a duty to protect.

Indeed, the European Court of Justice has pointed out that the TFEU did not only create reciprocal obligations among Member States but also intended to enact

> a juridical system of new kind in the field of international law, applying to States which have given up, even if in limited sectors, to their sovereign power, law system which recognizes as subjects not only member States but also their citizens.

What follows is that rights attributed to single citizens by EU law can also impose definite obligations on member States or European Institutions, in the sense that to a State's clear and unconditioned prohibition corresponds a right for each single citizen to have it respected.

Let's take a more in-depth look at the Van Gend Loos case:

> The first question of the tariefcommissie is whether article 12 of the treaty has direct application in national law in the sense that nationals of member states may on the basis of this article lay claim to rights which the national court must protect.
>
> To ascertain whether the provisions of an international treaty extend so far in their effects it is necessary to consider the spirit, the general scheme and the wording of those provisions.
>
> The objective of the eec treaty, which is to establish a common market, the functioning of which is of direct concern to interested parties in the community, implies that this treaty is more than an agreement which merely creates mutual obligations between the contracting states . this view is confirmed by the preamble to the treaty which refers not only to governments but to peoples . it is also confirmed more specifically by the establishment of institutions endowed with sovereign rights, the exercise of which affects member states and also their citizens . furthermore, it must be noted that the nationals of the states brought to-

---

9 See Lopez De Gonzalo M., *La «regola della separazione» nella disciplina dei servizi portuali ed aeroportuali*, in *Dir. Mar.*, 2005, p. 670 ff.

gether in the community are called upon to cooperate in the functioning of this community through the intermediary of the european parliament and the economic and social committee.

In addition the task assigned to the court of justice under article 177, the object of which is to secure uniform interpretation of the treaty by national courts and tribunals, confirms that the states have acknowledged that community law has an authority which can be invoked by their nationals before those courts and tribunals . the conclusion to be drawn from this is that the community constitutes a new legal order of international law for the benefit of which the states have limited their sovereign rights, albeit within limited fields, and the subjects of which comprise not only member states but also their nationals . independently of the legislation of member states, community law therefore not only imposes obligations on individuals but is also intended to confer upon them rights which become part of their legal heritage . these rights arise not only where they are expressly granted by the treaty, but also by reason of obligations which the treaty imposes in a clearly defined way upon individuals as well as upon the member states and upon the institutions of the community.

With regard to the general scheme of the treaty as it relates to customs duties and charges having equivalent effect it must be emphasized that article 9, which bases the community upon a customs union, includes as an essential provision the prohibition of these customs duties and charges . this provision is found at the beginning of the part of the treaty which defines the 'foundations of the community. it is applied and explained by article 12 .

The wording of article 12 contains a clear and unconditional prohibition which is not a positive but a negative obligation . this obligation, moreover, is not qualified by any reservation on the part of states which would make its implementation conditional upon a positive legislative measure enacted under national law . the very nature of this prohibition makes it ideally adapted to produce direct effects in the legal relationship between member states and their subjects.

The implementation of article 12 does not require any legislative intervention on the part of the states. the fact that under this article it is the member states who are made the subject of the negative obligation does not imply that their nationals cannot benefit from this obligation.

In addition the argument based on articles 169 and 170 of the treaty put forward by the three governments which have submitted observations to the court in their statements of case is misconceived. the fact that these articles of the treaty enable the commission and the member states to bring before the court a state which has not fulfilled its obligations does not mean that individuals cannot plead these obligations, should the occasion arise, before a national court, any more than the fact that the treaty places at the disposal of the commission ways of ensuring that obligations imposed upon those subject to the treaty are observed, precludes the possibility, in actions between individuals before a national court, of pleading infringements of these obligations.

A restriction of the guarantees against an infringement of article 12 by member states to the procedures under article 169 and 170 would remove all direct legal protection of the individual rights of their nationals. there is the risk that recourse to the procedure under these articles would be inneffective if it were to occur after the implementation of a national decision taken contrary to the provisions of the treaty.

The vigilance of individuals concerned to protect their rights amounts to an effective supervision in addition to the supervision entrusted by articles 169 and 170 to the diligence of the commission and of the member states.

It follows from the foregoing considerations that, according to the spirit, the general scheme and the wording of the treaty, article 12 must be interpreted as producing direct effects and creating individual rights which national courts must protect.

In other words, each indvidual citizen can assert this right, which derives from EU law, before a national judge (see the Case 4) Van Gend en Loos,). Moreover, this principle of direct effect has been ratified by the Court of Justice with reference to EC Treaty norms. With respect to primary law, the Court of Justice, in the Van Gend en Loos decision, ratified the principle of direct effect, provided, however, that the obligations be precise, clear, and unconditional and do not require complementary national or EU measures. In the Becker decision of January 19, 1982, case 8/81, the Court of Justice precluded the application of direct effect where States have even a minimal discretional margin in enacting the considered disposition (Kaefer and Procacci decision, December 12, 1990).

The Court of Justice has clarified that among the articles of the Treaty instituting the European Community (EC Treaty) the following have direct effect: article 12 (prohibiting discrimination based on nationality); article 25 (prohibiting customs tolls and taxes having the equivalent effect); articles 28 and 29 (prohibiting quantitative restrictions); article 39 (on free circulation of workers); article 43 (on the right of establishment); article 50 (on free circulation of services); article 81 (prohibiting agreements) and article 82 (prohibiting abuse of dominant potion); article 88 (on State help); article 95 (prohibiting fiscal discrimination towards imported articles); and article 141 (on equality between sexes)[10].

The Court of Justice has recognized that some of the Treaty's dispositions have full direct effect (e.g., internal market and competition rules). Direct effect has, in fact, two aspects: vertical and horizontal. Direct vertical effect is explained in the relationships between single citizens and the State: single citizens can assert EU law before the State. Direct horizontal effect is expressed in relationships among single citizens, i.e., where a single person invokes an EU norm against another single person. Depending on the EU law, the Court of Justice has differentiated between full direct effect (horizontal and vertical) and partial direct effect (only vertical). Moreover, the Court of Justice has unequivocally clarified that EU law must not only be applied in merely internal situations, but also in suits concerning internal relationships[11]. We here quote, as an example, the case of Cipolla and Calafiori ECJ, December 5, 2006, Federico Cipolla vs Rosaria Portolese in Fazari (C-94/04) and Stefano Macrino and Claudia Capoparte vs Roberto Meloni (C-202/04), point 30 (Case 5) in which the Court held that

---

10 See: ECJ, April 4th 1968, Molkerei Zentrale, case 28/67; ECJ, January 19th 1982, Becker, case 8/81; ECJ, September 20th 2001, Courage and Crehan, case C-453/99, ECJ, November 19th 1991, Francovich, case 6 and 9/90, ECJ, October 5th 2004, Pfeiffer and others, case C-397-403/01.

11 For a rigorous deepen on mutual recognition see Barnard C., *The Law of the Single European Market: Unpacking the Premises*, Oxford, 2002, p. 227 ff. and Swann D., *European Economic Integration: The Common Market, European Union and Beyond*, Edward Elgar, 1996.

In what concerns more specifically matters relative to the interpretation of article 49 EC, although it is pacific that all elements of the controversy brought before the judge for adjournment are limited within a single member State, an answer can however be useful for the judge for adjournment, in particular in case national law imposes, in a procedure as the one examined, that an Italian citizen have the same rights a citizen of a State other from the Italian Republic would have in the same situation, based on EU law.

2.3 The Regulation of Infrastructures Through Public Authorities and the "In House Providing"

According to the main principles present in national laws on infrastructures and public procurement, every State identifies a public body (mostly State agencies) in charge of construction, managing, and maintenance of facilities. Other private enterprises have the possibility of entering into such markets, but in some acceding States (such as Macedonia and Croatia) private companies are allowed carry out construction and management activities of infrastructures only as long as they are subcontractors of the public agency.

Anyway, performance of construction and management of infrastructures is an SGI and is subject to the requirements of TFEU articles 106 and 14[12]. EU allows a choice through a public tender of the specific subject for exercising SGI, because the markets for construction and management must be opened to every company that is interested. The subcontracting solution of less liberalized countries (including acceding countries but also the recent Italian praxis) seems to comply with TFEU art. 106 only insofar it allows the possibility of limiting competition through the role of the Agency, which is essentially a "*longa manus*" of the public administration.

Therefore, a generic provision that allows the Agency to subcontract determined services does not seem to satisfy the principle of proportionality for measures restricting competition. We must recall that the Altmark Court of Justice standard requires that the restrictions referred to in art. 106 can be allowed only when useful for reaching the mission of general interest and when they are proportionate. It is, in other words, required that exclusive rights assigned to companies in charge of Services of General Economic Interest do not obtain as a result damaging free access to the market and to competition.

Those prescriptions are, indeed, unbreakably linked to art. 56 of the TFEU, according to which any measure limiting freedom of circulation of services and

---

12 See Rodrigues S., *Les services public set le Traitè d'Amsterdam. Genès et portèe juridique du projet du nouvel article 16 du Traitè CE*, in *Revue du Marchè Commune r de l'Union Europèeenne*, 1998, p. 37 ff., Krajewski M. - Neergard U. - Van de Gronden J., *The changing legal framework for services of general interest in Europe. Between competition and solidarity*, Cambridge, 2009, Liston C., *Price-Cap versus Rate-of-Return Regulation*, in *Journal of Regulatory Economics*, 1995, p. 25 ff. and Gromnicka E., *Services of General Economic Interest in the State Aids Regime: Proceduralisation of Political Choices?*, in *European Public Law*, 2005, p. 429 ff.

companies causes a breach of European Union law. As the Court of Justice has often held (*ex multis* see Case 6) ECJ, October 5th 2004, Caixa Bank France, C-442/02), restraining measures are admissible only when they guarantee the pursuit of an imperative public need and do not go beyond what is necessary for protecting such needs.

The proportionality test was clearly applied in the Caixa Bank case:

7 It should be noted, as a preliminary point, that Directive 2000/12/EC of the European Parliament and of the Council of 20 March 2000 relating to the taking up and pursuit of the business of credit institutions (OJ 2000 L 126, p. 1) is not applicable in a case such as that at issue in the main proceedings, in particular because that directive does not refer to restrictions on the establishment of companies which, like Caixa-Bank, make use of freedom of establishment in a Member State as subsidiaries of credit institutions established in other Member States.

8 By its questions the national court essentially asks whether Article 43 EC precludes legislation of a Member State which prohibits a credit institution which is a subsidiary of a company from another Member State from remunerating sight accounts in euros opened by residents of the former Member State.

9 The freedom of establishment provided for in Article 43 EC, read in conjunction with Article 48 EC, is conferred both on natural persons who are nationals of a Member State and on legal persons within the meaning of Article 48 EC. Subject to the exceptions and conditions specified, it includes the right to take up and pursue all types of self-employed activity in the territory of any other Member State, to set up and manage undertakings, and to set up agencies, branches or subsidiaries (see, inter alia, Case C-255/97*Pfeiffer* [1999] ECR I-2835, paragraph 18).

10 The legal position of a company such as Caixa-Bank falls within the scope of Community law by virtue of the provisions of Article 43 EC.

11 Article 43 EC requires the elimination of restrictions on the freedom of establishment. All measures which prohibit, impede or render less attractive the exercise of that freedom must be regarded as such restrictions (see, inter alia, Case C-55/94 *Gebhard* [1995] ECR I-4165, paragraph 37, Case C-108/96 *Mac Quen and Others* [2001] ECR I-837, paragraph 26, and Case C-79/01 *Payroll and Others* [2002] ECR I-8923, paragraph 26).

12 A prohibition on the remuneration of sight accounts such as that laid down by the French legislation constitutes, for companies from Member States other than the French Republic, a serious obstacle to the pursuit of their activities via a subsidiary in the latter Member State, affecting their access to the market. That prohibition is therefore to be regarded as a restriction within the meaning of Article 43 EC.

13 That prohibition hinders credit institutions which are subsidiaries of foreign companies in raising capital from the public, by depriving them of the possibility of competing more effectively, by paying remuneration on sight accounts, with the credit institutions traditionally established in the Member State of establishment, which have an extensive network of branches and therefore greater opportunities than those subsidiaries for raising capital from the public.

14 Where credit institutions which are subsidiaries of foreign companies seek to enter the market of a Member State, competing by means of the rate of remuneration paid on sight accounts constitutes one of the most effective methods to that end. Access to the market by those establishments is thus made more difficult by such a prohibition.

15 While the French Government asserted at the hearing that there are forms of account comparable to sight accounts, such as 15-day accounts, which are not covered by the prohibition of remuneration and have helped credit institutions such as Caixa-Bank to compete with French credit institutions in raising funds from the public and increasing their market share in France, the Government conceded, however, that those accounts, unlike sight accounts, do not allow the use of bank cards or cheques. The prohibition at issue therefore entails a hindrance for credit institutions such as Caixa-Bank in their activity of raising capital from the public, which the existence of other forms of account with remunerated deposits cannot remedy.

16 The restriction on the pursuit and development of the activities of those subsidiaries resulting from the prohibition at issue is all the greater in that it is common ground that the taking of deposits from the public and the granting of credits represent the basic activities of credit institutions (see, to that effect, inter alia Article 1(1) of and Annex I to Directive 2000/12).

17 It is clear from settled case-law that where, as in the case at issue in the main proceedings, such a measure applies to any person or undertaking carrying on an activity in the territory of the host Member State, it may be justified where it serves overriding requirements relating to the public interest, is suitable for securing the attainment of the objective it pursues and does not go beyond what is necessary in order to attain it (see, inter alia, Case C-424/97 *Haim* [2000] ECR I-5123, paragraph 57, *Mac Quen*, paragraph 26, and Case C-439/99 *Commission* v *Italy* [2002] ECR I-305, paragraph 23).

18 It must therefore be examined whether the grounds put forward by the French Government meet those criteria.

19 To justify the restriction on freedom of establishment resulting from the prohibition at issue, the French Government prayed in aid both the protection of consumers and the encouragement of medium and long-term saving.

20 It submits, first, that the prohibition at issue in the main proceedings is necessary for maintaining the provision of basic banking services without charge. Introducing remuneration for sight accounts would substantially increase the operating costs of banks, which, to recover those costs, would increase charges and introduce charges for the various banking services currently provided free, in particular the issuing of cheques.

21 It must be observed, however, that while the protection of consumers is among the overriding requirements that can justify restrictions on a fundamental freedom guaranteed by the EC Treaty, the prohibition at issue in the main proceedings, even supposing that it ultimately presents certain benefits for the consumer, constitutes a measure which goes beyond what is necessary to attain that objective.

22 Even supposing that removing the prohibition of paying remuneration on sight accounts necessarily entails for consumers an increase in the cost of basic banking services or a charge for cheques, the possibility might be envisaged inter alia of allowing consumers to choose between an unremunerated sight account with certain basic banking services remaining free of charge and a remunerated sight account with the credit institution being

able to make charges for banking services previously provided free, such as the issuing of cheques.

23 As regards, next, the French authorities' concern to encourage long-term saving, it must be observed that, while the prohibition of remuneration on sight accounts is indeed suitable for encouraging medium and long-term saving, it nevertheless remains a measure which goes beyond what is necessary to attain that objective.

24 In the light of the above considerations, the answer to the questions referred for a preliminary ruling must be that Article 43 EC precludes legislation of a Member State which prohibits a credit institution which is a subsidiary of a company from another Member State from remunerating sight accounts in euros opened by residents of the former Member State.

Indeed, general provisions limiting the infrastructures market to subcontracts, in fact, restrain the giving of competitive advantages only to State-owned companies, without giving either any reason or any imperative need of general character that might justify such a strong and evident restriction.

Moreover, the absence of a call for tenders implies a lack of minimal control mechanisms from public institutions on the activity of such public enterprises; a direct and unconditional awarding of services to public enterprises also risks being incompatible with in-house providing norms. It is known that articles 56 and 49 of the TFEU provide the legal basis for governing all relations between member States and private companies offering themselves for performing services of general interest[13].

Given the absence of a uniform rule, EU law (and more precisely articles 49 and 56 of the TFEU) requires that each member State choose its own provider after having a public selection procedure, which allows an evaluation of the most efficient candidate (among all, Case 7) ECJ, December 7th 2000, Teleaustria, cause C-324/98). According to these decisions, the need for a comparative evaluation is critical to a fully functioning EU law in the field of establishment and free circulation of services and capital, and is especially essential since uniform norms on contracts and services (Directives n. 17/2004 and 18/2004) are not applicable.

Telaustria Case 7) is the first case where the Court declared that concessions[14] are subject to internal market rules even though they are not included in the field of application of public procurement directives:

---

[13] See Munari F., *La disciplina dei c.d. servizi essenziali tra diritto comunitario, prerogative degli Stati membri ed interesse generale*, in *Dir. Un. Eur.*, 2001, p. 39 ff. and Bovis C., *Financing Services of General Interest, Public Procurement and State Aid: The Delineation Between Market Forces and Protection*, in *Columbia Journal of European Law*, 2004, p. 419 ff.

[14] The concession model is a critical issue of European Union law as explanied in Guislain P. - Kerf M., *Concessions – The Way to Privatize Infrastructure Sector Monopolies, Viewpoint 59*, Finance and Private Sector Development Department, The World Bank, Washington D.C., 1995.

(...)

28 By the first and second questions, which can be examined together, the national court raises essentially two issues.

29 The first is whether a contract for pecuniary interest is covered, by reason of the contracting parties and its specific object, by Directives 92/50 or 93/38 where under that contract, which was concluded in writing between, on the one hand, an undertaking which is specifically responsible under the legislation of a Member State for operating a telecommunications service and whose capital is wholly held by the public authorities of that State and, on the other, a private undertaking, the first undertaking entrusts the second with the production and publication, for the purpose of distribution to the public, of printed and electronically accessible lists of telephone subscribers (telephone directories).

30 By the second issue raised, the national court seeks essentially to ascertain whether such a contract, whose specific object is the services mentioned in the preceding paragraph, although it is covered by one of those directives, is excluded, as Community law stands at present, from the scope of the directive which covers it, because, in particular, the consideration provided by the first undertaking to the second consists in the second obtaining the right to exploit for payment its own service.

31 In order to deal with the first issue raised, it should be noted at the outset that, as is clear from the 17th recital in the preamble to Directive 92/50, the provisions of that directive must not affect those of Directive 90/531 which, since it preceded Directive 93/38, also applied, like that directive, to procurement procedures in the water, energy, transport and telecommunications sectors.

32 Since Directive 90/531 was replaced by Directive 93/38, as is clear from Article 45(3) of that directive, and since the references to Directive 90/531 are to be construed, according to Article 45(4) of Directive 93/38, as referring to Directive 93/38, it must be concluded, as under the regime applicable when the sectoral Directive 90/531 was in force, that the provisions of Directive 92/50 must not affect those of Directive 93/38.

33 Consequently, where a contract is covered by Directive 93/38 governing a specific sector of services, the provisions of Directive 92/50, which are intended to apply to services in general, are not applicable.

34 In those circumstances, it is necessary only to examine whether the contract at issue in the main proceedings can be covered, by reason of the contracting parties and its specific object, by Directive 93/38.

35 In this respect, it is necessary to determine, first, whether an undertaking, such as Telekom Austria, falls within the scope ratione personae of Directive 93/38 and, second, whether a contract, whose object is the services mentioned in paragraph 26 above, comes within the material scope of that directive.

36 As regards the scope ratione personae of Directive 93/38, it is common ground, as is clear from the order for reference, that Telekom Austria, whose capital belongs entirely to the Austrian public authorities, constitutes a public undertaking over which those authorities may, by virtue of the fact that the Republic of Austria holds the entire capital, exercise a dominant influence. It follows that Telekom Austria must be regarded as a public undertaking for the purpose of Article 1(2) of that directive.

37 Furthermore, it is common ground that, under the Telekommunikationsgesetz under which it was founded, that public undertaking carries on the activity which consists in the provision of public telecommunications services. It follows that Telekom Austria constitutes a contracting entity for the purpose of Article 2(1)(a) of Directive 93/38 in conjunction with Article 2(2)(d) thereof.

38 Moreover, since it is also common ground that the aforementioned contract provides for the performance of services which are Telekom Austria's responsibility under the Telekommunikationsgesetz and consist in the provision of public telecommunications services, it is sufficient, in order to determine whether the contract at issue in the main proceedings comes within the material scope of Directive 93/38, to determine whether the specific object of that contract is covered by the provisions of Directive 93/38.

39 In this respect, it should be noted, as in the order for reference, that the services which are Herold's responsibility include:

- collecting, processing and arranging of subscriber data, in order to make them technically accessible, operations which require data gathering, data processing and tabulation, and services of data banks, which are in category 7, entitled Computer and related services, of Annex XVI A to Directive 93/38;
- production of printed telephone directories, which comes under category 15 of Annex XVI A to that directive, a category covering Publishing and printing services on a fee or contract basis;
- advertising services, which come under category 13 of Annex XVI A to Directive 93/38.

40 Since those services are directly linked to an activity relating to the provision of public telecommunications services, it must be concluded that the contract at issue in the main proceedings, whose specific object is the services referred to in the preceding paragraph, is covered by Directive 93/38.

41 In answering the second issue raised by the national court, it must be noted at the outset that the court links its questions to Proposal 91/C 23/01 of 13 December 1990 for a Council Directive relating to the coordination of procedures on the award of public service contracts (OJ 1991 C 23, p. 1; the proposal of 13 December 1990) and adopts the definition of public service concession proposed in that document by the Commission.

42 In that regard, it is necessary to state that the Court is in a position to deal with the second issue raised without its being necessary for it to adopt the definition of public service concession referred to in Article 1(h) of the proposal of 13 December 1990.

43 It should be noted at the outset that Article 1(4) of Directive 93/38 refers to contracts for pecuniary interest concluded in writing and, without making express reference to public service concessions, provides only indications about the contracting parties and about the object of the contract, defining them in particular in the light of the method of remunerating the service provider and without drawing any distinction between contracts in which the consideration is fixed and those in which the consideration consists in a right of exploitation.

44 Telaustria proposes that Directive 93/38 be interpreted as meaning that a contract under which the consideration consists in a right of exploitation also comes within its scope. In its submission, in order for Directive 93/38 to apply to such a contract, it is sufficient, in accordance with Article 1(4) of that directive, for the contract to be for pecuniary interest and concluded in writing. It would therefore be unjustified to infer that such contracts are excluded from the scope of Directive 93/38 simply because that directive is silent about the

method by which the service provider is to be remunerated. Telaustria adds that the fact that the Commission did not propose to include provisions about that type of contract within the scope of the Directive indicates that it considered that the Directive covers any contract for the provision of services, regardless of the arrangements for remunerating the provider.

45 Since Telekom Austria, the Member States which have submitted observations and the Commission dispute that interpretation, it is necessary to assess its merits in the light of the history of the relevant directives, in particular in the field of public service contracts.

46 In that regard, it should be recalled that both in its proposal of 13 December 1990 and in its amended proposal 91/C 250/05 of 28 August 1991 for a Council Directive relating to the coordination of procedures on the award of public service contracts (OJ 1991 C 250, p. 4; the proposal of 28 August 1991), which resulted in the adoption of Directive 92/50 which covers public service contracts in general, the Commission had expressly proposed that public service concessions be included within the scope of that directive.

47 Since that inclusion was justified by the intention to ensure coherent award procedures, the Commission stated, in the 10th recital in the preamble to the proposal of 13 December 1990, that public service concessions should be covered by this directive in the same way as Directive 71/305/EEC applies to public works concessions. Although the reference to Council Directive 71/305/EEC of 26 July 1971 concerning the coordination of procedures for the award of public works contracts (OJ, English Special Edition 1971 (II), p. 682) was withdrawn from the 10th recital in the preamble to the proposal of 28 August 1991, that proposal none the less expressly maintained the purpose of ensuring coherent award procedures in that recital.

48 However, during the legislative process, the Council eliminated all references to public service concessions, in particular because of the differences between the Member States as regards the delegation of the management of public services and modes of delegation, which could create a situation of very great imbalance in the opening-up of the public concession contracts (see point 6 of document No 4444/92 ADD 1 of 25 February 1992, entitled Statement of reasons of the Council and annexed to the common position of the same date).

49 The outcome was the same for the Commission's position expressed in its amended proposal 89/C 264/02 of 18 July 1989 for a Council Directive on the procurement procedures of entities operating in the water, energy, transport and telecommunications sectors (OJ 1989 C 264, p. 22), which resulted in the adoption of Directive 90/531, which was the first directive in those sectors on the award of public contracts and preceded Directive 93/38, in which the Commission had also proposed for those sectors certain provisions designed to govern public service concessions.

50 None the less, as is clear from point 10 of document No 5250/90 ADD 1 of 22 March 1990, entitled Statement of reasons of the Council and annexed to the Council's common position of the same date on the amended proposal for a Council Directive on the procurement procedures of entities operating in the water, energy, transport and telecommunications sectors, the Council did not act on that Commission proposal to include in Directive 90/531 rules on public service concessions, on the ground that such concessions existed in only one Member State and that it was inappropriate to proceed with their regulation in the absence of a detailed study of the various forms of public service concessions granted in the Member States in those sectors.

51 In view of those circumstances, the Commission did not propose the inclusion of public service concessions in its proposal 91/C 337/01 of 27 September 1991 for a Council Directive amending Directive 90/531 (OJ 1991 C 337, p. 1), which subsequently resulted in the adoption of Directive 93/38.

52 That finding is also supported by the way in which the scope of the directives on public works contracts evolved.

53 Article 3(1) of Directive 71/305, which was the first directive on the subject, expressly excluded concession contracts from its scope.

54 None the less, Council Directive 89/440/EEC of 18 July 1989 amending Directive 71/305 (OJ 1989 L 210, p. 1) inserted in Directive 71/305 Article 1b which expressly addressed public works concessions by making the advertising rules laid down in Articles 12(3), (6), (7), (9) to (13) and 15a thereof applicable to them.

55 Subsequently, Council Directive 93/37/EEC of 14 June 1993 concerning the coordination of procedures for the award of public works contracts (OJ 1993 L 199, p. 54), which replaced Directive 71/305 as amended, expressly refers to public works concessions among the contracts within its scope.

56 On the other hand, Directive 93/38, adopted on the same day as Directive 93/37, provided for no rule on public service concessions. It follows that the Community legislature decided not to include such concessions within the scope of Directive 93/38. If it had wished to, it would have done so expressly, as it did when adopting Directive 93/37.

57 Since public service concession contracts do not therefore come within the scope of Directive 93/38, it must be concluded that, contrary to the interpretation proposed by Telaustria, such contracts are not included in the concept of contracts for pecuniary interest concluded in writing appearing in Article 1(4) of that directive.

58 The answers to the first and second questions must therefore be that:

Directive 93/38 covers a contract for pecuniary interest concluded in writing between, on the one hand, an undertaking which is specifically responsible under the legislation of a Member State for operating a telecommunications service and whose capital is wholly held by the public authorities of that State and, on the other, a private undertaking, where under that contract the first undertaking entrusts the second with the production and publication, for the purpose of distribution to the public, of printed and electronically accessible lists of telephone subscribers (telephone directories);

although it is covered by Directive 93/38, such a contract is excluded, under Community law as it stands at present, from the scope of that directive by reason of the fact, in particular, that the consideration provided by the first undertaking to the second consists in the second obtaining the right to exploit for payment its own service.

59 However, the fact that such a contract does not fall within the scope of Directive 93/38 does not preclude the Court from helping the national court which has sent it a series of questions for a preliminary ruling. To that end, the Court may take into consideration other factors in making an interpretation which may assist the determination of the main proceedings.

60 In that regard, it should be borne in mind that, notwithstanding the fact that, as Community law stands at present, such contracts are excluded from the scope of Directive 93/38, the contracting entities concluding them are, none the less, bound to comply with the

fundamental rules of the Treaty, in general, and the principle of non-discrimination on the ground of nationality, in particular.

61 As the Court held in Case C-275/98 Unitron Scandinavia and 3-S [1999] ECR I-8291, paragraph 31, that principle implies, in particular, an obligation of transparency in order to enable the contracting authority to satisfy itself that the principle has been complied with.

62 That obligation of transparency which is imposed on the contracting authority consists in ensuring, for the benefit of any potential tenderer, a degree of advertising sufficient to enable the services market to be opened up to competition and the impartiality of procurement procedures to be reviewed.

63 It is for the national court to rule on the question whether that obligation was complied with in the case in the main proceedings and also to assess the materiality of the evidence produced to that effect.

In a few words, the awarding of the infrastructures constructor and manager can only take place through a selection procedure that makes everyone know the economic, juridical, and organizational frame of the contract. Indeed, private companies' interests and business plans can be completed only according to the specific opportunities offered by member States under a certainty of law standard.

This theory is called "in-house providing,"[15] which forbids member States from awarding public contracts without a public call unless two conditions are satisfied: (1) the awarding authority controls the company as if it were its own office, and (2) the awarded company must direct its activity mostly to the awarding authority. The leading cases are the Teckal decision (ECJ, 18th November 1999, case C-107/98, Teckal, in Rep., p. I-08121) and the Stadt Halle case (ECJ, 11 January 2005, case C-26/03, Stadt Halle, in Rep., p. I-00001); both judgments can be better understood reading the Coname case, case 8) ECJ, July 21st2005, Coname, case C-231/03, where the Courts clarified the meaning of "analougus control":

(...)

15 By its question, the referring court seeks, in essence, to ascertain whether Articles 43 EC and 49 EC preclude the direct award, that is to say without an invitation to tender, by a municipality of a concession for the management of the public gas-distribution service to a company with predominantly public capital in which that municipality holds a 0.97% share.

16 It must be remembered that the award of such a concession is not governed by any of the directives by which the Community legislature has regulated the field of public contracts. In the absence of any such legislation, the consequences in Community law of the award of such concessions must be examined in the light of primary law and, in particular, of the fundamental freedoms provided for by the Treaty.

17 In that regard, it must be pointed out that, in so far as the concession in question may also be of interest to an undertaking located in a Member State other than the Member State of the Comune di Cingia de' Botti, the award, in the absence of any transparency, of that

[15] See Comba, M., Steen Treumer St., *The In-House Providing in European Law*, Copenhagen, 2010.

concession to an undertaking located in the latter Member State amounts to a difference in treatment to the detriment of the undertaking located in the other Member State (see, to that effect, *Telaustria and Telefonadress*, paragraph 61).

18 In the absence of any transparency, the latter undertaking has no real opportunity of expressing its interest in obtaining that concession.

19 Unless it is justified by objective circumstances, such a difference in treatment, which, by excluding all undertakings located in another Member State, operates mainly to the detriment of the latter undertakings, amounts to indirect discrimination on the basis of nationality, prohibited under Articles 43 EC and 49 EC (see in particular, to that effect, Case C-111/91 *Commission* v *Luxembourg* [1993] ECR I-817, paragraph 17, Case C-337/97 *Meeusen* [1999] ECR I-3289, paragraph 27, and Case C-294/97 *Eurowings Luftverkehr* [1999] ECR I-7447, paragraph 33 and the case-law cited).

20 With regard to the case in the main proceedings, it is not apparent from the file that, because of special circumstances, such as a very modest economic interest at stake, it could reasonably be maintained that an undertaking located in a Member State other than that of the Comune di Cingia de' Botti would have no interest in the concession at issue and that the effects on the fundamental freedoms concerned should therefore be regarded as too uncertain and indirect to warrant the conclusion that they may have been infringed (see, to that effect, Case C-69/88 *Krantz* [1990] ECR I-583, paragraph 11; Case C-44/98 *BASF* [1999] ECR I-6269, paragraph 16; and the order in Case C-431/01 *Mertens* [2002] ECR I-7073, paragraph 34).

21 In those circumstances, it is for the referring court to satisfy itself that the award of the concession by the Comune di Cingia de' Botti to Padania complies with transparency requirements which, without necessarily implying an obligation to hold an invitation to tender, are, in particular, such as to ensure that an undertaking located in the territory of a Member State other than that of the Italian Republic can have access to appropriate information regarding that concession before it is awarded, so that, if that undertaking had so wished, it would have been in a position to express its interest in obtaining that concession.

22 If that is not the case, it must be concluded that there was a difference in treatment to the detriment of that undertaking.

23 With regard to the objective circumstances that could justify such a difference in treatment, it must be pointed out that the fact that the Comune di Cingia de' Botti has a 0.97% holding in the share capital of Padania does not, by itself, constitute one of those objective circumstances.

24 Even if the need for a municipality to exercise control over a concessionaire managing a public service may constitute an objective circumstance capable of justifying a possible difference in treatment, it must be pointed out that the 0.97% holding is so small as to preclude any such control, as the referring court itself observes.

25 At the hearing, the Italian Government submitted, in essence, that, in contrast to some large Italian cities, most municipalities lack the resources to provide, through in-house structures, public services such as that of gas distribution within their territory, and are therefore obliged to resort to structures, such as that of Padania, in the share capital of which several municipalities have holdings.

26 In that regard, it must be held that a structure such as that of Padania may not be treated in the same way as a structure through which a municipality or a city manages, on an in-house basis, a public service. As is apparent from the file, Padania is a company open, at least in part, to private capital, which precludes it from being regarded as a structure for the 'in-house' management of a public service on behalf of the municipalities which form part of it.

27 The Court has not been made aware of any other objective circumstance capable of justifying any difference in treatment.

28 In those circumstances, the answer to the question referred must be that Articles 43 EC and 49 EC preclude, in circumstances such as those at issue in the main proceedings, the direct award by a municipality of a concession for the management of the public gas-distribution service to a company in which there is a majority public holding and in which the municipality in question has a 0.97% holding, if that award does not comply with transparency requirements which, without necessarily implying an obligation to hold an invitation to tender, are, in particular, such as to enable an undertaking located in the territory of a Member State other than that of the municipality in question to have access to appropriate information regarding that concession, so that, if that undertaking had so wished, it would have been in a position to express its interest in obtaining that concession.

The indicated ECJ decisions don't allow even so-called "in-house contracts," except in the case of companies totally controlled by the State or by a public entity by virtue of "*control analogous to the one exercised over its own departments.*" In the law being considered, instead, direct contracts are made with no trace of dispositions relative to requirements imposed by legitimate direct assignment, i.e., (a) control analogous to the one exercised over its own departments, and (b) the prevailing destination of the activity for the State. It must in fact be reminded that "the sole circumstance that a public authority holds the entire social capital of a stock company deriving from transformation of a special company does not suffice to demonstrate the existence of 'analogous control.' According to the most important decision in this field (Case 9) ECJ, October 13th 2005, case C-458/03, Parking Brixen, in Rep., p. I-8612)":

44 By its second question, the referring court is asking, in essence, whether the award of a public service concession without it being put out to competition is compatible with Community law, if the concessionaire is a company limited by shares resulting from the conversion of a special undertaking of a public authority, a company whose share capital is at the time of the award 100% owned by the concession-granting public authority, but whose administrative board enjoys all extensive powers of routine administration and can effect independently, without the agreement of the shareholders' meeting, certain transactions up to a value of EUR 5 million.

45 That question refers, first, to the conduct of the concession-granting authority in relation to the award of a specific concession and, second, to the national legislation which permits the award of such a concession without a call for tenders.

46 Notwithstanding the fact that public service concession contracts are, as Community law stands at present, excluded from the scope of Directive 92/50, the public authorities concluding them are, none the less, bound to comply with the fundamental rules of the EC Treaty, in general, and the principle of non-discrimination on the ground of nationality, in

particular (see, to that effect, Case C-324/98 *Telaustria and Telefonadress* [2000] ECR I-10745, paragraph 60, and Case C-231/03 *Coname* [2005] ECR I-0000, paragraph 16).

47 The prohibition on any discrimination on grounds of nationality is set out in Article 12 EC. The provisions of the Treaty which are more specifically applicable to public service concessions include, in particular, Article 43 EC, the first paragraph of which states that restrictions on the freedom of establishment of nationals of a Member State in the territory of another Member State are to be prohibited, and Article 49 EC, the first paragraph of which provides that restrictions on freedom to provide services within the Community are to be prohibited in respect of nationals of Member States who are established in a State of the Community other than that of the person for whom the services are intended.

48 According to the Court's case-law, Articles 43 EC and 49 EC are specific expressions of the principle of equal treatment (see Case C-3/88 *Commission* v *Italy* [1989] ECR 4035, paragraph 8). The prohibition on discrimination on grounds of nationality is also a specific expression of the general principle of equal treatment (see Case 810/79 *Überschär* [1980] ECR 2747, paragraph 16). In its case-law relating to the Community directives on public procurement, the Court has stated that the principle of equal treatment of tenderers is intended to afford equality of opportunity to all tenderers when formulating their tenders, regardless of their nationality (see, to that effect, Case C-87/94 *Commission* v *Belgium* [1996] ECR I-2043, paragraphs 33 and 54). As a result, the principle of equal treatment of tenderers is to be applied to public service concessions even in the absence of discrimination on grounds of nationality.

49 The principles of equal treatment and non-discrimination on grounds of nationality imply, in particular, a duty of transparency which enables the concession-granting public authority to ensure that those principles are complied with. That obligation of transparency which is imposed on the public authority consists in ensuring, for the benefit of any potential tenderer, a degree of advertising sufficient to enable the service concession to be opened up to competition and the impartiality of procurement procedures to be reviewed (see, to that effect, *Telaustria and Telefonadress*, cited above, paragraphs 61 and 62).

50 It is for the concession-granting public authority to evaluate, subject to review by the competent courts, the appropriateness of the detailed arrangements of the call for competition to the particularities of the public service concession in question. However, a complete lack of any call for competition in the case of the award of a public service concession such as that at issue in the main proceedings docs not comply with the requirements of Articles 43 EC and 49 EC any more than with the principles of equal treatment, non-discrimination and transparency.

51 Furthermore, Article 86(1) EC provides that, in the case of public undertakings and undertakings to which Member States grant special or exclusive rights, Member States shall neither enact nor maintain in force any measure contrary to the rules contained in the Treaty, in particular to those laid down in Articles 12 EC and 81 EC to 89 EC.

52 It follows therefrom that the Member States must not maintain in force national legislation which permits the award of public service concessions without their being put out to competition since such an award infringes Article 43 EC or 49 EC or the principles of equal treatment, non-discrimination and transparency.

53 Two arguments are deployed to maintain that the provisions of the Treaty and the general principles mentioned in paragraphs 46 to 52 of this judgment do not apply to a public service concession awarded in circumstances such as those of the main proceedings.

54 First, Stadtwerke Brixen AG argues that Articles 43 EC to 55 EC do not apply to a situation such as that in the main proceedings, because it is a situation purely internal to a single Member State, given that Parking Brixen, Stadtwerke Brixen AG and the Gemeinde Brixen all have their seats in Italy.

55 That argument cannot be accepted. It is possible that, in the main proceedings, undertakings established in Member States other than the Italian Republic might have been interested in providing the services concerned (see, to that effect, *Commission* v *Belgium*, cited above, paragraph 33). In the absence of advertising and the opening to competition of the award of a public service concession such as that at issue in the main proceedings, there is discrimination, at least potentially, against undertakings of the other Member States which are prevented from making use of the freedom to provide services and of the freedom of establishment provided for by the Treaty (see, to that effect, *Coname*, cited above, paragraph 17).

56 Secondly, the Italian Republic, Stadtwerke Brixen AG and the Gemeinde Brixen contend that the application of the rules of the Treaty and of the general principles of Community law to a situation such as that in the main proceedings is precluded by the fact that Stadtwerke Brixen AG is not an entity independent of that municipality. In support of that argument, they rely on the judgment in Case C-107/98*Teckal* [1999] ECR I-8121, paragraphs 49 to 51.

57 In that regard, it is important to recall that, in *Teckal*, cited above, the Court held that Council Directive 93/36/EEC of 14 June 1993 coordinating procedures for the award of public supply contracts (OJ 1993 L 199, p. 1) is applicable where a contracting authority, such as a local authority, plans to conclude in writing, with an entity which is formally distinct from it and independent of it in regard to decision-making, a contract for pecuniary interest for the supply of goods.

58 As regards the existence of such a contract, the Court stated, in paragraph 50 of the judgment in *Teckal*, that, in accordance with Article 1(a) of Directive 93/36, it is in principle sufficient if the contract was concluded between, on the one hand, a local authority and, on the other, a person legally distinct from that local authority. The position can be otherwise only in the case where the local authority exercises over the person concerned a control which is similar to that which it exercises over its own departments and, at the same time, that person carries out the essential part of its activities with the controlling local authority or authorities.

59 The Court has confirmed that the same considerations apply to Directive 92/50 on public service contracts and Council Directive 93/37/EEC of 14 June 1993 concerning the coordination of procedures for the award of public works contracts (OJ 1993 L 199, p. 54) (see, respectively, Case C-26/03 *Stadt Halle and RPL Lochau* [2005] ECR I-1, paragraphs 48, 49 and 52, and Case C-84/03*Commission* v *Spain* [2005] ECR I-139, paragraph 39).

60 Those considerations are based on the premiss that the application of Directives 92/50, 93/36 and 93/37 depends on the existence of a contract concluded between two distinct persons (see *Teckal*, paragraphs 46 and 49). Yet the application of Articles 12 EC, 43 EC and 49 EC, as well as the principles of equal treatment, non-discrimination and transparency associated with them, does not depend on the existence of a contract. As a result, the considerations developed in the case-law cited in paragraphs 56 to 59 of this judgment do not apply automatically either to those provisions of the Treaty or to those principles.

61 Nevertheless, it must be held that those considerations may be transposed to the Treaty provisions and to the principles which relate to public service concessions excluded from the scope of the directives on public procurement. Indeed, in the field of public procurement and public service concessions, the principle of equal treatment and the specific expressions of that principle, namely the prohibition on discrimination on grounds of nationality and Articles 43 EC and 49 EC, are to be applied in cases where a public authority entrusts the supply of economic activities to a third party. By contrast, it is not appropriate to apply the Community rules on public procurement or public service concessions in cases where a public authority performs tasks in the public interest for which it is responsible by its own administrative, technical and other means, without calling upon external entities (see, to that effect, *Stadt Halle and RPL Lochau*, paragraph 48).

62 Consequently, in the field of public service concessions, the application of the rules set out in Articles 12 EC, 43 EC and 49 EC, as well as the general principles of which they are the specific expression, is precluded if the control exercised over the concessionaire by the concession-granting public authority is similar to that which the authority exercises over its own departments and if, at the same time, that entity carries out the essential part of its activities with the controlling authority.

63 Since it is a matter of a derogation from the general rules of Community law, the two conditions stated in the preceding paragraph must be interpreted strictly and the burden of proving the existence of exceptional circumstances justifying the derogation to those rules lies on the person seeking to rely on those circumstances (see *Stadt Halle and RPL Lochau*, paragraph 46).

64 It is appropriate to examine, first, whether the concession-granting public authority exercises a control over the concessionaire which is similar to that which it exercises over its own departments.

65 That assessment must take account of all the legislative provisions and relevant circumstances. It must follow from that examination that the concessionaire in question is subject to a control enabling the concession-granting public authority to influence the concessionaire's decisions. It must be a case of a power of decisive influence over both strategic objectives and significant decisions.

66 It is clear from the order for reference that under Article 1 of the statutes of the special undertaking, Stadtwerke Brixen, it was a municipal body whose specific function was the uniform and integrated provision of local public services. The municipal council laid down the general guidelines, allocated the start-up capital, ensured that any social costs were covered, monitored the operating results and exercised strategic supervision, the undertaking being guaranteed the necessary independence.

67 By contrast, Stadtwerke Brixen AG became market-oriented, which renders the municipality's control tenuous. Militating in that direction are:

(a) the conversion of Stadtwerke Brixen – a special undertaking of the Gemeinde Brixen – into a company limited by shares (Stadtwerke Brixen AG) and the nature of that type of company;

(b) the broadening of its objects, the company having started to work in significant new fields, particularly those of the carriage of persons and goods, as well as information technology and telecommunications. It must be noted that the company retained the wide range of activities previously carried on by the special undertaking, particularly those of water supply and waste water treatment, the supply of heating and energy, waste disposal and road building;

(c) the obligatory opening of the company, in the short term, to other capital;

(d) the expansion of the geographical area of the company's activities, to the whole of Italy and abroad;

(e) the considerable powers conferred on its Administrative Board, with in practice no management control by the municipality.

68 In fact, as regards the powers conferred on the Administrative Board, it is clear from the decision of reference that the statutes of Stadtwerke Brixen AG, particularly Article 18 thereof, give the board very broad powers to manage the company, since it has the power to carry out all acts which it considers necessary for the attainment of the company's objective. In addition, the power, under the said Article 18, to provide guarantees up to EUR 5 million or to effect other transactions without the prior authority of the shareholders' meeting shows that the company has broad independence vis-à-vis its shareholders.

69 The decision of reference also states that the Gemeinde Brixen has the right to appoint the majority of the members of Stadtwerke Brixen AG's Administrative Board. However, the referring court notes that the control exercised by the municipality over Stadtwerke Brixen AG is limited, essentially, to those measures which company law assigns to the majority of shareholders, which considerably attenuates the relationship of dependence which existed between the municipality and the special undertaking Stadtwerke Brixen, in the light, above all, of the broad powers possessed by Stadtwerke Brixen AG's Administrative Board.

70 Where a concessionaire enjoys a degree of independence characterised by elements such as those noted in paragraphs 67 to 69 of this judgment, it is not possible for the concession-granting public authority to exercise over the concessionaire control similar to that which it exercises over its own departments.

71 In those circumstances, and without it being necessary to consider the question whether the concessionaire carries out the essential part of its activities with the concession-granting public authority, the award of a public service concession by a public authority to such a body cannot be regarded as a transaction internal to that authority, to which the rules of Community law do not apply.

72 It follows that the reply to the second question referred for a preliminary ruling must be as follows:

Articles 43 EC and 49 EC, and the principles of equal treatment, non-discrimination and transparency, are to be interpreted as precluding a public authority from awarding, without putting it out to competition, a public service concession to a company limited by shares resulting from the conversion of a special undertaking of that public authority, a company whose objects have been extended to significant new areas, whose capital must obligatorily be opened in the short term to other capital, the geographical area of whose activities has been extended to the entire country and abroad, and whose Administrative Board possesses very broad management powers which it can exercise independently.

Many member States' legislation (for example Italy and Germany) give Services of General Interest companies the possibility to have shares in other companies. This kind of provision seems to contrast with both the requirement for analogous control and the requirement of prevailing destination of service. This disposition also appears to be in conflict with ECJ decisions Carbotermo May 11th 2006, in case C-340/04, in Rep., p. I-04137 (Case 10) and Parking Brixen October 13th 2005, in case C-458/03, where it was clarified that analogous control means not only shares ownwership resulting from public holding of the entire stock, but also the requirement of strict control over boards' and companies' decision-making power. European judges think public entities must have even greater and more involved control and power over the board of directors than those normally given by company law to the majority of members[16]. Furthermore the presence of analogous control has been excluded when the company has "*acquired a commercial vocation which makes control unstable*" and which results from the existence of elements such as: enhancement of social object; mandatory short term opening of the company to other capitals; and territorial expansion of companies' activities.

According to the Carbotermo decision, the second condition of the in-house providing, consisting in carrying out most of the activity with the awarding authority, can be clearly understood:

48 The second question comprises two parts.

49 First, the national court asks whether it is necessary to apply Article 13 of Directive 93/38 to assess the requirement that the undertaking to which a supply contract was directly awarded must carry out the essential part of its activities with the controlling authority. Second, it asks whether that requirement may be regarded as being fulfilled when such an undertaking carries out the essential part of its activities with the controlling authority or when it carries out the essential part of its activities in the territory of that authority.

First part of the second question

50 The order for reference indicates that the contract at issue in the main proceedings falls within the scope of Directive 93/36.

51 The issue is thus whether the exception provided for in Article 13 of Directive 93/38 should be applied by analogy in the scope of application of Directive 93/36.

52 The exception provided for in Article 13 relates only to service contracts and does not include supply contracts.

53 Article 13 of Directive 93/38 covers entities, particularly joint ventures and undertakings whose annual accounts are consolidated and whose methods of operating are different from those of the contracting authorities covered by Directive 93/36.

54 That article, moreover, contains a mechanism for notifying the Commission, which cannot be transposed to Directive 93/36 because there is no legal basis for doing so.

55 As exceptions must be interpreted restrictively, the Court does not find it appropriate to extend the application of Article 13 of Directive 93/38 to the scope of application of Directive 93/36.

---

[16] See Button K.J., *Privatization and Deregulation: Its Implications for Negative Transport Externalities*, in *The Annals of Regional Science*, 1994, p. 125 ff.

56 This finding is supported by the fact that, during the reform of the public procurement directives in 2004, the Community legislature, whilst maintaining that exception in Article 23 of Directive 2004/17/EC of the European Parliament and of the Council of 31 March 2004 coordinating the procurement procedures of entities operating in the water, energy, transport and postal services sectors (OJ 2004 L 134, p. 1), chose not to incorporate an analogous exception in Directive 2004/18/EC of the European Parliament and of the Council of 31 March 2004 on the coordination of procedures for the award of public works contracts, public supply contracts and public service contracts (OJ 2004 L 134, p. 114), which replaced Directive 93/36.

57 In the light of all of the foregoing, the answer to the first part of the second question must be that Article 13 of Directive 93/38 must not be applied in the assessment of the requirement relating to the inapplicability of Directive 93/36, according to which the undertaking to which a supply contract was awarded directly must carry out the essential part of its activities with the controlling authority.

Second part of the second question

58 It should be borne in mind that the principal objective of the Community rules in the field of public procurement is the free movement of services and the opening-up to undistorted competition in all the Member States (see, to that effect, Case C-26/03 *Stadt Halle and RPL Lochau* [2005] ECR I-1, paragraph 44).

59 The conditions laid down in *Teckal* for a finding that Directive 93/36 is inapplicable to the contracts concluded between a local authority and a person legally distinct from it, according to which the local authority must exercise over the person in question a control similar to that which it exercises over its own departments and that person must carry out the essential part of its activities with the controlling authority or authorities, are aimed precisely at preventing distortions of competition.

60 The requirement that the person in question must carry out the essential part of its activities with the controlling authority or authorities is aimed precisely at ensuring that Directive 93/36 remains applicable in the event that an undertaking controlled by one or more authorities is active in the market and therefore likely to be in competition with other undertakings.

61 An undertaking is not necessarily deprived of freedom of action merely because the decisions concerning it are controlled by the controlling authority, if it can still carry out a large part of its economic activities with other operators.

62 It is still necessary that that undertaking's services be intended mostly for that authority alone. Within such limits, it appears justified that that undertaking is not subject to the restrictions of Directive 93/36, since they are in place to preserve a state of competition which, in that case, no longer has any *raison d'être*.

63 In applying those principles, the undertaking in question can be viewed as carrying out the essential part of its activities with the controlling authority within the meaning of *Teckal* only if that undertaking's activities are devoted principally to that authority and any other activities are only of marginal significance.

64 In order to determine if that is the case, the competent court must take into account all the facts of the case, both qualitative and quantitative.

65 As to the issue of whether it is necessary to take into account in that context only the turnover achieved with the supervisory authority or that achieved within its territory, it should be held that the decisive turnover is that which the undertaking in question achieves pursuant to decisions to award contracts taken by the supervisory authority, including the turnover achieved with users in the implementation of such decisions.

66 The activities of a successful undertaking which must be taken into account are all those activities which that undertaking carries out as part of a contract awarded by the contracting authority, regardless of who the beneficiary is: the contracting authority itself or the user of the services.

67 It is also irrelevant who pays the undertaking in question, whether it be the controlling authority or third-party users of the services provided under concessions or other legal relationships established by that authority. The issue of in which territory those services are provided is also irrelevant.

68 If, in the main proceedings, the share capital of the successful undertaking is held indirectly by several authorities, it may be relevant to consider whether the activities to be taken into account are those which the successful undertaking carries out with all of the controlling authorities or only the activities carried out with the authority which in the present case acts as the contracting authority.

69 It should be borne in mind in this connection that the Court has stated that the legally distinct person in question must carry out the essential part of its activities with 'the controlling local authority or authorities' (*Teckal*, paragraph 50). It thus envisaged the possibility that the exception provided for could apply not only in cases where a single authority controls such a legal person, but also where several authorities do so.

70 Where several authorities control an undertaking, the condition relating to the essential part of its activities may be met if that undertaking carries out the essential part of its activities, not necessarily with one of those authorities, but with all of those authorities together.

71 Accordingly, the activities to be taken into account in the case of an undertaking controlled by one or more authorities are those which that undertaking carries out with all of those authorities together.

72 It follows from the foregoing that the answer to the second part of the second question must be that, in order to determine whether an undertaking carries out the essential part of its activities with the controlling authority, for the purpose of deciding on the applicability of Directive 93/36, account must be taken of all the activities which that undertaking carries out on the basis of an award made by the contracting authority, regardless of who pays for those activities, whether it be the contracting authority itself or the user of the services provided; the territory where the activities are carried out is irrelevant.

Other member States' legislation contain rules that allow Service of General Interest companies to perform activities different from the ones for which they were founded.

It is therefore not possible for the choice of public enterprises as managers of infrastructures or, generally speaking, of Services of General Interest, to take place by law without a call for tenders. Public enterprises are not State administrations called to perform as "pieces of the Public Administration"; nor are they are external portions for the State to controls as an internal office (so called analogous control and typical of the economic public body). Public enterprises are commercial enterprises that, according to the annexed decisions, can perform a service only after a comparative procedure allowing the ascertainment of efficiency conditions. Awarding a public contract, especially in a context so strongly against the EU spirit, risks violating EU internal market and competition laws.

In the same context it is of the outmost importance to guarantee respect for fundamental rights; a breach of internal market rules[17] could also imply the violation of the principle of certainty of law, and in itself breaks the principle of transparency, traditionally sustained by the European Court. It could, indeed, happen that the awarding authority should desire, for precise reasons, that certain conditions of the call for tenders be modified after choosing the contractor[18]. In this case it must expressly foresee such a possibility, as well as the application modalities, in all calls for tenders, limiting the boundaries within which the procedure must take place, so that all companies interested in bidding are aware of what they are engaging in from the beginning of the procedure.

Since this matter has immediate relevance from an EU law point of view it is plausible that the indicated principle, as summarized in the cited decision, is also applicable in the case of member States. And, therefore, the same standard of transparency and juridical certainty must be expected from them too when called to adopt administrative or legislative measures relevant from an EU law point of view.

It is known, in this concern, that the single market standard – summarizing rules in the fields of circulation of service, of company establishment, and capital – has evidenced a precise synthesis concerning measures which, even though not (directly or indirectly) discriminatory, produce a restrictive effect on free circulation, thereby discouraging foreign investments and the ability of foreign companies to bring services or establish themselves in the single member States.

Consequently, EU law has turned away from a law that avoids or sanctions discrimination (originally on the basis of nationality), as today, "living" EU law goes well beyond national treatments, forbidding measures which might disable the functioning of the internal market (as well as free circulation of services, capital, and establishments). For example, national measures *de facto* limiting the profitability of certain companies, and consequently the shares circulation, are certainly significant from the perspective of EU law.

As previously observed, the decisions of the Court of Justice have gone beyond the principle of non-discrimination (direct or indirect), configuring a real right to

---

17 See the complete study on Internal market rules that underlines the consequences of a member State breach: Barnard C., *The Law of the Single European Market: Unpacking the Premises*, Oxford, 2002.

18 See the economic analysis of cost pricing made by Braeutigam R., *An Analysis of Fully Distributed Cost Pricing in Regulated Industries*, in *The Bell Journal of Economics*, 1980, p. 182 ff. The birllant reasoning of Braeutigam perfectly fits concerning transport sector.

access the services and capital market[19]. This reasoning was held by the European Court of Justice in the Kraus case, Case 11) ECJ, March 31st 1993, case C-19/93, Kraus:

17 The appellants maintain that the contested judgment is vitiated by erroneous reasoning. The Court of First Instance held that if the subject-matter of the complaint had been within the exclusive purview of the Commission, the complainants would have been entitled to obtain a definitive decision from the Commission as to the existence of the infringement alleged for the period subsequent to the entry into force of the Electricity Law. In that connection the Court of First Instance rejected the view that the Commission had exclusive competence to apply the first sentence of Article 90(2) of the Treaty, without having regard to the second sentence of that provision.

18 It should be noted that, set in the context of the reasoning of the Court of First Instance, the reference to the first sentence of Article 90(2) of the Treaty cannot be interpreted as meaning that the Court of First Instance sought to make a distinction between those two sentences and acknowledge that the Commission has exclusive competence to apply the second sentence.

19 As the Commission rightly points out, this ground of appeal is based on an inaccurate reading of paragraph 99 of the judgment of the Court of First Instance before which, moreover, the question of the application of the second sentence of Article 90(2) of the Treaty did not arise.

20 It follows from the foregoing that this ground of appeal must be rejected.

Failure to state reasons for the priority accorded to the procedure under Article 169 of the Treaty

21 The appellants maintain that the Court of First Instance did not adequately explain the reasons why the Commission was entitled to accord priority to the procedure under Article 169 of the Treaty as opposed to that provided for in Article 3 of Regulation No 17.

22 In that connection, it must be emphasized that the Court of First Instance merely stated, in paragraphs 105 to 107 of the contested judgment, that the finding that the OVS is incompatible with the Treaty cannot have any practical effect so long as it has not been established that the Electricity Law is incompatible with the Treaty. The proper procedure to establish the inconsistency of that Law with the Treaty is that provided for in Article 169 of the Treaty.

23 It follows from those considerations that the Court of First Instance did not seek to establish an order of priority as between the procedure provided for in Regulation No 17 and the procedure against a State for failure to fulfil its obligations, which, moreover, concern separate persons and separate acts, but held that the Commission was entitled to take the view that the most appropriate procedure for examining the question whether the Electricity Law was consistent with the Treaty was the initiation of proceedings for failure to fulfil obligations.

24 Accordingly, this ground of appeal must also be rejected.

---

[19] See Swann D., *European Economic Integration: The Common Market, European Union and Beyond*, Edward Elgar, 1996.

An error of law in the judgment

25 The appellants maintain that the Court of First Instance misdirected itself with regard to the classification of the contested decision by holding that it does not in any way rule on the import restrictions applicable during the period prior to the entry into force of the Electricity Law, whereas the Commission itself acknowledged, according to paragraph 34 of the contested judgment, "that the contested decision contains a partial, implied rejection of the applicants' complaint". The Court of First Instance accordingly erred in declaring the action inadmissible on that point.

26 In that connection, it should be noted that the classification of an act for legal purposes by the Court of First Instance, in particular a finding that the act has no legal effect, is a question of law which may be raised in an appeal.

27 In order to determine the merits of this ground of appeal, it should be borne in mind that the Court of Justice has had occasion to hold that, even if the Commission is not obliged to adopt a decision establishing the existence of an infringement of the rules on competition or to investigate a complaint brought before it under Regulation No 17, it is none the less required to examine closely the matters of fact and of law raised by the complainant in order to ascertain whether there has been any anti-competitive conduct. Moreover, where an investigation is terminated without any action being taken, the Commission is required to state reasons for its decision in order to enable the Court of First Instance to verify whether the Commission committed any errors of fact or of law or is guilty of a misuse of powers.

28 In those circumstances, an institution empowered to find that there has been an infringement and to impose a sanction in respect of it and to which private persons may make complaint, as is the case with the Commission in the field of competition, necessarily adopts a measure producing legal effects when it terminates, wholly or in part, an investigation initiated upon a complaint by such a person (see the judgment in Case C-39/93 P SFEI and Others v Commission [1994] ECR I-2681, paragraph 27, and the case-law cited).

29 It follows from the foregoing that the Court of First Instance misdirected itself in law by holding that the contested decision had had no legal effect as regards the import restrictions applicable during the period prior to the entry into force of the Electricity Law and by declaring the application inadmissible on that point.

30 The plea is therefore well founded, with the result that the judgment must be set aside on this point.

The same reasoning was clarified, and since then never more discussed, in the Gebhard case, case 12) ECJ, November 30th 1995, case C-55/94, Gebhard:

31 The provisions relating to the right of establishment cover the taking-up and pursuit of activities (see, in particular, the judgment in Reyners, paragraphs 46 and 47). Membership of a professional body may be a condition of taking up and pursuit of particular activities. It cannot itself be constitutive of establishment.

32 It follows that the question whether it is possible for a national of a Member State to exercise his right of establishment and the conditions for exercise of that right must be determined in the light of the activities which he intends to pursue on the territory of the host Member State.

33 Under the terms of the second paragraph of Article 52, freedom of establishment is to be exercised under the conditions laid down for its own nationals by the law of the country where establishment is effected.

34 In the event that the specific activities in question are not subject to any rules in the host State, so that a national of that Member State does not have to have any specific qualification in order to pursue them, a national of any other Member State is entitled to establish himself on the territory of the first State and pursue those activities there.

35 However, the taking-up and pursuit of certain self-employed activities may be conditional on complying with certain provisions laid down by law, regulation or administrative action justified by the general good, such as rules relating to organization, qualifications, professional ethics, supervision and liability (see Case C-71/76 Thieffry v Conseil de l' Ordre des Avocats à la Cour de Paris [1977] ECR 765, paragraph 12). Such provisions may stipulate in particular that pursuit of a particular activity is restricted to holders of a diploma, certificate or other evidence of formal qualifications, to persons belonging to a professional body or to persons subject to particular rules or supervision, as the case may be. They may also lay down the conditions for the use of professional titles, such as avvocato.

36 Where the taking-up or pursuit of a specific activity is subject to such conditions in the host Member State, a national of another Member State intending to pursue that activity must in principle comply with them. It is for this reason that Article 57 provides that the Council is to issue directives, such as Directive 89/48, for the mutual recognition of diplomas, certificates and other evidence of formal qualifications or, as the case may be, for the coordination of national provisions concerning the taking-up and pursuit of activities as self-employed persons.

37 It follows, however, from the Court' s case-law that national measures liable to hinder or make less attractive the exercise of fundamental freedoms guaranteed by the Treaty must fulfil four conditions: they must be applied in a non-discriminatory manner; they must be justified by imperative requirements in the general interest; they must be suitable for securing the attainment of the objective which they pursue; and they must not go beyond what is necessary in order to attain it (see Case C-19/92 Kraus v Land Baden-Wuerttemberg [1993] ECR I-1663, paragraph 32).

38 Likewise, in applying their national provisions, Member States may not ignore the knowledge and qualifications already acquired by the person concerned in another Member State (see Case C-340/89 Vlassopoulou v Ministerium fuer Justiz, Bundes- und Europaangelegenheiten Baden-Wuerttemberg [1991] ECR I-2357, paragraph 15). Consequently, they must take account of the equivalence of diplomas (see the judgment in Thieffry, paragraphs 19 and 27) and, if necessary, proceed to a comparison of the knowledge and qualifications required by their national rules and those of the person concerned (see the judgment in Vlassopoulou, paragraph 16).

39 Accordingly, it should be stated in reply to the questions from the Consiglio Nazionale Forense that:

- the temporary nature of the provision of services, envisaged in the third paragraph of Article 60 of the EC Treaty, is to be determined in the light of its duration, regularity, periodicity and continuity;
- the provider of services, within the meaning of the Treaty, may equip himself in the host Member State with the infrastructure necessary for the purposes of performing the services in question;

- a national of a Member State who pursues a professional activity on a stable and continuous basis in another Member State where he holds himself out from an established professional base to, amongst others, nationals of that State comes under the provisions of the chapter relating to the right of establishment and not those of the chapter relating to services;
- the possibility for a national of a Member State to exercise his right of establishment, and the conditions for his exercise of that right, must be determined in the light of the activities which he intends to pursue on the territory of the host Member State;
- where the taking-up of a specific activity is not subject to any rules in the host State, a national of any other Member State will be entitled to establish himself on the territory of the first State and pursue that activity there. On the other hand, where the taking-up or the pursuit of a specific activity is subject to certain conditions in the host Member State, a national of another Member State intending to pursue that activity must in principle comply with them;
- however, national measures liable to hinder or make less attractive the exercise of fundamental freedoms guaranteed by the Treaty must fulfil four conditions: they must be applied in a non-discriminatory manner; they must be justified by imperative requirements in the general interest; they must be suitable for securing the attainment of the objective which they pursue; and they must not go beyond what is necessary in order to attain it;
- likewise, Member States must take account of the equivalence of diplomas and, if necessary, proceed to a comparison of the knowledge and qualifications required by their national rules and those of the person concerned.

The European Court of Justice, in the Gebhard case observed that:

national acts limiting the exercise of fundamental freedom guaranteed by the Treaty must satisfy four conditions: be applied in non discriminatory way, answer to imperative reasons of public interest, be adapt to guarantee the attainment of the pursued aim and not go past what is necessary for attaining it.

2.4 Infrastructures Construction and Management Through the Concession Model: Awarding Procedures and Fundamental Freedoms

Concessions are contracts according to which the State awards a company the right to build and manage a public facility through remuneration obtained by a user fee[20].

Concessions are now included in the field of application of Uniform Directives on Public Procurement, but, before their amending, the competence was limited to ordinary public contracts.

In the Telaustria Case, we see a clear distinction between concessions and contracts:

---

[20] For a complete explanation of European directives on public contracts, see Bovis H., *EU Public Procurement Law*, Edward Elgar, 2008, p. 52 ff.

43 It should be noted at the outset that Article 1(4) of Directive 93/38 refers to contracts for pecuniary interest concluded in writing and, without making express reference to public service concessions, provides only indications about the contracting parties and about the object of the contract, defining them in particular in the light of the method of remunerating the service provider and without drawing any distinction between contracts in which the consideration is fixed and those in which the consideration consists in a right of exploitation.

However, member States can award concessions related to Services of General Interest. Such a choice of limiting *ex lege* the number of operators falls in the field of application of Internal Market law, described in the first chapter. In order to assure and guarantee fundamental freedoms, the EU has adopted several normative acts instrumental to the creation of an internal market. They are based on art. 114 of the TFEU, which allows the adoption of EU norms to harmonize national legislations as far as it is necessary to open the European common market.

Several EU directives based on art. 114 of the TFEU have been adopted concerning procedures of assigning public calls for tenders. Finally, the directives of the European Parliament and of the Council 2004/18/EC (and 2004/17/EC) of 31.03.2004 have established norms of harmonization relativel to public calls for tenders for works, services, and supplies.

Nowadays, scholars and national courts agree that when the European Union has, according to the Treaties, a competitive competence with that of member states, the latter may make laws when the EU has not exercised its own competence or has stopped doing so[21]. This principle has only been crystallized in the Lisbon treaty and through specific provisions in the European Union Treaty.

According to the European Union Treaty, when the Treaties give the European Union a competence that competes with that of member states in a determinate sector, the Union and the States may promulgate laws and adopt juridically binding acts in that sector. The member States enact their own competences to the extent that the Union has not exercised its own or has stopped doing so[22].

The best doctrine holds that, in substance, the realization of the common market, represented by the four fundamental liberties, is an exclusive competence of the European Union, States being called to the role – however important – of concretely adopting acts necessary to ensure liberalization.

In jurisprudence, EU norms of harmozing legislation are interpreted by the Court as implying prohibitions for State to proceed autonomously in protecting certain interests where EU discipline has intervened.

---

[21] The relation between the Monopolies and Internal Market rules is well explained in Buendia Sierra J.L., *Exclusive Rights and State Monopolies under EC Law*, Oxford, 2000.

[22] For a description of the European Union competence in the Internal Market sector, see Barnard C., *The Law of the Single European Market: Unpacking the Premises*, Oxford, 2002.

In the Denkavit case (Case 13) the Court discusses the European Union compentence in the internal market sector:

(...)

13 As far as concerns the field of application of article 36 the national court asks , in the first place , whether that provision may still be invoked by a member state even though community directives or regulations make arrangements for supervision having the same objectives as those provided for by the national provisions adopted in accordance with the said article 36 .

14 The court of justice has held in its judgment of 5 october 1977 in case 5/77 carlo tedeschi v denkavit commerciale s . r . l . (1977) ecr 1556 that article 36 is not designed to reserve certain matters to the exclusive jurisdiction of member states but only permits national laws to derogate from the principle of the free movement of goods to the extent to which such derogation is and continues to be justified for the attainment of the objectives referred to in that article . consequently when , in application of article 100 of the treaty , community directives provide for the harmonization of the measures necessary to guarantee the protection of animal and human health and when they establish procedures to check that they are observed , recourse to article 36 is no longer justified and the appropriate checks must be carried out and the protective measures adopted within the framework outlined by the harmonizing directive .

15 Consideration of the directives referred to by the plaintiff and considered by the national court shows - as moreover that court rightly believes - that they do not deal with , and in any case at the time when the events giving rise to the main action occurred did not deal with , the harmonization of veterinary and public health prevention and supervision of the presence of salmonellae in feeding-stuffs of animal origin and especially in compound feeding-stuffs including milk products and animal fats .

16 This is in the first place the position in the case of council directive no 70/524/eec of 23 november 1970 concerning additives in feeding stuffs (official journal , english special edition 1970 (iii), p . 840) and of council directive no 74/63/eec of 17 december 1973 on the fixing of maximum permitted levels for undesirable substances and products in feeding-stuffs (official journal 1974 , l 38 , p . 31). in fact the wording of those directives as well as the objectives which they seek to attain show that they are in no way concerned with the presence of pathogenic agents in the feeding-stuffs in question since the said agents clearly can neither be regarded as additives nor as undesirable substances and products in respect of which a maximum level would be permitted .

17 The same applies to council directive no 70/373/eec of 20 july 1970 on the introduction of community methods of sampling and analysis for the official control of feeding-stuffs (official journal , english special edition 1970 (ii), p . 535) and of the various commission directives adopted for the implementation thereof . in fact the heading and content of those directives indicate that they do not relate to the physical requirements which are contemplated for the harmonization of national animal health measures relating to feeding-stuffs but only to the community methods making it possible to check whether the feeding-stuffs comply with the physical requirements which have been or are to be laid down in the future .

18 These physical requirements are inter alia dealt with in council directive no 77/101/eec of 23 november 1976 on the marketing of straight feeding-stuffs (official journal 1977 , l 32 , p . 1) and council directive no 79/373/eec of 2 april 1979 on the marketing of compound feeding-stuffs (official journal 1979 , l 86 , p . 30). it is the second of those directives which deals with the type of feeding-stuffs the importation whereof gave rise to the main action . in any case neither of them was in force when the main action originated and the second of them moreover allows member states a period not expiring until 1 january 1981 within which to adopt the laws , regulations and administrative provisions necessary to comply therewith . the consequence is therefore that those directives cannot in fact have overridden or override the powers which article 36 confers on the member states to except the goods at issue from free circulation . there is the further consequence that it is unnecessary to consider the question whether those directives deal with the presence of pathogenic elements in feeding-stuffs or not .

19 The court must also reject the argument of the plaintiff in the main action that it follows from the council resolutions of 12 march 1968 and 22 july 1974 on the veterinary , plant health and animal feeding-stuffs sectors (journal officiel 1968 , c 22 , p . 18 and official journal 1974 , c 92 , p . 2) that the harmonization programme introduced by these resolutions shows that the council did not think there was any point in adopting specific measures to combat salmonellosis and that the various directives taken together are exhaustive and the effect of their implementation is to forbid member states in the entire field of animal health measures concerning feeding-stuffs to have recourse to article 36 . this argument fails to take into account the gradual and methodical action taken by the council for the harmonization of national veterinary and public health laws and , on the other hand , the fact that in any case at the time when the events which gave rise to the dispute occurred the whole of the harmonization programme had not yet been completed .

20 it follows from the foregoing considerations that the conditions making it impossible for member states to justify having recourse to the exceptions permitted by article 36 of the eec treaty were not present when the events occurred which gave rise to the main action relating to compound animal feeding-stuffs of animal origin , as regards in particular measures against pathogenic agents.

In the same judgement, the Court clarified the concept of justified restriction of the market[23], first giving an outline of what member States are now subject to:

(…)

21 having regard to the foregoing considerations it is necessary , with reference to the question put by the national court , to ascertain next whether the restrictions of the kind laid down by the viehseuchenverordnung 1957 keep within the restrictions placed by article 36 of the treaty on the exceptions to the free movement of goods permitted by that provision . in fact it is clear from the wording thereof that the prohibitions or restrictions which it permits must be justified , that is to say necessary for attainment of its objective and may not constitute a means of arbitrary discrimination or a disguised restriction on trade between member states.

---

[23] For possbile justifications on the grounds of a cost-benefit reason, see Layard R. - Glaister S. (ed.), *Introduction to Cost-Benefit Analysis, Cambridge*, 1994 and Baumol W.J., *On the Proper Cost Tests for Natural Monopoly in a Multiproduct Industry*, in *American Economic Review*, 1977, p. 810 ff.

22 in this connexion the first question is whether a double check , which consists on the one hand of the requirement of a certificate from the competent authority in the exporting country to the effect that the animal feeding-stuffs in question have been subjected to a process whereby salmonellae have been destroyed and , on the other hand , of a systematic inspection at the frontier following which importation is only permitted after confirmation that the goods are free of salmonellae, exceeds what article 36 permits

23 the court held in its judgment of 20 may 1976 in case 104/75 , adriaan de peijper , managing director of centrafarm bv (1976) ecr 613 , at p . 636 that national rules or practices do not fall within the exception specified in article 36 if the health and life of humans can be effectively protected by measures which do not restrict intra-community trade so much and that in particular , article 36 cannot be relied on to justify rules or practices which , even though they are beneficial , contain restrictions which are explained primarily by a concern to lighten the administration's burden or reduce public expenditure , unless , in the absence of the said rules or practices , this burden or expenditure clearly would exceed the limits of what can reasonably be required moreover that judgment shows that if co-operation between the authorities of the member states makes it possible to facilitate and simplify frontier checks, which continue to be permissible by virtue of the exception provided for by article 36 of the eec treaty , the authorities responsible for veterinary and public health inspections must ascertain whether the substantiating documents issued as part of such co- operation do not raise a presumption that the imported goods comply with the requirements of national veterinary and public health legislation intended to simplify the checks carried out when the goods pass from one member state to another.

24 it is in each case for the national courts to apply these criteria in the light of all the circumstances relating to the actions brought before them taking into account the fact that it must always be the duty of a national authority relying on article 36 to prove that the measures which it enforces satisfy these criteria.

25 the national court also wishes to know whether a system of granting import licences, the issue whereof is left to the discretion of the competent authority and is subject to the conditions described in the question put by the national court may be regarded as keeping within the limits laid down by article 36.

26 the court held in its judgment of 15 december 1976 in case 41/76 (suzanne criel , nee donckerwolcke and henri schou v procureur de la republique au tribunal de grande instance , lille and director general of customs (1976) ecr 1921 , at p . 1936) that the application to intra-community trade of a national provision which requires , even purely as a formality , import licences or any other similar procedure is a measure having an effect equivalent to a quantitative restriction and is consequently prohibited . nevertheless this prohibition does not apply to those cases where prohibitions or restrictions on trade may in fact be kept in being under the terms of article 36 of the treaty provided that they are justified within the meaning of that provision . the special licence at issue in the main action is an exception to the general rule of a double check laid down by articles 1 and 2 of the viehseuchen-verordnung 1957 and is by definition deemed to be less restrictive than the general rule from which it derogates . consequently a system of import licences which derogates to a large extent from a general system of veterinary and public health restrictions which is compatible with article 36 complies itself with that provision . if it only made possible a relaxation of a general supervisory system which went beyond what article 36 permits is would be necessary to consider it on its own merits in the light of the exceptions permitted by article 36 of the treaty to the prohibition of measures having an effect equivalent to quantitative restrictions .

27 from this it follows that article 26 of the treaty cannot be interpreted as meaning that it forbids in principle a national authority , which has imposed by a general rule veterinary and public health restrictions on imports of animal feeding-stuffs , from providing that it will be possible to derogate therefrom by individual measures left to the discretion of the administration if such derogations assist the simplification of the restrictions imposed by the general rules and if this power of derogation does give rise to arbitrary discrimination between traders of different member states.

28 nevertheless it does not automatically follow that each of the conditions to which the national authority subjects the grant of such authorization itself complies with what is permitted by article 36 . it is in each case for the national courts , as has been indicated above , to determine whether these conditions are necessary to attain the objective which article 36 allows to be sought, taking into account the rule already mentioned above that it must be the duty of a national authority relying on article 36 to prove that the measures which it imposes satisfy these criteria.

2.5 The Principle of Separation and Violations of the Freedom of Establishment: The Proportionality Test

The separation between the manager of infrastructures and the service provider (i.e., the maintenance company) is not always present in national legislation. It is common, for example, to see praxis according to which Services of General Interest providers have the possibility to keep the property of the assets, thus risking to compromise free access to infrastructures and resulting minimal levels of service provided. The principle of separation derives from the application of article 102 of the TFEU and requires that the manager of goods and networks be autonomous and independent from the service provider. The owner of the networks must allow access to every potential enterprise so as to allow regular competition in the services market. This is the transposition of the U.S. Essential Facility Doctrine[24].

It is here reminded, indeed, that Public Authorities, when participating in business activities, like every public enterprise, are subject to the competition discipline:

As established by consolidated EU principles, for the competition discipline a company is any entity exercising an economic activity independently from its juridical status and how it is financed.

In the same case, case 14) ECJ, April 23, 1991, case 41/90, Klaus Hoefner e Fritz Elser - Macrotron GmbH, in Rep., I--1979), the European Court of Justice made an interpretation of Services of General Interest rules in connection with the competition policy of the European Union:

[24] The complete comparison of the services of general interest rules with the essential facility doctrine was carried out by Graham C., *Essential facilities and services of general interest*, in *Dir. e Pol. Un Eur.*, 2007, p. 22 ff.

16 In its fourth question, the national court asks more specifically whether the monopoly of employment procurement in respect of business executives granted to a public employment agency constitutes an abuse of a dominant position within the meaning of Article 86, having regard to Article 90(2). In order to answer that question, it is necessary to examine that exclusive right also in the light of Article 90(1), which is concerned with the conditions that the Member States must observe when they grant special or exclusive rights. Moreover, the observations submitted to the Court relate to both Article 90(1) and Article 90(2) of the Treaty.

17 According to the appellants in the main proceedings, an agency such as the Bundesanstalt is both a public undertaking within the meaning of Article 90(1) and an undertaking entrusted with the operation of services of general economic interest within the meaning of Article 90(2) of the Treaty. The Bundesanstalt is therefore, they maintain, subject to the competition rules to the extent to which the application thereof does not obstruct the performance of the particular task assigned to it, and it does not in the present case. The appellants also claim that the action taken by the Bundesanstalt, which extended its statutory monopoly over employment procurement to activities for which the establishment of a monopoly is not in the public interest, constitutes an abuse within the meaning of Article 86 of the Treaty. They also consider that any Member State which makes such an abuse possible is in breach of Article 90(1) and of the general principle whereby the Member States must refrain from taking any measure which could destroy the effectiveness of the Community competition rules.

18 The Commission takes a somewhat different view. The maintenance of a monopoly on executive recruitment constitutes, in its view, an infringement of Article 90(1) read in conjunction with Article 86 of the Treaty where the grantee of the monopoly is not willing or able to carry out that task fully, according to the demand existing on the market, and provided that such conduct is liable to affect trade between Member States.

19 The respondent in the main proceedings and the German Government consider on the other hand that the activities of an employment agency do not fall within the scope of the competition rules if they are carried out by a public undertaking. The German Government states in that regard that a public employment agency cannot be classified as an undertaking within the meaning of Article 86 of the Treaty, in so far as the employment procurement services are provided free of charge. The fact that those activities are financed mainly by contributions from employers and employees does not, in its view, mean that they are not free, since those contributions are general and have no link with each specific service provided.

20 Having regard to the foregoing considerations, it is necessary to establish whether a public employment agency such as the Bundesanstalt may be regarded as an undertaking within the meaning of Articles 85 and 86 of the Treaty.

21 It must be observed, in the context of competition law, first that the concept of an undertaking encompasses every entity engaged in an economic activity, regardless of the legal status of the entity and the way in which it is financed and, secondly, that employment procurement is an economic activity.

22 The fact that employment procurement activities are normally entrusted to public agencies cannot affect the economic nature of such activities. Employment procurement has not always been, and is not necessarily, carried out by public entities. That finding applies in particular to executive recruitment.

23 It follows that an entity such as a public employment agency engaged in the business of employment procurement may be classified as an undertaking for the purpose of applying the Community competition rules.

24 It must be pointed out that a public employment agency which is entrusted, under the legislation of a Member State, with the operation of services of general economic interest, such as those envisaged in Article 3 of the AFG, remains subject to the competition rules pursuant to Article 90(2) of the Treaty unless and to the extent to which it is shown that their application is incompatible with the discharge of its duties (see judgment in Case 155/73 Sacchi [1974] ECR 409).

25 As regards the manner in which a public employment agency enjoying an exclusive right of employment procurement conducts itself in relation to executive recruitment undertaken by private recruitment consultancy companies, it must be stated that the application of Article 86 of the Treaty cannot obstruct the performance of the particular task assigned to that agency in so far as the latter is manifestly not in a position to satisfy demand in that area of the market and in fact allows its exclusive rights to be encroached on by those companies.

26 Whilst it is true that Article 86 concerns undertakings and may be applied within the limits laid down by Article 90(2) to public undertakings or undertakings vested with exclusive rights or specific rights, the fact nevertheless remains that the Treaty requires the Member States not to take or maintain in force measures which could destroy the effectiveness of that provision (see judgment in Case 13/77 Inno [1977] ECR 2115, paragraphs 31 and 32). Article 90(1) in fact provides that the Member States are not to enact or maintain in force, in the case of public undertakings and the undertakings to which they grant special or exclusive rights, any measure contrary to the rules contained in the Treaty, in particular those provided for in Articles 85 to 94.

27 Consequently, any measure adopted by a Member State which maintains in force a statutory provision that creates a situation in which a public employment agency cannot avoid infringing Article 86 is incompatible with the rules of the Treaty.

28 It must be remembered, first, that an undertaking vested with a legal monopoly may be regarded as occupying a dominant position within the meaning of Article 86 of the Treaty (see judgment in Case 311/84 CBEM [1985] 3261) and that the territory of a Member State, to which that monopoly extends, may constitute a substantial part of the common market (judgment in Case 322/81 Michelin [1983] ECR 3461, paragraph 28).

29 Secondly, the simple fact of creating a dominant position of that kind by granting an exclusive right within the meaning of Article 90(1) is not as such incompatible with Article 86 of the Treaty (see Case 311/84 CBEM, above, paragraph 17). A Member State is in breach of the prohibition contained in those two provisions only if the undertaking in question, merely by exercising the exclusive right granted to it, cannot avoid abusing its dominant position.

30 Pursuant to Article 86(b), such an abuse may in particular consist in limiting the provision of a service, to the prejudice of those seeking to avail themselves of it.

31 A Member State creates a situation in which the provision of a service is limited when the undertaking to which it grants an exclusive right extending to executive recruitment activities is manifestly not in a position to satisfy the demand prevailing on the market for activities of that kind and when the effective pursuit of such activities by private companies is rendered impossible by the maintenance in force of a statutory provision under which such

activities are prohibited and non-observance of that prohibition renders the contracts concerned void.

32 It must be observed, thirdly, that the responsibility imposed on a Member State by virtue of Articles 86 and 90(1) of the Treaty is engaged only if the abusive conduct on the part of the agency concerned is liable to affect trade between Member States. That does not mean that the abusive conduct in question must actually have affected such trade. It is sufficient to establish that that conduct is capable of having such an effect (see Case 322/81 Michelin, above, paragraph 104).

33 A potential effect of that kind on trade between Member States arises in particular where executive recruitment by private companies may extend to the nationals or to the territory of other Member States.

34 In view of the foregoing considerations, it must be stated in reply to the fourth question that a public employment agency engaged in employment procurement activities is subject to the prohibition contained in Article 86 of the Treaty, so long as the application of that provision does not obstruct the performance of the particular task assigned to it. A Member State which has conferred an exclusive right to carry on that activity upon the public employment agency is in breach of Article 90(1) of the Treaty where it creates a situation in which that agency cannot avoid infringing Article 86 of the Treaty. That is the case, in particular, where the following conditions are satisfied:

- the exclusive right extends to executive recruitment activities;
- the public employment agency is manifestly incapable of satisfying demand prevailing on the market for such activities;
- the actual pursuit of those activities by private recruitment consultants is rendered impossible by the maintenance in force of a statutory provision under which such activities are prohibited and non-observance of that prohibition renders the contracts concerned void;
- the activities in question may extend to the nationals or to the territory of other Member States.

The interpretation of Article 59 of the EEC Treaty

35 In its third question, the national court seeks essentially to determine whether a recruitment consultancy company in a Member State may rely on Articles 7 and 59 of the Treaty regarding the procurement of nationals of that Member State for posts in undertakings in the same State.

36 It must be recalled, in the first place, that Article 59 of the EEC Treaty guarantees, as regards the freedom to provide services, the application of the principle laid down in Article 7 of that Treaty. It follows that where rules are compatible with Article 59 they are also compatible with Article 7 (judgment in Case 90/76 Van Ameyde [1977] ECR 1091, paragraph 27).

37 It must then be pointed out that the Court has consistently held that the provisions of the Treaty on freedom of movement cannot be applied to activities which are confined in all respects within a single Member State and that the question whether that is the case depends on findings of fact which are for the national court to make (see, in particular, the judgment in Case 52/79 Debauve]1980] ECR 833, paragraph 9).

38 The facts, as established by the national court in its order for reference, show that in the present case the dispute is between German recruitment consultants and a German undertaking concerning the recruitment of a German national.

39 Such a situation displays no link with any of the situations envisaged by Community law. That finding cannot be invalidated by the fact that a contract concluded between the recruitment consultants and the undertaking concerned includes the theoretical possibility of seeking German candidates resident in other Member States or nationals of other Member States.

40 It must therefore be stated in reply to the third question that a recruitment consultant in a Member State may not rely on Articles 7 and 59 of the Treaty regarding the procurement of nationals of that Member State for posts in undertakings in the same State.

41 In view of the above answer, it is unnecessary to consider the first two questions and the part of the fourth question concerned with the question whether Article 59 of the Treaty precludes a statutory prohibition of the pursuit, by private recruitment consultancy companies in a Member State, of the business of executive recruitment.

However, the juridical situation, as evident from the national laws considered, jeopardized violating the Treaties given the risk of discriminatory behaviors, especially regarding the public awarding of construction and management concessions. Such discrimination could imply a violation of the general principle of non-discrimination as interpreted by the Court of Justice and by norms related to freedom of access to the market, which are guaranteed to every company established within the European Union independently from the public or private nature of shareholders. The European Court of Justice, indeed, went beyond the principle of non discrimination considering unlawful also the "*indistinctly applicable*" measures which, according to EU law, requires member States to avoid rules that, though applicable to all citizens and companies, have the concrete effect of causing discrimination or restraining the free circulation of freights, services, or capital[25] (See the Casees: 11) ECJ, March 31st 1993, case C-19/93, Kraus, 12) ECJ, November 30th 1995, case C-55/94, Gebhard, and, in the same sense: ECJ October 17th 2002, case C-79/01, Payroll, ECJ, July 25th 1991, case C-288/89, Gouda, ECJ, July 9th 1997, case C-222/95, Parodi).

Indeed, in the Gebhard case, the Court held that

national acts limiting the exercise of fundamental freedoms guaranteed by the Treaty must satisfy four conditions: be applied in a non discriminatory manner, answer imperative reasons of public interest, be right for guaranteeing the reaching the aim and not go past what is necessary to attain it.

[25] See Butt-Philip A., *Implementing the European Internal Market: Problems and Prospects*, London, 1988, Calingaert M., *The 1992 Challenge from Europe: Development of the European Community's Internal Market*, Washington D.C., National Planning Association, 1988, Calori R. - Lawrence P. (ed.), *The Business of Europe: Managing Change,* Sage, 1991, Cecchini, P. - Catinat M. - Jacquemin A., *1992: The European Challenge: The Benefits of a Single Market*, Aldershot, 1992, Lord Cockfield, *The European Union: creating the single market*, Wiley Chancery Law, 1994, Coffey P. (ed.), *The Economic Policies of the Common Market*, London, 1979.

The lack of separation between the public administration and the enterprise also causes the restriction of the freedom of establishment. In other words, a company has the right to establish an office in another member State and carry out all the activities that, according to the European Union Law, it could carry out in its primary country.

In the Centros case ECJ (case 15 March 9th 1999, case C-212/97, Centros Ltd.) the right of establishment was clarified by the Court, which also discussed the risk of an abuse of European Union law:

14 By its question, the national court is in substance asking whether it is contrary to Articles 52 and 58 of the Treaty for a Member State to refuse to register a branch of a company formed in accordance with the legislation of another Member State in which it has its registered office but where it does not carry on any business when the purpose of the branch is to enable the company concerned to carry on its entire business in the State in which that branch is to be set up, while avoiding the formation of a company in that State, thus evading application of the rules governing the formation of companies which are, in that State, more restrictive so far as minimum paid-up share capital is concerned.

15 As a preliminary point, it should be made clear that the Board does not in any way deny that a joint stock or private limited company with its registered office in another Member State may carry on business in Denmark through a branch. It therefore agrees, as a general rule, to register in Denmark a branch of a company formed in accordance with the law of another Member State. In particular, it has added that, if Centros had conducted any business in England and Wales, the Board would have agreed to register its branch in Denmark.

16 According to the Danish Government, Article 52 of the Treaty is not applicable in the case in the main proceedings, since the situation is purely internal to Denmark. Mr and Mrs Bryde, Danish nationals, have formed a company in the United Kingdom which does not carry on any actual business there with the sole purpose of carrying on business in Denmark through a branch and thus of avoiding application of Danish legislation on the formation of private limited companies. It considers that in such circumstances the formation by nationals of one Member State of a company in another Member State does not amount to a relevant external element in the light of Community law and, in particular, freedom of establishment.

17 In this respect, it should be noted that a situation in which a company formed in accordance with the law of a Member State in which it has its registered office desires to set up a branch in another Member State falls within the scope of Community law. In that regard, it is immaterial that the company was formed in the first Member State only for the purpose of establishing itself in the second, where its main, or indeed entire, business is to be conducted (see, to this effect, Segers paragraph 16).

18 That Mrs and Mrs Bryde formed the company Centros in the United Kingdom for the purpose of avoiding Danish legislation requiring that a minimum amount of share capital be paid up has not been denied either in the written observations or at the hearing. That does not, however, mean that the formation by that British company of a branch in Denmark is not covered by freedom of establishment for the purposes of Article 52 and 58 of the Treaty. The question of the application of those articles of the Treaty is different from the question whether or not a Member State may adopt measures in order to prevent attempts by

certain of its nationals to evade domestic legislation by having recourse to the possibilities offered by the Treaty.

19 As to the question whether, as Mr and Mrs Bryde claim, the refusal to register in Denmark a branch of their company formed in accordance with the law of another Member State in which its has its registered office constitutes an obstacle to freedom of establishment, it must be borne in mind that that freedom, conferred by Article 52 of the Treaty on Community nationals, includes the right for them to take up and pursue activities as self-employed persons and to set up and manage undertakings under the same conditions as are laid down by the law of the Member State of establishment for its own nationals. Furthermore, under Article 58 of the Treaty companies or firms formed in accordance with the law of a Member State and having their registered office, central administration or principal place of business within the Community are to be treated in the same way as natural persons who are nationals of Member States.

20 The immediate consequence of this is that those companies are entitled to carry on their business in another Member State through an agency, branch or subsidiary. The location of their registered office, central administration or principal place of business serves as the connecting factor with the legal system of a particular State in the same way as does nationality in the case of a natural person (see, to that effect, Segers, paragraph 13, Case 270/83 Commission v France [1986] ECR 273, paragraph 18, Case C-330/91 Commerzbank [1993] ECR I-4017, paragraph 13, and Case C-264/96 ICI [1998] I-4695, paragraph 20).

21 Where it is the practice of a Member State, in certain circumstances, to refuse to register a branch of a company having its registered office in another Member State, the result is that companies formed in accordance with the law of that other Member State are prevented from exercising the freedom of establishment conferred on them by Articles 52 and 58 of the Treaty.

22 Consequently, that practice constitutes an obstacle to the exercise of the freedoms guaranteed by those provisions.

23 According to the Danish authorities, however, Mr and Mrs Bryde cannot rely on those provisions, since the sole purpose of the company formation which they have in mind is to circumvent the application of the national law governing formation of private limited companies and therefore constitutes abuse of the freedom of establishment. In their submission, the Kingdom of Denmark is therefore entitled to take steps to prevent such abuse by refusing to register the branch.

24 It is true that according to the case-law of the Court a Member State is entitled to take measures designed to prevent certain of its nationals from attempting, under cover of the rights created by the Treaty, improperly to circumvent their national legislation or to prevent individuals from improperly or fraudulently taking advantage of provisions of Community law (see, in particular, regarding freedom to supply services, Case 33/74 Van Binsbergen v Bedrijfsvereniging Metaalnijverheid [1974] ECR 1299, paragraph 13, Case C-148/91 Veronica Omroep Organisatie v Commissariaat voor de Media [1993] ECR I-487, paragraph 12, and Case C-23/93 TV 10 v Commissariaat voor de Media [1994] ECR I-4795, paragraph 21; regarding freedom of establishment, Case 115/78 Knoors [1979] ECR 399, paragraph 25, and Case C-61/89 Bouchoucha [1990] ECR I-3551, paragraph 14; regarding the free movement of goods, Case 229/83 Leclerc and Others v `Au Blé Vert' and Others [1985] ECR 1, paragraph 27; regarding social security, Case C-206/94 Brennet v Paletta [1996] ECR I-2357, `Paletta II', paragraph 24; regarding freedom of movement for

workers, Case 39/86 Lair v Universität Hannover [1988] ECR 3161, paragraph 43; regarding the common agricultural policy, Case C-8/92 General Milk Products v Hauptzollamt Hamburg-Jonas [1993] ECR I-779, paragraph 21, and regarding company law, Case C-367/96 Kefalas and Others v Greece [1988] ECR I-2843, paragraph 20).

25 However, although, in such circumstances, the national courts may, case by case, take account - on the basis of objective evidence - of abuse or fraudulent conduct on the part of the persons concerned in order, where appropriate, to deny them the benefit of the provisions of Community law on which they seek to rely, they must nevertheless assess such conduct in the light of the objectives pursued by those provisions (Paletta II, paragraph 25).

26 In the present case, the provisions of national law, application of which the parties concerned have sought to avoid, are rules governing the formation of companies and not rules concerning the carrying on of certain trades, professions or businesses. The provisions of the Treaty on freedom of establishment are intended specifically to enable companies formed in accordance with the law of a Member State and having their registered office, central administration or principal place of business within the Community to pursue activities in other Member States through an agency, branch or subsidiary.

27 That being so, the fact that a national of a Member State who wishes to set up a company chooses to form it in the Member State whose rules of company law seem to him the least restrictive and to set up branches in other Member States cannot, in itself, constitute an abuse of the right of establishment. The right to form a company in accordance with the law of a Member State and to set up branches in other Member States is inherent in the exercise, in a single market, of the freedom of establishment guaranteed by the Treaty.

28 In this connection, the fact that company law is not completely harmonised in the Community is of little consequence. Moreover, it is always open to the Council, on the basis of the powers conferred upon it by Article 54(3)(g) of the EC Treaty, to achieve complete harmonisation.

29 In addition, it is clear from paragraph 16 of Segers that the fact that a company does not conduct any business in the Member State in which it has its registered office and pursues its activities only in the Member State where its branch is established is not sufficient to prove the existence of abuse or fraudulent conduct which would entitle the latter Member State to deny that company the benefit of the provisions of Community law relating to the right of establishment.

30 Accordingly, the refusal of a Member State to register a branch of a company formed in accordance with the law of another Member State in which it has its registered office on the grounds that the branch is intended to enable the company to carry on all its economic activity in the host State, with the result that the secondary establishment escapes national rules on the provision for and the paying-up of a minimum capital, is incompatible with Articles 52 and 58 of the Treaty, in so far as it prevents any exercise of the right freely to set up a secondary establishment which Articles 52 and 58 are specifically intended to guarantee.

After having verified the presence of a restraint of the right of establishment, the Court proceeded to analyze every possible justification that could allow the member State to adopt such a measure. If the pursuing of the public need is proportionate, the measure doesn't cause a breach of European Union Law:

(...)

32 Referring both to Article 56 of the Treaty and to the case-law of the Court on imperative requirements in the general interest, the Board argues that the requirement that private limited companies provide for and pay up a minimum share capital pursues a dual objective: first, to reinforce the financial soundness of those companies in order to protect public creditors against the risk of seeing the public debts owing to them become irrecoverable since, unlike private creditors, they cannot secure those debts by means of guarantees and, second, and more generally, to protect all creditors, whether public or private, by anticipating the risk of fraudulent bankruptcy due to the insolvency of companies whose initial capitalisation was inadequate.

33 The Board adds that there is no less restrictive means of attaining this dual objective. The other way of protecting creditors, namely by introducing rules making it possible for shareholders to incur personal liability, under certain conditions, would be more restrictive than the requirement to provide for and pay up a minimum share capital.

34 It should be observed, first, that the reasons put forward do not fall within the ambit of Article 56 of the Treaty. Next, it should be borne in mind that, according to the Court's case-law, national measures liable to hinder or make less attractive the exercise of fundamental freedoms guaranteed by the Treaty must fulfil four conditions: they must be applied in a non-discriminatory manner; they must be justified by imperative requirements in the general interest; they must be suitable for securing the attainment of the objective which they pursue; and they must not go beyond what is necessary in order to attain it (see Case C-19/92 Kraus v Land Baden-Württemberg [1993] ECR I-1663, paragraph 32, and Case C-55/94 Gebhard v Consiglio dell'Ordine degli Avvocati e Procuratori di Milano [1995] ECR I-4165, paragraph 37).

35 Those conditions are not fulfilled in the case in the main proceedings. First, the practice in question is not such as to attain the objective of protecting creditors which it purports to pursue since, if the company concerned had conducted business in the United Kingdom, its branch would have been registered in Denmark, even though Danish creditors might have been equally exposed to risk.

36 Since the company concerned in the main proceedings holds itself out as a company governed by the law of England and Wales and not as a company governed by Danish law, its creditors are on notice that it is covered by laws different from those which govern the formation of private limited companies in Denmark and they can refer to certain rules of Community law which protect them, such as the Fourth Council Directive 78/660/EEC of 25 July 1978 based on Article 54(3)(g) of the Treaty on the annual accounts of certain types of companies (OJ 1978 L 222, p. 11), and the Eleventh Council Directive 89/666/EEC of 21 December 1989 concerning disclosure requirements in respect of branches opened in a Member State by certain types of company governed by the law of another State (OJ 1989 L 395, p. 36).

37 Second, contrary to the arguments of the Danish authorities, it is possible to adopt measures which are less restrictive, or which interfere less with fundamental freedoms, by, for example, making it possible in law for public creditors to obtain the necessary guarantees.

38 Lastly, the fact that a Member State may not refuse to register a branch of a company formed in accordance with the law of another Member State in which it has its registered office does not preclude that first State from adopting any appropriate measure for preventing or penalising fraud, either in relation to the company itself, if need be in cooperation with the Member State in which it was formed, or in relation to its members, where it has been established that they are in fact attempting, by means of the formation of the company, to evade their obligations towards private or public creditors established on the territory of a Member State concerned. In any event, combating fraud cannot justify a practice of refusing to register a branch of a company which has its registered office in another Member State.

2.6 The Relevance of the Notion of Undertaking in the Infrastructures Industry

An interesting point of the national laws is provided by a particular legislative technique according to which duties and competences of the public authorities for infrastructures are specifically listed. However, especially in acceding States (but not ony, see the Italian legislation), there are cases where the law list for the same Authority both regulation and direct management competences.

Compliance with the principle of separation emerging from EU Law makes it advisable that competences of control and regulation be exercised by independent Authorities for whom it should be prohibited to carry out any business activity[26]. Indeed, the European concept of enterprise includes any entity engaging in an economic activity, independently from its juridical status and from its means of financing, while economic activity encompasses any business consisting in the offering of goods or services in a specific market. The European Court of Justice, in one leading case (16) ECJ, June 18th 1998, Commission c. Italia, case C-35/96, in Rep., p. I-03851), held that Italian transport agents, even if physical persons, are undertakings:

(…)

33 In order to give judgment on the Commission's application for a declaration of failure to fulfil obligations, the question whether the tariff constitutes a decision of an association of undertakings within the meaning of Article 85 must first be examined.

34 At the hearing, the Italian Government contended that although, since they exercise a liberal profession like lawyers, surveyors or interpreters, customs agents are independent workers, they nevertheless cannot be regarded as being undertakings within the meaning of Article 85 of the Treaty because the services that they provide are of an intellectual nature and because the practice of their profession requires authorisation and entails compliance

---

[26] See Townley C., *The Concept of an 'Undertaking': The Boundaries of the Corporation - A Discussion of Agency, Employees and Subsidiaries*, London, 2009, Wils P.J.W., *The Optimal Enforcement of Ec Antitrust Law: Essays in Law & Economics,* Amsterdam, 2008, Ezrachi A., *EC competition law: an analytical guide to the leading cases*, Oxford, 2008, Korah V., *Cases and materials on EC competition law*, Oxford, 2006.

with certain conditions. Moreover, the Treaty makes a distinction between independent workers and undertakings, so that not all self-employed activity is necessarily carried on in the context of an undertaking. In addition, the indispensable organisational factor is lacking, that is to say, the combination of human, material and non-material resources permanently assigned to the pursuit of a specific economic goal.

35 Since independent customs agents are not undertakings, a fortiori the CNSD cannot constitute an association of undertakings within the meaning of Article 85 of the Treaty.

36 It must first be noted that, according to settled case-law, the concept of an undertaking covers any entity engaged in an economic activity, regardless of its legal status and the way in which it is financed (Case C-41/90 Höfner and Elser [1991] ECR I-1979, paragraph 21; Case C-244/94 Fédération Française des Sociétés d'Assurances and Others v Ministère de l'Agriculture et de la Pêche [1995] ECR I-4013, paragraph 14; and Case C-55/96 Job Centre [1997] ECR I-7119, paragraph 21), and that any activity consisting in offering goods and services on a given market is an economic activity (Case 118/85 Commission v Italy [1987] ECR 2599, paragraph 7).

37 The activity of customs agents has an economic character. They offer, for payment, services consisting in the carrying out of customs formalities, relating in particular to the importation, exportation and transit of goods, as well as other complementary services such as services in monetary, commercial and fiscal areas. Furthermore, they assume the financial risks involved in the exercise of that activity (Joined Cases 40/73 to 48/73, 50/73, 54/73 to 56/73, 111/73, 113/73 and 114/73 Suiker Unie and Others v Commission [1975] ECR 1663, paragraph 541). If there is an imbalance between expenditure and receipts, the customs agent is required to bear the deficit himself.

38 In those circumstances, the fact that the activity of customs agent is intellectual, requires authorisation and can be pursued in the absence of a combination of material, non-material and human resources, is not such as to exclude it from the scope of Articles 85 and 86 of the EC Treaty.

39 The next point to be considered is the extent to which a professional body such as the CNSD is acting as an association of undertakings, within the meaning of Article 85(1) of the Treaty, when compiling the tariff.

40 In this connection, it must be borne in mind that the public law status of a national body such as the CNSD does not preclude the application of Article 85 of the Treaty. According to its wording, that provision applies to agreements between undertakings and decisions by associations of undertakings. Accordingly, the legal framework within which such agreements are made and such decisions are taken and the classification given to that framework by the various national legal systems are irrelevant as far as the applicability of the Community rules on competition, and in particular Article 85 of the Treaty, are concerned (Case 123/83 BNIC v Clair [1985] ECR 391, paragraph 17).

41 Moreover, the members of the CNSD are the representatives of professional customs agents and nothing in the national legislation concerned prevents the CNSD from acting in the exclusive interest of the profession.

42 On the one hand, the members of the CNSD can only be registered customs agents, since they are elected from among the members of the Departmental Councils on which only customs agents sit (second paragraph of Article 13 of Law No 1612/1960 and second paragraph of Article 22 of the Decree of the Minister for Finance of 10 March 1964). On that point it should be noted that, since the amendment introduced by Decree-Law No

331/1992, the Director-General of Customs no longer acts as chairman of the CNSD. Lastly, the Italian Minister for Finance, who is responsible for the supervision of the professional organisation in question, cannot intervene in the appointment of the members of the Departmental Councils and the CNSD.

43 On the other hand, the CNSD is responsible for setting the tariff for the professional services of customs agents on the basis of proposals from the Departmental Councils (Article 14(d) of Law No 1612/1960). In that respect there is no rule in the national legislation in question obliging, or even encouraging, the members of either the CNSD or the Departmental Councils to take into account public-interest criteria.

44 It follows that the members of the CNSD cannot be characterised as independent experts (see, to that effect, Case C-185/91 Reiff [1993] ECR I-5801, paragraphs 17 and 19; Case C-153/93 Delta Schiffahrts- und Speditionsgesellschaft [1994] ECR I-2517, paragraphs 16 and 18; and Joined Cases C-140/94 to C-142/94 DIP and Others [1995] ECR I-3257, paragraphs 18 and 19) and that they are not required, under the law, to set tariffs taking into account not only the interests of the undertakings or associations of undertakings in the sector which has appointed them but also the general interest and the interests of undertakings in other sectors or users of the services in question (judgments cited above, Reiff, paragraphs 18 and 24; Delta Schiffahrts- und Speditionsgesellschaft, paragraph 17; and DIP and Others, paragraph 18).

45 Secondly, it must be held that the decisions by which the CNSD sets a uniform, compulsory tariff for all customs agents restrict competition within the meaning of Article 85 of the Treaty and are capable of affecting intra-Community trade.

46 The tariff directly sets the prices for customs agents' services. It provides, for each separate type of operation, the maximum and minimum prices which can be charged to customers. Furthermore, the tariff lays down various scales on the basis of the value or the weight of the goods to be cleared through customs or of the specific type of goods, or type of professional service (Article 1).

47 Lastly, the tariff is mandatory (Article 5), so that a customs agent may not depart from it on his own initiative. Only the CNSD is empowered to provide for derogations (Article 6).

48 As regards the question whether intra-Community trade is affected, it need merely be pointed out that an agreement extending over the whole of the territory of a Member State has, by its very nature, the effect of reinforcing the compartmentalisation of markets on a national basis, thereby holding up the economic interpenetration which the Treaty is designed to bring about (Case 8/72 Vereeniging van Cementhandelaren v Commission [1972] ECR 977, paragraph 29, and Case 42/84 Remia and Others v Commission [1985] ECR 2545, paragraph 22).

49 That effect is all the more appreciable in this case because the various types of import or export operations within the Community, as well as transactions between Community traders, require customs formalities to be carried out and may, in consequence, make it necessary for an independent registered customs agent to be involved.

50 That is true of so-called `internal transit' operations, covering the dispatching of goods from Italy to a Member State, that is to say from one point in the customs territory of the Community to another, by way of transit through a non-Member country (for example, Switzerland). That type of operation is particularly important for Italy, since a large propor-

tion of goods dispatched from regions in the north-east of the country to Germany and the Netherlands transit through Switzerland.

51 From the foregoing considerations, it follows that, in adopting the tariff, the CNSD infringed Article 85(1) of the Treaty.

52 Thirdly, the question of the extent to which that infringement can be attributed to the Italian Republic must be considered.

53 Although Article 85 of the Treaty is, in itself, concerned solely with the conduct of undertakings and not with measures adopted by Member States by law or regulation, the fact nevertheless remains that Article 85 of the Treaty, in conjunction with Article 5, requires the Member States not to introduce or maintain in force measures, even of a legislative nature, which may render ineffective the competition rules applicable to undertakings (for Article 85 of the Treaty, see Case 267/86 Van Eycke [1988] ECR 4769, paragraph 16; Reiff, cited above, paragraph 14; and Delta Schiffahrts-und Speditionsgesellschaft, cited above, paragraph 14; for Article 86 of the Treaty, see Case 13/77 GB-Inno-BM [1977] ECR 2115, paragraph 31).

54 Such would be the case if a Member State were to require or favour the adoption of agreements, decisions or concerted practices contrary to Article 85 or to reinforce their effects, or to deprive its own rules of the character of legislation by delegating to private economic operators responsibility for taking decisions affecting the economic sphere (see Case 267/86 Van Eycke [1988] ECR 4769, paragraph 16; Reiff, paragraph 14; and Delta Schiffahrts- und Speditionsgesellschaft, paragraph 14).

55 By adopting the national legislation in question, the Italian Republic clearly not only required the conclusion of an agreement contrary to Article 85 of the Treaty and declined to influence its terms, but also assists in ensuring compliance with that agreement.

56 First, Article 14(d) of Law No 1612/1960 requires the CNSD to compile a compulsory, uniform tariff for the services of customs agents.

57 Secondly, as is clear from paragraphs 41 to 44 of this judgment, the national legislation in question wholly relinquished to private economic operators the powers of the public authorities as regards the setting of tariffs.

58 Thirdly, the Italian legislation expressly prohibits registered customs agents from derogating from the tariff (Article 11 of Law No 1612/1960) on pain of exclusion, suspension or removal from the register (Articles 38 to 40 of the Decree of the Minister for Finance of 10 March 1964).

59 Fourthly, although no provision laid down by law or regulation confers on the Minister for Finance the power to approve the tariff, it remains the case that the Decree of the Minister for Finance of 6 July 1988 bestowed upon it the appearance of a public regulation. First, publication in the `General Series' of the Gazzetta Ufficiale della Repubblica Italiana gave rise to a presumption of knowledge of the tariff on the part of third parties, to which the CNSD's decision could never have laid claim. Second, the official character thus conferred on the tariff facilitates the application by customs agents of the prices that it sets. Lastly, its nature is such as to deter customers who might wish to contest the prices demanded by customs agents.

60 In the light of the foregoing considerations, it must be held that, by adopting and maintaining in force a law which, in granting the relative decision-making power, requires the CNSD to adopt a decision by an association of undertakings contrary to Article 85 of

the EC Treaty, consisting of setting a compulsory tariff for all customs agents, the Italian Republic has failed to fulfil its obligations under Articles 5 and 85 of the Treaty.

The European Court of Justice seems, nevertheless, to be more comprehensive in defining whether international organizations are considered public authorities (case 17) ECJ, 19th January 1994, case C-364/92, Eurocontrol:

15 SAT claims that Eurocontrol is an undertaking within the meaning of Articles 86 and 90 of the Treaty. The research and coordination activities carried on by that organization and the collection of route charges do not fall within the "jus imperii", but constitute economic activities that could be carried on by bodies governed by private law. Even air navigation control is an economic activity, as shown by the fact that in some Member States it is private undertakings that exercise such control. SAT claims, in the alternative, that at least the collection of charges, which gave rise to the dispute in the main proceedings, is a commercial activity as is demonstrated in particular by the fact that Eurocontrol has brought actions for recovery before the Brussels Commercial Court.

16 The French, German and Greek Governments, and the United Kingdom, on the other hand, base their reasoning on the public character of Eurocontrol' s activities, in denying that the latter is an undertaking within the meaning of the Treaty rules of competition. They are supported, in particular, by the judgments of the Court on the interpretation of the Convention of 27 September 1968 on Jurisdiction and the Enforcement of Judgments in Civil and Commercial Matters, from which it is apparent that Eurocontrol must be regarded as a public authority acting in the exercise of its powers (judgments in Case 29/76 LTU v Eurocontrol [1976] ECR 1541, and in Joined Cases 9/77 and 10/77 Bavaria Fluggesellschaft and Germanair v Eurocontrol [1977] ECR 1517). More particularly, they argue that air navigation control is a supervisory activity intended to ensure public safety. The collection of route charges, for its part, is an activity carried on on behalf of the Contracting States, the charges merely constituting the consideration for the air navigation services provided by those States.

17 The Commission also maintains that Eurocontrol does not constitute an undertaking, within the meaning of the relevant Treaty provisions, and in that connection puts forward the same arguments as those developed by the Member States so far as the collection of route charges is concerned. Furthermore, it considers that air navigation control, which is not directly at issue in the main proceedings, is a task involving the exercise of public authority and is not of an economic nature, since that activity constitutes a service in the public interest which is intended to protect both the users of air transport and the populations affected by aircraft flying over them.

18 It follows from the case-law of the Court (see especially the judgments in Case C41/90 Hoefner and Elser v Macrotron GmbH [1991] ECR I-1979, at paragraph 21, and in Joined Cases C-159/91 and C-160/91 Poucet et Pistre [1993] ECR I-637, at paragraph 17) that, in Community competition law, the concept of an undertaking encompasses every entity engaged in an economic activity, regardless of the legal status of the entity and the way in which it is financed.

19 In order to determine whether Eurocontrol' s activities are those of an undertaking within the meaning of Articles 86 and 90 of the Treaty, it is necessary to establish the nature of those activities.

20 Under Article 1 of the Convention on International Civil Aviation, signed at Chicago on 7 December 1944 (United Nations Treaty Series, Vol. 15, No 105): "The Contracting States recognize that every State has complete and exclusive sovereignty over the air space above its territory". It is in the exercise of that sovereignty that the States ensure, subject to compliance with the provisions of the applicable international conventions, the supervision of their air space and the provision of air navigation control services.

21 According to the Convention establishing it, Eurocontrol is a regionally-oriented international organization, whose aim is to strengthen cooperation between the Contracting States in the field of air navigation and develop joint activities in this field, making due allowance for defence needs and providing maximum freedom for all air space users consistent with the required level of safety. The organization is to act in cooperation with the civil and military authorities of the Contracting States (Article 1 of the amended Convention).

22 Eurocontrol' s tasks, as defined in Article 2 of the amended Convention, are concerned in the first place with research, planning, coordination of national policies and staff training.

23 Secondly, Eurocontrol is competent to establish and collect the route charges levied on users of air space. Eurocontrol settles, in accordance with the guidelines laid down by the International Civil Aviation Organization, the common formula on the basis of which the route charges are calculated. That formula takes into account the weight of the aircraft and the distance travelled, to which a "rate per unit" is applied. That rate is not fixed by Eurocontrol, but by each of the Contracting States for the use of its air space. A single charge, making up the sum of the charges payable, is calculated and collected by Eurocontrol for each flight. The charges are collected on behalf of the Contracting States to which they are paid over, after deduction of a proportion of the revenue corresponding to an "administrative rate" intended to cover collection costs.

24 Finally, as the Protocol of 12 February 1981 expressly provides, the operational exercise of air navigation control is limited since Eurocontrol can only carry on that activity at the request of the Contracting States. In that connection, it is common ground that Eurocontrol confines itself to providing air space control for the Benelux countries and the northern part of the Federal Republic of Germany from its Maastricht centre. For the purposes of such control, Eurocontrol is vested with rights and powers of coercion which derogate from ordinary law and which affect users of air space. In exercising those particular powers, it must ensure compliance with international agreements and national rules concerning access, overflying and the territorial security of the Contracting States concerned.

25 So far as the last-mentioned activity is concerned, it may be noted that it has not been disputed that Eurocontrol is required to provide navigation control in that air space for the benefit of any aircraft travelling through it, even where the owner of the aircraft has not paid the route charges owed to Eurocontrol.

26 Finally, Eurocontrol' s activities are financed by the contributions of the Contracting States.

27 Eurocontrol thus carries out, on behalf of the Contracting States, tasks in the public interest aimed at contributing to the maintenance and improvement of air navigation safety.

28 Contrary to SAT' s contention, Eurocontrol' s collection of route charges, which gave rise to the dispute in the main proceedings, cannot be separated from the organization' s other activities. Those charges are merely the consideration, payable by users, for the oblig-

atory and exclusive use of air navigation control facilities and services. As the Court has already held, specifically in connection with the interpretation of the abovementioned Convention of 27 September 1968, Eurocontrol must, in collecting the charges, be regarded as a public authority acting in the exercise of its powers (the LTU judgment, cited above, at paragraphs 4 and 5).

29 Eurocontrol acts in that capacity on behalf of the Contracting States without really having any influence over the amount of the route charges. Responsibility for the fact, relied upon by SAT before the national court, that the amounts of the charges vary in time or with respect to the areas overflown, cannot be attributed to Eurocontrol, which merely establishes and applies a common formula in the circumstances set out above, but to the Contracting States which set the amount of the rates per unit.

30 Taken as a whole, Eurocontrol' s activities, by their nature, their aim and the rules to which they are subject, are connected with the exercise of powers relating to the control and supervision of air space which are typically those of a public authority. They are not of an economic nature justifying the application of the Treaty rules of competition.

31 Accordingly, an international organization such as Eurocontrol does not constitute an undertaking subject to the provisions of Articles 86 and 90 of the Treaty.

32 On those grounds, the answer to the question submitted must be that Articles 86 and 90 of the Treaty are to be interpreted as meaning that an international organization such as Eurocontrol does not constitute an undertaking within the meaning of those articles.

The same arguments held by the Court concerning transport agents were carried out in a judgment (case 18) ECJ ,19th February 2002, case C-309/99, Wouters, in Rep., p. I-01577) where the BAR, the association of attorneys, was considered as an association of undertakings and the contract of association was subject to the competition law and, specifically, to article 101 of the TFEU. The question of the national court was:

(…)

(a) Is the term “association of undertakings” in Article 85(1) of the EC Treaty (now Article 81(1) EC) to be interpreted as meaning that there is such an association only if and in so far as it acts in the undertakings' interest, so that in applying that provision a distinction must be drawn between activities of the association carried out in the public interest and other activities, or is the mere fact that an association can also act in the undertakings' interest sufficient for it to be regarded as an association of undertakings within the meaning of the provision in respect of all its actions? Is the fact that the universally binding rules adopted by the relevant institution are adopted under a statutory power and in its capacity as a special legislature relevant as regards the application of Community competition law?

According to the European Court of Justice:

(…)

56 The question to be determined is whether, when it adopts a regulation such as the 1993 Regulation, a professional body is to be treated as an association of undertakings or, on the contrary, as a public authority.

57 According to the case-law of the Court, the Treaty rules on competition do not apply to activity which, by its nature, its aim and the rules to which it is subject does not belong to the sphere of economic activity (see, to that effect, Joined Cases C-159/91, C-160/91 Poucet and Pistre [1993] ECR I-637, paragraphs 18 and 19, concerning the management of the public social security system), or which is connected with the exercise of the powers of a public authority (see, to that effect, Case C-364/92 Sat Fluggesellschaft [1994] ECR I-43, paragraph 30, concerning the control and supervision of air space, and Case C-343/95 Diego Calì & Figli [1997] ECR I-1547, paragraphs 22 and 23, concerning anti-pollution surveillance of the maritime environment).

58 When it adopts a regulation such as the 1993 Regulation, a professional body such as the Bar of the Netherlands is neither fulfilling a social function based on the principle of solidarity, unlike certain social security bodies (Poucet and Pistre, cited above, paragraph 18), nor exercising powers which are typically those of a public authority (Sat Fluggesellschaft, cited above, paragraph 30). It acts as the regulatory body of a profession, the practice of which constitutes an economic activity.

59 In that respect, the fact that Article 26 of the Advocatenwet also entrusts the General Council with the task of protecting the rights and interests of members of the Bar cannot a priori exclude that professional organisation from the scope of application of Article 85 of the Treaty, even where it performs its role of regulating the practice of the profession of the Bar (see, to that effect, with regard to medical practitioners, Pavlov, cited above, paragraph 86).

60 Next, other indications support the conclusion that a professional organisation with regulatory powers, such as the Bar of the Netherlands, cannot escape the application of Article 85 of the Treaty.

61 First, it is clear from the Advocatenwet that the governing bodies of the Bar are composed exclusively of members of the Bar elected solely by members of the profession. The national authorities may not intervene in the appointment of the members of the Supervisory Boards, College of Delegates or the General Council (see, as regards a professional organisation of customs agents, CNSD, cited above, paragraph 42, and as regards a professional organisation of medical practitioners, Pavlov, paragraph 88).

62 Second, when it adopts measures such as the 1993 Regulation, the Bar of the Netherlands is not required to do so by reference to specified public-interest criteria. Article 28 of the Advocatenwet, which authorises it to adopt regulations, does no more than require that they should be in the interest of the proper practice of the profession (see, as regards a professional organisation of customs agents, CNSD, paragraph 43).

63 Lastly, having regard to its influence on the conduct of the members of the Bar of the Netherlands on the market in legal services, as a result of its prohibition of certain multi-disciplinary partnerships, the 1993 Regulation does not fall outside the sphere of economic activity.

64 In light of the foregoing considerations, it appears that a professional organisation such as the Bar of the Netherlands must be regarded as an association of undertakings within the meaning of Article 85(1) of the Treaty where it adopts a regulation such as the 1993 Regulation. Such a regulation constitutes the expression of the intention of the delegates of the members of a profession that they should act in a particular manner in carrying on their economic activity.

65 It is, moreover, immaterial that the constitution of the Bar of the Netherlands is regulated by public law.

Moreover, the European Court of Justice has applied the discipline of competition to several companies wholly participated in by public bodies that operated in activities with public relevance, i.e., Services of General Interest (See the Case: 19) ECJ, 11 December 1997, case C-55/96, Job Centre:

(…)

20 Having regard to the foregoing considerations, it is necessary to establish whether public placement offices such as those referred to in Article 11(1) of Law No 264 may be regarded as undertakings within the meaning of Articles 85 and 86 of the Treaty (see Höfner and Elser, cited above, paragraph 20).

21 It must be observed, in the context of competition law, first, that the concept of an undertaking encompasses every entity engaged in an economic activity, regardless of its status and the way in which it is financed and, second, that the placement of employees is an economic activity.

22 The fact that the placement of employees is normally entrusted to public offices cannot affect the economic nature of such activities. Placement of employees has not always been, and is not necessarily, carried out by public entities.

23 The Italian Government further contends that according to Joined Cases C-159/91 and C-160/91 Poucet and Pistre v Assurances Générales de France and Others [1993] ECR I-637, a social security body acting under a monopoly system is not an undertaking within the meaning of Article 86 of the Treaty; in paragraphs 18 and 19 of that judgment the Court held that such activity was not an economic activity, since it was based on the principle of national solidarity and was entirely non-profit-making.

24 However, although it is clear from that judgment that administering mandatory social security schemes such as those described in the references for a preliminary ruling in Poucet and Pistre, cited above, does not constitute an economic activity, that conclusion, in paragraph 17, was based on the same criteria as had been applied in Höfner and Elser when it was concluded that employment procurement must be described as a business activity within the meaning of the Community competition rules.

25 A body such as a public placement office may therefore be classed as an undertaking for the purposes of the Community competition rules.

26 Public placement offices entrusted under the legislation of a Member State with the operation of services of general economic interest, such as those envisaged in Article 11(1) of Law No 264, remain subject to the competition rules pursuant to Article 90(2) of the Treaty unless and to the extent to which it is shown that their application is incompatible with discharge of their duties (see Case 155/73 Sacchi [1974] ECR 409, paragraph 15, and Höfner and Elser, cited above, paragraph 24).

27 As regards the operation of public placement offices enjoying an exclusive right, compliance with which is ensured by a prohibition of any activity as an intermediary in employment relationships on pain of penal and administrative sanctions such as those provided for in Laws Nos 264 and 1369, it must be stated that the application of Article 86 of

the Treaty cannot obstruct the performance of the particular task assigned to those offices if they are manifestly not in a position to satisfy demand in that area of the market.

28 Whilst it is true that Article 86 concerns undertakings and may be applied within the limits laid down by Article 90(2) to public undertakings or undertakings vested with exclusive rights or specific rights, the Treaty nevertheless requires the Member States not to take or maintain in force measures which could destroy the effectiveness of that provision (see Case 13/77 Inno v ATAB [1977] ECR 2115, paragraphs 31 and 32, and Höfner and Elser, cited above, paragraph 26). Article 90(1) provides that the Member States are not to enact or maintain in force, in the case of public undertakings and the undertakings to which they grant special or exclusive rights, any measure contrary to the rules contained in the Treaty, in particular those provided for in Articles 85 to 94.

29 Consequently, any measure adopted by a Member State which maintains in force statutory provisions that create a situation in which public placement offices cannot avoid infringing Article 86 is incompatible with the rules of the Treaty.

30 In the first place, an undertaking vested with a legal monopoly may be regarded as occupying a dominant position within the meaning of Article 86 of the Treaty (see Case 311/84 CBEM v CLT and IPB [1985] ECR 3261, paragraph 16), and the territory of a Member State to which that monopoly extends may constitute a substantial part of the common market (see Case 322/81 Michelin v Commission [1983] ECR 3461, paragraph 28).

31 Secondly, the mere creation of such a dominant position by granting an exclusive right within the meaning of Article 90(1) is not as such incompatible with Article 86 of the Treaty (see CBEM, cited above, paragraph 17; Höfner and Elser, cited above, paragraph 29; Case C-320/91 Corbeau [1993] ECR I-2533, paragraph 11; and Case C-323/93 Centre d'Insémination de la Crespelle v Coopérative de la Mayenne [1994] ECR I-5077, paragraph 18). A Member State will contravene the prohibition contained in those two provisions only if the undertaking in question, merely by exercising the exclusive right granted to it, cannot avoid abusing its dominant position (see Case C-387/93 Banchero [1995] ECR I-4663, paragraph 51).

32 Pursuant to Article 86(b) of the Treaty, such abuse may in particular consist in limiting the provision of a service, to the prejudice of those seeking to avail themselves of it.

33 As the Commission has rightly pointed out, the market in the provision of services relating to the placement of employees is both very extensive and extremely diverse. Supply and demand on that market cover all sectors of production and relate to a range of jobs requiring anything from unskilled labour to the scarcest and most specialized professional qualifications.

34 On such an extensive and differentiated market, which is, moreover, subject to enormous changes as a result of economic and social developments, public placement offices may well be unable to satisfy a significant portion of all requests for services.

35 By prohibiting, on pain of penal and administrative sanctions, any activity as an intermediary between supply and demand on the employment market unless carried on by public placement offices, a Member State creates a situation in which the provision of a service is limited, contrary to Article 86(b) of the Treaty, if those offices are manifestly unable to satisfy demand on the employment market for all types of activity.

36 Thirdly, the question of the responsibility imposed on a Member State by virtue of Articles 86 and 90(1) of the Treaty arises only if the abusive conduct on the part of the placement agency concerned is liable to affect trade between Member States. That does not mean that the abusive conduct in question must actually have affected such trade. It is sufficient to establish that it is capable of having such an effect (see Michelin v Commission, cited above, paragraph 104).

37 A potential effect of that kind on trade between Member States arises in particular where the placement of employees by private companies may extend to the nationals or to the territory of other Member States.

38 In view of all the foregoing considerations, the reply to the national court must be that public placement offices are subject to the prohibition contained in Article 86 of the Treaty, so long as application of that provision does not obstruct the performance of the particular task assigned to them. A Member State which prohibits any activity as an intermediary between supply and demand on the employment market, whether as an employment agency or as an employment business, unless carried on by those offices, is in breach of Article 90(1) of the Treaty where it creates a situation in which those offices cannot avoid infringing Article 86 of the Treaty. That is the case, in particular, in the following circumstances:

- the public placement offices are manifestly unable to satisfy demand on the market for all types of activity; and
- the actual placement of employees by private companies is rendered impossible by the maintenance in force of statutory provisions under which such activities are prohibited and non-observance of that prohibition gives rise to penal and administrative sanctions; and
- the placement activities in question could extend to the nationals or to the territory of other Member States.

The revolution of the concept of undertakings was completed by the European Court of Justice in the Arduino Case, case 20) ECJ, September 26th 2000, case C-35/99, where the Court held that the competition rules are fully applicable to the States and to their legislative power:

(…)

32 By its questions, which it is appropriate to examine together, the national court seeks essentially to ascertain whether Article 5 of the EC Treaty (now Article 10 EC) and Article 85 of the Treaty preclude a Member State from adopting a law or regulation which approves, on the basis of a draft produced by a professional body of members of the Bar, a tariff fixing minimum and maximum fees for members of the profession, where that State measure forms part of a procedure such as that laid down in the Italian legislation.

33 As a preliminary point, the Court observes that, since that State measure extends to the whole of the territory of a Member State, it may affect trade between Member States within the meaning of Article 85(1) of the Treaty (see, to that effect, Commission v Italy, cited above, paragraph 48).

34 Although Article 85 of the Treaty is, in itself, concerned solely with the conduct of undertakings and not with laws or regulations emanating from Member States, that article, read in conjunction with Article 5 of the Treaty, none the less requires the Member States not to introduce or maintain in force measures, even of a legislative or regulatory nature, which may render ineffective the competition rules applicable to undertakings (Case 267/86

Van Eycke [1988] ECR 4769, paragraph 16; Case C-185/91 Reiff [1993] ECR I-5801, paragraph 14; Case C-153/93 Delta Schiffahrts- und Speditionsgesellschaft [1994] ECR I-2517, paragraph 14; Case C-96/94 Centro Servizi Spediporto [1995] ECR I-2883, paragraph 20; and Commission v Italy, cited above, paragraph 53; as to Article 86 of the EC Treaty (now Article 82 EC), see also Case 13/77 GB-Inno-BM [1977] ECR 2115, paragraph 31).

35 The Court has held that Articles 5 and 85 of the Treaty are infringed where a Member State requires or favours the adoption of agreements, decisions or concerted practices contrary to Article 85 or reinforces their effects, or where it divests its own rules of the character of legislation by delegating to private economic operators responsibility for taking decisions affecting the economic sphere (Van Eycke, paragraph 16; Reiff, paragraph 14; Delta Schiffahrts- und Speditionsgesellschaft, paragraph 14; Centro Servizi Spediporto, paragraph 21; and Commission v Italy, paragraph 54).

36 In that regard, the fact that a Member State requires a professional organisation to produce a draft tariff for services does not automatically divest the tariff finally adopted of the character of legislation.

37 That would be the case where the members of the professional organisation can be characterised as experts who are independent of the economic operators concerned and they are required, under the law, to set tariffs taking into account not only the interests of the undertakings or associations of undertakings in the sector which has appointed them but also the public interest and the interests of undertakings in other sectors or users of the services in question (see, to that effect, Reiff, paragraphs 17 to 19 and 24; Delta Schiffahrts- und Speditionsgesellschaft, paragraphs 16 to 18 and 23; Joined Cases C-140/94 to C-142/94 DIP and Others [1995] ECR I-3257, paragraphs 18 and 19; and Commission v Italy, paragraph 44).

The concrete application of the European Court of Justice decisions on the interpretation of public enterprises clearly suggests to member States that they must forbid public authorities from exercising any function consisting in the offering of goods or services in any market, placing emphasis, for example, on promotional and real estate activities.

It is certainly advisable for the government to provide for strong regulatory actions, but it is also advisable to prescribe that the determination of tolls by the public authority should be based on objective, transparent criteria that facilitate the right revenues for companies in accordance with the Altmark decision (See Case 3) ECJ, 24 July 2003, case C-280/00, Altmark). Such determination must, in particular, take into account all the duties regarding the public infrastructure manager, as well as the costs for maintenance of the facility.

Indeed, the main aim of the European law of competition is to protect consumers of Services of General Interest who, according to article 14 of the TFEU, can benefit from a real right concerning the efficiency and quality of Services of General Interest.

Bibliography

Barnard C., *The Law of the Single European Market: Unpacking the Premises*, Oxford, 2002.

Baumol W.J., *On the Proper Cost Tests for Natural Monopoly in a Multiproduct Industry*, in *American Economic Review*, 1977, p. 810 ff.

Bovis C., *Financing Services of General Interest, Public Procurement and State Aid: The Delineation Between Market Forces and Protection*, in *Columbia Journal of European Law*, 2004, p. 419 ff.

Bovis H., *EU Public Procurement Law*, Edward Elgar, 2008.

Braeutigam R., *An Analysis of Fully Distributed Cost Pricing in Regulated Industries*, in *The Bell Journal of Economics*, 1980, p. 182 ff.

Buendia Sierra J.L., *Exclusive Rights and State Monopolies under EC Law*, Oxford, 2000.

Butt-Philip A., *Implementing the European Internal Market: Problems and Prospects*, London, 1988.

Button K.J., *Privatization and Deregulation: Its Implications for Negative Transport Externalities*, in *The Annals of Regional Science*, 1994, p. 125 ff.

Calingaert M., *The 1992 Challenge from Europe: Development of the European Community's Internal Market*, Washington D.C., National Planning Association, 1988.

Calori R. - Lawrence P. (ed.), *The Business of Europe: Managing Change,* Sage, 1991.

Carbajo J.C. - Estache A. - Kennedy D., *Regulating the Quality of Privatized Transport Services*, The World Bank, Washington D.C., 1997.

Cassese S., *Lo spazio giuridico globale*, Roma-Bari, 2003, p. 39 ff.

Cecchini, P. - Catinat M. - Jacquemin A., *1992: The European Challenge: The Benefits of a Single Market*, Aldershot, 1992.

Coffey P. (ed.), *The Economic Policies of the Common Market*, London, 1979.

Comba, M., Steen Treumer St., *The In-House Providing in European Law*, Copenhagen, 2010.

Ezrachi A., *EC competition law: an analytical guide to the leading cases*, Oxford, 2008.

Flynn L., *Competition policy and public services in EC Law after the Maastricht and Amsterdam Treaties*, in Twomey P. - O'Keeffe D., *Legal Issues of the Amsterdam Treaty*, Oxford, 1999 p. 185 ff.

Graham C., *Essential facilities and services of general interest*, in *Dir. e Pol. Un Eur.*, 2007, p. 22 ff.

Guislain P. - Kerf M., *Concessions – The Way to Privatize Infrastructure Sector Monopolies, Viewpoint 59*, Finance and Private Sector Development Department, The World Bank, Washington D.C., 1995.

Gromnicka E., *Services of General Economic Interest in the State Aids Regime: Proceduralisation of Political Choices?*, in *European Public Law*, 2005, p. 429 ff.

Henry G. – Matheu M., *Des nouvelles régulations pour les services publics en concurrence,* in C. Henry - Matheu M. - Jeunmaitre A., *Réguler les services publics en réseau: l'expérience européenne*, Paris, 2003, p. 7 ff.

Karayigit T., *The Notion of Services of General Economic Interest Revisited*, in *European Public Law*, 2009, p. 575 ff.

Korah V., *Cases and materials on EC competition law*, Oxford, 2006.

Kovar R., *Droit Communautaire et service public: espritd'orthodoxie ou pensée laicisée*, in *Rev. trim. Doit eur.*, 1996, p. 493 ff.

Kovar R., *Les prises de partecipation publiques et le regime communautaire des aides d'Etat*, in *Rev. Trim. dr. Comn.*, 1992, p. 110 ff.

Krajewski M. - Neergard U. - Van de Gronden J., *The changing legal framework for services of general interest in Europe. Between competition and solidarity*, Cambridge, 2009.

Layard R. - Glaister S. (ed.), *Introduction to Cost-Benefit Analysis, Cambridge*, 1994.

Liston C., *Price-Cap versus Rate-of-Return Regulation*, in *Journal of Regulatory Economics*, 1995, p. 25 ff.

Lopez De Gonzalo M., *La «regola della separazione» nella disciplina dei servizi portuali ed aeroportuali*, in *Dir. Mar.*, 2005, p. 670 ff.

Lord Cockfield, *The European Union: creating the single market*, Wiley Chancery Law, 1994.

Maddalon P., *Paquet Altmark: quelle securité juridique?*, in *Contracts, concurrence, consommation*, 2006, p. 18 ff.

Maresca M., *L'accesso ai servizi di interesse generale, de-regolazione e ri-regolazione degli users' rights*, in *Dir. Un. Eur.* 2005, p. 441 ff.

Munari F., *La disciplina dei c.d. servizi essenziali tra diritto comunitario, prerogative degli Stati membri ed interesse generale*, in *Dir. Un. Eur.*, 2001, p. 39 ff.

Rodrigues S., *Les services public set le Traitè d'Amsterdam. Genès et portèe juridique du projet du nouvel article 16 du Traitè CE*, in *Revue du Marchè Commune r de l'Union Europèeenne*, 1998, p. 37 ff.

Ross M., *Article 16 EC and services of general interest: from derogation to obligation?*, in *European Law Review*, 2000, p. 22 ff.

Svane L.P., *Public service compensation in practice: Commission package on State aid for services of general economic interest*, in *Comp. Policy newsletter*, 2005, p. 34 ff.

Swann D., *European Economic Integration: The Common Market, European Union and Beyond*, Edward Elgar, 1996.

Tesauro G., *Diritto dell'Unione europea*, Padova, Padova 2010.

Thatcher M., *Institutions, Regulation and Change: New Regulatory Agencies in the British privatised utilities*, in *Britain in the 1990's*, 1998.

Townley C., *The Concept of an 'Undertaking': The Boundaries of the Corporation - A Discussion of Agency, Employees and Subsidiaries*, London, 2009.

Verhoeven A., *Privatisation and EC Law: Is the European Commission "Neutral" with Respect to Public Versus Private Ownership of Companies?*, in *International and Comparative Law Quarterly* 1996, p. 861 ff.

Wils P.J.W., *The Optimal Enforcement of Ec Antitrust Law: Essays in Law & Economics,* Amsterdam, 2008.

Wouters J. - Van Hees B., *Les enterprises publiques et le règles europèennes en matière d'aides d'Etat*, in *Revue du marchè unique europèen*, 1999, p. 35 ff.

Chapter 3 Seaports

3.1 The Principle of Separation in the Regulation of Ports: the Example of Italian Port Authorities

The international ports market needs innovative and modern legislative solutions in order to increase efficiency[1] through implementation of European Union competition principles and, particularly, to guarantee complete conformity with the rule of separation between port infrastructures management and services supply. Many legislative changes are therefore needed to clearly specify the content of the law in order to completely satisfy European principles.

According to the principle of separation, applicable on the legal basis of art. 102 of the Treaty on the Functioning of the European Union, it is important to give a concrete example of regulation through the description of the national legislation most evaluated by the European Court of Justice and the European Commission: the Italian law n. 84/1994. The port authority, identified as the Italian ports regulator, is defined as a non-economic public body charged with regulation of port business activities. The appointment procedure for the port authority's President is one of the most important features to try to understand if a public body is really to be independent: according to art. 8 of law n. 84/1994, the Transport Minister and the President of the Region should through a specific agreement choose the President from among three names designated by the municipality.

The introduction of public-private partnership financing schemes is another key feature of European ports law: the project financing procedure is generally considered the only way by which it is possible to build strategic port infrastructures, especially concerning the Trans-European Network of Transport.

---

[1] Ubbel B., *Institutional barriers to efficient policy intervention in the european port sector*, in *IATSS Review*, 2005 p. 40 ff.. For a comparative analysis see: US Department of Transportation (USDOT), *An Assessment of the US Marine Transportation System: A Report to Congress*, Washington, 1999, US Maritime Administration (USMA), 1998, *A Report to Congress on the Status of The Public Ports of the United States*, Washington DC, 1996–1997, Ircha, M. C., *US ports: evolution and structure*, in *Maritime Policy & Management*, 1995, p. 281 ff., Schenker, E., *Port Development in the United States*, Washington, 1976 and Marcus, H. S., Short, J. E. - Kuypers, J. C. - Roberts, P. O., *Federal Port Policy in the United States*, Cambridge, 1976.

The current law on port authority[2] is the result of a significant and historic evolution spurred by numerous debates about the most appropriate kind of public administration to be in charge of the Italian ports' governance. The logical consequence of the political and scientific discussions has been a number law proposals providing both the public and private models of governance.

The previous discipline consisted only in the laws contained in the *Maritime Code* and in the *Regulations on Maritime Navigation.* There was also a substantial number of special laws providing for specific governance of the main port authorities. These were economic public bodies entitled to manage the administrative functions of the port areas, but also with the faculty to carry out business activities. In the past, and in some member States, the ports managers had an exclusive competence in exercising both public and business functions. The contemporary exercise of public and business activities lead to the approval of the 1994 law, in order to provide private companies with a greater opportunity to compete and to avoid the confusion brought by such a complex and varied legal framework.

The legal framework described above, together with the confusion of regulatory and business functions, as well as the complex evolution of maritime traffic (including ro-ro and container ships), were indeed real barriers to competition in the maritime transport and port operations markets. The separation between public functions and business activities became the key feature of the new ports' reform proposals, as it was for law n. 84/1994 as well. What is really needed in the actual port market is to make real and effective what law n. 84/1994 didn't succeed in causing. Indeed, according to law n. 84/1994, port operations are reserved to private companies, while the port authority is responsible for port administration, excepting those competencies that the Maritime Code and law n. 84/1994 reserve to the maritime authority.

That this separation is a key feature of the ports' governance[3], is confirmed by the recent reform proposals currently being discussed in the Parliament and the Ministry of Transport. Clearly, the port authority should also be prevented from exercising business activities through indirect participation in other companies (art. 6 par. 6 law n 84/1994).

The non-economic nature of the port authority should confine the public body within the State organizational structure, estranging it from performing business activities either inside or outside the port. From this point of view, it becomes greatly important to maintain art. 6 par. 6, which becomes more concrete through the express provision of the non-economic nature of the entity. Anyway, the same

---

2 See Carbone S.M., *L'equilibrio tra Autorità portuale e mercato*, in *Dir. trasp.*, 1994 p. 823 ff., Carbone S.M. - Munari F., *La disciplina dei porti tra diritto comunitario e diritto interno*, Milano, 2006 and Maresca M., *La regolazione dei porti tra diritto interno e diritto comunitario*, Torino, 2001.

3 See Lopez De Gonzalo M., *La «regola della separazione» nella disciplina dei servizi portuali ed aeroportuali*, in Dir. Mar., 2005, p. 670 ff.

article recognizes the possibility for participation with other companies connected to ports activities and services.

The same provision must be also read referring to the recent laws (art. 3 budget law for 2008) about public participation in business activities, which, if they are apparently restrictive, prevent the port authority from creating or participating in any company except when the production of goods or services can be considered as necessary for the fulfillment of institutional aims. It is necessary to understand which activities are prohibited to the public administration and consider this prohibition also according art. 6 par. 6 of law n. 84/1994. It seems correct to identify the activities prohibited according to the art. 3 of the budget law for 2008 as a whole contained within the wider block of activities included in art. 6 par. 6 of law n. 84/1994.

The competence of control and regulation, substantially confirmative of the regulatory trend of port authority functions, complies with the principle of separation, thereby strengthening the features of *Landlord Port Authority* for the public body. This is a port where a public entity is responsible for the governance and development of the territory, providing, in the meanwhile, all the activities bound to the creation and regulation of infrastructures without any involvement in business activities, which are reserved to private companies. The *Tool Port* is another model of governance in which the port authority regulates and manages the infrastructures, while the *Operating Port* model provides for a port authority that is entitled to exercise every business activity inside the port and to carry out the loading and unloading of freights[4].

According to Italian law, port authorities have to administer ports accompanied by the maritime authority, that is the traditional body in charge of controlling safety within the port. It is difficult to understand the real limit of action between the port authority and the maritime authority, but it is necessary to consider the limits imposed on maritime authority functions, which are intended only to guarantee the fair exercise of port activities. Contrast this with the port authority, which is entitled to wield the larger power of controlling and regulating the business activities exercised inside the port. This conclusion is confirmed by the prescription describing the port authority as the only entity that can exercise the power of coordination over all ports activities within the port and the exclusive administration of port areas. It is also necessary to highlight the fact that the Navigation Code entitles the maritime authority to provide everything that is necessary for port security and police.

The relationship between the port authority and the maritime authority has always been discussed inside the judgments and the literature. The basic principle to grasp is that the port authority has the ground-competences and the maritime au-

---

4 Van Hooydonk E., *The regime of Port Authorities under European Law including an analysis of the Port Services Directive,* in *European Seaports Law, EU Law of Ports and Ports Services in the Port Package,* Antwerpen-Apeldoorm, Maklu, 2003.

thority has the sea-competences. There are, indeed, a lot of discussions divided in two.

The President of the port authority is both a representative and the technical person at the head of the public body. Different reform proposals, especially the one shown last autumn, seem to increment the technical requirements that must be held by the candidates for President, in addition to the requirement of managerial competence.

The appointment procedure of the President of the port authority nowadays consists of an agreement, through a decree, between the Ministry of Transport and the President of the Region about a name chosen from the proposals made by the Municipality, the Province, and Chamber of Commerce.

The law prescribes a marginal role for the territorial public bodies. Indeed, if there is the same agreement between the President of the Region and the Ministry, then the Municipality, the Province, and the Chamber of Commerce remain in the background of this appointment through specific agreement. If the agreement between the President of the Region and the Ministry fails twice, the President of the Ministers Council appoints the President of the port authority, but only after the vote of the Ministers Council and the opinion of the *Conferenza permanente per i rapport tra lo Stato, le Regioni e le Province autonome di Trento e Bolzano*.

It must be stressed that some previous reform proposals wished a complete exclusion of the smaller public bodies from the appointment procedure, although this posed a high risk of violating the subsidiary principle prescribed by art. 118 of the Italian Constitution and European Union law. The principle of subsidiarity is found in art. 5 of the Treaty on European Union and implies that policy decisions are taken as closely as possible to the citizen and that constant checks are made to verify that action at Union level is justified in light of the possibilities available at the national, regional, or local level. Specifically, it is the principle whereby the Union does not take action unless it is more effective than action taken at the national, regional, or local level. It is closely bound up with the principle of proportionality, which requires that any action by the Union should not go beyond what is necessary to achieve the objectives of the Treaties. The Treaty of Amsterdam took up the approach that followed from this declaration in a Protocol on the application of the principles of subsidiarity and proportionality. The new Protocol of the Lisbon Treaty now requires the principle of subsidiarity to be respected in all draft legislative acts and allows national parliaments to object to a proposal on the grounds that it breaches the principle, as a result of which the proposal may be maintained, amended, or withdrawn by the Commission, or blocked by the European Parliament or the Council.

The same principle must be adopted through legislation in the member States, and this is why, in the last port reform proposal in Italy, the agreement had been inserted as a way to involve the Municipality, Province, and Chamber of Commerce in the appointment procedure of the President of the port authority.

Nevertheless, it is important to highlight that several problems arose from conflicts among the public bodies during the appointment procedures in past years.

More than once, the three smallest public bodies involved proposed to the Minister and to the President of the Region only one candidate and not three different names as the law prescribes. Through many judgments, the mentioned praxis has been declared illegal because it limited the discretional power of the Minister of Transport.

The law in force offers a long list of functions of the President even if it establishes that the President can exercise every other competence not expressly attributed to other institutions. The new rule contained in art. 8 could provides the President with a wider range of power in the port administration, increasing the possibility to adopt urgent acts that must be, anyway, ratified by the port committee within fifteen days. Notwithstanding these changes, the real increase in the power of the President can be better understood through the diminution of functions attributed to the port committee.

The Port Committee is the body composed of all the representatives of every industrial and stakeholder category operating in the port, including the President, the Chief of the Port, the customs manager, the President of the Province, the Mayor, the Chamber of Commerce Chairman, six representatives of the main industrial categories of the port, six representatives of the employees, and a representative of the railway companies. While the heterogeneous composition of the Committee has been a real obstacle for the efficiency of the body, the reform proposals do not put forward any solutions to this problem.

The Committee holds planning and management functions. The current list of functions contained in art. 9 of the law n. 84/1994 is long and an eventual reduction would increase the competences of the President, who has every power not attributed to the Committee by the law.

The Auditors of Account College is composed of three effective members and three substitutes appointed through a Minister of Transport decree. It verifies and controls the port authority's acts and management. The reform proposals may abrogate the substitute members.

3.2 Planning and Environmental Protection in European Ports

One of the most important issue of Seaports regulation is the of the port planning competence and the related procedure. The "Port Plan" is the planning act which defines the spatial limits of the port areas, their industrial destination, and the port infrastructure's organization[5]. National policies, on the grounds of European Union law, tends to simplify the actual praxis, introducing some changes most of which portend to the approval procedure aspect. A key feature is the definition of

[5] See Becet J.M., *La notion d'«extension limitée de l'urbanisation» (article L.146-4 II du Code de l'urbanisme)*, in *Annuaire de droit maritime et océanique* 2000, p. 31 ff.

the planning act. For example, a generic definition seems to allow a wider planning power over the port areas by the port authority, although the object of the planning act will remain reasonably the same: the port area's destination.

Port authorities can wield their regulatory power within a certain area delineated by the Port Plan Act. The Port Plan Act controls the port areas' territorial and functional aspects. For example, in the Guidelines provided by the Infrastructure Department of the Italian Government, the faculty to extend the competence area beyond the specific borders identified by the same Department is expressly provided. The geographical planning borders given to the Ministry can be raised when there is the strategic need to intervene in private areas located near the port. This provision leads to a definition of relevant market that can go beyond the ports' areas and gives the port authority the opportunity to wield its competences outside the spatial limits prescribed by the national laws in case of port development needs. The Port Planning Act also prescribes the kind of activities that are allowed in every single zone.

To understand whether the Port Plan can determine an unjustified restriction of Internal market rules of European Union, it is important to check the national approval procedures. For example, the approval procedure of the Italian Port Planning Act, art. 5 of law n. 84/1994, is within the competence of the Port Committee, while the reform proposal provides the need to obtain a mandatory opinion of the Infrastructure Ministry and of the President of the Region within sixty days. It also provides the need for an opinion of the Municipality within ninety days; a delay will imply tacit consent. In the case of objections, the Region will promote a *Conferenza di servizi*, i.e., a round table with the presence of a delegate from each public administration, in order to achieve the agreement with every competent administration.

The most important feature of the Port Planning Act is the regulation of the environment within the port areas. An important decision of the Court of Justice made a balance between the freedom to provide services, competition rules, and environmental protection. This is, indeed, an important European goal and entitles member States to adopt measures that do not fall in the field of application of the competition rules (case 1) ECJ, 18 March 1997, Case C-343/95, - Diego Calì & Figli Srl v Servizi ecologici porto di Genova SpA, in Rep. p. I-01547):

(...)

1 By decision of 12 October 1995, which was received at the Court on 30 October 1995, the Tribunale di Genova referred to the Court for a preliminary ruling under Article 177 of the EC Treaty three questions concerning the interpretation of Article 86 of the Treaty.

2 Those questions were raised in a dispute between Diego Calì & Figli Srl (hereinafter `Calì') and Servizi Ecologici Porto di Genova SpA (hereinafter `SEPG') regarding the payment to be made by Calì for preventive anti-pollution services performed by SEPG in the oil port of Genoa.

3 At the material time, the port of Genoa was managed by the Consorzio Autonomo del Porto (hereinafter `CAP'), which was replaced in 1994 by the Autorità Portuale (Port Authority). The CAP was a public body upon which both the administrative and economic functions relating to the management of the port had been conferred by legislation.

4 By Order No 14 of 1 July 1986, the President of the CAP, in his capacity as delegate of the Government, approved the regulations governing the harbour police and security at the oil port of Genoa-Multedo.

5 By Order No 32 of 23 August 1991, the President of the CAP amended those regulations by creating a compulsory surveillance and rapid intervention service intended to protect maritime areas against any pollution caused by accidental discharges of hydrocarbons into the sea.

6 Article 1 of Order No 32 defines the service in the following terms: `The service shall be responsible for the following functions and intervention procedures:

(a) constant surveillance of the waters on account of the presence of tankers laying alongside or berthed at quays in order to identify at once any risk of spills of hydrocarbons or other pollutants arising from criminal acts or negligence;

(b) in cases of pollution, whether from a ship or from dry land, occurring during loading or unloading operations or in any other circumstances:

(1) immediate reporting of the incident to the responsible authorities, together with the provision of any information which could be of use in evaluating the incident;

(2) taking all such action at the appropriate time, subject to those responsible for the pollution being liable for the costs thereby incurred, as is necessary and advisable for the purpose of containing the spill and associated risks and for removing and/or neutralizing the spilled substances and fully cleansing the waters in question.'

7 By Decree No 1186 of 30 August 1991, the President of the CAP entrusted that service, in the form of an exclusive concession, to SEPG.

8 By Decree No 1191 of 30 August 1991, the President of the CAP approved the tariffs which SEPG was authorized to apply, in respect of the service in question, to vessels using the installations of the oil terminal. Those tariffs were established in accordance with the tonnage of the vessels, the quantities transported and the duration of the intervention.

9 On several occasions between 1992 and 1994, Calì, which transports, for third parties, petrochemical products by sea in tankers, used the oil port of Genoa-Multedo for the purpose of loading and unloading products, including acetone.

10 The operations themselves were carried out not by Calì, but, on payment of a fee, by the harbour company Porto Petroli di Genova SpA. The vessels used were equipped with anti-pollution devices and systems.

11 SEPG invoiced Calì for a total amount of LIT 8 708 928 in respect of the anti-pollution surveillance services performed on Calì's behalf. The latter refused to pay on the ground that it had never requested nor had recourse to services of that type during the operations carried out in the oil port of Genoa.

12 On 22 December 1994 SEPG obtained an order from the Tribunale di Genova which required Calì to pay the disputed invoices.

13 In the course of the proceedings contesting that order, the Tribunale di Genova stayed proceedings until the Court of Justice had given a preliminary ruling on the following questions:

`1. Can a "dominant position within the common market or in a substantial part of it" be said to exist where a limited company, set up by a national port authority, is given responsibility for and does actually carry out, pursuant to an administrative concession from that authority, the task of providing, with exclusive rights within a harbour sector specializing in loading and unloading petroleum products, an "anti-pollution surveillance" service, and where that company collects the relevant fee, which is set unilaterally by the port authority on the basis of the vessel's tonnage and the quantity of the product loaded or unloaded, from users of that service, that is to say vessels which dock at the wharves to carry out those operations?

2. Having regard to the situation set out in Question 1 and if there is a dominant position within the common market or a substantial part of it, is there an abuse of the aforesaid "dominant position" within the meaning of Article 86 of the Treaty, in particular of subparagraphs (a), (c) and (d), and are there related practices, when an undertaking holding the exclusive concession for a service (even though on the basis of a decision of the authority granting the concession) charges fees:

- which are compulsory and independent of the provision of an efficient surveillance and/or intervention service, merely because a vessel berths in a mooring in the Porto Petroli and loads/unloads goods, whether petroleum products or chemicals and petrochemicals, according to the contractual terms imposed;
- the amount of which depends solely on the tonnage of the vessel, the amount of the product and also, in the event of any actual intervention, the duration thereof, but not on the product's nature, quality or capacity to pollute;
- which, since they are imposed exclusively on the vessel (which is merely passively loaded and unloaded), affect a subject other than those whose responsibility it is to carry out the necessary technical operations (in this case Porto Petroli di Genova SpA and the laders/receivers of the product), resulting in an inevitable discrepancy between the responsibility for any pollution and the bearing of the cost of the anti-pollution service;
- which, given the nature of the product and/or its existence, represent an unnecessary service for vessels equipped with their own anti-pollution devices and systems adapted to the type of product to be loaded or unloaded;
- which impose on the vessel a charge, and an associated extra cost, in addition to those provided for by the landing contract between the carrier and the company operating the wharves, and have no practical connection with the subject-matter of the contract.

3. If, in the situations set out in Questions 1 and 2, there are one or more practices amounting to abuse of a dominant position by an undertaking for the purposes of Article 86 of the Treaty, does this lead to a potential adverse effect on trade between Member States of the Union?'

14 In order to answer the first question, concerning the existence of a dominant position, it must be established whether an activity of the kind carried on by SEPG in this case falls within the scope of Article 86 of the Treaty.

15 Such activities are carried on under an exclusive concession granted to SEPG by a public body.

16 As regards the possible application of the competition rules of the Treaty, a distinction must be drawn between a situation where the State acts in the exercise of official authority and that where it carries on economic activities of an industrial or commercial nature by offering goods or services on the market (Case 118/85 Commission v Italy [1987] ECR 2599, paragraph 7).

17 In that connection, it is of no importance that the State is acting directly through a body forming part of the State administration or by way of a body on which it has conferred special or exclusive rights (Case 118/85 Commission v Italy, cited above, paragraph 8).

18 In order to make the distinction between the two situations referred to in paragraph 16 above, it is necessary to consider the nature of the activities carried on by the public undertaking or body on which the State has conferred special or exclusive rights (Case 118/85 Commission v Italy, cited above, paragraph 7).

19 On this point, it is clear from the order for reference and the wording of the first question that the main proceedings concern the payment to be made by Calì for anti-pollution surveillance exercised by SEPG in relation to the loading and unloading of acetone products transported by Calì in the oil port of Genoa.

20 Furthermore, it is common ground that the dispute in the main proceedings does not concern the invoicing of any action by SEPG necessitated by pollution actually produced during loading or unloading operations.

21 Article 1 of Order No 32 of the President of CAP referred to above expressly distinguishes, moreover, between surveillance intended to prevent pollution and intervention in a case where pollution has occurred and it provides (Article 1(b)(2)) that those responsible for the pollution are to bear the costs arising from any action deemed necessary or advisable.

22 The anti-pollution surveillance for which SEPG was responsible in the oil port of Genoa is a task in the public interest which forms part of the essential functions of the State as regards protection of the environment in maritime areas.

23 Such surveillance is connected by its nature, its aim and the rules to which it is subject with the exercise of powers relating to the protection of the environment which are typically those of a public authority. It is not of an economic nature justifying the application of the Treaty rules on competition (Case C-364/92 SAT Fluggesellschaft v Eurocontrol [1994] ECR I-43, paragraph 30).

24 The levying of a charge by SEPG for preventive anti-pollution surveillance is an integral part of its surveillance activity in the maritime area of the port and cannot affect the legal status of that activity (Case C-364/92 SAT Fluggesellschaft v Eurocontrol, cited above, paragraph 28). Moreover, as stated in paragraph 8 of this judgment, the tariffs applied by SEPG have been approved by the public authorities.

25 In the light of the foregoing considerations, the answer to Question 1 must be that Article 86 of the EC Treaty is to be interpreted as not being applicable to anti-pollution surveillance with which a body governed by private law has been entrusted by the public authorities in an oil port of a Member State, even where port users must pay dues to finance that activity.

3.3 The Financing of Ports Infrastructures Between Public-private Partnerships and Public Policies

The introduction of public-private partnership financing schemes is another key feature of European ports law, as the project financing procedure is considered the only way through which it is possible to build strategic port infrastructures, especially considering the Trans-European Network of Transport[6].

The main problem regards the port's infrastructure. Italian law, for example, indicated the Ministry of Public Works as the public body with the duty to finance works, construction, and maintenance of ports, while law n. 84/1994 designates the port authority as the one in charge for routine and extra-routine maintenance of the port, in accordance with the Department of Public Works.

Thanks to Directive 2004/17/EC and to the Green Paper of the European Commission, many member States approved new rules to innovate the financing framework of public works in the ports through the introduction of the project financing procedure. Indeed, ports infrastructures are almost an economic resource both for the managing subject and the users (carriers), implying the need to introduce new private financing methods with the aim to guarantee enough cash flow to fund the whole amount of works[7].

The project financing allows, on one hand, private investors to participate in the facilities construction and, on the other hand, to reduce business risk through the adjudication of the managing concession to private companies. Through the special procedure described by European laws (especially the Green Paper on Private-Public Partnerships), private companies can finance the infrastructure building with the advantage of obtaining its future management (case 2) European Commission, 15 November 2005, Communication on Public-Private Partnerships and Community Law on Public Procurement and Concessions, in www.eurlex.eu):

(...)

A key feature of concessions is the right of the concessionaire to exploit the construction or service granted as a consideration for having erected the construction or delivered the service. The main difference to public procurement is the risk inherent in such exploitation which the concessionaire, usually providing the funding of at least parts of the relevant projects, has to bear. Such private capital involvement is considered to be one of the key incentives for public authorities to enter into PPPs. In spite of their practical importance, only few provisions of secondary Community legislation coordinate the award procedures for

---

6 The construction of the Trans European Network of Transport presupposes an intermodal policy of transports: See Hayuth, Y., *Intermodality: Concept and Practice*, London, 1987, Haralambides, H.E., *Competition, Excess Capacity, and the Pricing of Port Infrastructure*, in *International Journal of Maritime Economics*, 2002, p. 323 ff. and Luberoff, D. - Walder, J., *US Ports and the Funding of Intermodal Facilities: An Overview of Key Issues*, Cambridge, 2000.

7 See Notteboom T., Ducruet C., De Langen P.W., *Ports in Proximity: Competition and Coordination Among Adjacent Seaports*, Ashgate, 2009.

works concessions. For their part, the rules governing the award of service concessions apply only by reference to the principles resulting from Articles 43 and 49 of the EC Treaty, in particular the principles of transparency, equality of treatment, proportionality and mutual recognition. Against this background, the Green Paper (question 6) asked whether in the view of stakeholders a Community legislative initiative designed to regulate the procedure for awarding concessions was desirable.

The great majority of stakeholders participating in the consultation confirmed the demand for greater legal certainty as regards the Community rules governing the award of concessions. Opinions on how to provide such legal certainty – via legislation or a non-binding, interpretative instrument – were, however, divided.

3.2. Options to provide legal certainty on concessions

The consultation showed the demand for a stable, consistent legal environment for the award of concessions at EU level, in particular to reduce transaction costs (by decreasing legal risks) and more generally to enhance competition. Many stakeholders argued that increasing legal certainty and effective competition in the area of concessions would be a practical way of promoting PPPs, thereby increasing the contribution that private project financing can make in times of tight public budgets. Private stakeholders particularly underlined that only EU level action could provide such legal certainty avoiding at the same time the problems posed by the patchwork of national legislation, especially with regard to the new Member States which need private finance most. There are basically two ways to meet this demand: (1) non-binding guidance, in particular in the form of an Interpretative Communication, and (2) legislation spelling out the obligations emanating from general EC Treaty principles.

Interpretative Communication

The Commission has already (in April 2000) adopted an Interpretative Communication on Concessions under Community Law which explains the scope and content of the EC Treaty principles applicable to the award of concessions. Many stakeholders argued that an Interpretative Communication was a quick and effective tool to provide clarification. However, comments made by key stakeholders in the course of the debate indicate that the existing Interpretative Communication on concessions has failed to spell out in a sufficiently clear manner the implications of EC Treaty principles for the award of concessions. Contributions from several important stakeholders were – surprisingly – still based on the assumption that existing EC law obligations do not require the award of concessions to be opened up to competition, in particular by enabling all undertakings to express their interest in obtaining concessions.

Other stakeholders considered an Interpretative Communication to be an ideal instrument to provide a clearer delimitation between public procurement contracts and concessions. However, the scope for certainty provided by an Interpretative Communication is limited, as it merely construes existing law. In many cases a lack of precision in the law can hardly be overcome by means of interpretation. It therefore seems likely that – while providing some added value – an update of the April 2000 Interpretative Communication on concessions would probably fall short of meeting the request for more legal certainty.

Legislative initiative

The reported misunderstandings regarding the scope and content of Community law obligations for contracting authorities who award concessions confirm the view of stakeholders that the general EC Treaty principles, even clarified by an interpretative document from the Commission, do not provide enough legal certainty. They are considered to leave too much discretion to contracting authorities and cannot therefore guarantee equal treatment of European companies throughout the EU. Indeed, both legal practice and doctrine show that – in spite of clarification provided by the European Court of Justice (See the case Telaustria) – the requirements of the EC Treaty are understood in different ways. It was reported that this created particular difficulties for bidders bringing a case against the award of concessions for review by national courts. Clearly, this situation could discourage firms from bidding for concessions and might diminish competition for PPPs and ultimately jeopardise their success.

On a more general note, it is difficult to understand why service concessions which are often used for complex and high value projects are entirely excluded from EC secondary legislation. Some arguments explaining this lack of detailed award procedures at EC level have been submitted in the course of the PPP Green Paper consultation. They include the flexibility supposedly needed in the area of concessions and the subsidiarity principle. These arguments against a binding Community initiative in this area are, however, unconvincing: adopting Community legislation on the award of concessions does not imply that public authorities should lack flexibility when choosing a private partner for PPPs. A legislative initiative on the award of concessions needs to take the possible complexity of concessions and the need for negotiations between the contracting authority and the bidders into account. Against this background, it is difficult to see why spelling out the rules applicable to the award of concessions would *per se* unduly limit the flexibility of contracting authorities when awarding service concessions. Likewise, the precise content of such initiative should determine whether or not it is compliant or non-compliant with the subsidiarity principle. There is no reason to consider such an initiative *per se* as being non-compliant with this principle.

Having carefully considered all arguments and the factual information submitted in the course of the PPP Green Paper consultation, it would currently appear that a legislative initiative is the preferable option as regards concessions. However, as mentioned above, before formally proposing legislation further in-depth analysis will need to be undertaken in accordance with the principles of "Better Regulation", in order (1) to determine whether indeed a Community initiative to regulate procedures for awarding concessions is necessary, (2) if so, to shape such an initiative, and (3) to better understand its possible impact.

3.3. Content of a possible Community initiative on concessions

As explained above, the general principles derived from the EC Treaty may need to be clearly spelt out by means of Community legislation on the award of concessions. The legislation which should cover both works and service concessions would provide a clear delineation between concessions and public procurement contracts. It would require adequate advertising of the intention to award a concession and fix the rules governing the selection of concessionaires on the basis of objective, non-discriminatory criteria. More generally, the rules should aim at applying the principle of equality of treatment of all participants to the award of concessions. Also, problems relating to the long duration of concessions, such as the need for their adaptation over time, as well as questions on PPPs established to build and operate cross-border infrastructures might be dealt with by such initiative.

One consequence of such legislation on concessions would be a qualitative leap in the protection of bidders in most of the Member States, as concessions, once they are covered by Community secondary legislation, would fall within the scope of the Community Directives on review procedures for the award of public procurement contracts, which provide for more effective and adequate remedies than the basic principles of jurisdictional protection developed by the European Court of Justice.

It is not possible to give details on the content of a potential Community initiative on concessions at this stage. The existence and shape of such rules depends on further research the Commission needs to undertake in the course of a full impact assessment. It is therefore premature to express an opinion on the overall scope of such rules, including the definition of threshold values above which such rules would apply. In any case, such initiative would not aim at amending existing sector-specific Community regulation covering the award of concessions in the respective sectors.

Some member States, nevertheless, still identify the Central State as the subject with the competence and duty to finance the works related to international infrastructures and with the faculty to authorize the intervention of regions, municipalities, and port authorities through the introduction of new taxes or the increasing of leaseholds and concessions fees. The project financing discipline directly seeks to reach the same objectives by leaving the realization costs on private companies, reducing the heavy burden of public contribution, and giving private investors a new profit opportunity[8].

Many European port authorities have the faculty to increase or reduce the concession fees also in consequence of works realized by concessionaires. In other words, if today the port's infrastructure financing is a public competence with the possibility to charge the costs on private companies through taxes and concessions fees, the European model tries to move the works funding on private subjects that will be able to reach good profits through the management of the infrastructure built.

3.4 The Regulation of Port Areas According to the European Common Market and Fundamental Freedoms

After the adoption of the European Community Treaty, national laws initiated important privatizations of ports through the adjudication of concessions of port areas to the most efficient and profitable private companies. The choice of the concession model (or of the leasehold model in common law countries) is more and

8 See Maresca M. (ed.), *Lo spazio mediterraneo della mobilità*, Udine, 2010, Van Hooydonk E., *The regime of Port Authorities under European Law including an analysis of the Port Services Directive,* in *European Seaports Law, EU Law of Ports and Ports Services in the Port Package,* Antwerpen-Apeldoorm, Maklu, 2003 and Suykens, F. - Van de Voorde E., *Port Management in Europe*, in *Maritime Policy and Management*, 1998, p.251 ff.

more based on criterion aimed to select the best business investor through a public tender in full compliance with European Union rules such as transparency, impartiality, proportionality, efficiency, and non-discrimination. These principles are, indeed, binding under the European Union legal order that qualifies them as general principles fully applicable to every concrete situation falling in the field of EU law. The internalization of these principles, through their inclusion in some national laws, promoted the effectiveness of European rules in the Italian legal order[9]. An important issue not always clear in national judgments is the field of application of European Union Law in the harbor market. The European Court of Justice held that they are undoubtedly subject to Internal Market rules (case 3) ECJ, 29 April 1999, Case C-224/97, Erich Ciola v Land Vorarlberg, in Rep., p. I-02517):

(…)

10 By its first question, the national court essentially asks whether the Treaty provisions on freedom to provide services are to be interpreted as precluding a Member State from establishing a maximum quota of moorings which may be rented to boat-owners resident in another Member State.

11 It should be observed at the outset that, as the national court has pointed out, first, the right freely to provide services may be relied on by an undertaking as against the State in which it is established if the services are provided for persons established in another Member State (Case C-70/95 Sodemare and Others v Regione Lombardia [1997] ECR I-3395, paragraph 37) and, second, in accordance with Joined Cases 286/82 and 26/83 Luisi and Carbone v Ministero del Tesoro [1984] ECR 377, paragraph 16, and Case 186/87 Cowan v Trésor Public [1989] ECR 195, paragraph 15, that right includes the freedom for recipients of services to go to another Member State in order to receive a service there, without being obstructed by restrictions.

12 Consequently, Articles 59 to 66 of the Treaty apply to a service such as that which the company of which Mr Ciola is manager provides, by means of a contract for the rental of a mooring, to a boat-owner resident in another Member State who receives and enjoys the service in a Member State other than that in which he resides.

13 In those circumstances, a restriction on moorings of the kind at issue in the main proceedings infringes the prohibition under the first paragraph of Article 59 of the Treaty of all discrimination, even indirect, with regard to providers of services.

14 While the restriction of the number of moorings which may be allocated to non-resident boat-owners is not based on their nationality, and so may not be regarded as direct discrimination, it does, however, use as the distinguishing criterion their place of residence. It is settled case-law that national rules under which a distinction is drawn on the basis of residence are liable to operate mainly to the detriment of nationals of other Member States, as non-residents are in the majority of cases foreigners (see Case C-350/96 Clean Car Autoservice v Landeshauptmann von Wien [1998] ECR I-2521, paragraph 29).

---

[9] See Maresca D. – Pelleriti S., *La regolazione del diritto di accesso alle infrastrutture portuali ed aeroportuali*, in *Dir. e Pol. Un. Eur.*, 2009, p. 107 ff.

15 To justify imposing a quota on moorings reserved for nationals of other Member States on mandatory grounds in the general interest, the Land of Vorarlberg relied at the hearing on the need to reserve access to the moorings for local boat-owners, as there is a risk of such moorings being monopolised by persons resident in other Member States and willing to pay higher rental charges. Because of the limitation of the total number of moorings available, for reasons concerning protection of the environment, lifting the quota would increase the pressure on the authorities of the Land of Vorarlberg.

16 National rules which are not applicable to services without distinction whatever the place of residence of the recipient, and which are therefore discriminatory, are compatible with Community law only if they can be brought within the scope of an express derogation, such as Article 56 of the EC Treaty (see Case 352/85 Bond van Adverteerders and Others v Netherlands State [1988] ECR 2085, paragraph 32); however, economic aims cannot constitute grounds of public policy within the meaning of that provision (Case C-288/89 Collectieve Antennevoorziening Gouda v Commissariaat voor de Media [1991] ECR I-4007, paragraph 11).

17 Since the Land of Vorarlberg has justified the imposition of a quota on moorings for non-resident owners not on grounds of public policy, public security or public health, but for economic reasons for the benefit of local owners, Article 56 of the Treaty cannot be applied; in those circumstances, it must be ascertained whether the existence of an exception in the Act of Accession authorized the Land of Vorarlberg to take measures such as the quota at issue in the main proceedings in order to limit the influx of boat-owners from other Member States.

18 On this point, it suffices to note that Article 70 of the Act of Accession lays down an express derogation, for a limited time, only for existing legislation regarding secondary residences.

19 Consequently, the establishment by a Member State of a maximum quota for moorings which may be rented to boat-owners resident in another Member State is contrary to the principle of freedom to provide services.

20 The answer to Question 1 must therefore be that Article 59 of the Treaty is to be interpreted as precluding a Member State from prohibiting the manager of a boat harbour, on pain of prosecution, from renting moorings in excess of a specified quota to boat-owners who are resident in other Member States.

Question 2

21 By its second question, the Verwaltungsgerichtshof essentially asks whether a prohibition which is contrary to the freedom to provide services, laid down before a Member State's accession to the European Union not by a general abstract rule but by a specific individual administrative decision that has become final, must be disregarded when assessing the validity of a fine imposed for failure to comply with that prohibition after the date of accession.

22 It appears from the grounds of the order for reference that in a case of failure to comply with general abstract rules which were not compatible with a fundamental principle of the Treaty, the Verwaltungsgerichtshof would have set aside such rules in favour of Community law on the basis of the Court's judgment in Case 106/77 Amministrazione delle Finanze dello Stato v Simmenthal [1978] ECR 629.

23 However, as the case-law to date, according to the Verwaltungsgerichtshof, lays down only the principle of the primacy of Community law over general rules of national law, that court asks whether that principle also applies to a specific individual administrative decision that is not in conformity with Community law such as, in the main proceedings, the Bescheid of 9 August 1990.

24 The Austrian Government submits that there is no reason why the case-law on the primacy of Community law should be applied, automatically and without restriction, to specific individual administrative acts. In support of its argument, it relies on the enforceability of administrative acts and refers in that connection to the case-law on what is known as the `procedural autonomy of the Member States'. In its view, to hold that Community law takes precedence over an enforceable administrative act would be liable to call into question the principles of legal certainty, protection of legitimate expectations or protection of lawfully acquired rights.

25 It must be observed at the outset, as the Advocate General does in points 40 to 43 of his Opinion, that the dispute concerns not the fate of the administrative act itself, in this case the decision of 9 August 1990, but the question whether such an act must be disregarded when assessing the validity of a penalty imposed for failure to comply with an obligation thereunder, because of its incompatibility with the principle of freedom to provide services.

26 Next, since thc provisions of the EC Treaty are directly applicable in the legal systems of all Member States and Community law takes precedence over national law, those provisions create rights for the persons concerned which the national authorities must observe and safeguard, and any conflicting provision of national law therefore ceases to be applicable (see Case 167/73 Commission v France [1974] ECR 359, paragraph 35).

27 Since the essential requirements of Article 59 of the Treaty became directly and unconditionally applicable at the end of the transitional period (see Case 279/80 Webb [1981] ECR 3305, paragraph 13), that provision consequently precludes the application of any conflicting measure of national law.

28 As regards the Republic of Austria, it is apparent from Article 2 of the Act of Accession that the provisions of the EC Treaty apply as from accession, that is, 1 January 1995, the date from which Article 59 of the Treaty thus became a direct source of law.

29 While the Court initially held that it is for the national court to refuse if necessary to apply any conflicting provision of national law (see Simmenthal, cited above, paragraph 21), it subsequently refined its case-law in two respects.

30 Thus it appears from the case-law, first, that all administrative bodies, including decentralised authorities, are subject to that obligation as to primacy, and individuals may therefore rely on such a provision of Community law against them (Case 103/88 Fratelli Costanzo v Comune di Milano [1989] ECR 1839, paragraph 32).

31 Second, provisions of national law which conflict with such a provision of Community law may be legislative or administrative (see, to that effect, Case 158/80 Rewe v Hauptzollamt Kiel [1981] ECR 1805, paragraph 43).

32 It is consistent with that case-law that those administrative provisions of national law should include not only general abstract rules but also specific individual administrative decisions.

33 There is no reason why the legal protection which individuals derive from the direct effect of provisions of Community law and which the national courts must ensure (see Case C-213/89 R v Secretary of State for Transport ex parte Factortame and Others [1990] ECR I-2433, paragraph 19) should be refused to those individuals in cases where the dispute concerns the validity of an administrative measure. The existence of such protection cannot depend on the nature of the conflicting provision of national law.

34 It follows from the foregoing that a prohibition which is contrary to the freedom to provide services, laid down before the accession of a Member State to the European Union not by a general abstract rule but by a specific individual administrative decision that has become final, must be disregarded when assessing the validity of a fine imposed for failure to comply with that prohibition after the date of accession.

Most national laws expressly prescribe that port authorities concede the port areas to private companies through public tenders in order to facilitate the best business development of the port. Investments and new infrastructures projects, they are able to guarantee to all port activities managers the biggest profit possible. There are, nevertheless, countries that limit the faculty to concede ports areas to private subjects[10].

In most of civil law countries (Italy, France, Germany) port areas are currently considered as public assets that cannot be the object of private law contracts[11]. Italy provides an administrative procedure through which port areas can become free from this regime (the *sdemanializzazione* contained in art. 35 of the *Maritime Code*), but it is actually very complex and it ends with a Decree of the Minister of Transport after a concrete evaluation of the public use potential of the specific port area.

The public regime of port areas has the power to preserve their essential nature as door to the sea. Indeed every potential user has the right to access the port facilities according to the principle of non-discrimination. Under European law, this regime is guaranteed through the application of competition rules, primarily art. 102 of the TFEU, which, according to the European Commission, fully applies to the essential facilities doctrine (case 4) European Commission, 21 December 1993, IV/34.689, 94/19/EC, Sea Containers v. Stena Sealink, in OJEU L15 of 5th January 1994):

(61) To determine whether an undertaking is dominant, it is necessary first to identify the 'relevant market', i. e. the relevant geographical and service markets in which to assess the market power of the allegedly dominant undertaking.

---

10 For a complete perspective of ports' areas regulation in Europe see Van Hooydonk E., *The regime of Port Authorities under European Law including an analysis of the Port Services Directive,* in *European Seaports Law, EU Law of Ports and Ports Services in the Port Package,* Antwerpen-Apeldoorm, Maklu, 2003.

11 In common law countries the same objective is reached through the essential facility doctrine: Waller S.W. - Frischmann B.M., *The essential nature of infrastructure or the infrastructural nature of essential facilities*, Chicago, 2007.

(62) The essence of the complaint is that what amounts to refusal of access to the port of Holyhead on reasonable and non-discriminatory terms will protect and lead to the strengthening of Sealink's position on the market for the provision of maritime transport services for cars and passengers on the 'central corridor' route between the United Kingdom and Ireland (see recital 11 above).

(63) The port of Holyhead is the only British port now serving this market. The nearest alternative port to Holyhead is Liverpool; the journey from Dublin to Liverpool is approximately twice the length of that from Dublin to Holyhead. This makes the Dublin to Liverpool journey so much longer that the Liverpool port is not substitutable for Holyhead for the purpose of passenger and car ferry services.

(64) In the present circumstances Sea Containers could not, if they wished to introduce a ferry service on the central corridor route, do so without substantially increasing the length of the crossing or building a new port themselves. The latter course of action would not be economically or physically realistic.

(65) Therefore Sealink, in its capacity as port authority, has a dominant position in the market for the provision of port facilities for car and passenger ferry operations on the central corridor route between the United Kingdom and Ireland.

(c) Abuse of dominant position

(66) An undertaking which occupies a dominant position in the provision of an essential facility and itself uses that facility (i. e. a facility or infrastructure, without access to which competitors cannot provide services to their customers), and which refuses other companies access to that facility without objective justification or grants access to competitors only on terms less favourable than those which it gives its own services, infringes Article 86 if the other conditions of that Article are met (6). An undertaking in a dominant position may not discriminate in favour of its own activities in a related market. The owner of an essential facility which uses its power in one market in order to protect or strengthen its position in another related market, in particular, by refusing to grant access to a competitor, or by granting access on less favourable terms than those of its own services, and thus imposing a competitive disadvantage on its competitor, infringes Article 86.

(67) This principle applies when the competitor seeking access to the essential facilities is a new entrant into the relevant market. In the Hoffmann-La Roche case (7), the Court said:

"The concept of abuse is an objective concept relating to the behaviour of an undertaking in a dominant position which is such as to influence the structure of a market where, as a result of the very presence of an undertaking in question, the degree of competition is weakened and which, through recourse to methods different to those which condition normal competition in products or services on the basis of the transactions of commercial operators, has the effect of hindering the maintenance of the degree of competition still existing in the market or the growth of that competition"

(…)

(70) Sealink consistently delayed and raised difficulties concerning SC's possible use of existing facilities on the west side of the port. It was not until 21 June 1993 that Sealink stated its willingness to permit SC to operate from temporary facilities, at its own expense, on the eastern side on the port, until such time as the redevelopment works required them to be moved. At the hearing, it became clear that redevelopment work was intended to start before SC's fast ferry service, thus rendering the offer meaningless. The Commission con-

siders that Sealink did not conduct its negotiations with Sea Containers by proposing or seeking solutions to the problems it was raising and that its rejection of all of SC's proposals without making any counter offer or attempting to negotiate was not consistent with the obligations on an undertaking which enjoys a dominant position in relation to an essential facility. Neither was it the conduct which would have been expected from an independent port authority. This is borne out by the fact that Sealink gave itself rapid approval for its own fast ferry service. To sum up, SSP treated the request by SC in a discriminatory manner in comparison with that of SSL.

(71) At no stage during the negotiations which took place between June 1992 and March 1993 did Sealink set out any proposals of its own concerning SC's proposal to solve the problems raised by Sealink by constructing, at SC's own expense, temporary facilities in the port. Its actions in this respect were entirely negative and consisted of raising difficulties associated with each of the four options put forward by SC.

(72) Until 1 October 1993, Sealink was unwilling to provide Sea Containers with the slots it had requested to commence a service from existing facilities.

(73) Sealink did not consult the two ferry operators at the port of Holyhead on its redevelopment plans.

(74) Sealink never set up any procedures for dealing with its responsibilities as harbour operator to ensure that it carried out its duties to other ferry operators. Sealink never consulted SC about ways of solving the difficulties Sealink identified. Sealink approved promptly its own timetable for its ferry operations in 1993 and 1994 but refused to discuss SC's 1994 timetable until the autumn of 1993. During 1993 Sealink altered its development plan for the east side of the harbour several times without consultation with SC, often in order to suit its own needs, although later versions of the plan made it more difficult to allow SC to install temporary facilities in 1994 on the east side. Sealink itself admitted that its other proposals to SC for 1994 might lead to congestion, but it refused to allow SC to have its own facilities. Although SC said that the timetable suggested to it by Sealink for 1994 was unsatisfactory, until October 1993 Sealink never claimed to have considered any modification in its own 1994 timetable. At the hearing Sealink argued that it had no duty to let in a new entrant if the overall service at the port would deteriorate as a result, but Sealink never had consultations with SC to see if this alleged result was unavoidable. It appears that Sealink also omitted to consult B& I about its plans to redevelop the port of Holyhead.

(75) It is the Commission's view that in the circumstances of the present case an independent harbour authority, which would of course have had an interest in increasing revenue at the port, would at least have considered whether the interests of existing and proposed users of the port could best be reconciled by a solution involving modest changes in the allocated slot times or in any plans for the development of the harbour. In situations such as the present one, unless a solution is considered fully and discussed with all the interests involved, it is likely that a port authority which is not independent will prefer an arrangement which minimizes inconvenience to itself (especially in relation to its own operations as a user) but which does not necessarily provide non-discriminatory access to the new entrant. If Sealink, in drawing up the various versions of its redevelopment plan for the east side, had always duly consulted SC (and B& I), it might have been possible to avoid the difficulty of reconciling the plan with SC's wish for temporary facilities there.

(76) While SC has no right to insist on obtaining a preferential position in any respect, the Commission concludes that until 1 October 1993, Sealink did not offer access to Holyhead on non-discriminatory terms to SC. In the context of this decision it does not seem neces-

sary to examine in detail the relevance of the considerations put forward by Sealink and described in recitals 23, 27 and 40 above. This question would be further examined in the context of any final decision in this case.

The many reform proposals under the Parliament's examination last summer dealt with this feature through different approaches. In the earliest text of the reform, a simple way of *sdemanializzazione* was provided for every kind of port area after the deliberation of a conference of public administrations; in a second proposal, this faculty was limited to touristic harbors, while in the last versions every trace of this procedure had been removed[12].

3.5 The Liberalization of Terminal Activities: The Non-Discrimination Principle and the Determination of the Relevant Market

The ports' business activities discipline, according to most of European Commission decisions, identifies the market structure in three main parts. First of all there is the terminal operator market made of those companies that load and unload freights using specific equipment[13] and, except for some special cases, hold the exclusive right to use a port area pursuant to a concession or leasehold. The second port business market is represented by those companies that, thanks to a specific port authority authorization, can serve terminal operators' activities. The third market is made of those private subjects that provide temporary employment in order to guarantee the full effectiveness of the port when the ordinary workforce of a terminal operator is not sufficient to guarantee the loading and unloading of the whole freights in a specific harbor. The liberalization of ports began from a famous judgment of the European Court of Justice regaring temporary employment regulation in Italy (case 5) ECJ, 10 December 1991, case C-179-90, Merci convenzionali porto di Genova SpA v Siderurgica Gabrielli SpA, in Rep., p. I-05889):

---

[12] Reading the report of the World Bank, *Alternative port management structures and ownership models*, Washington, 2007, it is natural to understand that the perspective of a sdemanialization of ports' areas (especially in Italy and France) would bring the possibility to use contracts scheme more flexible than concessions: the most used in the greatest ports (ex. Rottedam) is the leasehold that can be studied in: Templeman L., *Landlord and Tenant*, in Halsbury's, *Laws of England*, London, 1980, p. 1 ff., South J., *Leasehold: the case for reform*, Croydon, 2006, Lawson F.H. - Rudden B., *The Law of Property*, Oxford, 1982, Bryant J., *Straightforward Guide to Leaseholders and Commonholders Rights*, Lewes, 2005, Burn. E.H., *Modern Law of real property*, London, 1988, Callo K., *Making Sense of Leasehold Property*, London, 2005.

[13] To understand the tendency of freights ports towards the containerization of traffics, see Chilcote, P. W., *The containerization story.* in *Urban Ports and Harbor Management*, Hershman M.J. (ed.), New York, 1988.

(...)

8 By its first question the national court is essentially asking whether Article 90(1) of the Treaty, in conjunction with Articles 7, 30 and 86 thereof, precludes rules of a Member State which confer on an undertaking established in that State the exclusive right to organize dock work and require it, for the performance of such work, to have recourse to a dock-work company formed exclusively of nationals, and whether those articles give rise to rights for individuals which the national courts must protect.

9 To answer this question, as it has been reformulated, it should be noted in limine that a dock-work undertaking enjoying the exclusive right to organize dock work for third parties, as well as a dock-work company having the exclusive right to perform dock work must be regarded as undertakings to which exclusive rights have been granted by the State within the meaning of Article 90(1) of the Treaty.

10 That article provides that in the case of such undertakings Member States shall neither enact nor maintain in force any measure contrary to the rules contained in the Treaty, in particular those provided for in Article 7 and the articles relating to competition.

11 As regards, in the first place, the nationality condition imposed on the workers of the dock-work company, it should be recalled, to begin with, that according to the case-law of the Court, the general prohibition of discrimination on grounds of nationality laid down in Article 7 of the Treaty applies independently only to situations governed by Community law in regard to which the Treaty lays down no specific prohibition of discrimination (see for example Case 305/87 Commission v Greece [1989] ECR 1461, paragraphs 12 and 13; Case C-10/90 Masgio v Bundesknappschaft [1991] ECR I-1119, paragraph 12).

12 As regards workers, that principle has been specifically applied by Article 48 of the Treaty.

13 In this respect it should be recalled that Article 48 of the Treaty precludes, first and foremost, rules of a Member State which reserve to nationals of that State the right to work in an undertaking of that State, such as the Port of Genoa company which is at issue before the national court. As the Court has already declared (see, for example, the judgment in Case 66/85 Lawrie-Blum v Land Baden-Wuerttemberg [1986] ECR 2121, paragraph 17) the concept of "worker" within the meaning of Article 48 of the Treaty pre-supposes that for a certain period of time a person performs services for and under the direction of another person in return for which he receives remuneration. That description is not affected by the fact that the worker, whilst being linked to the undertaking by a relationship of employment, is linked to other workers by a relationship of association.

14 In the second place, as to the existence of exclusive rights, it should be stated first that with regard to the interpretation of Article 86 of the Treaty the Court has consistently held that an undertaking having a statutory monopoly over a substantial part of the common market may be regarded as having a dominant position within the meaning of Article 86 of the Treaty (see the judgments in Case C-41/90 Hoefner and Elser v Macrotron [1991] ECR I-1979, paragraph 28; Case C-260/89 ERT v DEP [1991] ECR I-2925, paragraph 31).

15 As regards the definition of the market in question, it may be seen from the order for reference that it is that of the organization on behalf of third persons of dock work relating to ordinary freight in the Port of Genoa and the performance of such work. Regard being had in particular to the volume of traffic in that port and its importance in relation to maritime import and export operations as a whole in the Member State concerned, that market may be regarded as constituting a substantial part of the common market.

16 It should next be stated that the simple fact of creating a dominant position by granting exclusive rights within the meaning of Article 90(1) of the Treaty is not as such incompatible with Article 86.

17 However, the Court has had occasion to state, in this respect, that a Member State is in breach of the prohibitions contained in those two provisions if the undertaking in question, merely by exercising the exclusive rights granted to it, cannot avoid abusing its dominant position (see the judgment in Case C-41/90 Hoefner, cited above, paragraph 29) or when such rights are liable to create a situation in which that undertaking is induced to commit such abuses (see the judgment in Case C-260/89 ERT, cited above, paragraph 37).

18 According to subparagraphs (a), (b) and (c) of the second paragraph of Article 86 of the Treaty, such abuse may in particular consist in imposing on the persons requiring the services in question unfair purchase prices or other unfair trading conditions, in limiting technical development, to the prejudice of consumers, or in the application of dissimilar conditions to equivalent transactions with other trading parties.

19 In that respect it appears from the circumstances described by the national court and discussed before the Court of Justice that the undertakings enjoying exclusive rights in accordance with the procedures laid down by the national rules in question are, as a result, induced either to demand payment for services which have not been requested, to charge disproportionate prices, to refuse to have recourse to modern technology, which involves an increase in the cost of the operations and a prolongation of the time required for their performance, or to grant price reductions to certain consumers and at the same time to offset such reductions by an increase in the charges to other consumers.

20 In these circumstances it must be held that a Member State creates a situation contrary to Article 86 of the Treaty where it adopts rules of such a kind as those at issue before the national court, which are capable of affecting trade between Member States as in the case of the main proceedings, regard being had to the factors mentioned in paragraph 15 of this judgment relating to the importance of traffic in the Port of Genoa.

21 As regards the interpretation of Article 30 of the Treaty requested by the national court, it is sufficient to recall that a national measure which has the effect of facilitating the abuse of a dominant position capable of affecting trade between Member States will generally be incompatible with that article, which prohibits quantitative restrictions on imports and all measures having equivalent effect (see the judgment in Case 13/77 GB-INNO-BM v ATAB [1977] ECR 2115, paragraph 35) in so far as such a measure has the effect of making more difficult and hence of impeding imports of goods from other Member States.

22 In the main proceedings it may be seen from the national court' s findings that the unloading of the goods could have been effected at a lesser cost by the ship' s crew, so that compulsory recourse to the services of the two undertakings enjoying exclusive rights involved extra expense and was therefore capable, by reason of its effect on the prices of the goods, of affecting imports.

23 It should be emphasized in the third place that even within the framework of Article 90, the provisions of Articles 30, 48 and 86 of the Treaty have direct effect and give rise for interested parties to rights which the national courts must protect (see in particular, as regards Article 86 of the Treaty, the judgment in Case 155/73 Sacchi [1974] ECR 409, paragraph 18).

24 The answer to the first question, as reformulated, should therefore be that:

Article 90(1) of the EEC Treaty, in conjunction with Articles 30, 48 and 86 of the Treaty, precludes rules of a Member State which confer on an undertaking established in that State the exclusive right to organize dock work and require it for that purpose to have recourse to a dock-work company formed exclusively of national workers;

Articles 30, 48 and 86 of the Treaty, in conjunction with Article 90, give rise to rights for individuals which the national courts must protect.

The second question

25 In its second question the national court is in essence asking whether Article 90(2) of the Treaty must be interpreted as meaning that a dock-work undertaking and/or company in the situation described in the first question must be regarded as being entrusted with the operation of services of general economic interest within the meaning of that provision.

26 For the purpose of answering that question it should be borne in mind that in order that the derogation to the application of the rules of the Treaty set out in Article 90(2) thereof may take effect, it is not sufficient for the undertaking in question merely to have been entrusted by the public authorities with the operation of a service of general economic interest, but it must be shown in addition that the application of the rules of the Treaty obstructs the performance of the particular tasks assigned to the undertaking and that the interests of the Community are not affected (see the judgments in Case 311/84 CBEM v Compagnie Luxembourgeoise [1985] ECR 3261, paragraph 17, and in Case C-41/90 Hoefner, cited above, paragraph 24).

27 In that respect it must be held that it does not appear either from the documents supplied by the national court or from the observations submitted to the Court of Justice that dock work is of a general economic interest exhibiting special characteristics as compared with the general economic interest of other economic activities or, even if it were, that the application of the rules of the Treaty, in particular those relating to competition and freedom of movement, would be such as to obstruct the performance of such a task.

28 The answer to the second question should therefore be that Article 90(2) of the Treaty must be interpreted as meaning that a dock-work undertaking and/or company in the position described in the first question may not be regarded, on the basis only of the factors set out in that description, as being entrusted with the operation of services of general economic interest within the meaning of that provision.

The main thrust of European Union port law is the improvement and maintenance of a high level of competition inside the port's markets. It is important to make reference to the decisions and praxis of the EU Commission, which in most cases, identified the relevant port market, in order to evaluate a violation of European competition rules, to a wider area than the port one, including also those ports that are located near the area where the behavior under investigation by the Commission is executed.

The European Commission, during its antitrust investigations, adopted a larger interpretation of the "geographic area" of a single port, clarifying, for example, that Northern European ports have to be considered as a whole geographic market including hinterland markets, i.e., those overland connections among the ports and the inland and hinterland terminals[14] (case 6) COMP/JV. 56-Hutchinson/ECT, in OJEU C 293 of 19th October 2001, p. 2):

(…)

A Relevant Market

1. Product markets

12. Hutchison and ECT are both container terminal operators providing stevedoring services to deep-sea container vessels in Northern Europe. There is no, or only very marginal, overlap between the parties to the concentration with regard to other business activities.

13. Deep-sea container terminal throughput can be broken down by traffic flow as follows:

(a) hinterland traffic (also known as ëdirect deep-seaí), that is containers transported directly onto/from a deep-sea container vessel to/from the hinterland (via barge, truck or train), and

(b) transhipment traffic, that is containers destined for onward transportation to other ports. Transhipment traffic can in turn be sub-divided into relay traffic and feeder traffic. ëRelayí refers to containers moved between deep-sea vessel and deep-sea vessel (for example, containers transferred from a Far East liner shipping service to a transatlantic service). ëFeederí concerns the movement to or from deep-sea vessels from or to short-sea vessels (feeder vessels).

14. In its decision of 3 July 2001 in Hutchison/RCPM/ECT, the Commission concluded that the provision of stevedoring services in respect of hinterland traffic and transhipment traffic each constituted a discrete relevant product market. It also concluded that there was insufficient evidence to justify a further breakdown of the transhipment market into discrete feeder and relay markets.

15. There have been no changes in the market in the five months that have elapsed since July 2001 that might cast doubt on the continuing validity of the above conclusion.

16. The parties agree with the above product market definitions.

2. Geographic dimension

Hinterland

17. In its decision in Hutchison/RCPM/ECT the Commission concluded that it was possible to distinguish a United Kingdom/Ireland market (on which Hutchison was present) and several North Continental markets (on which ECT was present). In view of the limited degree of overlap between the North Continent and the United Kingdom/Ireland hinterland markets, the Commission considered that the concentration. It should be noted that the notifying parties have agreed that the Commission may use all of the information (including market studies and statistics) submitted by the parties in Case JV.55 for the purposes of assessing the instant operation would neither create nor strengthen a dominant position on any hinterland market. There was therefore no need to further assess the impact of the concentration on these markets.

---

[14] A complete overview of the competition between ports can be read in Fleming, D. K., *Port rivalry, co-operation, merger*, in *Maritime Policy & Management*, 1983 p. 207 ff.

18. The available evidence indicates that the above conclusion is still valid. The market studies cited in support of that conclusion are still the most recent reliable and comprehensive source of information on the services and markets in question. There is no evidence to suggest that either the hinterland markets or the parties presence on those markets have undergone any significant change in the period since July 2001.

19. The parties agree with the Commissionís conclusion that as there is little or no overlap between Hutchison and ECT on any conceivable hinterland market there is no need to assess further the impact of the concentration on these markets.

Transhipment

20. The available market studies and other evidence indicate that the potential substitutes for transhipment traffic in Northern Europe include all main deep-sea ports in the Gothenburg ñ Le Havre range;

21. The parties have argued that the geographic market for the provision of stevedoring services to transhipment traffic should be extended to encompass ports in Southern Europe. The parties point in particular to growth in the volumes handled by these ports as evidence of increasing competition to Northern European ports for transshipment traffic.

22. In the Commissionís view, with the possible exception of Algeciras, Southern European ports do not pose any serious threat to Northern European ports in respect of transhipment traffic. The growth in volumes is largely explained by the fact that a number of Mediterranean ports now act as regional hubs from which cargoes are fed to those Southern European ports that generate insufficient volumes to justify a direct call by a deep-sea container service. There is little overlap between Northern and Southern European ports with respect to that traffic. As for Algeciras, [Ö] of the throughput of the main container terminal, which is controlled by the A.P. M¯ller Group, is accounted for by Maersk Sealand, an A.P. M¯ller subsidiary. These volumes represent captive production, which should not be included in the market when determining market shares. The inclusion of Algeciras in the relevant market would therefore have little or no impact on the structure of that market.

Conclusion on the relevant market

23. It is concluded that the relevant market to be considered in this case is the market for the provision in Northern Europe of stevedoring services for transhipment traffic carried by deep-sea container vessels.

The port's market border have, therefore, to be determined taking into account both the products and the geographical features as clarified by the EC Commission praxis.

The application of European Union law to terminal operators guarantees a more efficient market with the clear aim to promote the competitiveness of European ports. For example, in another important case we see that European Commission evaluated the legality of a concentration considering port range made by Alexandria-Port Piraeus, Greece and East Coast of Italy[15]. The relevant market of prod-

---

15 For a comparative analysis of competition in the United States, see Moody's Investors Service, *Competition among West Coast ports pressures credit outlook*, New York, 1998.

ucts was divided in: short-sea traffic, feeder traffic, hinterland traffic and transshipment traffic (case 7) European Commission, COMP/M. 1674, in OJEC, C 253 of 4th september 1999, Maersk/ECT):

(…)

9. According to the parties, the relevant product market is that of the provision of container terminal services, i.e. loading and unloading, storing, etc. These services may also be referred to as stevedoring services. Deep-sea container ships transport goods between continents, whereas smaller short sea vessels are generally used for transport over shorter distances (short-sea traffic) and for transshipping containers from and to deep-sea ports ('feeder' traffic). Given the different berthing and landside equipment facilities needed for deep-sea and short-sea vessels, a distinction for stevedoring services may be made according to the size of the vessels which require handling, i.e. deep-sea or short-sea vessels. Furthermore, container traffic may be related to a particular hinterland that is connected to the port of origin or final destination. ('hinterland traffic'), but traffic may also be brought to a port for further sea transportation to and from other ports ('transshipment traffic'). Although the ability to attract a particular kind of traffic may be relevant to determine the particular competitive strengths of a container terminal, it is considered that different markets for hinterland- and transshipment traffic of containers do not exist, given that demand and supply involves the same players and the same equipment and processes. In any event, the exact definition of the product market may be left aside because in all alternative product definitions considered, the merger will not lead to the creation or reinforcement of a dominant position.

Geographic aspects

10. As stated, ports serve a particular hinterland or serve as hub ports for smaller transshipment ports. The geographic area that they generally serve determines the geographic scope related to their services. One can therefore determine the geographic ranges (or catchment areas) which are served form a particular group of ports. For example, all deep sea container ports in Northern Europe are considered to belong to a single geographic market, due to the routes undertaken by shipping lines (see the Commission decision in P&O/Royal Nedlloyd). In that case the Commission came to the conclusion that substitution between Northern European and Mediterranean ports does not take place to any considerable degree, because of their different catchment areas.

11. In this case, the new Port Said terminal is mainly to serve Egypt for hinterland traffic and the eastern part of the Mediterranean Sea and the Black Sea area for transshipment purposes (also referred to as the 'EastMed/Black Sea range'). This is generally recognized by the industry as a separate geographic area for container terminal services. The port range involved, according to the parties, is that of Alexandria-Port Piraeus, and therefore includes Greece. Independent sources also include ports on the East Coast of Italy in the market. This indicates that the market possibly extends to a larger amount of ports in the Eastern Mediterranean area. However, the question of what range constitutes the exact relevant geographic area can be left aside, because the operation will not create or strengthen a dominant position in the Community or the EEA, as demonstrated below.

V ASSESSMENT

12. In case the market to consider is the range of the eastern part of the Mediterranean Sea and the Black Sea excluding Italian ports, the merger will not lead to any addition in market shares, neither Maersk nor ECT being active in this area. In any event, the market share which the new entity may attain over the next five years on the basis of its planned capacity will not surpass some [between 10 - 20 %] (figures based on the overall capacity currently available in that range and an expected 1 million TEU4 capacity at Port Said). Much of the traffic handled at the terminal is expected to consist of transhipment traffic. In the transshipment segment in the Eastmed/Black Sea range, according to the business plan, the new entity is expected to achieve a share of transshipment of some [between 25 - 35 %] by the year 2005.

13. If Italian ports on the East Coast of Italy are included in the market, account should be taken of a container terminal in Trieste, in which ECT has a controlling interest. However, Maersk has no activities in this range, so also on this wider market definition there is no effect on competition relating to an overlap of activities of Maersk and ECT. In any event, if the capacity of ECT in Trieste is added to the planned capacity of the new Port Said terminal, the share of capacity attributable to ECT/Maersk is expected not attain more than [between 15 - 25 %] in the EastMed/Black Sea range until 2005.

14. Given the above data, the merger will not lead to the creation or strengthening of a dominant position on any of the alternative markets considered.

According to the above principles, it is important to describe the limits on the ability to use the ports area imposed by terminal operators and the organization rules imposed by European Union law. Indeed, European Union law placed great weight on the prevention of abusive behavior, *ex* art. 102 TFUE, cartels *ex* art. 101 TFUE and mergers[16]. Many discussions have referred to the power of concessionaires to avail themselves of the infrastructures and facilities located in different port areas in order to satisfy their business needs. Indeed the European Commission clarified that the use of an infrastructure has to be guaranteed to everyone who is interested and on a non-discriminatory basis if there are not similar facilities in the same relevant market (case 8) European Commission, 21 December 1993, port of Rødby, in OJEC L 55 , 26th february1994, p. 52):

(…)

Similarly, the Roedby-Puttgarden route cannot easily be substituted by the other passenger sea routes between Sweden and Germany. In view of the excellent motorway connections between Roedby and Helsingoer, which is only fifteen minutes by boat from the Swedish port of Helsingborg, the direct link between Germany and Sweden, Travemuende-Trelleborg, in 1991 only accounted for 1 102 463 passengers and 159 484 cars, while the Roedby-Puttgarden route accounted for 8 024 654 passengers and 1 209 065 cars during the

16 See Fleming, D. K., *Port rivalry, co-operation, merger*, in *Maritime Policy & Management*, 1983 p. 207 ff. and Van Hooydonk E., *The regime of Port Authorities under European Law including an analysis of the Port Services Directive,* in *European Seaports Law, EU Law of Ports and Ports Services in the Port Package,* Antwerpen-Apeldoorm, Maklu, 2003.

same period. This indicates that passengers prefer the Puttgarden-Helsingborg route, regarded as more direct and faster (the Travemuende-Trelleborg crossing between Sweden and Germany takes from seven to nine hours). Similarly, while the Goeteborg-Frederikshavn crossing meets some of the traffic demand on the route between Sweden, on the one hand, and Denmark and the rest of western Europe, on the other, it still has drawbacks compared with the Roedby-Puttgarden route due to the duration of the crossing (three and a quarter hours instead of one hour) and poorer motorway connections.

Lastly, the route across the Great Belt (between the islands of Zealand and Fyn to Jutland) involves a sea crossing of the same duration of Roedby-Puttgarden but adds 165 km to the distance to be travelled on land between Copenhagen and Hamburg. This alternative route is thus not as advantageous as the main Helsingoer-Copenhagen-Roedby-Puttgarden route.

It is true that, once the proposed fixed link across the Great Belt between Zealand and Fyn is built, it will be easier to divert some of the traffic between Sweden and Copenhagen, on the one hand, and Germany, on the other hand, through Jutland. However:
- the fixed link is not yet in service (the rail link is to open in 1995, the motorway link in 1998),
- a charge will in any event be made for the Great Belt link, as for the sea crossings.

Accordingly, the Commission considers that the Roedby-Puttgarden crossing is an important link and cannot easily be substituted by the other existing forms of transport and routes between Denmark and Sweden, on the one hand, and Germany, on the other.

(…)

The relevant market

(7) The relevant market is the market for the organization of port services in Denmark for ferry services operating on the Roedby-Puttgarden route (passengers and vehicles).

As the Court of Justice has stated, the organization on behalf of a third party of port operations in a single port can constitute a relevant market within the meaning of Article 86 (Porto di Genova judgment of 10 December 1991, Case C 179/90, paragraph 15).

This is due to the fact that operators wishing to provide a transport service on a given sea route must have access to the port facilities located at both ends of the crossing in order to attain their objective.

In the case in question, there is no real alternative with the same advantages as those offered by the port of Roedby for sea transport between eastern Denmark, on the one hand, and Germany and the rest of western Europe, on the other (see point (5) above).

(8) Roedby handles over 70,8 % of passengers and 87,9 % of lorries travelling by sea between Denmark and Germany. In 1991 8 024 654 passengers and 207 255 lorries transited through Roedby, representing a turnover of DM 320 million. The port of Roedby thus constitutes a substantial part of the common market.

(9) In addition, the maritime transport services between Roedby and Puttgarden constitute a neighbouring but separate market which may be affected by the behaviour of an undertaking on the market for the organization of port services.

As emerges from the particulars given in point 5, the Roedby-Puttgarden route has specific characteristics as a result of which it is not a straightforward alternative to the other transport routes and faces only limited competition from them (see Ahmed Saeed judgment (1)).

Dominant position

(10) According to the case-law of the Court, an undertaking with a legal monopoly of supply of certain services may hold a dominant position within the meaning of Article 86 of the Treaty (Télémarketing case, No C-311/84).

DSB is a public undertaking which, by virtue of the exclusive right granted by the State in its capacity as port authority, holds a dominant position in Denmark on the market for the organization of port operations with regard to the transport of passengers and vehicles by ferry between Roedby and Puttgarden. This is dominant position which is relevant in considering the compatibility with the Treaty of the state measures referred to in this decision.

(11) DSB also operates, in conjunction with DB, as a carrier on the Roedby-Puttgarden route. The Court of First Instance recently found that the links between the members of a liner conference (within the meaning of Council Regulation (EEC) No 4056/86 laying down detailed rules for the application of Articles 85 and 86 of the Treaty to maritime transport) may be such that the positions of the member undertakings must be considered jointly in order to determine the existence of an abuse of dominant position within the meaning of Article 86 of the EC Treaty (2).

The links established by DSB and DB in order to operate the Roedby-Puttgarden route (see paragraph 4) are similar to those between members of a conference (fixing of common rates, coordination of timetables, joint marketing).

Consequently, the position of DB and DSB on the route in question must be assessed jointly.

DB and DSB are the only ferry companies operating between Roedby and Puttgarden and therefore hold a joint dominant position on that route. This dominant position on the market for transport services is protected by state measures related to the market for the organization of port operations on which the dominant position referred to in point 10 is exercised.

Abuse of dominant position

(12) The refusal to allow 'Euro-Port A/S', a subsidiary of the Swedish group 'Stena Rederi AB' (Stena) to operate from Roedby has the effect of eliminating a potential competitor on the Roedby-Puttgarden route and hence of strengthening the joint dominant position of DSB and DB on that route.

According to the case law of the Court, an abuse within the meaning of Article 86 is committed in cases where, without any objective necessity, an undertaking holding a dominant position on a particular market reserves to itself an ancillary activity which might be carried out by another undertaking as part of its activities on a neighbouring but separate market, with the possibility of eliminating all competition from such undertaking (Case 311/84 CBEM v. CLT and IPB [1985] ECR 3261, paragraph 27).

Thus an undertaking that owns or manages and uses itself an essential facility, i.e. a facility or infrastructure without which its competitors are unable to offer their services to customers, and refuses to grant them access to such facility is abusing its dominant position.

Consequently, an undertaking that owns or manages an essential port facility from which it provides a maritime transport service may not, without objective justification, refuse to grant a shipowner wishing to operate on the same maritime route access to that facility without infringing Article 86.

(13) According to the case-law of the Court (judgment of 13 December 1991 in Case C-18/88, paragraphs 20 and 21), Article 90 (1) prohibits Member States from placing, by law, regulation or administrative provision, public undertakings and undertakings to which they grant exclusive rights in a position in which those undertakings could not place themselves by their own conduct without infringing Article 86. The Court added that, where the extension of the dominant position of a public undertaking or an undertaking to which the State has granted exclusive rights resulted from a State measure, such a measure constituted an infringement of Article 90, read in conjunction with Article 86 of the Treaty. This principle was confirmed in the judgment of 17 November 1992 in Cases C-271, 281 and 289/90 (paragraph 36).

Thus, for the reasons given above, any firm in the same position as DSB which refused to grant another shipping operator access to the port it controlled would be abusing a dominant position. Where, as in the present case, a Member State has refused such access and has strengthened the effects of the refusal by also refusing to authorize the construction of a new port, it constitutes a State measure in breach of Article 90, read in conjunction with Article 86.

(14) The reasons given by the Danish Transport Ministry for rejecting both requests of 'Euro-Port A/S', a subsidiary of the Swedish group 'Stena Rederi AB' (Stena) are the following:
- the plan of 'Euro-Port A/S', a subsidiary of the Swedish group 'Stena Rederi AB' (Stena), to build a new terminal is not acceptable as that undertaking has allegedly 'not established that there is an unsatisfied demand for a ferry service' and it is 'most unlikely that such a demand would arise' (letter of 9 May 1990 referred to in paragraph 1),
- 'Euro-Port A/S', a subsidiary of the Swedish group 'Stena Rederi AB' (Stena) could not operate from the existing port facilities as this would have the effect of preventing the companies already operating in the port from expanding their activities.

This line of resoning was set out in the letter dated 8 August 1990 from the Danish Transport Minister, by the summer of 1991, DSB and DB had increased the number of daily sailings between Roedby and Puttgarden from 98 to 112.

The Commission concludes from the foregoing that:
- there was indeed an unsatisfied demand for ferry services in May 1990 since one year later DSB and DB had expanded their services,
- the increase in the activities of DB and DSB in 1991 confirms that the port of Roedby was not saturated.

(15) The Commission also considers that there is no evidence that the existing facilities at Roedby would today be saturated or that, subject to alterations which Stena has informed the Commission it is prepared to finance, existing port capacity is unable to cope with an increase in trade.

The Commission also notes that the Swedish group 'Stena Rederi AB' (Stena) has acquired land adjacent to the port facilities of Roedby which is perfectly suitable for development as a terminal by Stena.

It therefore concludes that there are no technical constraints preventing the Stena group from sailing between Roedby and Puttgarden.

(16) In their letter of 22 February 1993 which constitutes the reply to the letter of formal notice sent by the Commission on 24 November 1992, the Danish authorities rejected the latter's request, stressing that their refusals were justified under Community law. They stated that it would be impossible to allow Stena access to the existing facilities, giving tech-

nical reasons and referring for the first time, without any further details, to obligations incumbent upon DB and DSB in the general interest.

This would appear to indicate that, in the view of the Danish authorities, the technical feasibility of access to the port is not a problem or is not the only problem and that they also have a duty to protect the public undertaking DSB from a competitor on the market for ferry services.

Nor can the Commission share the view of the Danish authorities that the alleged saturation of the existing port facilities would make pointless any attempt to introduce competition since this could not in any event lead to an increase in the number of sailings between Roedby and Puttgarden.

Even on a saturated market, an improvement in the quality of products or services offered or a reduction in prices as a result of competition is a definite advantage for consumers; this could also lead to an increase in demand which, in the present case, could be met by expanding the port.

It is clear from the foregoing that the statement by the Danish authorities that they would be prepared to re-examine the request to build a new port made by the Stena subsidiary in 1989 and rejected in 1990 does not constitute a firm commitment either to approve the request or to allow the Stena subsidiaries access to the existing port. Refusing to acknowledge that they have any obligation under Community law, the Danish authorities are prepared only to review the case without stating whether or when the Stena subsidiaries will be granted the right to operate on the route in question on comparable terms to those offered to operators already present on the market. This position, which in any case further defers recognition of the legitimate rights of the Stena subsidiaries, does not constitute a satisfactory reply to the letter of formal notice sent by the Commission to the Danish Government.

Effects on trade between Member States

(17) The double refusal referred to in this decision has the effect of preventing the entry of new operators on the market for ferry services between Denmark and Germany. Therefore it has an appreciable effect on trade between Member States, taking account of the volume of traffic on the Roedby-Puttgarden route (see paragraphs 5 and 8 above).

3.6 The Technical Nautical Services Ancillary to Navigation: Liberalization and Self-Consumption

Technical nautical services are those activities, different from loading and unloading, which serves the ships arriving to and leaving from the port, in order to guarantee safe navigation inside the port and on the coast, including the protection of infrastructures, persons, and the environment[17].

[17] See Carbone S.M. – Munari F., *Safety of navigation and efficiency in port from the view of technical-nautical services ancillary to navigation: remarks on the European Commission green paper on ports and maritime infrastructure,* in *Dir. Mar.*, 1998, p. 902 ff. and Carbone S.M. - Munari F., *The regime of technical-nautical services (pilotage, towage, mooring-men) under European law,* in *Comunicazioni e studi,* 2002, p. 177 ff.

There are four technical nautical services ancillary to navigation: pilotage, towage, mooring, and maneuvering. In Italy, the Maritime Authority is the competent public administration in the matter of navigation with the power to regulate and monitor the entry of ships into the port as well as their exit. According to the specific national laws, those services can be mandatory in case of emergency under the proportionality principle.

Nevertheless, European Court of Justice judgments liberalized them. In this legal context member States' restrictions on the provision of these services are unlawful. The first case that needs to be read concerns pilotage (case 9) ECJ, 17 May 1994, Case C-18/93, Corsica Ferries Italia Srl v Corpo dei Piloti del Porto di Genova, in Rep., p. I-01783):

(...)

17 In questions 1 and 3 the Tribunale essentially wishes to know whether Community law precludes the application in a Member State, for identical piloting services, of different tariffs depending on whether or not the undertaking which provides shipping services between two Member States operates a vessel which is authorized for maritime cabotage, that being reserved to vessels flying the flag of that State.

18 The Court notes to begin with that Article 5 of the Treaty, referred to in question 1, which provides that Member States must ensure fulfilment of their obligations arising out of the Treaty, is worded so generally that there can be no question of applying it autonomously when the situation concerned is governed by a specific provision of the Treaty (see the judgment in Joined Cases C-78/90 to C-83/90 Compagnie Commerciale de l' Ouest and Others v Receveur Principal des Douanes de La Pallice Port [1992] ECR I-1847, paragraph 19).

19 Secondly, the Court has consistently held that Article 7 of the EEC Treaty (Article 6 of the EC Treaty), which lays down the general principle of the prohibition of discrimination on grounds of nationality, applies independently only to situations governed by Community law in respect of which the Treaty lays down no specific prohibition of discrimination (see the judgment in Case C-179/90 Merci Convenzionali Porto di Genova v Siderurgica Gabrielli [1991] ECR I-5889, paragraph 11).

20 In the field of freedom to provide services, the principle of the prohibition of discrimination is given specific expression in Article 59 of the Treaty.

21 As regards the determination of the services to which Article 59 of the Treaty is to be applied, it should be noted that a system of differential tariffs for piloting services affects a transport undertaking such as Corsica Ferries in two ways. Piloting services are services provided for consideration to the shipping undertakings by the corporation, and differences in tariffs affect those undertakings as recipients of the services. However, the differences in tariffs affect the undertakings primarily in their capacity as providers of maritime transport services, in so far as they have an effect on the cost of those services and thus place them at a disadvantage in comparison with economic operators who benefit from the preferential tariffs.

22 In assessing the tariff system at issue before the national court from the point of view of the freedom to provide maritime transport services, the Court must consider, firstly, to what extent the principle of non-discrimination laid down in Article 59 of the Treaty ap-

plies in the maritime transport sector and, secondly, whether such a system causes discrimination on the grounds of nationality.

23 Article 61(1) of the Treaty provides that freedom to provide services in the field of transport is to be governed by the provisions of the title of the Treaty relating to transport (see in particular the judgments in Case 13/83 Parliament v Council [1985] ECR 1513, paragraph 62, and Case C-49/89 Corsica Ferries France v Direction Générale des Douanes Françaises [1989] ECR 4441, paragraph 10).

24 It follows that, as the Court held in its judgments in Corsica Ferries France, cited above, paragraph 11, and in Joined Cases 209 to 213/84 Ministère Public v Asjes [1986] ECR 1425, paragraph 37, in the transport sector the objective laid down in Article 59 of the Treaty of abolishing during the transitional period restrictions on freedom to provide services should have been attained in the framework of the common policy provided for in Articles 74 and 75 of the Treaty.

25 With regard in particular to maritime transport, Article 84(2) of the Treaty provides that the Council may decide whether, to what extent and by what procedure appropriate provisions may be laid down for that kind of transport.

26 Thus the Council, on the basis of those provisions, adopted Regulation (EEC) No 4055/86 of 22 December 1986 applying the principle of freedom to provide services to maritime transport between Member States and between Member States and third countries (OJ 1986 L 378, p. 1), which entered into force on 1 January 1987.

27 Article 1(1) of that regulation provides that:

"Freedom to provide maritime transport services between Member States and between Member States and third countries shall apply in respect of nationals of Member States who are established in a Member State other than that of the person for whom the services are intended."

28 As regards the substantive scope of Regulation No 4055/86, the wording of Article 1 makes it clear that the regulation applies to maritime transport services between Member States of the kind at issue in the main proceedings.

29 As to the persons covered by Regulation No 4055/86, Article 1 refers to nationals of Member States who are established in a Member State other than that of the person for whom the services are intended, and does not mention the registration of or the flag flown by the vessels operated by the transport undertakings.

30 Moreover, the freedom to provide maritime transport services between Member States, and in particular the prohibition of discrimination on grounds of nationality, may be relied on by an undertaking as against the State in which it is established, if the services are provided for persons established in another Member State. In a case such as that in point in the main proceedings, an undertaking established in one Member State and operating a liner service, covered by Regulation No 4055/86, to another State, provides those services, by reason of their very nature, inter alia for persons established in the latter State.

31 Consequently, the situation at issue in the main proceedings is not a purely national matter, and the Italian Government' s argument on this point must be rejected.

32 In considering next whether the tariff system at issue in the main proceedings is compatible with Regulation No 4055/86, it should be noted that paragraphs 6 and 7 of this judgment show that the system gives preferential treatment to vessels permitted to engage in maritime cabotage, in other words, those flying the Italian flag.

33 Such a system indirectly discriminates between economic operators according to their nationality, since vessels flying the national flag are generally operated by national economic operators, whereas transport undertakings from other Member States as a rule do not operate ships registered in the State applying that system.

34 That finding is not affected by the fact that the class of less favourably treated economic operators may also include national transport undertakings which operate vessels not registered in their State, or by the fact that the class of operators given favourable treatment may include transport undertakings from other Member States which operate vessels registered in the aforesaid State, since the class receiving favourable treatment consists essentially of nationals of that State.

35 It follows that Article 1(1) of Regulation No 4055/86 prohibits a Member State from applying different tariffs for identical piloting services, depending on whether or not an undertaking, even one from that Member State, which provides maritime transport services between that Member State and another Member State operates a vessel authorized to engage in maritime cabotage, which is reserved to vessels flying the flag of that State.

36 The corporation and the Italian Government are wrong in attempting to justify the different tariffs on grounds of navigational safety, national transport policy or protection of the environment. Even if those objectives were capable of justifying intervention by the public authorities in the transport sector, a discriminatory tariff system such as that at issue before the national court does not appear necessary for attaining those objectives.

37 The answer to questions 1 and 3 must therefore be that Article 1(1) of Regulation No 4055/86, which gives effect to the principle of freedom to provide services, and in particular to the prohibition of discrimination, in the field of maritime transport between Member States, precludes the application in a Member State of different tariffs for identical piloting services, depending on whether or not the undertaking which provides maritime transport services between two Member States operates a vessel authorized to engage in maritime cabotage, which is reserved to vessels flying the flag of that State.

The rules on competition

38 By question 5(1) and (2) the national court essentially wishes to know whether Articles 90(1) and 86 of the Treaty prohibit a national authority from enabling an undertaking which has the exclusive right of providing compulsory piloting services in a substantial part of the common market to apply different tariffs to maritime transport undertakings, depending on whether they operate transport services between Member States or between ports situated on national territory.

39 It should be noted that the corporation, the defendant in the main proceedings, has received from the public authorities the exclusive right to provide compulsory piloting services in the port of Genoa.

40 An undertaking which has a legal monopoly in a substantial part of the common market may be regarded as occupying a dominant position within the meaning of Article 86 of the Treaty (see the judgments in Case C-41/90 Hoefner and Elser v Macrotron [1991] ECR

I-1979, paragraph 28; Case C-260/89 ERT v DEP and Kouvelas [1991] ECR I-2925, paragraph 31; and Merci Convenzionali Porto di Genova, cited above, paragraph 14).

41 The market in question is that of piloting services in the port of Genoa. Having regard in particular to the volume of traffic in that port and its importance in relation to maritime import and export operations as a whole in the Member State concerned, that market may be regarded as constituting a substantial part of the common market (see the judgment in Merci Convenzionali Porto di Genova, cited above, paragraph 15).

42 The mere fact of creating a dominant position by granting exclusive rights within the meaning of Article 90(1) is not in itself incompatible with Article 86 of the Treaty.

43 However, a Member State infringes the prohibitions in those two articles if, by approving the tariffs adopted by the undertaking, it induces it to abuse its dominant position inter alia by applying dissimilar conditions to equivalent transactions with its trading partners, within the meaning of Article 86(c) of the Treaty.

44 Inasmuch as the discriminatory practices referred to in the order for reference affect undertakings providing transport services between two Member States, they may affect trade between Member States.

45 The answer to question 5(1) and (2) must therefore be that Article 90(1) and Article 86 of the Treaty prohibit a national authority from inducing an undertaking which has been granted the exclusive right of providing compulsory piloting services in a substantial part of the common market, by approving the tariffs adopted by it, to apply different tariffs to maritime transport undertakings, depending on whether they operate transport services between Member States or between ports situated on national territory, in so far as trade between Member States is affected.

However, European Union law allows member States to approve a detailed discipline of technical nautical services in each port, prescribing, for example, the public service standards through which the specific port's regulations can be approved in accordance with the opinion of the port authority. Such legislation must therefore comply with European law standards on state aids. Indeed, the obligation to pay a fixed fee for services has to be provided with specific motivation concerning the compensation related to public service duties, again in accordance with the European principles prescribed by the Court of Justice in the *Altmark* judgment, (See chapter 2, case 2) which allow the imposition of public service duties when there is an effective and transparent definition of the tasks, and the compensation is proportionate[18]. Indeed, according to the Court of Justice decisions, the amount of money given for the compensation of public service duties is not an illegal state aid according to art. 107 of the TFUE when it is limited to the effective costs necessary for the service supply (see case 10), ECJ, 22 November 2001, cause C-53/00, *Ferring S.A.* c. *ACOSS,* in Rep., p. I-9067):

---

[18] An identification of public goals to be pursued for the port development, see Kagan, R. A., *Patterns of Port Development: Government, Intermodal Transportation and Innovation in the United States, China and Hong Kong*, Berkeley, 1990.

(...)
30 In the event that the advantage for wholesale distributors in not being assessed to the tax on direct sales of medicines exceeds the additional costs that they bear in discharging their public service obligations, the national court asks, essentially, whether an advantage of that kind is covered by Article 90(2) of the Treaty.

31 Under Article 90(2) of the Treaty, undertakings entrusted with the operation of services of general economic interest or having the character of a revenue-producing monopoly shall be subject to the rules contained in the Treaty in so far as the application of such rules does not obstruct the performance, in law or in fact, of the particular tasks assigned to them. The development of trade must not be affected to such an extent as would be contrary to the interests of the Community.

32 If it is the case that the advantage for wholesale distributors in not being assessed to the tax on direct sales of medicines exceeds the additional costs that they bear in discharging the public service obligations imposed on them by national law, that advantage, to the extent that it exceeds the additional costs mentioned, cannot, in any event, be regarded as necessary to enable them to carry out the particular tasks assigned to them.

33 Consequently, the answer must be that Article 90(2) of the Treaty is to be interpreted as meaning that it does not cover a tax advantage enjoyed by undertakings entrusted with the operation of a public service such as those concerned in the main proceedings in so far as that advantage exceeds the additional costs of performing the public service.

Bibliography

Becet J.M., *La notion d'«extension limitée de l'urbanisation» (article L.146-4 II du Code de l'urbanisme)*, in *Annuaire de droit maritime et océanique* 2000, p. 31 ff.

Bryant J., *Straightforward Guide to Leaseholders and Commonholders Rights*, Lewes, 2005.

Burn. E.H., *Modern Law of real property*, London, 1988.

Callo K., *Making Sense of Leasehold Property*, London, 2005.

Carbone S.M., *L'equilibrio tra Autorità portuale e mercato*, in *Dir. trasp.*, 1994 p. 823 ff.

Carbone S.M. - Munari F., *Safety of navigation and efficiency in port from the view of technical-nautical services ancillary to navigation: remarks on the European Commission green paper on ports and maritime infrastructure,* in *Dir. Mar.*, 1998, p. 902 ff.

Carbone S.M. - Munari F., *La disciplina dei porti tra diritto comunitario e diritto interno*, Milano, 2006.

Carbone S.M. - Munari F., *The regime of technical-nautical services (pilotage, towage, mooring-men) under European law,* in *Comunicazioni e studi,* 2002, p. 177 ff.

Chilcote, P. W., *The containerization story.* in *Urban Ports and Harbor Management*, Hershman M.J. (ed.), New York, 1988.

Fleming, D. K., *Port rivalry, co-operation, merger*, in *Maritime Policy & Management*, 1983 p. 207 ff.

Hayuth, Y., *Intermodality: Concept and Practice*, London, 1987.

Haralambides, H.E., *Competition, Excess Capacity, and the Pricing of Port Infrastructure*, in *International Journal of Maritime Economics*, 2002, p. 323 ff.

Ircha, M. C., *US ports: evolution and structure*, in *Maritime Policy & Management*, 1995, p. 281 ff.

Kagan, R. A., *Patterns of Port Development: Government, Intermodal Transportation and Innovation in the United States, China and Hong Kong*, Berkeley, 1990.

Lawson F.H. - Rudden B., *The Law of Property*, Oxford, 1982.

Luberoff, D. - Walder, J., *US Ports and the Funding of Intermodal Facilities: An Overview of Key Issues*, Cambridge, 2000.

Marcus, H. S., Short, J. E. - Kuypers, J. C. - Roberts, P. O., *Federal Port Policy in the United States*, Cambridge, 1976.

Maresca D. – Pelleriti S., *La regolazione del diritto di accesso alle infrastrutture portuali ed aeroportuali*, in *Dir. e Pol. Un. Eur.*, 2009, p. 107 ff.

Maresca M., *La regolazione dei porti tra diritto interno e diritto comunitario*, Torino, 2001.

Maresca M. (ed), *Lo spazio mediterraneo della mobilità*, Udine, 2010.

Moody's Investors Service, *Competition among West Coast ports pressures credit outlook*, New York, 1998.

Notteboom T., Ducruet C., De Langen P.W., *Ports in Proximity: Competition and Coordination Among Adjacent Seaports*, Ashgate, 2009.

Schenker, E., *Port Development in the United States*, Washington, 1976.

Slack, B., Comtois, C. and Sletmo, G., *Shipping lines as agents of change in the port industry*, in *Maritime Policy & Management*, 1996, p. 289 ff.

South J., *Leasehold: the case for reform*, Croydon, 2006.

Suykens, F. - Van de Voorde E., *Port Management in Europe*, in *Maritime Policy and Management*, 1998, p.251 ff.

Templeman L., *Landlord and Tenant*, in Halsbury's, *Laws of England*, London, 1980, p. 1 ff.

Thienel T., *International Maritime Law Aspects of Sea Ports,* in *International Commercial Arbitration and International Maritime Law from a German and Russian Perspective*, Trunk A. - Musin A.V. (ed.), Münster, 2004, p. 79 ff.

Ubbel B., *Institutional barriers to efficient policy intervention in the european port sector*, in *IATSS Review*, 2005 p. 40 ff.

US Department of Transportation (USDOT), *An Assessment of the US Marine Transportation System: A Report to Congress*, Washington, 1999.

US Maritime Administration (USMA), 1998, *A Report to Congress on the Status of The Public Ports of the United States*, Washington DC, 1996–1997.

Van Hooydonk E., *The regime of Port Authorities under European Law including an analysis of the Port Services Directive,* in *European Seaports Law, EU Law of Ports and Ports Services in the Port Package,* Antwerpen-Apeldoorm, Maklu, 2003.

Waller S.W. - Frischmann B.M., *The essential nature of infrastructure or the infrastructural nature of essential facilities*, Chicago, 2007.

World Bank, *Alternative port management structures and ownership models*, Washington, 2007.

Chapter 4 Railways

4.1 The Application of Antitrust Law to the Railway Sector in the United States Legal System

The fundamental problem in the railway market is the tension between administrative burdens and the traditional tendency of courts to apply reasonableness tests in the common law process[1]. This tradition tends to direct courts towards an inquiry into the economic reasonableness[2] of a defendant's conduct. The rule of reason usually leads to the deregulation of the markets, but we will see that in its European application it leads to re-regulation in light of important new goals[3].

An important case is *United States v. Trans-Missouri Freight Ass'n*, 166 U.S. 290 (1897). There, the railroads along the Mississippi had created the Trans-Missouri Freight Association to establish fixed freight fees for all participants. The Association admitted it was a restraint on competition, but claimed that they were exempt from the Sherman Act on grounds that they were regulated under the Interstate Commerce Act (case 1) Supreme Court. *United States v. Trans-Missouri*, part. I):

(…)

The first answer to this argument is that in our opinion the commerce act does not authorize an agreement of this nature. It may not in terms prohibit, but it is far from conferring, either directly or by implication, any authority to make it. If the agreement be legal, it does not owe its validity to any provision of the commerce act; and, if illegal, it is not made so by that act. The fifth section prohibits what is termed 'pooling,' but there is no express provi-

---

1 For an overview on the United States railways regulation, see Winston C., *United States: Private and deregulated*, in Gómez - Ibañez, J.A. - de Rus G. (ed), *Competition in the railway industry: An international comparative analysis*, Edward Elgar, 2006.While, a global analysis of the problem can be read in Budin K.J., *Global Trend to Railway Concessions Delivering Positive Results*, in *Public Policy for the Private Sector*, 134, The World Bank. Washington D.C., 1997.

2 To understand the economic structure of the Railways market, see Oum T. H. - Yu C., *Economic efficiency of railways and implications for public policy: A comparative study of the OECD countries' railways*, in *Journal of Transport Economics and Policy*, 1994, p. 121 ff.

3 The pursuit of new goals passes through the necessary application of the principle of separation: World Bank, *The benefits of separating rail Infrastructure from operations,* note no.135 December 1997.

sion in the act prohibiting the maintenance of traffic rates among competing roads by making such an agreement as this, nor is there any provision which permits it. Prior to the passage of the act the companies had sometimes endeavored to regulate competition and to maintain rates by pooling arrangements, and in the act that kind of an arrangement was forbidden. After its passage other devices were resorted to for the purpose of curbing competition and maintaining rates. The general nature of a contract like the one before us is not mentioned in or provided for by the act. The provisions of that act look to the prevention of discrimination; to the furnishing of equal facilities for the interchange of traffic; to the rate of compensation for what is termed the 'long and the short haul'; to the attainment of a continuous passage from the point of shipment to the point of destination, at a known and published schedule, and, in the language of counsel for defendants, 'without reference to the location of those points or the lines over which it is necessary for the traffic to pass'; to procuring uniformity of rates charged by each company to its patrons; and to other objects of a similar nature. The act was not directed to the securing of uniformity of rates to be charged by competing companies, nor was there any provision therein as to a maximum or minimum of rates. Competing and nonconnecting roads are not authorized by this statute to make an agreement like this one.

As the commerce act does not authorize this agreement, argument against a repeal by implication of the provisions of the act which it is alleged grant such authority becomes ineffective. There is no repeal in the case, and both statutes may stand, as neither is inconsistent with the other.

It is plain, also, that an amendment of the commerce act would not be an appropriate method of enacting the legislation contained in the trust act, for the reason that the latter act includes other subjects in addition to the contracts of or combinations among railroads, and is addressed to the *316 prohibition of other contracts besides those relating to transportation. The omission, therefore, to amend the commerce act, furnishes no reason for claiming that the later statute does not apply to railroad transportation. Although the commerce statute may be described as a general code for the regulation and government of railroads upon the subjects treated of therein, it cannot be contended that it furnishes a complete and perfect set of rules and regulations which are to govern them in all cases, and that any subsequent act in relation to them must, when passed, in effect amend or repeal some provision of that statute. The statute does not cover all cases concerning transportation by railroad and all contracts relating thereto. It does not purport to cover such an extensive field.

The existence of agreements similar to this one may have been known to congress at the time it passed the commerce act, although we are not aware, from the record, that an agreement of this kind had ever been made and publicly known prior to the passage of the commerce act. Yet, if it had been known to congress, its omission to prohibit it at that time, while prohibiting the pooling arrangements, is no reason for assuming that when passing the trust act it meant to except all contracts of railroad companies in regard to traffic rates from the operation of such act. Congress, for its own reasons, even if aware of the existence of such agreements, did not see fit, when it passed the commerce act, to prohibit them with regard to railroad companies alone, and the act was not an appropriate place for general legislation on the subject. And at that time, and for several years thereafter, congress did not think proper to legislate upon the subject at all. Finally it passed this trust act, and in our opinion no obstacle to its application to contracts relating to transportation by railroads is to be found in the fact that the commerce act had been passed several years before, in which the entering into such agreements was not in terms prohibited.

It is also urged that the debates in congress show beyond a doubt that the act as passed does not include railroads. Counsel*317 for the defendants refer in considerable detail to its history from the time of its introduction in the senate to its final passage. As the act originally passed the senate, the first section was in substance as it stands at present in the statute. On its receipt by the house that body proposed an amendment by which it was, in terms, made unlawful to enter into any contract for the purpose of preventing competition in the transportation of persons or property. As thus amended the bill went back to the senate, which itself amended the amendment by making the act apply to any such contract as tended to raise prices for transportation above what was just and reasonable. This amendment by the senate of the amendment proposed by the house was disagreed to by that body. The amendments were then considered by conference **550 committees, and the first conference committee reported to each house in favor of the amendment of the senate. This report was disagreed to, and another committee appointed, which agreed to strike out both amendments and leave the bill as it stood when it first passed the senate; and that report was finally adopted, and the bill thus passed.

Our attention is also called to one of the rules for the construction of statutes which has been approved by this court,-that, while it is the duty of courts to ascertain the meaning of the legislature from the words used in the statute and the subject-matter to which it relates, there is an equal duty to restrict the meaning of general words whenever it is found necessary to do so in order to carry out the legislative intent. Brewer v. Blougher, 14 Pet. 178, 198; Petri v. Bank, 142 U. S. 644, 650, 12 Sup. Ct. 325; McKee v. U. S., 164 U. S. 287, 17 Sup. Ct. 92. It is therefore urged that if, by a strict construction of the language of this statute, it may be made to include railroads, yet it is evident from other considerations now to be mentioned that the real meaning of the legislature would not include them, and they must for that reason be excluded. It is said that this meaning is plainly to be inferred because of fundamental differences, both in an economic way and before the law, between trade and manufacture, on the one hand, and railroad transportation, on the other. Among these differences are the public character of railroad business, and, as a result, the peculiar power of control and regulation possessed by the state over railroad companies. The trader or manufacturer, on the other hand, carries on an entirely private business, and can sell to whom he pleases; he may charge different prices for the same article to different individuals; he may charge as much as he can get for the article in which he deals, whether the price be reasonable or *321 unreasonable; he may make such discrimination in his business as he chooses, and he may cease to do any business whenever his choice lies in that direction; while, on the contrary, a railroad company must transport all persons and property that come to it, and it must do so at the same price for the same service, and the price must be reasonable, and it cannot at its will discontinue its business. It is also urged that there are evils arising from unrestricted competition in regard to railroads which do not exist in regard to any other kind of property; that it is so admitted by the latest and best writers on the subject, and that practical experience of the results of unrestricted competition among railroads tends directly to the same view; that the difference between railroad property, on the one hand, and all other kinds of property, on the other hand, is so plain that entirely different economic results follow from unrestricted competition among railroads from those which obtain in regard to all other kinds of business. It is also said that the contemporaneous industrial history of the country, the legal situation in regard to railroad properties at the time of the enactment of this statute, its legislative history, the ancient and constantly maintained different legal effect and policy regarding railway transportation and ordinary trade and manufacture, together with a just regard for interests of such enormous magnitude as are represented by the railroads of the country, all tend to show that congress, in passing the anti-trust act, never could have contemplated the inclusion of railroads within its provisions. It is therefore claimed to be the duty of the court, in carrying out the rule of statutory construction above stated, to restrict the meaning of these general words of the statute which would include railroads, because, from the considerations above mentioned, it is plain that congress never intended, that railroads should be included.

Many of the foregoing assertions may be well founded, while at the same time the correctness of the conclusions sought to be drawn therefrom need not be conceded. The points of difference between the railroad and other corporations are many and great. It cannot be disputed that a railroad *322 is a public corporation, and its business pertains to and greatly affects the public, and that it is of a public nature. The company may not charge unreasonable prices for transportation, nor can it make unjust discriminations, nor select its patrons, nor go out of business when it chooses, while a mere trading or manufacturing company may do all these things. But the very fact of the public character of a railroad would itself seem to call for special care by the legislature in regard to its conduct, so that its business should be carried on with as much reference to the proper and fair interests of the public as possible. While the points of difference just mentioned and others do exist between the two classes of corporations, it must be remembered they have also some points of resemblance. Trading, manufacturing, and railroad corporations are all engaged in the transaction of business with regard to articles of trade and commerce, each in its special sphere,-either in manufacturing or trading in commodities, or in their transportation by rail. A contract among those engaged in the latter business, by which the prices for the transportation of commodities traded in or manufactured **552 by the others is greatly enhanced from what it otherwise would be if free competition were the rule, affects, and to a certain extent restricts, trade and commerce, and affects the price of the commodity. Of this there can be no question. Manufacturing or trading companies may also affect prices by joining together in forming a trust or other combination, and by making agreements in restraint of trade and commerce, which, when carried out, affect the interests of the public. Why should not a railroad company be included in general legislation aimed at the prevention of that kind of agreement made in restraint of trade, which may exist in all companies, which is substantially of the same nature wherever found, and which tends very much towards the same results whether put in practice by a trading and manufacturing or by a railroad company? It is true the results of trusts, or combinations of that nature, may be different in different kinds of corporations, and yet they all have an essential similarity, and have been induced by motives of individual or corporate aggrandizement*323 as against the public interest. In business or trading combinations they may even temporarily, or perhaps permanently, reduce the price of the article traded in or manufactured, by reducing the expense inseparable from the running of many different companies for the same purpose. Trade or commerce under those circumstances may nevertheless be badly and unfortunately restrained by driving out of business the small dealers and worthy men whose lives have been spent therein, and who might be unable to readjust themselves to their altered surroundings. Mere reduction in the price of the commodity dealt in might be dearly paid for by the ruin of such a class and the absorption of control over one commodity by an all-powerful combination of capital. In any great and extended change in the manner or method of doing business it seems to be an inevitable necessity that distress, and, perhaps, ruin, shall be its accompaniment, in regard to some of those who were engaged in the old methods. A change from stagecoaches and canal boats to railroads threw at once a large number of men out of employment. Changes from hand labor to that of machinery, and from operating machinery by hand to the application of steam for such purpose, leave behind them, for the time, a number of men who must seek other avenues of livelihood. These are misfortunes which seem to be the necessary accompaniment of all great industrial changes. It takes time to effect a readjustment of industrial life so that those who are thrown out of their old employment by reason of such changes as we have spoken of may find opportunities for labor in other departments than those to which they have been accustomed. It is a misfortune, but yet in such cases it seems to be the inevitable accompaniment of change and improvement.

It is wholly different, however, when such changes are effected by combinations of capital whose purpose in combining is to control the production or manufacture of any particular article in the market, and by such control dictate the price at which the article shall be sold; the effect being to drive out of business all the small dealers in the commodity, and to render the public subject to the decision of the combination*324 as to what price shall be paid for the article. In this light, it is not material that the price of an article may be lowered. It is in the power of the combination to raise it, and the result in any event is unfortunate for the country, by depriving it of the services of a large number of small but independent dealers, who were familiar with the business, and who had spent their lives in it, and who supported themselves and their families from the small profits realized therein. Whether they be able to find other avenues to earn their livelihood is not so material, because it is not for the real prosperity of any country that such changes should occur which result in transferring an independent business man, the head of his establishment, small though it might be, into a mere servant or agent of a corporation for selling the commodities which he once manufactured or dealt in; having no voice in shaping the business policy of the company, and bound to obey orders issued by others. Nor is it for the substantial interests of the country that any one commodity should be within the sole power and subject to the sole will of one powerful combination of capital. Congress has, so far as its jurisdiction extends, prohibited all contracts or combinations in the form of trusts entered into for the purpose of restraining trade and commerce. The results naturally flowing from a contract or combination in restraint of trade or commerce, when entered into by a manufacturing or trading company such as above stated, while differing somewhat from those which may follow a contract to keep up transportation rates by railroads, are nevertheless of the same nature and kind, and the contracts themselves do not so far differ in their nature that they may not all be treated alike and be condemned in common. It is entirely appropriate generally to subject corporations or persons engaged in trading or manufacturing to different rules from those applicable to railroads in their transportation business, but when the evil to be remedied is similar in both kinds of corporations, such as contracts which are unquestionably in restraint of trade, we see no reason why similar rules should not be promulgated in regard to both, and both be covered in the same *325 statute by general language sufficiently broad to include them both. We see nothing, either in contemporaneous history, in the legal situation at the time of the passage of the statute, in its legislative history, or in any general difference in the nature or kind of these trading or manufacting companies from **553 railroad companies, which would lead us to the conclusion that it cannot be supposed the legislature, in prohibiting the making of contracts in restraint of trade, intended to include railroads within the purview of that act.

Neither is the statute, in our judgment, so uncertain in its meaning, or its language so vague, that it ought not to be held applicable to railroads. It prohibits contracts, combinations, etc., in restraint of trade or commerce. Transporting commodities is commerce, and, if from one state to or through another, it is interstate commerce. To be reached by the federal statute, it must be commerce among the several states or with foreign nations. When the act prohibits contracts in restraint of trade or commerce, the plain meaning of the language used includes contracts which relate to either or both subjects. Both trade and commerce are included, so long as each relates to that which is interstate or foreign. Transportation of commodities among the several states or with foreign nations falls within the description of the words of the statute with regard to that subject, and there is also included in that language that kind of trade in commodities among the states or with foreign nations which is not confined to their mere transportation. It includes their purchase and sale. Precisely at what point in the course of the trade in or manufacture of commodities the statute may have effect upon them, or upon contracts relating to them, may be somewhat difficult to determine, but interstate transportation presents no difficulties. In U. S. v. E. C. Knight Co., 156 U. S. 1, 15 Sup. Ct. 249, heretofore cited, it was in substance held, reiterating the language of Mr. Justice Lamar in Kidd v. Pearson, 128 U. S. 1, 9 Sup. Ct. 6, that the intent to manufacture of export a manufactured article to foreign nations, or to send it to another state, did not determine the time when the article or product passed from the control of the state and *326 belonged to commerce. The difficulty in determining that question, however, is no reason for denying effect to language which, by its terms, plainly includes the transportation of commodities among the several states or with foreign nations, and which may also be the subject of contracts or combination in restraint of such commerce. The difficulty of the subject, so far as the trade in or the manufacture of commodities is concerned, arises from the limited control which congress has over the matter of trade or manufacture. It was said by Mr. Justice Lamar in Kidd v. Pearson, supra: 'If it be held that the term 'commerce' includes the regulation of all such manufactures as are intended to be the subject of commercial transactions in the future, it is impossible to deny that it would also include the productive industries that contemplate the same thing. The result would be that congress would be invested, to the exclusion of the states, with the power to regulate, not only manufactures, but also agriculture, horticulture, stock raising, domestic fisheries, and mining,-in short, every branch of human industry.'

In the Knight Company Case, supra, it was said that this statute applied to monopolies in restraint of interstate or international trade or commerce, and not to monopolies in manufacture even of a necessary of life. It is readily seen from these cases that, if the act do not apply to the transportation of commodities by railroads from one state to another or to foreign nations, its application is so greatly limited that the whole act might as well be held inoperative.

Still another ground for holding the act inapplicable is urged, and that is that the language covers only contracts or combinations like trusts, or those which, while not exactly trusts, are otherwise of the same form or nature. This is clearly not so.

While the statute prohibits all combinations in the form of trusts or otherwise, the limitation is not confined to that form alone. All combinations which are in restraint of trade or commerce are prohibited, whether in the form of trusts or in any other form whatever.

We think, after a careful examination, that the statute *327 covers, and was intended to cover, common carriers by railroad.

Second. The next question to be discussed is as to what is the true construction of the statute, assuming that it applies to common carriers by railroad. What is the meaning of the language, as used in the statute, that 'every contract, combination in the form of trust or otherwise, or conspiracy in restraint of trade or commerce among the several states or with foreign nations, is hereby declared to be illegal'? Is it confined to a contract or combination which is only in unreasonable restraint of trade or commerce, or does it include-what the language of the act plainly and in terms covers-all contracts of that nature?

We are asked to regard the title of this act as indicative of its purpose to include only those contracts which were unlawful at common law, but which require the sanction of a federal statute in order to be dealt with in a federal court. It is said that when terms which are known to the common law are used in a federal statute, those terms are to be given the same meaning that they received at common law; and that, when the language of the title is 'to protect trade and commerce against unlawful restraints and monopolies,' it means those restraints and monopolies which the common law regarded as unlawful, and which were to be prohibited by the federal statute. We are of opinion that the language used in the title refers to and includes, and was intended to include, those restraints and monopolies which are made unlawful in the body of the statute. It is to the statute itself that resort must be had to learn the meaning thereof, though a resort tot he title here creates no doubt about **554 the meaning of, and does not alter the plain language contained in, its text.

It is now with much amplification of argument urged that the statute, in declaring illegal every combination in the form of trust or otherwise, or conspiracy in restraint of trade or commerce, does not mean what the language used therein plainly imports, but that it only means to declare illegal any such contract which is in unreasonable restraint of trade, while leaving all others unaffected by the provisions of the *328 act; that the common-law meaning of the term 'contract in restraint of trade' includes only such contracts as are in unreasonable restraint of trade; and when that term is used in the federal statute it is not intended to include all contracts in restraint of trade, but only those which are in unreasonable restraint thereof.

The term is not of such limited signification. Contracts in restraint of trade have been known and spoken of for hundreds of years, both in England and in this country, and the term includes all kinds of those contracts which in fact restrain or may restrain trade. Some of such contracts have been held void and unenforceable in the courts by reason of their restraint being unreasonable, while others have been held valid because they were not of that nature. A contract may be in restraint of trade, and still be valid at common law. Although valid, it is nevertheless a contract in restraint of trade, and would be so described either at common law or elsewhere. By the simple use of the term 'contract in restraint of trade,' all contracts of that nature, whether valid or otherwise, would be included, and not alone that kind of contract which was invalid and unenforceable as being in unreasonable restraint of trade. When, therefore, the body of an act pronounces as illegal every contract or combination in restraint of trade or commerce among the several states, etc., the plain and ordinary meaning of such language is not limited to that kind of contract alone which is in unreasonable restraint of trade, but all contracts are included in such language, and no exception or limitation can be added without placing in the act that which has been omitted by congress.

Proceeding, however, upon the theory that the statute did not mean what its plain language imported, and that it intended in its prohibition to denounce as illegal only those contracts which were in unreasonable restraint of trade, the courts below have made an exhaustive investigation as to the general rules which guide courts in declaring contracts to be void as being in restraint of trade, and therefore against the public policy of the country. In the course of their discussion *329 of that subject they have shown that there has been a gradual, though great, alteration in the extent of the liberty granted to the vendor of property in agreeing, as part consideration for his sale, not to enter into the same kind of business for a certain time or within a certain territory. So long as the sale was the bona fide consideration for the promise, and was not made a mere excuse for an evasion of the rule itself, the later authorities, both in England and in this country, exhibit a strong tendency towards enabling the parties to make such a contract in relation to the sale of property, including an agreement not to enter into the same kind of business, as they may think proper, and this with the view to granting to a vendor the freest opportunity to obtain the largest consideration for the sale of that which is his own. A contract which is the mere accompaniment of the sale of property, and thus entered into for the purpose of enhancing the price at which the vendor sells it, which, in effect, is collateral to such sale, and where the main purpose of the whole contract is accomplished by such sale, might not be included within the letter or spirit of the statute in question. But we cannot see how the statute can be limited, as it has been by the courts below, without reading into its text an exception which alters the natural meaning of the language used, and that, too, upon a most material point, and where no sufficient reason is shown for believing that such alteration would make the statute more in accord with the intent of the lawmaking body that enacted

4.2 The Reasonableness Test Applied to Railroads Services: From the Per-Se Rule to the Rule of Reason

An important defense of Trans-Missouri Freight Association was that the rates fixed[4] were legal because they were reasonable and therefore valid under common law[5]. The lower court accepted this argument, but the Supreme Court did not. It held that since that kind of contract was not explicitly regulated by the Interstate Commerce Act, the Sherman Act applied (case 2) Supreme Court. *United States v. Trans-Missouri*, part II):

(…)

The great stress of the argument for the defendants on this branch of the case has been to show, if possible, some reason in the attendant circumstances, or some fact existing in the nature of railroad property and business, upon which to found the claim that, although by the language of the statute agreements or combinations in restraint of trade or commerce are included, the statute really means to declare illegal only those contracts, etc., which are in unreasonable restraint of trade. In order to do this, the defendants call attention to many facts which they have already referred to in their argument, upon the point that railroads were not included at all in the statute. They again draw attention to the fact of the peculiar nature of *330 railroad property. When a railroad is once built, it is said, it must be kept in operation. It must transport property, when necessary in order to keep its business, at the smallest price, and for the narrowest profit, or even for no profit, provided running expenses can be paid, rather than not to do the work; that railroad property cannot be altered for use for any other purpose, at least without such loss as may fairly be called destructive; that competition, while perhaps right and proper in other business, simply leads in railroad business to financial ruin and insolvency, and to the operation of the road by receivers in the interest of its creditors, instead of in that of its owners and the public; that a contest between a receiver of an insolvent corporation and one which is still solvent tends to ruin the latter company, **555 while being of no benefit to the former; that a receiver is only bound to pay operating expenses so he can compete with the solvent company, and oblige it to come down to prices incompatible with any profit for the work done, and until ruin overtakes it, to the destruction of innocent stockholders, and the impairment of the public interests.

---

4 The most of *Supreme Court* cases concerned price fixing practices, that are completely explained in Peppin J.C., *Price Fixing Agreements under the Sherman Antitrust law*, in *28 California Law Review*, 1940, p. 297 ff

5 An explanation of the regulation of tariffs in the United States, under the common law, can be read in Ratner S., *The tariff in American History*, New York, 1972.

To the question why competition should necessarily be conducted to such an extent as to result in this relentless and continued war, to eventuate only in the financial ruin of one or all of the companies indulging in it, the answer is made that, if competing railroad companies be left subject to the sway of free and unrestricted competition, the results above foreshadowed necessarily happen from the nature of the case; that, competition being the rule, each company will seek business to the extent of its power, and will underbid its rival, in order to get the business, and such underbidding will act and react upon each company until the prices are so reduced as to make it impossible to prosper or live under them; that it is too much to ask of human nature for one company to insist upon charges sufficiently high to afford a reasonable compensation, and, while doing so, to see its patrons leave for rival roads, who are obtaining its business by offering less rates for doing it than can be afforded, and a fair profit obtained therefrom. Sooner than experience ruin from mere inanition, efforts will *331 be made in the direction of meeting the underbidding of its rival, until both shall end in ruin. The only refuge, it is said, from this wretched end lies in the power of competing roads agreeing among themselves to keep up prices for transportation to such sums as shall be reasonable in themselves, so that companies may be allowed to save themselves from themselves, and to agree not to attack each other, but to keep up reasonable and living rates for the services performed. It is said that, as railroads have a right to charge reasonable rates, it must follow that a contract among themselves to keep up their charges to that extent is valid. Viewed in the light of all these facts, it is broadly and confidently asserted that it is impossible to believe that congress, or any other intelligent and honest legislative body, could ever have intended to include all contracts or combinations in restraint of trade, and, as a consequence thereof, to prohibit competing railways from agreeing among themselves to keep up prices for transportation to such a rate as should be fair and reasonable.

These arguments, it must be confessed, bear with much force upon the policy of an act which s should prevent a general agreement upon the question of rate among competing railroad companies to the extent simply of maintaining those rates which reasonable and fair.

There is another side to this question, however, and it may not be amiss to refer to one or two facts which tend to somewhat modify and alter the light in which the subject should be regarded. If only that kind of contract which is in unreasonable restraint of trade be within the meaning of the statute, and declared therein to be illegal, it is at once apparent that the subject of what is a reasonable rate is attended with great uncertainty. What is a proper standard by which to judge the fact of reasonable rates? Must the rate be so high as to enable the return for the whole business done to amount to a sum sufficient to afford the shareholder a fair and reasonable profit upon his investment? If so, what is a fair and reasonable profit? That depends sometimes upon the risk incurred, and the rate itself differs in different localities. Which is the one to which reference is to be made as the standard? Or is *332 the reasonableness of the profit to be limited to a fair return upon the capital that would have been sufficient to build and equip the road, if honestly expended? Or is still another standard to be created, and the reasonableness of the charges tried by the cost of the carriage of the article, and a reasonalbe profit allowed on that? And, in such case, would contribution to a sinking fund to make repairs upon the roadbed and renewal of cars, ect., be assumed as a proper item? or is the reasonableness of the charge to be tested by reference to the charges for the transportation of the same kind of property made by other roads similarly situated? If the latter, a combination among such roads as to rates would, of course, furnish no means of answering the question. It is quite apparent, therefore, that it is exceedingly difficult to formulate even the term of the rule itself which should qovern in the matter of determining what would be reasonable rates for transporting: while, even after the standard should be determined, there is such an infinite variety of facts entering into the question of what is a reasonable rate, no matter what standard is adopted, that any individual shipper would in most cases be apt to abandon the effort to show the unreasonable character of a charge, sooner than hazard the great expense in time and money necessary to prove the fact, and at the same time incur the ill will of the road itself in all his future dealings with it. to say, therefore, that the act excludes agreements which are not in unreasonable restraint of trade, and which tend simply to keep up reasonable rates for transportation, is substantially to leave the question of reasonableness to the companies themselves.

However, the Supreme Court definitely turned to the application of the rule of reason in *Chicago Board of Trade v. United States*, 246 U.S. 231 (1918), case 3). The Chicago Board of Trade[6] required members to establish their off-hour trading price for "to arrive" grain at a special session referred to as the "Call." All trades that took place after the Call and before the opening of the Board on the next business day had to use the price set at the end of the Call. The government brought suit for price fixing. According to the Court, the true test of legality was whether the restraint imposed was such that it merely regulated and thereby promoted competition, or whether it was of a character that would suppress or even destroy competition. To determine that question the Court must ordinarily consider the facts peculiar to the business to which the restraint is applied[7]. The Court stated that in evaluating reasonableness, it would consider: the nature of the rule, the scope of the rule, and the effect of the rule. In this case, there was no effect on market prices, and moreover, the rule improved market competition:

(…)

The government proved the existence of the rule and described its application and the change in business practice involved. It made no attempt to show that the rule was designed to or that it had the effect of limiting the amount of grain shipped to Chicago; or of retarding or accelerating shipment; or if raising or depressing prices; or of discriminating against any part of the public; or that it resulted in hardship to anyone. The case was rested upon the bald proposition, that a rule or agreement by which men occupying positions of strength in any branch of trade, fixed prices at which they would buy or sell during an important part of the business day, is an illegal restraint of trade under the Anti-Trust Law. But the legality of an agreement or regulation cannot be determined by so simple a test, as whether it restrains competition. Every agreement concerning trade, every regulation of trade, restrains. To bind, to restrain, is of their very essence. The true test of legality is whether the restraint imposed is such as merely regulates and perhaps thereby promotes competition or whether

6 See the development of the law and economics theory held in Chicago Board of Trade, in: Dewey D., *Monopoly in Economics and Law*, 1959, Chicago, p. 112 ss., Letwin W., *Law and Economic Policy in America: the evolution of the Sherman act*, 1965, Chicago, Thorelli H.B., *The Federal Antitrust Policy: origination of an American tradition*, 1955, Baltimore

7 For a specific analysis of competition in the railroads sector, see Waters II W.G., *Evolution of railroad economics*, in Dennis S.M. – Talley W.K. (ed.), *Railroad economics. Research in transportation economics*, Elsevier, 2007.

it is such as may suppress or even destroy competition. To determine that question the court must ordinarily consider the facts peculiar to the business to which the restraint is applied; its condition before and after the restraint was imposed; the nature of the restraint and its effect, actual or probable. The history of the restraint, the evil believed to exist, the reason for adopting the particular remedy, the purpose or end sought to be attained, are all relevant facts. This is not because a good intention will save an otherwise objectionable regulation or the reverse; but because knowledge of intent may help the court to interpret facts and to predict consequences. The District Court erred, therefore, in striking from the answer *239 allegations concerning the history and purpose of the call rule and in later excluding evidence on that subject. But the evidence admitted makes it clear that the rule was a reasonable regulation of business consistent with the provisions of the Anti-Trust Law.

First. The nature of the rule: The restriction was upon the period of price-making. It required members to desist from further price-making after the close of the call until 9:30 a. m. the next business day; but there was no restriction upon the sending out of bids after close of the call. Thus it required members who desired to buy grain 'to arrive' to make up their minds before the close of the call how much they were willing to pay during the interval before the next session of the Board. The rule made it to their interest to attend the call; and if they did not fill their wants by purchases there, to make the final bid high enough to enable them to purchase from country dealers.

Second. The scope of the rule: It is restricted in operation to grain 'to arrive.' It applies only to a small part of the grain shipped from day to day to Chicago, and to an even smaller part of the day's sales; members were left free to purchase grain already in Chicago from any one at any price throughout the day. It applies only during a small part of the business day; members were left free to purchase during the sessions of the Board grain 'to arrive,' at any price, from members anywhere and from nonmembers anywhere except on the premises of the Board. It applied only to grain shipped to Chicago; members were left free to purchase at any price throughout the day from either members or non-members, grain 'to arrive' at any other market. Country dealers and farmers had available in practically every part of the territory called tributary to Chicago some other market for grain 'to arrive.' Thus Missouri, Kansas, Nebraska*240 and parts of Illinois are also tributary to St. Louis; Nebraska and Iowa, to Omaha; Minnesota, Iowa, South and North Dakota, to Minneapolis or Duluth; Wisconsin and parts of Iowa and of Illinois, to Milwaukee; Ohio, Indiana and parts of Illinois, to Cincinnati; Indiana and parts of Illinois, to Louisville.

Third. The effects of the rule: As it applies to only a small part of the grain shipped to Chicago and to that only during a part of the business day and does not apply at all to grain shipped to other markets, the rule had no appreciable effect on general market prices; nor did it materially affect the total volume of grain coming to Chicago. But within the narrow limits of its operation the rule helped to improve market conditions thus:

(a) It created a public market for grain 'to arrive.' Before its adoption, bids were made privately. Men had to buy and sell without adequate knowledge of actual market conditions. This was disadvantageous to all concerned, but particularly so to country dealers and farmers.

(b) It brought into the regular market hours of the Board sessions, more of the trading in grain 'to arrive.'

(c) It brought buyers and sellers into more direct relations; because on the call they gathered together for a free and open interchange of bids and offers.

(d) It distributed the business in grain 'to arrive' among a far larger number of Chicago receivers and commission merchants than had been the case there before.

(e) It increased the number of country dealers engaging in this branch of the business; supplied them more regularly with bids from Chicago; and also increased the number of bids received by them from competing markets.

(f) It eliminated risks necessarily incident to a private market, and thus enabled country dealers to do business on a smaller margin. In that way the rule made it possible for them to pay more to farmers without raising the price to consumers.

(g) It enabled country dealers to sell some grain to arrive which they would otherwise have been obliged either to ship to Chicago commission merchants or to sell for 'future delivery.'

(h) It enabled those grain merchants of Chicago who sell to millers and exporters, to trade on a smaller margin and by paying more for grain or selling it for less, to make the Chicago market more attractive for both shippers and buyers of grain.

(i) Incidentally it facilitated trading 'to arrive' by enabling those engaged in these transactions to fulfill their contracts by tendering grain arriving at Chicago on any railroad, whereas formerly shipments had to be made over the particular railroad designated by the buyer.

The restraint imposed by the rule is less severe than that sustained in Anderson v. United States, 171 U. S. 604, 19 Sup. Ct. 50, 43 L. Ed. 300. Every Board of Trade and nearly every trade organization imposes some restrainst upon the conduct of business by its members. Those relating to the hours in which business may be done are common; and they make a special appeal where, as here, they tend to shorten the working day or, at least, limit the period of most exacting activity. The decree of the District Court is reversed with directions to dismiss the bill.

4.3 The Rejection of the Public Utility Argument as a Justification for Restraint of Trade

The Supreme Court rejected the public utility argument[8] proffered by Trans-Missouri. According to this defense, if the rail enterprises competed vigorously, they would not be able to cover fixed costs, which would lead to a failure to maintain equipment and structures, as well as bankruptcy for some businesses and inconvenience to customers[9]. Competition would drive out all competitors leaving

---

[8] The public Utility argument cane be referred to the European doctrine of Services of General Interest: Gathon H. J. - Pestieau P., *Decomposing efficiency into its managerial and its regulatory components: The case of European railways*, in *European Journal of Operational Research*, 1995, p. 500 ff., Friebel, G. - Ivaldi, M. - Vibes, *Railway (de) regulation: A European efficiency comparison. IDEI report no 3 on passenger rail transport,* Toulouse, 2003.

[9] The incidence of the competition of passenger welfare can be studied in See Monami E., *European Passenger Rail Reforms: A Comparative Assessment of the Emerging Models*, in *Transport Reviews*, 2000, p. 91 ff. and Nash, C.A., *Passenger railway re-*

one firm, which would then raise its prices[10] on account of its monopoly[11]. The Court said that it could not determine if the rates were reasonable because it had insufficient information. Indeed, the framers of the Act did not envision this level of supervision and intervention by the courts (case 4) Supreme Court. *United States v. Trans-Missouri*, part III):

(…)

It must also be remembered that railways are public corporations organized for public purposes, granted valuable franchises and privileges, among which the right to take the private property of the citizen in invitum is not the least (Cherokee Nation v. Southern Kan. Ry. Co., 135 U. S. 641, 657, 10 Sup. Ct. 965); that many of them are the donees of large tracts of public lands, and of gifts of money by municipal corporations, and that they all primarily owe duties to the public of a higher nature even than that of earning large dividends for their shareholders. The business which the railroads do is of a public nature, closely affecting almost all classes in the community,-the farmer, the artisan, the manufacturer, and the trader. It is of such a public nature that it may well be doubted, to say the least, whether any contract which imposes any restraint upon its business would not be prejudicial to the public interest.

We recognize the argument upon the part of the defendants that restraint upon the business of railroads will not be prejudicial to the public interest so long as such restraint provides for reasonable rates for transportation, and prevents the deadly competition so liable to result in the ruin of the roads, and to thereby impair their usefulness to the public, and in that way to prejudice the public interest. But it must be remembered that these results are by no means admitted with unanimity; on the contrary, they are earnestly and warmly denied on the part of the public and by those who assume to defend its interests both in and out of

---

form in the last 20 years – European experience reconsidered, in *Research in Transport Economics*, 2008, p. 61 ff.

10 The importance of price determination is set in the balance of a business plan for the financing of infrastructures; for an International and comparative outlook, see: Thompson L.S., *Directions of Railway Reform. International Railway Congress Association*, Vienna, 2001, Oum T. H. – Waters W.G. II - Yu C., *A survey of productivity and efficiency measurement in rail transport*, in *Journal of Transport Economics and Policy*, 1999, p. 9 ff., Meeddat - Sesp, *Les comptes des transports en 2007 (tome 1). Les transferts de l'État et des collectivités locales: Ministère de l'écologie, de l'énergie, du développement durable et de l'aménagement du territoire*, Paris, 2008, Link H., *Rail infrastructure charging and on-track competition in Germany*, in *International Journal of Transport Management*, 2004 p. 17 ff.

11 The same debates is now carried out in Europe where the different model of public intervention lead to a market made of many national carriers who monopolize the cabotage traffic: International Chamber of Commerce, *The liberalization of rail transport in Europe*, 2007, Glaister S. (2006). *Competition undermined by politics*, in Gómez - Ibañez, J.A. - de Rus G. (ed), *Competition in the railway industry: An international comparative analysis*. Edward Elgar, 2006, Campos, Cantos, *Regulating privatized rail transport*, Police research working paper 2064, The World Bank, Economic Development Institute, 1999, Bergmann - Rawlings, *Trasport management. Future directions: redefining the role of transport*, in *Strategic Supply Chain Management: Best Pratice in Supply Chain Management*, Aldershot, 1998, p. 369 ff.

congress. Competition, they urge, is a necessity for the purpose of securing in the end just and proper rates. It was said in Gibbs v. Gas Co., 130 U. S. 396, at page 408, 9 Sup. Ct. 557, by Mr. Chief Justice Fuller, as follows: 'The supply of illuminating gas is a business of a public nature to meet a public necessity. It is not a business like that of an ordinary corporation engaged in the manufacture of articles that may be furnished by individual effort. New Orleans Gaslight Co. v. Louisiana Light & Heat Producing & Manufacturing Co., 115 U. S. 650, 6 Sup. Ct. 252; Louisville Gas Co. v. Citizens' Gaslight Co., 115 U. S. 683, 6 Sup. Ct. 265; Shepard v. Milwaukee Gas Co., 6 Wis. 539; Chicago Gaslight & Coke Co. v. People's Gaslight & Coke Co., 121 Ill. 530, 13 N. E. 169; St. Louis v. St. Louis Gaslight Co., 70 Mo. 69. Hence, while it is justly urged that those rules which say that a given contract is against public policy should not be arbitrarily extended so as to interfere with the freedom of contract (Registering Co. v. Samson, L. R. 19 Eq. 462), yet, in the instance of business of such a character that it presumably cannot be restrained to any extent whatever without prejudice to the public interest, courts decline to enforce or *334 sustain contracts imposing such restraint, however partial, because in contravention of public policy. This subject is much considered, and the authorities cited, in West Virginia Transp. Co. v. Ohio River Pipe-Line Co., 22 W. Va. 600; Chicago Gaslight & Coke Co. v. People's Gaslight & Coke Co., 121 Ill. 530, 13 N. E. 169; W. U. Tel. Co. v. American Union Tel. Co., 65 Ga. 160.'

It is true, in the Gibbs Case there was a special statute, which prohibited the company from entering into any consolidation, combination, or contract with any other gas company whatever, and it was provided that any attempt to do so, or to make such combination or contract, should be utterly null and void. The above extract from the opinion of the court is made for the purpose of showing the difference which exists between a private and a public corporation; that kind of a public corporation which, while doing business for remuneration, is yet so connected in interest with the public as to give a public character to its business; and it is seen that while, in the absence of a statute prohibiting them, contracts of private individuals or corporations touching upon restraints in trade must be unreasonable in their nature to be held void, different considerations obtain in the case of public corporations like those of railroads, where it well may be that any restraint upon a business of that character, as affecting its rates of transportation, must thereby be prejudicial to the public interests.

The plaintiffs are, however, under no obligation in order to maintain this action to show that by the common law all agreements among competing railroad companies to keep up rates to such as are reasonable were void as in restraint of trade or commerce. There are many cases which look in that direction, if they do not precisely decide that point. Some of them are referred to in the opinion in the Baltimore Gas Co. Case, above cited. The case of Steamship Co. v McGregor, 21 Q. B. Div. 544, 23 Q. B. Div. 598, and [1892] App. Cas. 25, has been cited by the courts below as holding in principle that contracts of this nature are valid at common law. The agreement held valid there was *335 an agreement for lowering rates of transportation among the parties thereto, and it was entered into for the purpose of driving out of trade rival steamships, in order that thereafter the rates might be advanced. The English courts held that the agreement was not a conspiracy, and that it was valid, although the result aimed at was to drive a rival out of the field, because, so long as the injury to such rival was not the sole reason for the agreement, but self-interest the predominating motive, there was nothing wrong in law with an agreement of that kind. But, assuming that agreements of this nature are not void at common law, and that the various cases cited by the learned courts below show it, the answer to the statement of their validity now is to be found in the terms of the statute under consideration. The provisions of the interstate commerce act relating to reasonable rates, discriminations, etc., do not authorize such an agreement as this, nor do they authorize any other agreements which would be inconsistent with the provisions of this act.

The general reasons for holding agreements **557 of this nature to be invalid, even at common law, on the part of railroad companies, are quite strong, if not entirely conclusive.

Considering the public character of such corporations, the privileges and franchises which they have received from the public in order that they might transact business, and bearing in mind how closely and immediately the question of rates for transportation affects the whole public, it may be urged that congress had in mind all the difficulties which we have before suggested of proving the unreasonableness of the rate, and might, in consideration of all the circumstances, have deliberately decided to prohibit all agreements and combinations in restraint of trade or commerce, regardless of the question whether such agreements were reasonable or the reverse.

It is true that, as to a majority of those living along its line, each railroad is a monopoly. Upon the subject now under consideration, it is well said by Judge Oliver P. Shiras, United States district judge, Northern district of Iowa, in his very able dissenting opinion in this case is the United States circuit court of appeals, as follows:

*336 'As to the majority of the community living along its line, each railway company has a monopoly of the business demanding transportation as one of its elements. By reason of this fact, the action of this corporation in establishing the rates to be charged largely influences the net profit coming to the farmer, the manufacturer, and the merchant, from the sale of the products of the farm, the workshop and manufactory, and of the merchandise purchased and resold, and also largely influences the price to be paid by every one who consumes any of the property transported over the line of railway. There is no other line of business carried on in our midst which is so intimately connected with the public as that conducted by the railways of the country. * * * A railway corporation engaged in the transportation of the persons and property of the community is always carrying on a public business which at all times directly affects the public welfare. All contracts or combinations entered into between railway corporations intended to regulate the rates to be charged the public for the service rendered must, of necessity, affect the public interests. By reason of this marked distinction existing between enterprises inherently public in their character and those of a private nature, and, further, by reason of the difference between private persons and corporations engaged in private pursuits, who owe no direct or primary duty to the public and public corporations created for the express purpose of carrying on public enterprises, and which, in consideration of the public powers exercised in their behalf, are under obligation to carry on the work intrusted to their management primarily in the interest and for the benefit of the community, it seems clear to me that the same test is not applicable to both classes of business and corporations in determining the validity of contracts and combinations entered into by those engaged therein. * * * In the opinion of the court are found citations from the reports of the interstate commerce commission in which are depicted the evils that are occasioned to the railway companies and the public by warfares over rate charges, and the advantages that are gained in many directions by proper conference and concert of action among the competing*337 lines. It may be entirely true that, as we proceed in the development of the policy of public control over railway traffic, methods will be devised and put in operation by legislative enactment whereby railway companies and the public may be protected against the evils arising from unrestricted competition, and from rate wars which unsettle the business of the community; but I fail to perceive the force of the argument that because railway companies, through their own action, cause evils to themselves and the public by sudden changes or reductions in tariff rates, they must be permitted to deprive the community of the benefit of competition in securing reasonable rates for the transportation of the products of the country. Competition, free and unrestricted, is the general rule which governs all the ordinary business pursuits and transactions of life. Evils, as well as benefits, result therefrom. In the fierce heat of competition, the stronger competitor may crush out the weaker; fluctuations in prices may be caused that result in wreck and disaster; yet, balancing the benefits as against the evils, the law of competition remains as a controlling element in the business world. That free and unrestricted competition in the matter of railroad charges may be productive of evils does not militate against the fact that such is the law now governing the subject. No law can be enacted nor system be devised for the control of human affairs that in its enforcement does not produce some evil results, no matter how beneficial its general purpose may be. There are benefits and there are evils which result from the operation of the law of free competition between railway companies. The time may come when the companies will be relieved from the operation of this law, but they cannot, by combination and agreements among themselves, bring about this change. The fact that the provisions of the interstate commerce act may have changed in many respects the conduct of the companies in the carrying on of the public business they are engaged in does not show that it was the intent of congress, in the enactment of that statute, to clothe railway companies with the right to combine together for the purpose of avoiding the effects of competition on the subject of rates.'

*338 The whole opinion is a remarkably strong presentation of the views of the learned judge who wrote it.

Still, again, it is answered that the effects **558 of free competition among railroad companies, as described by the counsel for the companies themselves in the course of their argument, are greatly exaggerated. According to that argument, the moment an agreement of this nature is prohibited the railroads commence to cut their rates, and they cease only with their utter financial ruin, leaving, perhaps, one to raise rates indefinitely when its rivals have been driven away. It is said that this is a most overdrawn statement, and that, while absolutely free competition may have in some instances and for a time resulted in injury to some of the railroads, it is not at all clear that the general result has been other than beneficial to the whole public, and not in the long run detrimental to the prosperity of the roads. It is matter of common knowledge that agreements as to rates have been continually made of late years, and that complaints of each company in regard to the violation of such agreements by its rivals have been frequent and persistent. Rate wars go on notwithstanding any agreement to the contrary, and the struggle for business among competing roads keeps on, and, in the nature of things, will keep on, and alleged agreement to the contrary notwithstanding; and it is only by the exercise of good sense, and by the presence of a common interest, that railroads, without entering into any affirmative agreement in regard thereto, will keep within the limit of exacting a fair and reasonable return for services rendered. These agreements have never been found really effectual for any extended period.

The interstate commerce commission, from whose reports quotations have been quite freely made by counsel for the purpose of proving the views of its learned members in regard to this subject, has never distinctly stated that agreements among competing railroads to maintain prices are to be commended, or that the general effect is to be regarded as beneficial. They have stated in their fourty annual report that competition may degenerate into rate wars, and that such wars are as unsetting to the business of the country *339 as they are mischievous to the carriers, and that the spirit of existing law is against them. They then add: 'Agreements between railroad companies which from time to time they have entered into with a view to prevent such occurrences have never been found effectual, and for the very sufficient reason that the mental reservations in forming them have been quite as numerous and more influential than the written stipulations.' It would seem true, therefore, that there is no guaranty of financial health to be found in entering into agreements for the maintenance of rates, nor is financial ruin or insolvency the necessary result of their absence.

The claim that the company has the right to charge reasonable rates, and that, therefore, it has the right to enter into a combination with competing roads to maintain such rates, cannot be admitted. The conclusion does not follow from an admission of the premise. What one company may do in the way of charging reasonable rates is radically different from entering into an agreement with other and competing roads to keep up the rates to that point. If there be any competition, the extent of the charge for the service will be seriously affected by that fact. Competition will itself bring charges down to what may be reasonable, while, in the case of an agreement to keep prices up, competition is allowed no play. It is shut out, and the rate is practically fixed by the companies themselves by virtue of the agreement, so long as they abide by it.

As a result of this review of the situation, we find two very widely divergent views of the effects which might be expected to result from declaring illegal all contracts in restraint of trade, etc.; one side predicting financial disaster and ruin to competing railroads, including thereby the ruin of shareholders, the destruction of immensely valuable properties, and the consequent prejudice to the public interest; while on the other side predictions equally earnest are made that no such mournful results will follow, and it is urged that there is a necessity, in order that the public interest may be fairly and justly protected, to allow free and open competition among railroads upon the subject of the rates for the transportation of persons and property.

*340 The arguments which have been addressed to us against the inclusion of all contracts in restraint of trade, as provided for by the language of the act, have been based upon the alleged presumption that congress, notwithstanding the language of the act, could not have intended to embrace all contracts, but only such contracts as were in unreasonable restraint of trade. Under these circumstances, we are therefore asked to hold that the act of congress excepts contracts which are not in unreasonable restraint of trade, and which only keep rates up to a reasonable price, notwithstanding the language of the act makes no such exception. In other words, we are asked to read into the act, by way of judicial legislation an exception that is not placed there by the lawmaking branch of the government, and this is to be done upon the theory that the impolicy of such legislation is so clear that it cannot be supposed congress intended the natural import of the language it used. This we cannot and ought not to do. That impolicy is not so clear, nor are the reasons for the exception so potent, as to permit us to interpolate an exception into the language of the act, and to thus materially alter its meaning and effect. It may be that the policy evidenced by the passage of the act itself will, if carried out, result **559 in disaster to the roads, and in a failure to secure the advantages sought from such legislation. Whether that will be the result or not we do not know and cannot predict. These considerations are, however, not for us. If the act ought to read as contended for by defendants, congress is the body to amend it, and not this court, by a process of judicial legislation wholly unjustifiable. Large numbers do not agree that the view taken by defendants is sound or true in substance, and congress may, and very probably did, share in that belief in government is to be found in its statutes, government is to be found in its statutes and, when they have not directly spoken, then in the decisions of the courts and the constant practice of the government officials; but when the lawmaking power speaks upon a particular subject, over which it has constitutional power to legislate, public policy in such a case is what the statute enacts. If the law prohibit any contract*341 or combination in restraint of trade or commerce, a contract or combination made in violation of such law is void, whatever may have been theretofore decided by the courts to have been the public policy of the country on that subject.

The conclusion which we have drawn from the examination above made into the question before us is that the anti-trust act applies to railroads, and that it renders illegal all agreements which are in restraint of trade or commerce, as we have above defined that expression, and the question then arises whether the agreement before us is of that nature.

Although the case is heard on bill and answer, thus making it necessary to assume the truth of the allegations in the answer which are well pleaded, yet the legal effect of the agreement itself cannot be altered by the answer, nor can its violation of law be made valid by allegations of good intention or of desire to simply maintain reasonable rates; nor can the plaintiffs' allegations as to the intent with which the agreement was entered into be regarded, as such intent is denied on the part of the defendants; and, if the intent alleged in the bill were a necessary fact to be proved in order to maintain the suit, the bill would have to be dismissed. In the view we have taken of the question, the intent alleged by the government is not necessary to be proved. The question is one of law in regard to the meaning and effect of the agreement itself, namely, does the agreement restrain trade or commerce in any way so as to be a violation of the act? We have no doubt that it does. The agreement on its face recites that it is entered into 'for the purpose of mutual protection by establishing and maintaining reasonable rates, rules, and regulations on all freight traffic, both through and local.' To that end the association is formed, and a body created which is to adopt rates, which, when agreed to, are to be the governing rates for all the companies, and a violation of which subjects the defaulting company to the payment of a penalty; and, although the parties have a right to withdraw from the agreement on giving 30 days' notice of a desire so to do, yet while in force, and assuming it to be lived up to, there can be no doubt *342 that its direct, immediate, and necessary effect is to put a restraint upon trade or commerce as described in the act.

For these reasons, the suit of the government can be maintained without proof of the allegation that the agreement was entered into for the purpose of restraining trade or commerce, or for maintaining rates above what was reasonable. The necessary effect of the agreement is to restrain trade or commerce, no matter what the intent was on the part of those who signed it.

One or two subsidiary questions remain to be decided.

It is siad that to grant the injunction prayed for in this case is to give the statute a retroactive effect; that the contract, at the time it was entered into, was not prohibited or declared illegal by the statute, as it had not then been passed, and to now enjoin the doing of an act which was legal at the time it was done would be improper. We give to the law no retroactive effect. The agreement in question is a continuing one. The parties to it adopt certain machinery, and agree to certain methods for the purpose of establishing and maintaining in the future reasonable rates for transportation. Assuming such action to have been legal at the time the agreement was first entered into, the continuation of the agreement, after it has been declared to be illegal, becomes a violation of the act. The statute prohibits the continuing or entering into such an agreement for the future, and, if the agreement be continued, it then becomes a violation of the act. There is nothing of an ex post facto character about the act. The civil remedy by injunction and the liability to punishment under the criminal provisions of the act are entirely distinct, and there can be no question of any act being regarded as a violation of the statute which occurred before it was passed. After its passage, if the law be violated, the parties violating it may render themselves liable to be punished criminally, but not otherwise.

It is also argued that the United States have no standing in court to maintain this bill; that they have no pecuniary interest in the result of the litigation, or in the question to be decided by the court. We think that the fourth section of *343 the act invests the government with full power and authority to bring such an action as this, and, if the facts be proved, an injunction should issue. Congress, having the control of interstate commerce, has also the duty of protecting it, and it is entirely competent for that body to give the remedy by injunction, as more **560 efficient than any other civil remedy. The subject is fully and ably discussed in the case of In re Debs, 158 U. S. 564, 15 Sup. Ct. 900. See, also, Cincinnati, N. O. & T. P. Ry. Co. v. Interstate Commerce Commission, 162 U. S. 184, 16 Sup. Ct. 700; Texas & P. R. Co. v. Interstate Commerce Commission, 162 U. S. 197, 16 Sup. Ct. 666.

For the reasons given, the decrees of the United States circuit court of appeals and of the circuit court for the district of Kansas must be reversed, and the case remanded to the circuit court for further proceedings in conformity with this opinion.

4.4 Private Party Autonomy in the Rail Sector and Ruinous Competition: The Joint Traffic Case

The same kind of motivation was discussed by the Court in *McLean Trucking v. United States*, 321 U.S. 67 (1944), where, evaluating a merger between two trucking companies, it was affirmed that there are three kinds of exemptions: (1) exemptions implied by federal regulation; (2) express exemptions; and (3) exemptions implied by state regulation[12]. An exemption will be implied when the state has created a scheme that displaces competition according to a clearly articulated state policy. *See Parker v. Brown*, 317 U.S. 341 (1943). Recall the *Trans-Missouri* case, and specifically the second argument regarding the absence of a violation of the Sherman Act[13] because of the reasonableness of the rates. They substantially said that the Court should have applied to the Sherman Act the same standard applied under the common law. The Court rejected this argument because the Sherman Act punishes "every contract in restraint of trade."

The Court repeated the reasoning of *Trans-Missouri in United States v. Joint Traffic Ass'n*, 171 U.S. 505 (1898) (case 5). *Joint Traffic*'s defense was based on the theory of ruinous competition, according to which in a market with fixed costs, the average cost declines as output expands. This leads to a price war that will

---

12 A deep analysis of the boundaries for the intervention of public authorities can be studied in: Landes W., *Optimal Sanctions for antitrust violations,* in 50 *University of Chicago Law Review*, 1983, p. 652 ff.

13 The violation of the Sherman Act can cause both damages and criminal sanctions: Sidak G., *Note, Rethinking antitrust damages*, in *33 Stanford L. Review*, 1981, p. 329 ff. and Becker G.S., *Crime and Punishment: an economic approach,* in *76 J. Pol. Econ.*, 1968 p. 169 ff. In the most of the European countries antitrust vialoations don't imply a criminal proceeding.

continue until only one firm remains in the market. Yet if this theory were valid, the Court's decision should have led to the decline of the railroad industry. But it did not:

(…)
Notwithstanding the general liberty of contract which is possessed by the citizen under the constitution, we find that there are many kinds of contracts which, while not in themselves immoral or mala in se, may yet be prohibited by the ***573** legislation of the states, or, in certain cases, by congress. The question comes back whether the statute under review is a legitimate exercise of the power of congress over interstate commerce, and a valid regulation thereof. The question is, for us, one of power only, and not of policy. We think the power exists in congress, and that the statute is therefore valid.

Finally, we are asked to reconsider the question decided in the Trans-Missouri Case, and to retrace the steps taken therein, because of the plain error contained in that decision, and the widespread alarm with which it was received, and the serious consequences which have resulted, or may soon result, from the law as interpreted in that case.

It is proper to remark that an application for a reconsideration of a question but lately decided by this court is usually based upon a statement that some of the arguments employed on the original hearing of the question have been overlooked or misunderstood, or that some controlling authority has been either misapplied by the court or passed over without discussion or notice. While this is not strictly an application for a rehearing in the same case, yet in substance it is the same thing. The court is asked to reconsider a question but just decided after a careful investigation of the matter involved. There have heretofore been in effect two arguments of precisely the same questions now before the court, and the same arguments were addressed to us on both those occasions. The report of the Trans-Missouri Case shows a dissenting opinion delivered in that case, and that the opinion was concurred in by three other members of the court.

That opinion, it will be seen, gives with great force and ability the arguments against the decision which was finally arrived at by the court. It was after a full discussion of the questions involved, and with the knowledge of the views entertained by the minority as expressed in the dissenting opinion, that the majority of the court came to the conclusion it did. Soon after the decision a petition for a rehearing of the case was made, supported by a printed argument in its favor, and pressed with an earnestness and vigor and at a length which were certainly commensurate with the importance of the case. ***574**

This court, with care and deliberation, and also with a full appreciation of their importance, again considered the questions involved in its former decision.

A majority of the court once more arrived at the conclusion it had first announced, and accordingly it denied the application. And now, for the third time, the same arguments are employed, and the court is again asked to recant its former opinion, and to decide the same question in direct opposition to the conclusion arrived at in the Trans-Missouri Case.

The learned counsel, while making the application, frankly confess that the argument in opposition to the decision in the case above named has been so fully, so clearly, and so forcibly presented in the dissenting opinion of Mr. Justice WHITE that it is hardly possible to add to it, nor is it necessary to repeat it.

The fact that there was so close a division of opinion in this court when the matter was first under advisement, together with the different views taken by some of the judges of the lower courts, led us to the most careful and scrutinizing examination of the arguments advanced by both sides, and it was after such an examination that the majority of the court came to the conclusion it did.

It is not now alleged that the court on the former occasion overlooked any argument for the respondents or misapplied any controlling authority. It is simply insisted that the court, notwithstanding the arguments for an opposite view, arrived at an erroneous result, which, for reasons already stated, ought to be reconsidered and reversed.

As we have twice already deliberately and earnestly considered the same arguments which are now for a third time pressed upon our attention, it could hardly be expected that our opinion should now change from that already expressed. ***34***

While an erroneous decision might be in some cases properly reconsidered and overruled, yet it is clear that the first necessity is to convince the court that the decision was erroneous. It is scarcely to be assumed that such a result could be ****575*** secured by the presentation for a third time of the same arguments which had twice before been unsuccessfully urged upon the attention of the court.

We have listened to them now because the eminence of the counsel engaged, their earnestness and zeal, their evident belief in the correctness of their position, and, most important of all, the very grave nature of the questions argued, called upon the court to again give to those arguments strict and respectful attention. It is not matter for surprise that we still are unable to see the error alleged to exist in our former decision, or to change our opinion regarding the questions therein involved.

Upon the point that the agreement is not in fact one in restraint of trade, even though it did prevent competition, it must be admitted that the former argument has now been much enlarged and amplified, and a general and most masterly review of that question has been presented by counsel for the respondents. That this agreement does in fact prevent competition, and that it most have been so intended, we have already attempted to show. Whether stifling competition tends directly to restrain commerce in the case of naturally competing railroads is a question upon which counsel have argued with very great ability. They acknowledge that this agreement purports to restrain competition, although, they say, in a very slight degree, and on a single point. They admit that, if competition and commerce were identical, being but different names for the same thing, then, in assuming to restrain competition even so far, it would be assuming in a corresponding degree to restrain commerce. Counsel then add (and therein we entirely agree with them) that no such identity can be pretended, because it is plain that commerce can and does take place on a large scale, and in numerous forms, without competition. The material considerations therefore turn upon the effects of competition upon the business of railroads,-whether they are favorable to the commerce in which the roads are engaged, or unfavorable, and in restraint of that commerce. Upon that question it is contended that agreements between railroad companies of the ****576*** nature of that now before us are promotive, instead of in restraint, of trade.

This conclusion is reached by counsel after an examination of the peculiar nature of railroad property, and the alleged baneful effects of competition upon it and also upon the public. It is stated that the only resort open to railroads to save themselves from the effects of a ruinous competition is that of agreements among themselves to check and control it. A ruinous competition is, as they say, apt to be carried on until the weakest of the combatants goes to destruction. After that the survivor, being relieved from competition, proceeds to raise its prices as high as the business will bear. Commerce, it is said, thus finally becomes restrained by the effects of competition, while at the same time otherwise valuable railroad property is thereby destroyed, or greatly reduced in value. There can be no doubt that the general tendency of competition among competing railroads is towards lower rates for transportation, and the result of lower rates is generally a greater demand for the articles so transported, and this greater demand can only be gratified by a larger supply, the furnishing of which increases commerce. This is the first and direct result of competition among railroad carriers.

In the absence of any agreement restraining competition, this result, it is argued, is neutralized, and the opposite one finally reached, by reason of the peculiar nature of railroad property, which must be operated, and the capital invested in which cannot be withdrawn, and the railroad managers are therefore, as is claimed, compelled to not only compete among themselves for business, but also to carry on the war of competition until it shall terminate in the utter destruction or the buying up of the weaker roads, after which the survivor will raise the rates as high as is possible. Thus the indirect but final effect of competition is claimed to be the raising of rates, and the consequent restraint of trade, and it is urged that this result is only to be prevented by such an agreement as we have here. In that way alone it is said that competition is overcome, and general uniformity and reasonableness of rates securely established. ***577***

The natural, direct, and immediate effect of competition is, however, to lower rates, and to thereby increase the demand for commodities, the supplying of which increases commerce; and an agreement whose first and direct effect is to prevent this play of competition restrains, instead of promoting, trade and commerce. Whether, in the absence of an agreement as to rates, the consequences described by counsel will in fact follow as a result of competition, is matter of very great uncertainty, depending upon many contingencies, and in large degree upon the voluntary action of the managers of the several roads. Railroad companies may, and often do, continue in existence and engage in their lawful traffic at some profit, although they are competing railroads, and are not acting under any agreement or combination with their competitors upon the subject of rates. It appears from the brief of counsel in this case that the agreement in question does not embrace all of the lines or systems engaged in the business of railroad transportation between Chicago and the Atlantic coast. It cannot be said that destructive competition, or, in other words, war to the death, is bound ****35*** to result unless an agreement or combination to avoid it is entered into between otherwise competing roads.

It is not only possible, but probable, that good sense and integrity of purpose would prevail among the managers, and, while making no agreement and entering into no combination by which the whole railroad interest as herein represented should act as one combined and consolidated body, the managers of each road might yet make such reasonable charges for the business done by it as the facts might justify. An agreement of the nature of this one, which directly and effectually stifles competition, must be regarded under the statute as one in restraint of trade, notwithstanding there are possibilities that a restraint of trade may also follow competition that may be indulged in until the weaker roads are completely destroyed, and the survivor thereafter raises rates and maintains them.

Coming to the conclusion we do in regard to the various questions herein discussed, we think it unnecessary to ***578*** further allude to the other reasons which have been advanced for a reconsideration of the decision in the Trans-Missouri Case.

The judgments of the circuit court of the United States for the Southern district of New York and of the circuit court of appeals for the Second circuit are reversed, and the case remanded to the circuit court, with directions to take such further proceedings therein as may be in conformity with this opinion.

4.5 Rail Liberalization in the European Union and the Refusal to Deal

After the adoption of Directive 91/440/CE, the European rail sector was liberalized through the introduction of the rule of separation between the owner of the network and the transport companies[14]. The aim of the European Commission, through this opening of competition in a sector that was structured by historic public-integrated monopolies, was to open the markets for both infrastructures management and transport services[15]. But after more than two years, the balance is very different according to the member States. The German railway[16], for example, is becoming the first European railway enterprise, while the French[17] and Italian[18] ones have not managed to expand beyond their borders and do not allow other companies to join in their networks[19]. Nevertheless, the right of access to

---

[14] For a complete view on rail liberalization, see: European conference of ministers of transport(ECMT), R*ailway accounts for effective regulation*, march 2007, Id, *European integration of rail freight transport: Conclusions of Round Table 125,* Paris, 28-29 November 2002, Id, *Rail reform and charges for the use of infrastructure*, 2005, Chabalier, *The Europeanization of the railway sector*, Bilgi University, Istanbul, 21-23 September 2006, Carpaneto L., *Il diritto comunitario dei trasporti tra sussidiarità e mercato. Il caso del trasporto ferroviario*, Torino, 2009.

[15] For an economic analysis of railway liberalization, see: Institute for Transport Studies, *European Railway Comparisons, Final Report*, ITS Working Paper 418, Freeman, M (1999) *Review article. 'Trains of thought': steam railway capitalism and the law in 19th-century England*, in *Oxford Journal of Legal Studies* 1999, p. 99 ff., Friedlander A. - Berndt E.R., Chiang J. S. - M. Showalter M. - Vellturro C.A., *Rail Costs and Capital Adjustments in a Quasi-Regulated Environment*, in *Journal of Transport Economics and Policy*, 1993, p. 131 ff.

[16] See Lalive S., Working Paper No. 0609, *Entry in liberalized railway markets: The German experience,* Zurich, 2007 and Häfner P., *The Effects of Railroad Reform in Germany*, in *Japan Railways and Transport Review*, 1996, 15, p. 27 ff.

[17] See Quinet E., *France: Avoiding competition*, in Gómez - Ibañez, J.A. - de Rus G. (ed), *Competition in the railway industry: An international comparative analysis*. Edward Elgar, 2006.

[18] See Celli - L. Pettinari L. - Piazza R., *La liberalizzazione del trasporto ferroviario*, Torino, 2007.

[19] For a comparative perspective of the rail liberalization see: Campos, J, *Spain: The end of an era*, in Gómez - Ibañez, J.A. de Rus G. (ed.), *Competition in the railway industry: An international comparative analysis*. Edward Elgar, 2006, Carbajo J.C. - Estache A., *Railway Concessions – Heading down the Right Track in Argentina, Viewpoint, 88. Finance and Private Sector Development Department*, The World Bank, Washington D.C., 1998, Beria P. - Quinet E. - De Rus G. - Schulz, C., *A comparison of rail liberalisation levels across four European countries*, Munich, 2010, European Council of Ministers of Transport, *National Policies towards shifting freight form road to rail: the case of Switzerland, the United kingdom and France*, 2002, European Commission (2009b). *Report from the Commission to the Council and the European Parliament. Second report on monitoring development of the rail market*, SEC(2009)1687. European Commission, Gomez-Ibanez, J.A. - Pittman, R. (2004). *Chinese Railway Reform and*

infrastructures is now consolidated in the European legal framework due to the application of the essential facility doctrine.

In the European Nights Services case, the European Commission distinguished two relevant service markets: (1) the market for the transport of business travelers, for whom scheduled air travel, high-speed rail travel, and the rail services to be operated by ENS are interchangeable modes of transport; and (2) the market for the transport of leisure travelers, for whom substitute services may include economy-class air travel, train, coach, and possibly private motor car.

The European Commission held that the behavior of an international joint venture (ENS) operating the Channel tunnel and refusing to provide traction services to other operators, causes a restriction of the competition. It stated that ENS's parent undertakings were not withdrawing permanently from the relevant market, since their technical and financial resources could easily enable them to set up an international grouping within the meaning of Article 3 of Directive 91/440 and to provide overnight passenger transport services. Furthermore, they continued to operate primarily in a market upstream from ENS's market, namely the market in necessary rail services, which the railway undertakings sold to transport operators such as ENS. Indeed, new railway companies are held to the rights of access conferred by that provision, although member States may enact domestic legislation that is more generous in the access it allows to infrastructures (case 6) ECJ, 15 September 1998, Joined cases T-374/94, T-375/94, T-384/94 and T-388/94, European Night Services Ltd (ENS), in Rep., p. II-03141):

(…)

90 First of all, it must be noted that, in order to assess the effects of the ENS agreements on competition and on trade between Member States, the Commission defined two relevant service markets in the decision: the market for the transport of business travelers, for whom scheduled air travel and high-speed rail travel are interchangeable modes of transport (the `intermodal' market for business travel), and the market for the transport of leisure travelers, for whom substitute services may include economy-class air travel, train, coach and possibly private motor car (the `intermodal' market for leisure travel) (see points 26 and 27 of the decision).

91 The Commission went on to consider, referring to Case 66/86 Ahmed Saeed Flugreisen and Silver Line Reisebüro v Zentrale zur Bekämpfung unlauteren Wettbewerbs [1989] ECR 803, that the relevant geographical market should be confined to the routes actually to be served by ENS (points 28 and 29 of the decision), namely:

- London-Amsterdam, - London-Frankfurt/Dortmund, - Paris-Glasgow/Swansea and - Brussels-Glasgow/Plymouth.

Competition, in *Journal of Transport Economics and Policy*, 2004 p. 309 ff., Kirchner, *Rail Liberalisation Index 2004: Comparison of the Market Opening in the Rail Markets of the Member States of the European Union, Switzerland and Norway*, Humboldt University, Berlin, 2004.

92 As that definition of the geographical market has not been challenged by the applicants, it follows that the ENS agreements fell to be assessed solely on the basis of the four separate geographical markets listed above and solely in the context of an intermodal market comprising various modes of transport such as rail, air, coach and motor car. On that basis, therefore, it is necessary to examine whether the Commission correctly evaluated ENS's market shares in order to arrive at the conclusion that the ENS agreements would have an appreciable effect on trade between Member States, bearing in mind that, according to the applicants' notification, those market shares would not exceed the critical threshold of 5% and would, in any event, be insignificant.

93 It is to be noted here that the contested decision makes no reference to the market shares of ENS or of any other operators competing with ENS and also present on the various intermodal markets taken by the Commission as the relevant markets for the purposes of applying Article 85(1) of the Treaty. Consequently, even if - contrary to the applicants' submission - the ENS agreements were to restrict competition, the Court is not in a position, in the absence of any such data concerning the analysis of the relevant market in the contested decision, to make any finding as to whether the supposed restrictions on competition have an appreciable effect on trade between Member States and are thus caught by Article 85(1) of the Treaty, having regard, in particular, to the intermodal competition which is, according to the decision itself, a feature of the two service markets in question.

94 It was not until the stage of the proceedings before the Court that the Commission first referred to the notification submitted by the parties in support of its contention that `even on the basis of the conservative - and by nature therefore restrictive - forecasts of ENS which are based on a narrower definition of the market, the Night Services' share of the business segment of the market is 7%, and 8% in the case of the leisure segment of the market'. It was also during the written procedure that it first asserted that ENS's market share should be calculated, for the business segment, in relation to early morning and late evening flights rather than by reference to all the flights available round the clock on a given route and is thus in fact much larger.

95 It is settled law that whilst, in stating the reasons for the decisions which it takes to enforce the rules on competition, the Commission is not required to discuss all the issues of fact and law and the considerations which have led it to adopt its decision, it is none the less required under Article 190 of the Treaty to set out at least the facts and considerations having decisive importance in the context of the decision in order to make clear to the Court and the persons concerned the circumstances in which it has applied the Treaty (Case C-360/92 P Publishers Association v Commission [1995] ECR I-23, paragraph 39, Case T-290/94 Kaysersberg v Commission [1997] ECR II-2137, paragraph 150, and Joined Cases T-369/94 and T-85/95 DIR International Film and Others v Commission [1998] ECR II-357, paragraph 117). It is also clear from the case-law that, other than in exceptional circumstances, the statement of reasons must be contained in the decision itself, and it is not sufficient for it to be explained subsequently for the first time before the Court (Case T-61/89 Dansk Pelsdyravlerforening v Commission [1992] ECR II-1931, paragraph 131, Case T-230/94 Farrugia v Commission [1996] ECR II-195, paragraph 36, and Case T-16/91 RV Rendo and Others v Commission [1996] ECR II-1827, paragraph 45).

96 It follows from the abovementioned case-law that when a Commission decision applying Article 85(1) of the Treaty suffers from serious omissions, such as the absence of any reference to the market shares of the undertakings concerned, the Commission may not remedy that defect by adducing for the first time before the Court figures and other analytical data from which it may be concluded that the essential elements of a situation in which

Article 85(1) applies are in fact present unless none of the parties had challenged the analytical data in question during the prior administrative procedure.

97 Here, according to the estimates put forward by the applicants in the notification, ENS's market shares were not expected to exceed 4%, and it was only on the basis of a narrower market definition that they might reach 7% for the business travel market and 8% for the leisure travel market (see point 2.1.2 of the summary of the notification), without even then having an appreciable effect on competition. It is thus clear that, as regards the effect of the ENS agreements on trade between Member States, the applicants and the Commission were starting from different premisses, the applicants considering that the agreements did not have an appreciable effect on intra-Community trade. The Commission was thus required to provide an adequate statement of its reasons for finding that the ENS agreements had an appreciable effect on trade between Member States.

98 Furthermore, even on the assumption that the Commission may adduce figures and other analytical data for the first time before the Court in order to show that its decision was well founded, the conclusions which it draws from the notification (see paragraph 94 above) are incorrect. According to Table 17 on page 26 of the notification, ENS's market shares for the business travel segment were to be under 5% on all the routes concerned:

- London-Amsterdam : 3% - London-Frankfurt/Dortmund : 3% - Paris-Glasgow/Swansea : 4% - Brussels-Glasgow/Plymouth : 1%.

99 Again according to Table 17 in the notification, ENS's market share in the leisure travel segment was expected to exceed 5% on only two of the four routes to be served by it, without on any route exceeding the 8% threshold put forward by the Commission:

- London-Amsterdam : 7% - London-Frankfurt/Dortmund : 6% - Paris-Glasgow/Swansea : 4% - Brussels-Glasgow/Plymouth : 4%.

100 It is further stated in the notification that ENS's market shares in the leisure travel segment were likely to remain fixed or even, in view of its limited possibilities for increasing capacity, to fall as the market as a whole grew. Whilst it is true, as has been pointed out above, that the Commission was not required to discuss all the issues of fact and law raised during the course of the administrative procedure prior to the adoption of the contested decision, this latter consideration put forward by the notifying parties was an essential part of their argument that the ENS agreements had an insignificant effect on trade between Member States. It is thus not possible to conclude, as the Commission maintains, that according to the notification ENS's market share on the leisure travel segment was 8%, or even that it exceeded 5%.

101 It must be noted here that whilst at points 2.1.2 of the summary of the notification and II.4.c.5.2(d) of the notification itself the parties stated, inter alia, that ENS's market share might reach 7% in the business travel segment and 8% in the leisure travel segment, they nevertheless made it clear that those shares would only apply in the context of a narrower definition of the market, based on `city to city flows' and excluding residual competition from cars and coaches. Moreover, those estimates put forward by the parties related to average shares of an overall geographical market and not to the four routes actually to be served by ENS and specifically regarded by the Commission as the different relevant geographical markets within which the ENS agreements fell to be assessed. Consequently, since the contested decision defined the relevant markets by reference not to `city to city flows' but to flows involving more than one destination (for example, from Paris to Glasgow and Swansea), since it did not exclude residual competition from cars and coaches from its definition of the market and since it did not assess the effects of the ENS agree-

ments on the basis of an overall geographical market but on that of the four routes actually to be served by ENS, the Commission was not entitled to rely on the abovementioned market shares of 7% and 8%.

102 In any event, even if, as noted above, ENS's share of the tourist travel market was in fact likely to exceed 5% on certain routes, attaining 7% on the London-Amsterdam route and 6% on the London-Frankfurt/Dortmund route (see paragraph 94 above), it must be borne in mind that, according to the case-law, an agreement may fall outside the prohibition in Article 85(1) of the Treaty if it has only an insignificant effect on the market, taking into account the weak position which the parties concerned have on the product or service market in question (Case 5/69 Völk v Vervaecke [1969] ECR 295, paragraph 7). With regard to the quantitative effect on the market, the Commission has argued that, in accordance with its notice on agreements of minor importance, cited above, Article 85(1) applies to an agreement when the market share of the parties to the agreement amounts to 5%. However, the mere fact that that threshold may be reached and even exceeded does not make it possible to conclude with certainty that an agreement is caught by Article 85(1) of the Treaty. Point 3 of that notice itself states that `the quantitative definition of "appreciable" given by the Commission is, however, no absolute yardstick' and that `in individual cases ... agreements between undertakings which exceed these limits may ... have only a negligible effect on trade between Member States or on competition, and are therefore not caught by Article 85(1)' (see also Langnese-Iglo, cited above, paragraph 98). It is noteworthy, moreover, if only as an indication, that that analysis is corroborated by the Commission's 1997 notice on agreements of minor importance (OJ 1997 C 372, p. 13) replacing the notice of 3 September 1986, cited above, according to which even agreements which are not of minor importance can escape the prohibition on agreements on account of their exclusively favourable impact on competition.

103 That being so, where, as in the present case, horizontal agreements between undertakings reach or only very slightly exceed the 5% threshold regarded by the Commission itself as critical and such as to justify application of Article 85(1) of the Treaty, the Commission must provide an adequate statement of its reasons for considering such agreements to be caught by the prohibition in Article 85(1) of the Treaty. Its obligation to do so is all the more imperative here, where, as the applicants stated in their notification, ENS has to operate on markets largely dominated by other modes of transport, such as air transport, and where, on the assumption of an increase in demand on the relevant markets and having regard to the limited possibilities for ENS to increase its capacity, its market shares will either fall or remain stable. In addition, such a statement of reasons is necessary in the present instance in view of the fact that, as the Court of Justice held at paragraph 86 of its judgment in Musique Diffusion Française, cited above, an agreement is capable of exercising an appreciable influence on the pattern of trade between Member States even where the market shares of the undertakings concerned do not exceed 3%, provided that those market shares exceed those of most of their competitors.

104 There is, however, no such statement of reasons in the present case.

105 It must be concluded from the foregoing that the contested decision does not contain a sufficient statement of reasons to enable the Court to make a ruling on the shares held by ENS on the various relevant markets and, consequently, on whether the ENS agreements have an appreciable effect on trade between Member States, and the decision must therefore be annulled on that ground.

(...)

135 According to the contested decision, the ENS agreements have effects restricting existing and potential competition (a) among the parent undertakings, (b) between the parent undertakings and ENS and (c) vis-à-vis third parties; furthermore (d), those restrictions are aggravated by the presence of a network of joint ventures set up by the parent undertakings.

136 Before any examination of the parties' arguments as to whether the Commission's analysis as regards restrictions of competition was correct, it must be borne in mind that in assessing an agreement under Article 85(1) of the Treaty, account should be taken of the actual conditions in which it functions, in particular the economic context in which the undertakings operate, the products or services covered by the agreement and the actual structure of the market concerned (judgments in Delimitis, cited above, Gottrup-Klim, cited above, paragraph 31, Case C-399/93 Oude Luttikhuis and Others v Verenigde Coöperatieve Melkindustrie [1995] ECR I-4515, paragraph 10, and Case T-77/94 VGB and Others v Commission [1997] ECR II-759, paragraph 140), unless it is an agreement containing obvious restrictions of competition such as price-fixing, market-sharing or the control of outlets (Case T-148/89 Tréfilunion v Commission [1995] ECR II-1063, paragraph 109). In the latter case, such restrictions may be weighed against their claimed pro-competitive effects only in the context of Article 85(3) of the Treaty, with a view to granting an exemption from the prohibition in Article 85(1).

137 It must also be stressed that the examination of conditions of competition is based not only on existing competition between undertakings already present on the relevant market but also on potential competition, in order to ascertain whether, in the light of the structure of the market and the economic and legal context within which it functions, there are real concrete possibilities for the undertakings concerned to compete among themselves or for a new competitor to penetrate the relevant market and compete with the undertakings already established (Delimitis, cited above, paragraph 21). Furthermore, according to the Commission notice of 1993 concerning the assessment of cooperative joint ventures pursuant to Article 85 of the Treaty: `The assumption of potential competitive circumstances presupposes that each parent alone is in a position to fulfil the tasks assigned to the [joint venture] and that it does not forfeit its capabilities to do so by the creation of the [joint venture]. An economically realistic approach is necessary in the assessment of any particular case' (point 18).

138 It is in the light of those considerations, therefore, that it is necessary to examine whether the Commission's assessment of the restrictive effects of the ENS agreements was correct.

- *Restrictions on competition among the parent undertakings*

139 It is clear from the documents before the Court that, prior to the adoption of Directive 91/440, the railway undertakings in the Member States were neither actually nor potentially in competition with each other because most Member States provided for exclusive rights precluding, de jure or de facto, both the provision of international passenger services and access to the infrastructure (the national rail networks). Prior to the adoption of that directive, as the parties have stressed, the only basis on which such services were provided in the Community was that of the traditional cooperation agreements between the railway undertakings operating on the various networks concerned. However, following the adoption of Directive 91/440, conditions of competition on the market for rail transport changed and the railway undertakings operating on their national networks became to a certain extent potential competitors for international passenger services, provided that they formed `international groupings' with other railway undertakings established in other Member States for

the purpose of providing international transport services between those Member States (Articles 3 and 10 of the directive).

140 It would appear from the Commission's arguments that the possibility of providing international services via international groupings is open not only to existing railway undertakings but also to new railway undertakings, including subsidiaries of existing railway undertakings, and that it was on the basis of that premiss that the Commission considered that the ENS agreements restricted competition among the parent undertakings inasmuch as (a) each of the parties to those agreements could form an international grouping either with an undertaking established in the United Kingdom or with its own subsidiary there and thus compete with ENS, (b) each of those parties could set up a subsidiary specialising as a `transport operator' and buy from those parties the same necessary rail services as they sold to ENS and (c) each railway undertaking could itself take on the role of transport operator and provide international night passenger services by buying the necessary rail services from the railway undertakings concerned.

141 With regard to the possibility for each of the parties to the ENS agreements to form an international grouping either with a railway undertaking in the United Kingdom or with its own subsidiary there and thus compete with ENS, it must first of all be borne in mind that since, in accordance with Article 10 of Directive 91/440, an international route may be served only by an international grouping formed by the railway undertakings established in each of the countries concerned, the only `obligatory trading partners' for the constitution of such an international grouping on each route are necessarily the railway undertakings established in each Member State concerned. As the applicants have pointed out, with regard to the example of the London-Amsterdam route, the only obligatory trading partners at the material time were NS and EPS; the fact that SNCF and DB were also members of the grouping could thus have no effect on existing competition since, in the context created by Directive 91/440, neither of those two railway undertakings could compete with EPS and NS on that route. The situation is the same for each of the three other routes actually to be served by ENS (see paragraph 9 above). Consequently, the fact that the four routes in question are operated jointly by EPS, DB, SNCF and NS cannot have the effect of an appreciable restriction of existing competition among the parent undertakings.

142 As regards the view that potential competition is restricted by the fact that each of the parent undertakings could set up subsidiaries in the Member States of the other parent undertakings and form, either with its own subsidiaries or with other railway undertakings established in the other Member States concerned, international groupings in direct competition with ENS, the Court considers this to be a hypothesis unsupported by any evidence or any analysis of the structures of the relevant market from which it might be concluded that it represented a real, concrete possibility. There is no indication either in the contested decision or in the documents before the Court that there are any railway undertakings with subsidiaries in other Member States having themselves the status of railway undertakings, such as to demonstrate any actual exercise of the right to freedom of establishment on the market for rail transport in the Community.

143 It should be stressed here that, as a measure of organisation of the procedure, the Court requested the Commission to indicate whether any railway undertakings established in the Member States had subsidiaries in other Member States having the status of railway undertakings within the meaning of Directive 91/440 and, if so, to specify which railway undertakings had been set up since the entry into force of Directive 91/440. In its answer, the Commission admitted that it had no knowledge of other subsidiaries set up by ENS's parent undertakings either before or after the adoption of Directive 91/440, reiterating,

however, its view that the right of establishment is conferred directly on any interested railway undertaking by Article 52 of the Treaty.

144 The Court considers that the Commission's argument in this regard, to the effect that there is in theory no legal obstacle precluding railway undertakings from exercising their right of establishment in a Member State other than that in which they have their registered office, fails to take account of the economic context and characteristics of the relevant market as they appear from the documents in the case and is thus not sufficient, without further support, to establish the existence of restrictions of potential competition among the parent undertakings or between them and ENS.

145 As the applicants have explained at length in their pleadings, it would be unrealistic, given the novelty and the specific features of the night rail services in question, for the parent undertakings to set up other subsidiaries in other Member States having the status of railway undertakings for the sole purpose of forming a new joint venture to compete with ENS. The prohibitive cost of the investment required for such services through the Channel Tunnel and the fact that there are no economies of scale in the operation of a single route, as opposed to the four routes to be operated together by ENS, show how unrealistic potential competition is among the parent undertakings and between them and ENS. It is, moreover, clear from the documents before the Court that, following the publication in the Official Journal of the European Communities of the Commission's notice inviting interested parties to submit their observations on the ENS agreements as summarised in that notice, no third parties took any steps during the administrative procedure to submit observations as a potential competitor capable of being affected or concerned by the implementation of the ENS agreements (see paragraph 17 above). Finally, it may also be seriously questioned whether ENS has any existing or potential competitors in this context in view of the fact that, as the Commission acknowledged in its answers to the written questions put by the Court, no subsidiaries have yet been set up in other Member States by any Community railway undertakings, whether before or after the adoption of Directive 91/440.

146 On the basis of the foregoing considerations, the Commission's finding that the ENS agreements are such as appreciably to restrict existing and/or potential competition among the parent undertakings and between them and ENS must be held to be vitiated by inadequate reasoning and/or error of assessment.

147 As regards the view that competition among the parent undertakings is restricted because each of the railway undertakings participating in the ENS agreements could either set up a subsidiary specialising as a transport operator or itself take on the role of transport operator and compete with ENS by buying the same necessary rail services, the Court considers that the Commission's assessment is here again based on an analysis of the market which does not correspond to the real situation. The Commission takes as its starting-point the assumption that in the market for rail passenger services there is in addition to railway undertakings another category of economic operators - transport operators - providing the same services as railway undertakings - passenger transport - but by buying or hiring `necessary rail services' - locomotives, crews and access to infrastructure - from those undertakings. ENS, being, according to the decision, a transport operator, could thus be exposed to competition either from specialised subsidiaries set up by railway undertakings as transport operators or by those undertakings themselves acting directly on the market as transport operators, and its creation therefore restricts the parties' freedom to operate individually as transport operators on the relevant market.

148 However, the Commission's assessment in that regard cannot be examined without first answering the question whether international passenger services are provided not only by international groupings as provided for in Directive 91/440 but also by transport operators. As that question is raised, in substance, by the applicants in the context of their second plea in law, it will therefore be examined in that context (see paragraphs 161 to 189 below).

- Restrictions on competition vis-à-vis third parties

149 The contested decision stresses that third-party access to the relevant markets is likely to be impeded by the existence of a special relationship between ENS and its parent undertakings, placing other operators at a disadvantage in competition for the necessary rail services provided by the parent undertakings, and by the Channel Tunnel usage agreement entered into by BR, SNCF and Eurotunnel, which allows BR and SNCF to retain a significant proportion - 75% - of the path capacity reserved for international train services.

150 With regard, first, to the special relationship between ENS and the railway undertakings concerned, it must be noted that the Commission's analysis is based on the premiss that the market for rail passenger transport is split into two parts: an upstream market in the provision of `necessary rail services' (train paths, special locomotives and train crews) and a downstream market in passenger transport, on which transport operators such as ENS operate alongside railway undertakings. According to the decision, the parent undertakings could abuse their dominant position on the upstream market by refusing to provide necessary rail services to third parties competing with ENS on the downstream market.

151 Here again, however, the Commission's assessment cannot be examined without first answering the question whether there are also, in addition to international groupings, transport operators on the relevant markets, which will be examined in the context of the second plea in law, and the question whether the services provided to ENS by the parent undertakings may be categorised as `necessary or essential facilities', which falls within the scope of the third plea and must therefore be examined in that context (see paragraphs 190 to 221 below).

152 As regards, second, any restrictive effects arising out of the Channel Tunnel usage agreement, it must be borne in mind that the Commission's decision exempting that agreement from the prohibition in Article 85(1) of the Treaty (`the Eurotunnel decision') was annulled by judgment of the Court of First Instance of 22 October 1996 in Joined Cases T-79/95 and T-80/95 SNCF and British Railways v Commission [1996] ECR II-1491, on the ground that the Commission had made a factual error in its interpretation of the provisions of that agreement governing the allocation of train paths in the tunnel as between SNCF and BR on the one hand and Eurotunnel on the other.

153 As a measure of organisation of the procedure, the Court requested the parties to state their position on the relevance of that judgment for the present case. In its answer, the Commission considered that it was irrelevant for the appraisal of the legality of the contested decision, point 47 of which indicates that even if BR and SNCF did not hold all the available paths for international trains they would still control a significant proportion of them. The applicants, however, took the view that the judgment confirms that access to the Channel Tunnel is not closed and that the Commission incorrectly assessed the restrictive effects of the tunnel usage agreement vis-à-vis third parties.

154 The Court considers that, since the Commission specifically took the `Eurotunnel agreement' as its basis in order to demonstrate in the contested decision that SNCF's and BR's allegedly privileged access to train paths in the tunnel placed undertakings competing with ENS at a competitive disadvantage, and since the Eurotunnel decision has been annulled by the Court of First Instance on the ground that it contained an error of fact in the interpretation of the provisions of the agreement relating to the allocation of train paths, the Commission cannot derive any valid argument from it with regard to the assessment of the ENS agreements.

- Aggravation of the restrictive effects on competition caused by the presence of a network of joint ventures

155 With regard, finally, to the alleged aggravation of the restriction of competition caused by the presence of networks of joint ventures (points 49 to 53 of the decision), it should first be noted that, according to the Commission's 1993 communication, special attention must be paid to the presence of networks of joint ventures set up by the same parents, by one parent with different partners or by different partners in parallel (point 17 of the communication). In particular, networks of joint ventures can restrict competition where competing parents set up several joint ventures for complementary products which they themselves intend to process or for non-complementary products which they themselves distribute, thus increasing the extent and intensity of the restriction of competition. Those considerations are also valid for the service sector (point 29 of the communication).

156 In the contested decision, the Commission considered that to be the case in the present instance, inasmuch as BR/EPS, SNCF, DB and NS were taking part to varying degrees in a network of joint ventures for the transport of both goods and passengers, in particular through the Channel Tunnel. It referred to the joint venture ACI, set up by, inter alia, BR and SNCF to provide combined transport of goods (Commission Decision 94/594/EC of 27 July 1994 relating to a proceeding under Article 85 of the EC Treaty and Article 53 of the EEA Agreement (IV/34.518 - ACI) (OJ 1994 L 224, p. 28, hereinafter `the ACI decision')), and Autocare Europe, to which BR and SNCB are parties, which provides rail transport for motor vehicles. In its pleadings, the Commission referred for the first time in addition to the joint venture Intercontainer, set up by 26 railway undertakings, including BR and SNCF, and also operating on the market for combined transport of goods.

157 The contested decision does not, however, specify what joint ventures set up by the parent undertakings concern passenger transport services. As a measure of organisation of the procedure, the Court requested the Commission to specify the joint ventures operating on the passenger transport market in which, according to point 51 of the contested decision, ENS's parent undertakings are participating. In its answer, the Commission stated that it had no knowledge of any other joint ventures of ENS's parent undertakings for passenger transport. It noted, however, that `SNCF, SNCB and BR (subsequently to the latter's privatisation, London & Continental Railways Ltd) jointly take part in Eurostar for passenger transport between the United Kingdom and the Continent', although it did not assert that point 51 was in fact implicitly referring to Eurostar. The Court therefore considers that, as regards the alleged presence of a network of joint ventures set up by the parent undertakings, the contested decision is vitiated by an absence of reasoning.

158 As regards the participation of the parent undertakings in joint ventures for combined transport of goods, it follows from point 29 of the Commission's 1993 communication that when parent undertakings set up joint ventures for `non-complementary' services, competition may be restricted when those `non-complementary' services are marketed by the parent undertakings themselves.

159 There is no indication in the contested decision that the parent undertakings themselves market the services provided by ACI, Intercontainer and Autocare. As a measure of organisation of the procedure, the Court requested the applicants to specify whether the transport services provided by ACI, Intercontainer and Autocare were marketed by them or by another undertaking. From their answers it appears that none of the parent undertakings markets or sells services provided by any of those three undertakings. In any event, even if they did market those services, the contested decision does not explain how the participation of some or all of the parent undertakings in a network of joint ventures operating on markets different from that of ENS would restrict competition among them at the level of the creation of ENS. Consequently, the Commission's assessment of the aggravating effects on the restrictions of competition caused by the presence of a network of joint ventures does not contain a sufficient statement of reasons.

160 It follows from the foregoing that, as regards the assessment of the restrictions of competition arising out of the ENS agreements, the contested decision is vitiated by an absence or insufficiency of reasoning.

4.6 European Railway Markets Analysis: Transport Passengers, Traction, and Infrastructures Access

An important case, decided by the European Commission in 2003, provides a complete outline of the different markets involved in rail infrastructures management: passenger/freight transport, traction, and infrastructures access[20]. The European Commission, in concurrence with the European Court of Justice, applied the rule of reason, stating that the refusal to deal in each of these markets is considered an abuse of dominant position unless the restraining company justifies its conduct through reasonable and proportionate public interests[21]. This case was initiated by a complaint from the German railway company Georg Verkehrsorganisa-

---

20 For a complete study of the different services, see: Thompson L.S., *Directions of Railway Reform. International Railway Congress Association*, Vienna, 2001, Oum T. H. – Waters W.G. II - Yu C., *A survey of productivity and efficiency measurement in rail transport*, in *Journal of Transport Economics and Policy*, 1999, p. 9 ff., Meeddat - Sesp, *Les comptes des transports en 2007 (tome 1). Les transferts de l'État et des collectivités locales: Ministère de l'écologie, de l'énergie, du développement durable et de l'aménagement du territoire*, Paris, 2008 and Link H., *Rail infrastructure charging and on-track competition in Germany*, in *International Journal of Transport Management*, 2004 p. 17 ff.

21 The balance between competition and public policies is the key feature of rail liberalization: International Chamber of Commerce, *The liberalization of rail transport in Europe*, 2007, Glaister S. (2006). *Competition undermined by politics*, in Gómez - Ibañez, J.A. - de Rus G. (ed), *Competition in the railway industry: An international comparative analysis*, Edward Elgar, 2006, Campos, Cantos, *Regulating privatized rail transport*, Police research working paper 2064, The World Bank, Economic Development Institute, 1999, Bergmann - Rawlings, *Trasport management. Future directions: redefining the role of transport*, in *Strategic Supply Chain Management: Best Pratice in Supply Chain Management*, Aldershot, 1998, p. 369 ff.

tion GmbH (GVG) against Ferrovie dello Stato SpA (FS), the Italian national railway carrier. GVG complained that since 1995 FS had been refusing to provide access to the Italian infrastructure, to enter into negotiations for the formation of an international grouping, and to provide traction. This prevented GVG from providing an international rail passenger service from various points in Germany via Basle to Milan. The Commission held that by denying GVG access to the services in question, which are necessary for carrying out its business, FS has abused its dominant position within the meaning of Article 102 of the TFEU (case 7):

(...)

2.3. ACCESS TO INFRASTRUCTURE

(14) The railway undertaking also needs to be provided with infrastructure capacity, i.e. a certain time slot on the tracks of the railway networks on which it wishes to provide the cross-border service. Access to the infrastructure includes a number of different services and actions that take place at different points in time. In particular the following elements are important: information regarding the availability of train paths and related prices; the handling of requests for capacity; the permission to use track capacity; train control, including signalling, regulation and the provision of information on train movement; access to refuelling facilities; access to passenger stations; access to marshalling yards; access to storage sidings; and access to maintenance and other technical facilities(15).

(15) Some of these services need to be made available to a railway undertaking before it takes a formal decision to start a service. This holds in particular for the provision of all relevant technical information concerning the allocation of train paths, the reservation of a particular train path and information concerning infrastructure tariffs. Only on the basis of such information and the reservation of the necessary train path can the potential entrant establish a business plan. Based on the latter, the potential entrant takes its entry decision, which, if it is positive, then leads to a start of negotiations with potential partners.

(...)

2.4. ACCESS TO INTERNATIONAL TRAIN PATHS

(22) The provision of international rail transport services requires the coordination of train paths on the national railway networks. Such coordination is carried out by European railway companies in the working groups of Forum Train Europe (hereinafter "FTE"). During such meetings, railway companies discuss the time schedules of services to ensure that rolling stock and infrastructure capacity are available. Three meetings a year are organised on a regular basis(19). Railway companies wishing to provide international services make requests for train paths to the respective allocation bodies. Train paths are reserved on a temporary basis. If they are not taken up within a certain period of time the reservation is cancelled and a new request has to be made during the following FTE meeting. Before the train path can actually be used for a particular service, the allocation body has to verify whether the necessary technical and safety requirements for the rolling stock are fulfilled.

2.5. SAFETY CERTIFICATE

(24) Pursuant to Article 11 of Directive 95/19/EC, the railway undertakings in the international grouping must have a safety certificate to ensure safe service on the routes concerned. In order to obtain the safety certificate, the undertaking must comply with relevant

regulations under national law. In Italy, according to Article 5 of Decree No 277/98(20), the Ministry of Transport determines the relevant standards and regulations on the basis of a proposal made by the infrastructure manager. As the infrastructure manager, FS (RFI) grants the safety certificate to railway undertakings and international groupings.

2.6. TRACTION

(25) In order to be able to provide a rail transport service, a railway undertaking needs to have traction - i.e. a locomotive and a driver - to move the train on the network(21).

(26) At this stage in the process of liberalizing the rail transport sector in the EU, there are a number of technical, legal and economic barriers to the provision of traction for international rail transport services. For a century and a half, European railways have developed within national boundaries. Each national railway has adopted its own technical and administrative standards according to national requirements. As a result, there are 15 different national signalling systems and five different systems for electricity supply (voltage). National systems differ in their operating procedures, length of passing tracks, safety systems, driver training and route knowledge. The fact that different technical standards continue to exist has prevented interoperability in the European market for rail services. Therefore, unless they are equipped with multiple technology, locomotives have to be changed at borders. Similar barriers also exist for drivers, who need route knowledge, a national license and language skills. To provide traction for international services by itself, a railway undertaking would have to set up separate locomotive and driver pools in every Member State where it wishes to operate.

(…)

F. RELEVANT MARKETS

1. THE RELEVANT UPSTREAM MARKETS

(48) Two upstream markets can be identified: the market for access to the infrastructure and the traction market.

1.1. MARKET FOR ACCESS TO THE INFRASTRUCTURE

The product market

(49) The Court of First Instance has considered that there is "a market for access to and management of railway infrastructure"(34). In addition, EU directives, as transposed into Italian law, have established to whom and under what conditions infrastructure capacity can be sold. Directive 91/440/EEC establishes a right of access to the infrastructure for international groupings. In Italy, FS (RFI) sells network capacity to transport service providers such as FS (Trenitalia), Cisalpino, Rail Traction Company (hereinafter "RTC") and Ferrovie Nord Milano SpA (hereinafter "FNME"). It follows that providing access to the railway infrastructure is a discrete market capable of separate delineation.

The geographic market

(50) In order to provide its rail passenger service from German cities, as mentioned above, to Milan via Basle, GVG needs access to the Italian network between Domodossola and Milan. Thus, from the demand side, the relevant geographic market is an intercity railway path in Italy which is connected to the Swiss railway network and which allows GVG to run its train from Basle to Milan, i.e. the Domodossola-Milan segment. Trains originating

in Basle may also pass via Chiasso and via France. However, these other routes do not offer an alternative for GVG, as they would mean a longer travelling time. In any case, as FS (RFI) operates the only long-distance rail network in Italy any other possible connection between Basle and Milan would also imply that GVG has to rent network capacity from FS (RFI).

1.2. TRACTION MARKET

The product market

(51) Traction is defined as the provision of a locomotive and driver. This includes the ancillary service of a locomotive and driver back-up. In principle, traction can either be provided in-house, i.e. by GVG or its partner in the international grouping using their own personnel and locomotives, or traction can be rented from other railway companies.

(52) The provision of traction is linked to a specific rail transport service on the downstream market. In this case it is a passenger rail transport service from Basle to Milan via Domodossola. As the traction is provided with a view to carrying out this particular transport service, certain requirements have to be fulfilled by the traction supplier. In particular, the traction supplier has to provide a locomotive at a certain location (here: Milan/Domodossola), at a certain point in time (before the departure of the train) and for a certain time period (until the specific transport service is terminated). In the case of a scheduled train service, such as GVG's planned service between Basle and Milan, traction has to be provided on a regular basis (daily). The locomotive has to meet certain quality requirements (such as minimum speed) and it has to be fully operational. In this particular case, GVG requires an electric locomotive capable of speeds of at least 160 km/hour.

(53) A contract for traction must, if it is to be meaningful, include whatever back-up is necessary to ensure reasonable certainty in terms of punctuality, reliability and continuity of the service. Such back-up would need to include the maintenance and repair of the locomotive as well as the provision of a replacement locomotive, if necessary. With regard to the driver, the traction supplier has to ensure that the driver has the necessary licence and the route knowledge for the specific service. As in the case of the locomotive, the driver has to be provided at a certain location, a certain point in time and for a specified duration. A back-up requirement exists also for the driver.

(54) The market for traction is different from the market for the renting or purchasing of locomotives. Traction services can only be provided by railway companies, as they have a licence to do so. Locomotives can be rented or purchased from railway companies or from manufacturers. The renting or purchasing of a locomotive is not a substitute for traction as it concerns only the provision of rolling stock. Traction instead includes also the provision of a driver, maintenance and repair services and the back-up. These additional elements are necessary to ensure the continuity of a scheduled passenger transport service.

(55) In recent years, a readily identifiable traction market has developed in various Member States. In the UK, for instance, British freight train operators EWS, Freightliner, GB Railfreight and DRS provide Network Rail with traction for infrastructure trains. In Germany, DB and other private railway operators provide traction on a commercial basis to each other and to "private wagon owners" for passenger transport, and DB has provided traction to the GVG/SJ international grouping. On the basis of bilateral agreements and International Union of Railways (UIC) rules(35), national railway companies provide each other with traction for cross-border and "penetration" services(36). SNCF provides traction services on the French railway network for international passenger charter services of foreign railway companies and private wagon owners, and to DB for its "Autoreisezug"(37) on routes from

Germany to Avignon, Fréjus, Narbonne and Bordeaux. Société Nationale des Chemins de Fer Belges (SNCB) provides traction on the Belgian railway network for the passenger night train operated between Paris and Amsterdam by SNCF and Nederlandse Spoorwegen (NS).

(56) Similarly, based on UIC rules, FS (Trenitalia) regularly provides traction services to foreign railway companies. It provides traction, for instance, to SNCF for passenger transport from Milan and Turin to Lyon(38). On 13 different routes between Germany and Italy, DB regularly operates train services with its "Autoreisezug". FS (Trenitalia) provides traction and ancillary services to DB on the Italian network for a price of [...](39) and wagon. According to the contract between the parties, such services comprise a volume of at least [...] per year. In 2000 and 2001, FS (Trenitalia) provided traction for the Overnight Express which operated six nights a week between Amsterdam and Milan. The Overnight Express was a combined passenger/freight train which consisted of approximately five passenger wagons and seven freight wagons(40). FS (Trenitalia) also provides traction services to private wagon owners in Italy and to Intercontainer and European Rail Shuttle for international container transport services to Milan. In May 2001, FS (Trenitalia) provided traction to GVG for a passenger transport service from Chiasso to Monte Carlo.

The geographic market

(57) In all EU Member States, the locomotive has to comply with national technical standards and the crew (driver) needs special qualifications/training to be permitted to drive on the national railway network. For this particular service, neither the locomotive nor the crew of railway undertakings of another Member State can be used to provide traction in Italy. As a result, GVG can only rent traction from an undertaking that operates in Italy, i.e. which has locomotives and drivers that fulfil Italian technical criteria.

(58) Further, in order to provide back-up, the traction provider needs to be able to call upon a pool of locomotives at reasonably short notice in the event of technical failure. This means that the pool has to be sufficiently close to the Domodossola-Milan route, otherwise the time and cost incurred in providing the replacement locomotive will be disproportionate. The relevant geographic market is therefore confined to the region of Milan.

3. INTERNATIONAL RAIL PASSENGER TRANSPORT MARKET

The product market

(59) In air transport decisions, supported by case-law, the Commission has developed the point-of-origin/point-of-destination (O & D) pairs approach(41) for passenger transport services. This principle applies irrespective of the transport mode chosen by the individual passenger. GVG proposes to provide a rail passenger service from several German cities like Karlsruhe, Koblenz and Mannheim to Milan via Basle. Each of these routes can therefore be considered to be a relevant market on its own.

(60) In transport, under certain conditions passengers may consider air travel, high-speed rail travel, coach and car travel to be interchangeable modes of transport. This depends on the concrete characteristics of the service, for instance the travelling time. In this particular case, other transport modes such as car, coach or air transport, do not offer an alternative from the customer's point of view for the planned rail transport service for the reasons set out in recitals 61 to 67(42).

(61) GVG's proposed "Sprinter" service from German cities to Milan via Basle is directed toward business customers from Germany. The main advantage for the latter would arise from the shorter travelling time, since GVG's point-to-point service aims to be at least one hour faster than existing trains. GVG also plans to provide additional services for business customers on the train. For such customers, car and coach transport do not offer a valid alternative. For traffic between Karlsruhe, Koblenz and Mannheim to Milan, there is no scheduled coach service.

(62) In its written reply to the statement of objections, FS argued that the overall journey time of GVG's planned service would be more or less identical to the service operated by Cisalpino and not much shorter than that of traditional services, inter alia because the particular line does not allow a speed of 160 km/h to be exceeded. GVG's planned train would therefore not offer a new service for the customer. This assertion is not correct, as GVG's service is addressed mainly to passengers who are fed into Basle from Germany. For a comparison of travelling time for this group of passengers between GVG's train and existing connections it is important to consider two elements. The first element is the travelling time between Basle and Milan and the second element the interconnection with feeder trains from and to places in Germany.

(63) GVG's schedule, as set out in recital 9, does not require the train to operate at a higher speed than 160 km/h. The shorter travelling time of GVG's service in comparison with traditional services results in particular from the fact that GVG's planned train is a non-stop service. Existing trains operate with 14 stops between Basle and Milan. GVG's planned schedule furthermore saves time in comparison with existing connections due to a shorter stop in Domodossola for the exchange of locomotives.

(64) In comparison with the Cisalpino, for passengers from and to places in Germany, the main advantage of the planned GVG train is the interconnection in Basle. The Cisalpino operates in Basle from the "Basle SBB" railway station. Trains from Germany arrive in the Basle Bad railway station. Cisalpino passengers therefore have to transfer from one railway station to the other, which takes about 30 minutes. By way of contrast, GVG's train would operate directly into Basle Bad where, as set out in recital 9, passengers would have a connecting Intercity train to Germany within seven to eight minutes. More importantly, Cisalpino's departure time in Basle of 6.17 is too early for passengers who start the journey in cities like Koblenz, Karlsruhe or Mannheim. Such passengers would have to come to Basle the day before to catch the Cisalpino in the morning. Similarly, the Cisalpino from Milan arrives in Basle only at 21.44. The only possible connection is then a regional train from Basle Bad at 23.33 (which is slower than the Intercity train). As a result, for passengers taking the Cisalpino the overall travelling time to Germany would be almost three hours longer than with the planned GVG train.

(65) GVG's train offers a transport service that, if at all, is comparable only to a car transport service provided by a chauffeur. Car travel cannot be considered to be a transport service if the passenger drives the car himself. Moreover, the quality of transport differs considerably between the two transport modes(43). Trains enable congestion problems on the road to be avoided. It is possible to work on the train while it is difficult to do so in a car even if one has a driver. In addition, the estimated travelling cost would be significantly higher for the use of the car(44). On the other hand, the car offers more flexibility than the train, as regards the departure time and mobility after arrival. Thus, with regard to the present route, car and rail transport offer substantially different quality elements and therefore cannot be considered to be close substitutes on this market.

(66) Similarly, there are considerable quality differences between travelling by train and by aircraft. GVG aims to feed passengers into Basle from cities in Germany which either do not have an airport nearby or where no direct flights to Milan are available. If they wish to fly, passengers from such a place of origin would first have to travel to the airport. Thereafter they have to take the aircraft while changing to a bus or train to travel from Malpensa airport to the city centre of Milan(45). The frequent changes between the bus and the plane and the need to check in and to pass through controls at the airport cause numerous disruptions which prevent the traveller from working while travelling.

(67) In the case of point-to-point traffic between Basle and Milan, a price comparison demonstrates that transport by air and rail belong to different markets. A return ticket on the Cisalpino in the first and second class cost EUR 310 and EUR 194 respectively. On the same day, the corresponding price for a business class and economy class ticket on a direct flight offered by Swiss amounted to EUR 811,87 and EUR 749,14 respectively(46). Thus, air transport is at least about 2,6 times more expensive than existing train connections. On the other hand, in most cases the estimated travelling time of air transport is significantly shorter than the travelling time by train. In this particular case, between Basle and Milan the Cisalpino takes about four hours, 30 minutes. By way of comparison, if one takes into account the time needed to travel to and from the airport as well as check-in, air travel between the two cities may take about three hours(47). Thus, from the standpoint of the passenger, in this case train and air transport services cannot be regarded as substitutable due to their different characteristics, prices and intended use.

The geographic market

(68) It follows that for the relevant bundle of routes from Germany to Italy, i.e. Karlsruhe, Koblenz and Mannheim to Milan, transport by rail is not interchangeable from the customer's point of view and, as a result, the relevant downstream market in this case is rail passenger transport between the abovementioned German cities and Milan.

Access to the market

(69) As set out in recital 12, a particularity of the European rail passenger market is the legal requirement to form an international grouping for the provision of international passenger rail services. Article 10(1) of Directive 91/440/EEC establishes access and transit rights for international groupings to provide international rail transport services. Article 10(3) requires that such international groupings conclude the necessary administrative, technical and financial agreements with the infrastructure managers with a view to regulating traffic control and safety issues.

(70) Only after having concluded an international grouping with a railway undertaking established in Italy can GVG provide its service from Germany to Milan. Like access to the infrastructure, conclusion of the international grouping agreement is therefore a precondition for entering the market. However, while access to the infrastructure is to be provided by infrastructure managers, the international grouping agreement is to be concluded with railway undertakings which provide transport services. As argued by FS in its written reply to the statement of objections(48), it is therefore considered that the formation of an international grouping relates to the passenger rail transport market.

(71) It follows from the judgment of the Court of First Instance in the ENS case(49) that there is no specific mandatory form for an international grouping(50). In particular, an international grouping does not have to take the form of a traditional joint operation agreement in the railway sector. It also follows from that judgment that it is not unusual for railway undertakings to enter into agreements solely aimed at conferring a contractual right of

access to the railway infrastructure in the other railway undertaking's Member State, without necessarily also entering into other commercial agreements concerning the joint operation of services(51). Such agreements also fall under the definition of "international grouping" as they constitute an "association of at least two railway undertakings established in different Member States for the purpose of providing international transport services between Member States". The concept of an international grouping is therefore anything between a fully fledged commercial agreement under which the parties share risk more or less equally and an agreement under which parties only confer access rights to each other pursuant to Directive 91/440/EEC(52) without bearing any commercial risk.

(...)

H. ABUSE OF A DOMINANT POSITION

(117) FS has committed several abuses of its dominant position in the relevant upstream and downstream markets which have had the effect of foreclosing competition in international rail passenger transport on a number of routes from German cities to Milan via Basle.

(118) It is recalled that nothing in Italian law as described in recital 13 of this Decision prevents FS from providing information, entering into an international grouping(71) with, or granting a safety certificate, granting access to infrastructure and providing traction to a licensed railway undertaking established in another Member State.

1. ABUSE ON THE RELEVANT UPSTREAM MARKETS

1.1. REFUSAL TO GRANT ACCESS TO THE ITALIAN INFRASTRUCTURE

(119) FS holds a monopoly as the allocation body that has been designated by the Italian State to decide upon requests for infrastructure capacity on the Italian railway network. In this capacity, FS is responsible for assigning train paths to railway operators in Italy.

(120) In line with the Court of First Instance's Aéroports de Paris ruling(72), the railway infrastructure can be considered an essential facility. It fulfils the two main conditions for an essential facility, as established by the CFI in its ENS(73) decision, i.e. the indispensability of the facility and, if access is not granted, the elimination of all competition from the other operator(74). For any competitor it would be unfeasible to duplicate FS's long-distance railway network because of the prohibitive cost of such an investment and the impossibility of getting the right of way.

(121) Restricting access to the railway network constitutes an abuse of a dominant position if it excludes a potential competitor from the market. In its decision in the Port of Rødby case, the Commission concluded that an undertaking that owns or manages and uses itself an essential facility, i.e. a facility or infrastructure without which its competitors are unable to offer their services to customers, and refuses them access to such facility, is abusing its dominant position(75).

(122) In its judgment in the Télémarketing case(76), the Court ruled that "an abuse within the meaning of Article 86 [now 82] of the EC Treaty is committed where, without objective necessity, an undertaking holding a dominant position on a particular market reserves to itself or to an undertaking belonging to the same group an ancillary activity which might be carried out by another undertaking as part of its activities on a neighbouring but separate market, with the possibility of eliminating all competition from such undertaking".

(123) As pointed out in the Commission notice on the application of competition rules to access agreements in the telecommunications sector(77), a refusal to give access to facilities may be prohibited pursuant to Article 82 if the refusal is made by an undertaking which is dominant because of its control of facilities. An undue, inexplicable or unjustified delay in responding to a request for access to an essential infrastructure may also constitute an abuse.

(124) FS has made use of its power as allocation body to deny GVG, a potential competitor in the market for rail passenger transport services, train paths on the Domodossola-Milan route. It has both withheld from GVG information necessary to enable GVG to prepare an adequate business plan and it has effectively denied access to GVG without objective justification. It has thus prevented GVG from entering the market for the provision of rail passenger transport services on this route. In deciding to retain for itself the market for the provision of cross-border rail passenger transport services, FS has extended its dominant position on the market for the access to infrastructure to this neighbouring but separate market. In Decision 98/190/EC in the FAG-Flughafen Frankfurt case(78), the Commission concluded that an infringement of Article 86 (now 82) arose as soon as FAG's monopoly on the ramp-handling services market was maintained by a refusal on its part to authorise self-handling or third-party handling. The fact that FAG already held a dominant position on the ramp-handling market prior to committing the infringement could not justify FAG's decision to reserve for itself the market by denying ramp access to potential competitors.

(125) In the circumstances of the present case, an allocation body verifiably independent of any railway undertaking would certainly have actively considered all possible means, in terms of availability of time slots and other practical and technical issues, of granting GVG access to the infrastructure on fair and non-discriminatory terms. However, experience with previous cases suggests that an allocation body that is also active in the market for providing services on its own infrastructure is likely to prefer an arrangement which will minimise inconvenience to itself, especially in relation to its own operations as a user(79).

(126) Directive 91/440/EEC does not explicitly mention the right of access to technical information regarding access to infrastructure for railway companies that have not yet formed an international grouping. The Commission, however, rejects FS's argument that such information can only be provided and a train path can only be reserved after the applicant has entered into an international grouping. Directive 91/440/EEC does not prejudice the application of the competition rules of the EC Treaty. The allocation body cannot require the establishment of an international grouping before even providing information relating to prices of train paths and their availability, since that may have the effect of preventing market entry. Such information is necessary to enable the entrant to establish a business plan and to judge whether the planned service would be economically viable.

(127) FS was in a position to provide such information and give advice on related issues of access to infrastructure. Before the entry into force of Decree No 146/1999, FS (Infrastruttura(80)) was entitled pursuant to Article 8(5) of Decree No 277/1998 to issue a (temporary) safety certificate in accordance with Directive 95/19/EC. At that stage, as the infrastructure manager, instead of refusing to provide the requested information on the grounds that GVG did not have a safety certificate(81), FS (Infrastruttura) should have taken a proactive approach. For instance, in line with its obligations as the infrastructure manager, FS should have informed GVG that it is FS (Infrastruttura) itself which grants the safety certificate and advised it of what is required to obtain such a certificate.

(128) In addition, the Commission considers that Article 10(1) of Directive 91/440/EEC has direct effect. According to the relevant case-law of the Court of Justice, a provision may have direct effect if the obligation imposed on the Member States is sufficiently clear and precise, unconditional and does not leave any margin of discretion in its implementation(82).

(129) Article 10(1) of Directive 91/440/EEC is a provision that clearly indicates that international groupings have the right to obtain access to infrastructure. Such a provision in itself does not require any further implementation from Member States and can thus be considered sufficiently clear and precise in accordance with the abovementioned case-law.

(130) Railway undertakings such as GVG could rely directly on this provision to request from FS information necessary to enter into meaningful negotiations with railway undertakings established in Italy with a view to setting up an international grouping. Article 10(1) could therefore be invoked by GVG since the entry into force of Directive 91/440/EEC on 1 January 1993. GVG had the right to form an international grouping with a view to providing an international rail passenger transport service to Milan. Hence, it was entitled to request information from FS regarding train paths and prices with a view to obtaining access to the Italian infrastructure.

(131) It is concluded that during the period at least from September 1995(83) until July 2002, FS refused to provide the necessary information for access to the Italian railway infrastructure to GVG without any objective justification and thereby prevented GVG from entering the market in international rail passenger transport in breach of Article 82 of the EC Treaty.

1.2. REFUSAL TO PROVIDE TRACTION

(132) Recital 51 states that traction consists in the provision of a locomotive, a driver and ancillary services such as the back-up. There is a market for traction services, as such services are provided on a commercial basis in most Member States. Recitals 55 and 56 provide examples showing that FS is and has been active on the traction market. For instance, FS provides regular traction services to SNCF from Milan and Turin to Lyon and to DB for its international "Autoreisezug" on 13 different routes between Germany and Italy. On one occasion it also provided traction services to GVG for a rail passenger transit service. None of these rail transport services are competing with transport services provided by FS.

(133) As set out in recitals 86 to 109, the Commission has extensively examined whether GVG (or any other railway undertaking from another Member State) would have alternatives to renting traction from FS (Trenitalia) on the Italian segment of the planned passenger transport service between Basle and Milan. This examination has shown that there were no such commercially viable alternatives available to GVG or any other non-Italian railway undertaking. Therefore, in order to be able to provide an international rail passenger service between Germany and Milan, it is indispensable that GVG obtains traction from FS on the Italian railway network.

(134) As FS has not responded to GVG's requests for traction, since December 1998 it has effectively refused to provide traction services to GVG for this particular service. FS's refusal was not justified by any objective reason. For instance, FS does not lack spare capacity for traction services, there are no safety reasons preventing FS from providing traction to GVG, FS could obtain an adequate remuneration for the provision of such services and it does not operate under public service obligations which prevent it from providing traction services to GVG.

(135) No lack of spare capacity: Following the hearing, FS Trenitalia argued that it did not have spare locomotive capacity to provide traction services to GVG. However, after further investigation, FS Trenitalia finally declared by letter of 18 December 2002 that it had quantified its spare capacity for the supply of such traction services at one million km per year.

(136) No safety reasons: Once it has ensured traction and it has formed an international grouping, GVG would still have to obtain a safety certificate for the planned passenger transport service in Italy. This is therefore a separate and consecutive step. As the safety certificate is issued by the infrastructure manager, it is not the responsibility of FS (Trenitalia) to judge whether GVG fulfils the necessary safety requirements. A refusal to provide traction could therefore not be justified on the grounds of safety concerns.

(137) Adequate remuneration: FS has a right to adequate remuneration under normal commercial terms.

(138) No public service obligations: Finally, FS is under no explicit obligation to provide a public service the financial equilibrium of which could be jeopardised by the services that GVG intends to provide (see recitals 154 and 155).

(139) GVG's planned service between Basle and Milan competes with the Cisalpino, which is a joint venture of FS and SBB. This has been confirmed by FS's reply to the statement of objections. FS considers that GVG's planned service would have damaged its existing traffic on the Basle-Milan route(84).

(140) FS has therefore refused to provide traction to a potential competitor in a neighbouring market to the market for traction. FS is dominant not only in the latter (upstream) market but also in the downstream market for rail passenger transport. On the downstream market, there is no competition. By refusing to provide traction to GVG, FS is preventing a potential competitor from entering this market. It is thereby preserving its monopoly position on this separate downstream market by eliminating potential competition on that market(85).

(141) The Court has consistently held that the extension of a monopoly in a given market to a neighbouring market, without objective justification, is prohibited pursant to Article 82(86). In Télémarketing(87), the Court found that an abuse of Article 82 is committed where an undertaking holding a dominant position on a particular market reserves to itself, without any objective necessity, an ancillary activity which might be carried out by another undertaking and if it thereby eliminates all competition from such an undertaking. This applies even where the dominant position is due not to the activity of the undertaking itself but to the fact that by reason of provisions laid down by law there can be no competition or only very limited competition in that market(88).

(142) The Commission found in Decision 98/190/EC in the FAG-Flughafen Frankfurt case(89) that Frankfurt Airport had abused its dominant position in breach of Article 82 of the EC Treaty by denying, without objective justification, potential competitors access to the market for the provision of ramp-handling services at Frankfurt Airport. This market was considered to be a separate market from that of the provision of airport facilities. Until the adoption of that Decision, Frankfurt Airport had a monopoly on both the market for the provision of airport facilities and that of the provision of ramp-handling services.

(143) In the present case, although Italian law has appointed FS's subsidiary RFI as the infrastructure manager, it does not confer exclusive rights on FS for the provision of international passenger services, in particular on the route at stake. FS's refusal is therefore only based on its own commercial decision as an undertaking and not on State intervention(90).

(144) Finally, according to settled case-law(91), a refusal to supply also constitutes an abuse when it leads to the risk of elimination of competition on the part of the requesting undertaking in the relevant market or hindering competitors' development and when it is not objectively justified.

(145) FS's refusal to provide traction, an activity which it routinely performs, is not justified by any objective reason and it protects its monopoly position in the downstream market for international passenger rail services between Basle and Milan. It therefore constitutes an abuse of a dominant position. FS's refusal to provide traction to GVG eliminates a potential competitor and thereby hinders the growth of competition in the downstream market. This harms consumers, who will not benefit from alternatives to existing rail passenger services.

(146) The infringement took place between December 1998 and 27 June 2003. At least since December 1998, GVG requested FS to provide traction services for its planned service on the Domodossola-Milan route. FS did not make any offer to provide traction until August 2002. On 25 November 2002, FS (Trenitalia) offered GVG a draft contract for the provision of traction, including back-up, for its planned service on the Domodossola-Milan route. On 27 June 2003, GVG and FS (Trenitalia) concluded negotiations by agreeing on the traction price.

2. ABUSE ON THE MARKET IN RAIL PASSENGER TRANSPORT

2.1. REFUSAL TO NEGOTIATE THE FORMATION OF AN INTERNATIONAL GROUPING

(147) At the present stage in the liberalisation of the European rail passenger market, railway undertakings can only provide cross-border rail passenger services if they have formed an international grouping with a licensed railway undertaking established in another Member State. However, the existence of this European regulatory framework does not preclude the application of Article 82 of the EC Treaty to situations in which there is only one railway undertaking available to form an international grouping and which refuses to enter into negotiations with a view to the formation of such a grouping.

(148) In its judgment in ENS(92) the Court of First Instance held that a service may be regarded as "necessary" for entry to the relevant market if such a service is not "interchangeable" and if, by reason of its special characteristics - in particular the prohibitive cost of and/or time reasonably required for reproducing it - there are no viable alternatives available to potential competitors, who are therefore excluded from the market by the refusal to provide such a service.

(149) In the present case the formation of an international grouping with FS is indispensable for GVG if the undertaking is to be able to provide the international passenger transport service on the Domodossola-Milan route. It is not "interchangeable" with any other service in the sense that there are no other railway undertakings with which GVG could enter into an international grouping for the purposes of operating this route(93). As set out in recital 101, neither does the option exist at this stage for GVG to set up a subsidiary in Italy with a view to forming an international grouping with its own subsidiary.

(150) Therefore, unless the refusal by FS to enter into negotiations with GVG with a view to the formation of an international grouping is justified on the basis of objective reasons, it constitutes an abuse of a dominant position. While FS has pointed out in general that there is no obligation under EU law to form an international grouping and that it would enter into an international grouping only if it had a commercial interest in doing so, it has not provided concrete reasons why it could not enter into such negotiations. Instead, FS has argued

that its refusal to enter into negotiations with GVG was justified since GVG's planned service would compete with services already provided by FS, in particular the Cisalpino, on the Basle-Milan route(94). To preserve its monopoly on this route, however, is not an acceptable justification for FS's refusal.

(151) At least since August 1999, FS was aware that GVG wanted to enter into an international grouping with it to provide an international service between Basle and Milan. FS failed to deal with GVG's request until August 2002. On 27 June 2003, the parties signed an international grouping agreement.

(152) The Commission therefore concludes that by refusing to enter into an international grouping with GVG without any objective justification, during the period from August 1999 until 27 June 2003, FS abused its dominant position on the Italian market for passenger rail transport.

Bibliography

Becker G.S., *Crime and Punishment: an economic approach*, in *76 J. Pol. Econ.*, 1968 p. 169 ff.

Bergmann - Rawlings, *Trasport management. Future directions: redefining the role of transport,* in *Strategic Supply Chain Management: Best Pratice in Supply Chain Management,* Aldershot, 1998, p. 369 ff.

Beria P. - Quinet E. - De Rus G. - Schulz, C., *A comparison of rail liberalisation levels across four European countries*, Munich, 2010.

Boodoo, *An international comparison of railway organisational and planning frameworks,* Loughborough, 2002.

Campos, Cantos, *Regulating privatized rail transport*, Police research working paper 2064, The World Bank, Economic Development Institute, 1999.

Campos, J, *Spain: The end of an era*, in Gómez - Ibañez, J.A. de Rus G. (ed.), *Competition in the railway industry: An international comparative analysis.* Edward Elgar, 2006.

Carbajo J.C. - Estache A., *Railway Concessions – Heading down the Right Track in Argentina, Viewpoint, 88. Finance and Private Sector Development Department*, The World Bank, Washington D.C., 1998.

Carpaneto L., *Il diritto comunitario dei trasporti tra sussidiarità e mercato. Il caso del trasporto ferroviario*, Torino, 2009.

Celli - L. Pettinari L. - Piazza R., *La liberalizzazione del trasporto ferroviario*, Torino, 2007.

Chabalier, *The Europeanization of the railway sector*, Bilgi University, Istanbul, 21-23 September 2006.

Dewey D., *Monopoly in Economics and Law*, 1959, Chicago, p. 112 ff., Dodgson J., *Access Pricing in the Railway System*, in *Utilities Policy*, 1994,p. 205 ff.

European Commission (2009b). *Report from the Commission to the Council and the European Parliament. Second report on monitoring development of the rail market*, SEC(2009)1687. European Commission.

European Rail Infrastructure Managers (EIM) - Community of European Railway and Infrastructure Companies (CER) (2008). *Rail Charging and Accounting Schemes in Europe. Case studies from six countries*, May 2008.

European conference of ministers of transport(ECMT), R*ailway accounts for effective regulation*, march 2007.

European conference of ministers of transport (ECMT), *European integration of rail freight transport: Conclusions of Round Table 125,* Paris, 28-29 November 2002.

European Council of ministers of transport, *Rail reform and charges for the use of infrastructure*, 2005.

European Council of Ministers of Transport, *National Policies towards shifting freight form road to rail: the case of Switzerland, the United kingdom and France*, 2002.

European Investment Bank, *Evaluation of EIB financing of railway projects in the European Union*, 2005

Freeman, M (1999) *Review article. 'Trains of thought': steam railway capitalism and the law in 19th-century England*, in *Oxford Journal of Legal Studies* 1999, p. 99 ff.

Friebel, G. - Ivaldi, M. - Vibes, *Railway (de) regulation: A European efficiency comparison. IDEI report no 3 on passenger rail transport,* Toulouse, 2003.

Friedlander A. - Berndt E.R., Chiang J. S. - M. Showalter M. - Vellturro C.A., *Rail Costs and Capital Adjustments in a Quasi-Regulated Environment*, in *Journal of Transport Economics and Policy*, 1993, p. 131 ff.

Gomez-Ibanez, J.A. - Pittman, R. (2004). *Chinese Railway Reform and Competition*, in *Journal of Transport Economics and Policy*, 2004 p. 309 ff.

Gathon H. J. - Pestieau P., *Decomposing efficiency into its managerial and its regulatory components: The case of European railways*, in *European Journal of Operational Research*, 1995, p. 500 ff.

Glaister S. (2006). *Competition undermined by politics*, in Gómez - Ibañez, J.A. - de Rus G. (ed), *Competition in the railway industry: An international comparative analysis*. Edward Elgar, 2006.

Häfner P., *The Effects of Railroad Reform in Germany*, in *Japan Railways and Transport Review*, 1996, 15, p. 27 ff.

Institute for Transport Studies, *European Railway Comparisons, Final Report*, ITS Working Paper 418, University of Leeds., 1994.

International Chamber of Commerce, *The liberalization of rail transport in Europe,* 2007.

Kirchner, *Rail Liberalisation Index 2004: Comparison of the Market Opening in the Rail Markets of the Member States of the European Union, Switzerland and Norway*, Humboldt University, Berlin, 2004.

Lalive S., Working Paper No. 0609, *Entry in liberalized railway markets: The German experience,* Zurich, 2007.

Landes W., *Optimal Sanctions for antitrust violations,* in 50 *University of Chicago Law Review*, 1983, p. 652 ff.

Letwin W., *Law and Economic Policy in America: the evolution of the Sherman act*, 1965, Chicago.

Link H., *Rail infrastructure charging and on-track competition in Germany*, in *International Journal of Transport Management*, 2004 p. 17 ff.

Lundberg A., *Restructuring of the Swedish State Railways*, in *Japan Railways and Transport Review*, 1996, p. 22 ff.

Meeddat - Sesp, *Les comptes des transports en 2007 (tome 1). Les transferts de l'État et des collectivités locales: Ministère de l'écologie, de l'énergie, du développement durable et de l'aménagement du territoire*, Paris, 2008.

Monami E., *European Passenger Rail Reforms: A Comparative Assessment of the Emerging Models*, in *Transport Reviews*, 2000, p. 91 ff.

Nash C.A., *Europe: alternative models of restructuring*, in Gómez - Ibañez, J.A. - de Rus G. (ed), *Competition in the railway industry: An international comparative analysis*. Edward Elgar, 2006.

Nash, C.A., *Passenger railway reform in the last 20 years – European experience reconsidered,* in *Research in Transport Economics*, 2008, p. 61 ff.

Oum T. H. – Waters W.G. II - Yu C., *A survey of productivity and efficiency measurement in rail transport*, in *Journal of Transport Economics and Policy*, 1999, p. 9 ff.

Oum T. H. - Yu C., *Economic efficiency of railways and implications for public policy: A comparative study of the OECD countries' railways*, in *Journal of Transport Economics and Policy*, 1994, p. 121 ff.

Peppin J.C., *Price Fixing Agreements under the Sherman Antitrust law*, in *28 California Law Review*, 1940, p. 297 ff.

Pittman R., *Options for restructuring the state-owned monopoly railway,* in Dennis S.M. – Talley W.K. (ed.), *Railroad economics. Research in transportation economics*, Elsevier, 2007.

Quinet E., *France: Avoiding competition*, in Gómez - Ibañez, J.A. - de Rus G. (ed), *Competition in the railway industry: An international comparative analysis*. Edward Elgar, 2006.

Ratner S., *The tariff in American History*, New York, 1972.

Sidak G., *Note, Rethinking antitrust damages*, in *33 Stanford L. Review*, 1981, p. 329 ff.

Thompson L.S., *Directions of Railway Reform. International Railway Congress Association*, Vienna, 2001.

Thompson L.S., - Budin K.J., *Global Trend to Railway Concessions Delivering Positive Results*, in *Public Policy for the Private Sector*, 134, The World Bank. Washington D.C., 1997.

Thorelli H.B., *The Federal Antitrust Policy: origination of an American tradition*, 1955, Baltimore.

Winston C., *United States: Private and deregulated*, in Gómez - Ibañez, J.A. - de Rus G. (ed), *Competition in the railway industry: An international comparative analysis*, Edward Elgar, 2006.

Waters II W.G., *Evolution of railroad economics*, in Dennis S.M. – Talley W.K. (ed.), *Railroad economics. Research in transportation economics*, Elsevier, 2007.

World Bank, *The benefits of separating rail Infrastructure from operations,* note no.135 December 1997.

Chapter 5 Airports

5.1 The Importance of the Concept of Airport System

"Airport system" is the established way that allows the member States to allocate at their own discretion air traffic between specific airports, within the specific limits imposed by EU Law[1].

Legislation and case studies regarding airport systems are centered on the interpretation of the notion itself, on the basis of two different criteria. First, we have the concept of "interchangeability" of airports within the same system. This interchangeability is based on the fact that it makes no difference to the carriers to service anyone of the airports within the same system. Second, we must verify the allocation against the EU norms regulating internal markets. The norm that introduced this concept is article 8 of the Regulation (EEC) number 2408/92, that allows member States to create their respective air transportation policies even through authoritative allocation of traffic among different airports, as long as said airports serve the same "urban agglomeration".

The above mentioned norm was recently replaced by article 19 of the Regulation (EC) number 1008/2008, which specifies and defines the conditions that regulate the ability to allocate air traffic by a member State.

In order to comprehend the real scope of innovation of this norm, it is necessary to keep in mind how the previous norm was interpreted by the European Commission and the European Court of Justice. In short, we can already see how both authorities base their judgment regarding the legitimacy of the measures taken by individual member States on the presence of a true urban agglomeration, that is to say that they focus on the actual interchangeability of the airports in

---

1 A complete introduction to airport competition regulation can be read in: Müller-Rostin C., *Airport Entry and Exit: An European Analysis*, in Forsyth P. - Gillen D. (ed.), *Airport competition: the European experience*, Burlington, 2010, p. 31 ff., Kunz M., *Airport regulation: The policy framework*, in Pfähler, W. - Niemeier H.M.- Mayer O. (ed.), *Airports and air traffic – regulation, privatisation and competition*, Frankfurt, 1999, Graham A., *Managing Airports – an international perspective*, Amsterdam, 2005, Forsyth P., 2006, *Airport Competition: Regulatory Issues and Policy Implications*, in Lee D. (ed), *Advances in Airline Economics, Vol 1 Competition Policy and Antitrust*, Amsterdam, 2006, p. 343 ff., Forsyth P., *Locational and monopoly rents at airports: creating them and shifting them*, in *Journal of Air Transport Management*, 2004, 51 ff., Forsyth P., *Airport competition: A perspective and synthesis*, in Forsyth P. - Gillen D. (ed.), *Airport competition: the European experience*, Burlington, 2010.

question. In fact, we can talk about “urban agglomeration” only if within it there is a guaranteed mobility that allows for fast and efficient transfers from different points within the same area, and, specifically, from one airport to the other.

In order to evaluate the legitimacy of the measures for traffic allocation, and specifically that there is absence of discrimination that would give advantage to a carrier over another, it is necessary to have in place a series of infrastructures that meet the need for connections between the airports. One of the main parameters for the evaluation of the advantage of being “assigned” to an airport rather than another is the ease of access to the airport itself (infrastructure). We are talking about ground infrastructures that become the true acid test to establish the legitimacy of the qualification as “airport system” in each actual case (case 1), European Commission, 16 September 1998, Case VII/AMA/11/98, Italian traffic distribution rules for the airport system of Milan, in OJEU, L337, 12 december1998, p. 42):

(…)

40.3. An operational direct rail service from Milan to the airport

(41) According to the information transmitted by the Italian authorities, while the extension of the SS336 should be completed by 25 October 1998, the works for the modernization of the A8 motorway will not be completed until December 2000 (so far, only the additional lane has been constructed) and a direct rail service will probably not be operational until May 1999. This rail service will be a provisional service (two trains per hour - journey time: 39 minutes). The fully operational rail service ('Malpensa Express`: four trains per hour - journey time: 30 minutes) will be available only in 2001. No formal commitment has been given by the Italian authorities about the respect of this timetable.

(42) Hence, the level of available access infrastructures to Malpensa airport from 25 October 1998 will not be compatible with the traffic which the airport will have to handle as a result of the transfer of traffic from Linate, on the one hand, and of market growth, on the other. On the basis of the information available to the Commission, it seems that this will be the case at least until December 2000, when all the abovementioned infrastructure is planned to be completed.

(43) However, even when those infrastructures are completed, the level will not necessarily be sufficient to offset the less favourable geographic location of this airport as compared to Linate airport. In this regard, it will be necessary to take into account both the availability of various transport links and the quality of these links.

(44) Given the existing differences between Linate airport and Malpensa airport with regard to access conditions, the Commission is of the opinion that these airports will not be comparable from the point of vue of their attractiveness until the level of access infrastructures to Malpensa offsets the geographic location of this airport as compared to Linate airport.

(45) In view of the foregoing and taking into account the competitive situation between Alitalia and the other Community air carriers, the criteria set out in Decree No 46-T, by permitting only Alitalia to serve its Rome-Fiumicino hub from Linate airport while other Community air carriers will be obliged to serve their respective hubs from Malpensa airport, will in fact afford Alitalia a competitive advantage. This competitive advantage will

exist as long as Malpensa airport does not enjoy a level of access infrastructures such as to overcome the present situation which leads to consumer reluctance to use Malpensa airport.

(46) Therefore, the Commission considers that the application of the criteria set out in Decree No 46-T from 25 October 1998 by virtue of Decree 70-T will in practice produce discriminatory effects in favour of Alitalia. Consequently, the application of those criteria from 25 October 1998 is not compatible with the principle of non-discrimination on the grounds of the identity of the air carrier as provided for in Article 8(1) of Regulation (EEC) No 2408/92.

The principle of proportionality

(47) The Malpensa 2000 project, by extending and upgrading existing facilities at Malpensa airport, aims at creating a fully operational and viable hub at that airport. The Italian rules contribute to that objective by ensuring that a sufficient amount of traffic will be transferred from Linate airport to Malpensa airport so as to ensure the viability of the hub. Article 8(1) of Regulation (EEC) No 2408/92 expressly recognises the legitimacy of an active airport planning policy. It must however comply with the general principles of Community law and, in particular, the third package of measures for the liberalisation of air transport (see Decision 95/259/EC, page 31).

(48) Under the Italian rules, air carriers will no longer be allowed to choose Linate airport for the operation of air routes other than those meeting specific thresholds. In practice, this will apply to all air routes except Milan-Rome. Consequently, these rules will restrict the freedom to provide air services in the Community to and from Milan. Even if these rules were not regarded as being discriminatory, according to the consistent case-law of the Court of Justice (see in particular the abovementioned judgment in Case C-288/89 Collectieve Antenne voorziening Gouda) 'the application of national provisions to providers of services established in other Member States must be such as to guarantee the achievement of the intended aim and must not go beyond that which is necessary in order to achieve that objective. In other words, it must not be possible to obtain the same result by less restrictive rules` (paragraph 15 of the judgment).

(49) In this regard, the Commission notes that it has not been proven that the creation of a viable operational hub and the success of the trans-European networks project make such restrictive measures necessary. The contrary seems to be established by the factors set out in points 49.1 and 49.2.

49.1. The operational viability of the Malpensa 2000 project (including the timely operation of all flights and the prerequisite normal access of travellers thereto) does not necessitate the complete transfer on 25 October 1998 of such a volume of traffic as that provided by the Italian rules. The application of the criteria laid down by those rules will result in an estimated transferred traffic of 11,7 million passengers while only 2,5 million passengers will remain at Linate airport.

The operational viability of the Malpensa hub necessitates the transfer of a volume of traffic which is compatible with the level of airport facilities and access infrastructures. Otherwise, the development and future positioning of Malpensa airport as a successful hub in the Community could be threatened. As already indicated above, the necessary access infrastructures to the airport will not be ready on 25 October 1998; hence, at that date, existing access infrastructures will not be compatible with the volume of traffic which will be transferred. This would seem to be the case at least until December 2000 when the upgrading of the A8 motorway and a provisional rail service are planned to be operational according to the information transmitted by the Italian authorities, provided that the level of traffic of the airport at that time does not make further improvements necessary to the access infrastructures.

49.2. The financial arrangements for the Malpensa 2000 project do not require that the transfer of traffic from Linate airport to Malpensa airport be completed by 25 October 1998. In fact, according to the contract entered into between the EIB and SEA for the financing of the project, the concentration of traffic from Linate to Malpensa needs to be completed by 31 December 2000 at the latest.

(50) In view of the foregoing, the Commission is of the opinion that the creation of a fully viable and operational hub does not necessarily presuppose the transfer of 11,7 million passengers from 25 October 1998. A postponement of the transfer or a gradual transfer of that volume from 25 October 1998 onwards would be better suited to that objective and would also reduce the effect on freedom to provide air services to and from Milan. Therefore, the Italian rules are not indispensable to secure the objective pursued by the Italian authorities which could be attained with rules less restrictive of the freedom to provide air services.

(51) Lastly the Italian authorities also justified the imposition of high thresholds for traffic permitted to remain at Linate by indicating that only at these levels would airline operations be justified both at Malpensa and at Linate and that this would concern routes where traffic was predominantly point-to-point.

If one of the objectives of Decree No 46-T was really to keep at Linate routes where traffic was predominantly point-to-point which indeed appears to be the intention since the 12th recital in the preamble to that Decree refers 'in particular` to services between Milan and Rome, then the Decree cannot be regarded as appropriate to achieving the objective of retaining such routes at Linate since they impose unnecessary restrictions on all routes other than Milan-Rome by actually excluding them from Linate altogether.

Further the imposition of restrictions resulting in an immediate and drastic reduction of activities at Linate from 14,2 million passengers per year in 1997 to 2,5 million after the new measures take effect would not appear to be an appropriate measure to attain the objective indicated in the 11th recital in the preamble to the Decree, namely that Linate airport should in any event be kept in service.

(52) Consequently, the Commission considers that the traffic distribution rules set out in Decree No 46-T and Decree No 70-T are not compatible with the principle of proportionality.

5.2 Summary of the EU Norms that are Applicable to Air Transportation and Norms from Regulation Number 2408/92

Analysis of norms and case studies relating to airport systems must include a reference, even in a very brief format, to the essential trends of the EU policies towards air transportation deregulation.

In fact, even though this is not the place for an in depth examination of the subject, it would be useful to notice that air transportation is subject to the European guidelines on competition and freedom of circulation and market access.

Title VI of the Treaty on the Functioning of European Union (TFEU) deals with the European policy on transportation. General norms on provision of services refer to it, being a case of special discipline. Moreover, the sector of air transportation is configured in a special way, compared to ground transportation, since article 80, paragraph 2 of the European Treaty contemplates that it will be the Council's responsibility to decide, through qualified majority, if, to which extent and by which procedure appropriate provisions may be adopted to discipline maritime and air transportation[2].

However, the norms to which we can refer regarding the topic of our examination are those presented through various regulations collected in CD sets or in unified regulatory packages issued by the European Legislature on the topic of air transportation[3]. The "packet" that seems the most relevant in our case is certainly the one issued in 1992, consisting of five regulations[4]. The latest one to appear is Regulation (EC) number 1008/2008, which adapted the previously used norms to the conclusions reached by the Court of Justice.

According to article 8.1 of Regulation (EEC) 2408/92, members States have the power to *"regulate, without discrimination based on the nationality or identification of the air carrier, traffic allocation between airports located within an airport system"*. For this purpose, article 8.3 of the same Regulation gives the European Commission the power to supervise the application of said regulation, within very specific time limits and with the purpose to avoid *"discrimination based on the nationality or identification of the carriers"*.

In fact, the European Commission has systematically stated the illegitimacy of provisions introduced by member States regarding traffic allocation within an airport system whenever it was proved that such provisions, directly or indirectly, constituted discrimination between carriers. In most of the cases, it was a matter of

---

2 For a comparative perspective with the United States, see: Bhadra, D. - Texter, P., *Airline networks: an econometric framework to analyze domestic U.S. air travel*, in *Journal of Transportation and Statistics*, 2004, p. 87 ff.

3 A complete analisys of Air transportation under the perspective of Internal Market rules is explained in Tuo C., *Il trasporto aereo nell'Unione Europea tra diritti fondamentali e relazioni esterne,* Torino, 2008.

4 See the liberaliazation of Air transport in: Carbone S.M. – Munari F., *L'attuazione nell'ordinamento comunitario della direttiva sul libero accesso al mercato dei servizi aeroportuali*, in *Dir. Comm. Int.*, 2000, p. 95 ff., Francis G. – Humprheys I. – Ison S., *Airports' perspectives on the growth of low- cost airlines and the remodeling of the airport-airline relationship*, in *Tourism Management*, 2004, p. 507 ff., Franke M., *Competition between network carriers and low-cost carriers – retreat battle or breakthrough to a new level of efficiency?*, in *AirTransport Management,* 2004, p. 15 ff., Frenke K. - Van Terwisgam S. -Verburg T. - Burghouwt G., *Airline competition at European airports*, in *Tijdschrift voor Economische en Sociale Geografie,* 2004, p. 233 ff., Munari F., *La liberalizzazione del trasporto aereo nell'Unione europea tra lotta alle discriminazioni e compressione delle competenze statali*, in *Dir. Un. Eur.*, 1999, p. 207 ff., Tuo C., *Il trasporto aereo nell'Unione Europea tra diritti fondamentali e relazioni esterne,* Torino, 2008,

measures that would favor a domestic carrier over competitors from other member States.

Deregulation of air transportation has significantly changed the structure of the manner services are provided, replacing *"direct city-to-city connections with a more articulate system – radial pattern -, characterized by a series of connection to/from "regional" airports with nearby hubs. These hubs sort the traffic with other hubs, which are in turn connected with a series of regional airports within their own area"*[5].

Indeed, nowadays air transport is fully subject to the European Union laws on competition, and state aids (case 2) Court of First Instance, December 2000, Case T-296/97, Alitalia - Linee aeree italiane SpA v Commission of the European Communities, in Rep., p. II-03871):

(…)

61. According to the actual wording of the fifth paragraph of Article 173 of the Treaty (now, after amendment, the fifth paragraph of Article 230 EC), the criterion of the day on which a measure came to the knowledge of an applicant, as the starting point for the period prescribed for instituting proceedings, is subsidiary to the criteria of publication or notification of the measure.

(…)

63. Since the contested decision, which was not notified to the applicant, was published, it is the date of publication that started the period running.

(…)

81. A capital contribution from public funds satisfies the test of a private investor operating in the normal conditions of a market economy and does not imply the grant of State aid if, inter alia, it was made at the same time as a significant capital contribution on the part of a private investor made in comparable circumstances.

(…)

84. The employees' participation in an undertaking's capital, in the form of consent to a change in salary in return for shares in the undertaking corresponding to the annual saving in labour costs, does not in itself show that the capital contribution in the form of public funds satisfies the private investor test. The conduct of a private investor in a market economy is guided by prospects of profitability, whereas such participation on the part of employees is motivated by the desire to keep their jobs and therefore, above all, by considerations pertaining to the undertaking's viability and survival rather than by prospects of profitability.

(…)

---

5 See Baldwin R. - Cave, *Understanding regulation: Theory, strategy and practice*, Oxford, 1999, Bain J.S., *Barriers to new competition*. Cambridge, 1956 and Barrett S., *Airport competition in the deregulated European aviation market*, in *Journal of Air Transport Management*, 2000, p. 13 ff.

86. In the context of an action for annulment under Article 173 of the Treaty (now, after amendment, Article 230 EC), the legality of a Community measure must be assessed on the basis of the elements of fact and of law existing at the time when the measure was adopted. In particular, the complex assessments made by the Commission must be examined solely on the basis of the information available to the Commission at the time when those assessments were made.

(...)

105. The assessment by the Commission of the question whether an investment satisfies the private investor test involves a complex economic appraisal. When the Commission adopts a measure involving such a complex economic appraisal, it enjoys a wide discretion and judicial review of that measure, even though it is in principle a comprehensive review as to whether a measure falls within the scope of Article 92(1) of the Treaty (now Article 87(1) EC), is limited to verifying whether the Commission complied with the relevant rules governing procedure and the statement of reasons, whether the facts on which the contested finding was based have been accurately stated and whether there has been any manifest error of assessment or a misuse of powers. In particular, the Court is not entitled to substitute its own economic assessment for that of the author of the decision.

(...)

132. Even though the Commission is not required to answer all the arguments put forward during the administrative procedure by a company which, as a beneficiary of the contested aid measure, is an interested party for the purposes of Article 93(2) of the Treaty (now Article 88(2) EC), it is none the less required to provide in its decision an adequate statement of the reasons why the essential arguments of such a party cannot be upheld.

Therefore, having regard to the fact that a decision was the only precedent for the Commission's practice when taking decisions on the calculation of the minimum rate for an investment by the public authorities in an airline, it must be held that the interested parties argument that its situation must be distinguished from that of the company in respect of which the previous decision was taken formed an essential part of its case that the investment from public funds satisfied the private investor test. In those circumstances, the Commission was required to answer that argument in the contested decision, failing which it failed to fulfil its obligation to state reasons.

This change to the organizational structure of the way services are provided in the field of air transportation, deeply affects the trade logic of the carriers. They now tend to concentrate their attention on the market segment of "transit passengers".

It is a matter of ensuring continuity and efficiency in the transit operations (disembarking and boarding), in order to make the airport more "appetizing" to carriers. According to this perspective, air transportation services become more profitable as the number of transit passengers who can be "collected" increases. In turn, this factor depends on the number of connections that the airport can offer to the passengers. Essentially, it all becomes a virtuous cycle, where airports and carriers have an interest in becoming respectively traffic allocation centers and leading operators of the traffic.

In this contest, we can see how the connection infrastructure between airports within the same airport system takes on crucial importance. Member States have a major interest in concentrating the most profitable portions of the international[6] traffic in a single airport, in order to transform it into a more important point of reference for the European theater. However, the member States' power to allocate air traffic is far from being totally discretionary. It is limited by non-discrimination principles for equal treatment of the carriers, and its application is constantly under the scrutiny of the European Commission. As we highlighted in the premise, the main parameter for this scrutiny is the interchangeability of the airports within the system, in other words, the presence of efficient connections, not only between the airport and the center of the urban agglomeration, but also between the airports. Airport services (handling and ticket sales) are, in fact, essential facilities that are fully subject to the application of European competition rules[7]. An important decision of European Commission held that Sabena, Belgian World Airlines, had infringed Article 106 of the TFEU by abusing its dominant position on the computerized ticket reservations market in Belgium. The alleged abusive conduct involved the refusal by Sabena to grant London European Airways access to its Saphir computer reservation system which is managed by Sabena. According to the European Commission, Sabena, by refusing to grant access to the Saphir system, was using its power on the ticket reservations market to impose minimum air fares on London European Airways, or was attempting to make entry to the Saphir system subject to acceptance by London European Airways of services which had no connection with the reservation system. This is the legal assessment of the Decision (case 3) European Commission, 4 November 1988, case IV/32.318, 88/589/CEE, Sabena, in OJEU L 317, 24 November 1988, p. 47 ff.):

(…)

The relevant market

(a) The relevant product market

(13) In order to determine whether Sabena occupies a dominant position within the meaning of Article 86, it is necessary first to define the relevant market. This constitutes all substitute products existing in a given geographic area in which the conditions of competition are sufficiently uniform to enable the economic power of the undertakings in question to be judged.

---

6 An international overview of airport services is rigorously explained in Graham A., *Managing Airports – an international perspective*, Amsterdam, 2005.

7 For a complete overview of the application of antitrust rules to the airport services see: Forsyth P. - Gillen D. (ed.), *Airport competition: the European experience*, Burlington, 2010, Pfähler, W. - Niemeier H.M.- Mayer O. (ed.), *Airports and air traffic – regulation, privatisation and competition*, Frankfurt, 1999, Lee D. (ed), *Advances in Airline Economics, Vol 1 Competition Policy and Antitrust*, Amsterdam, 2006 and Forsyth P., *Airport competition: A perspective and synthesis*, in Forsyth P. - Gillen D. (ed.), *Airport competition: the European experience*, Burlington, 2010

(14) The Commission notes that all the major airlines in Europe have developed or concluded agreements on access to a computerized reservation system. Although as matters stand, other non-computerized methods of reserving seats still exist, computer reservation will in the near future replace all other forms of reservation. The advantages of a computerized system (speed, quantity of data, immediate reservation and issue of ticket, constantly up-dated information, etc.) are such that the other services still in existence cannot be regarded as equivalent, e.g. the consultation by travel agencies of schedules and tariffs or telephoned reservations through airlines. Although London European itself referred to the latter form of reservation in promoting its Brussels-Luton service, its insistence on gaining access to the Saphir system shows that such access is essential for a company wishing to compete with companies already on the market. Reservations by telephone can, however, still serve as a back-up system, especially for companies with few flights and lower fares than their competitors. Nonetheless, the ability to offer customers a computerized reservation service is an important feature of a marketing policy.

(15) The originality of the product in question is due to its situation, halfway between the travel agencies and the airlines. It is in the interests of the latter, and in London European's in the present case, to ensure their flights are displayed in a reservation system so that travel agencies using the system can offer the flights to their customers.

The market in question thus comprises two facets: the market for the provision of computerized reservation services by an operator of such systems to one or more air transport undertakings; second, the market for the supply of such systems by that operator to travel agencies. This is why when examining whether Sabena holds a dominant position on the market for the provision of computerized reservation services it is necessary to consider both the market share of the Saphir system in relation to other computerized reservation systems and that share in relation to the supply of the system to travel agencies.

(b) The relevant geographical market

(16) The geographical market to be taken into consideration is the Belgian market. It is on this territory that customers residing in Belgium reserve their air tickets. Transactions are conducted in one currency, the Belgian franc, and the travel agents operate in a single market, the Belgian national market.

The Commission and the Court of Justice have expressely recognized that 'the territories of both large and medium-sized countries' (1) constitute a substantial part of the common market. It can therefore be inferred that the territory in question meets the criterion of substantiatily.

The Commission therefore concludes that for the purposes of Article 86 the relevant market is that for the provision of computerized flight reservation services in Belgium.

Regulation No 17

(17) As regards the applicability of Regulation No 17 to computerized flight reservation systems, it should be noted that the scope of application of this Regulation is limited by Council Regulation (EEC) No 141/62 (2) only, and not by the provisions of Council Regulation (EEC) No 3975/87 of (EEC) No 3976/87 (3).

Article 1 of Regulation (EEC) No 141/62 excludes the application of Regulation (EEC) No 17 to dominant positions on the transport market.

This provision, since it is a limitation of the scope of Regulation No 17, must be interpreted strictly. There is therefore no doubt that activities ancillary to the transport market as such do not fall within this exception and therefore fall within the scope of Regulation No 17.

(18) It is necessary to examine whether the market as defined above falls within the scope of application of Regulation No 17.

(19) Since the relevant market comprises two parts, the matter can easily be resolved as regards the relationship between an operator of a computerized reservation system and travel agencies. It is clear that Regulation No 17 is applicable on this market. It is well established that the services provided by a travel agent do not comprise the provision of transport itself (4). Therefore travel agents do not provide a service which relates to the transport market as required by Regulation No 141/62 in order to avoid the application of Regulation No 17.

(20) As regards the second part of the market, Regulation No 17 is also applicable for similar reasons.

Although the provision of ticket reservation services is in many instances connected with the provision of air transport services, it is only indirectly connected and does not consist in the provision of air transport as such. One can clearly conceive of an air transport service being provided without a prior reservation, if seats are available. The sole purpose of a reservation is to ensure that a traveller leaves when he wishes, but it can certainly be separated from the transport service proper. As in many other sectors, the selling of tickets is separate from the service attached to the ticket.

Furthermore, the fact that airlines have themselves developed their own reservation systems does not mean that reservations are indissociable from transportation. There is nothing to prevent a company having no links with airline companies from developing and marketing a system.

While it is true that reservations are an integral part of marketing air transport services, the marketing is not in itself a transport service.

Commission Decision 85/121/EEC (1) (Olympic Airways Case), which specifies that ground handling services are not as such air transport services and thus come under Regulation No 17 supports the conclusion reached by the Commission in the present case. In the same way as handling services provided on the ground before and after the transport takes place, the provision of a reservation service prior to the actual provision of transportation cannot be regarded as forming part of the transport market; it therefore falls within the scope of Regulation No 17.

(21) It must also be remembered that at the time when the events which are the subject of this decision took place, Regulation (EEC) No 3976/87 had not yet been adopted. Yet an analysis of the origin of this Regulation reinforces the view of the Commission that Regulation No 17 is applicable to computerized reservation services.

In its proposal of 8 July 1984 (2) for an amendment to Council Regulation (EEC) No 2821/71 of 20 December 1971 on the application of Article 85 (3) of the Treaty to categories of agreements, decisions and concerted practices (3), the Commission adopted the principle that computerized reservations systems do not fall within the scope of Article 1 of Regulation No 141/62 and are already convered by Regulation No 17. The explanatory memorandum to the proposal clearly states that agreements on ticket reservations and the issue of tickets are not of a purely technical nature and are already covered by Regulation No 17. In addition, the recitals of the abovementioned proposal place agreements on computer reservation systems on the same footing as those relating to technical and other operations carried out on the ground in airports.

This Commission position is reflected in the first recital of Regulation (EEC) No 3976/87. The recital draws a clear distinction between agreements directly related to the provision of air transport services and those not directly related. The former are covered by Regulation (EEC) No 3975/87 and the latter by Regulation No 17.

(22) The fact that Article 2 (1) of Regulation (EEC) No 3976/87 empowers the Commission to adopt block exemption regulations 'without prejudice to the application of Regulation (EEC) No 3975/87' does not mean that all the activities listed in Article 2 (2) of Regulation (EEC) No 3976/87 fall within the scope of Regulation (EEC) No 3975/87. The purpose of Regulation (EEC) No 3976/87 is to specify the areas where the Commission may grant block exemptions. These areas relate to air transport as such as well as to services ancillary thereto.

These two categories of service are found in a single regulation only for the purposes of that regulation, which does not affect the scope of Regulations No 17 and No 141/62 in relation to individual cases. As regards the latter, Regulation (EEC) No 3975/87 applies to air transport as such while Regulation No 17 will remain applicable to all other areas which do not consist of the provision of transport services as such.

Moreover, this reasoning is confirmed in Commission Regulation (EEC) No 2672/88 of 26 July 1988 relating to the application of Article 85 (3) of the EEC Treaty to categories of agreements between undertakings relating to computerized reservation systems for air transport services (4). The penultimate recital of the Regulation states that agreements exempted automatically by virtue of that Regulation do not have to be notified to the Commission pursuant to Regulation No 17.

Furthermore, the scope of Regulations No 17 and No 141/62 is not affected by Article 6 of Regulation (EEC) No 3976/87 which provides for consulation of the Advisory Committee established by Article 8 (3) of Regulation (EEC) No 3975/87 before publication of the draft regulation as well as before its adoption. Article 6 of Regulation (EEC) No 3976/87 does not affect in any way the procedures laid down in Regulation No 17 for the investigation of infringements of the processing of requests for individual exemption or negative clearance inareas which do not relate directly to the transport sector.

Existence of a dominant position

(23) It must then be assessed whether Sabena holds a dominant position both in the market for the provision of computerzed services by an operator of such services to travel agencies and in that of the provision of such services to other air transport companies.

(24) As regards the former market Sabena estimates the market share held by Saphir at between 40 and 50 %.

Although the Court has ruled that a 45 % share does not automatically entail control of the market, it is necessary to assess the degree of control in relation to the strength and number of competitors (1), whilst the ratio of market shares held by the undertaking concerned to those held by its competitors is also a reliable indicator (2).

There are five other computerized systems in Belgium, used by no more than some 20 agencies. The fact that 118 agencies use the Saphir system can be regarded as proof of Sabena's pre-eminent strength in the market for the provision of such services to travel agents.

(25) It also emerged that, between June and September 1987, 47 % of seats reserved in Belgium on Brussels-Luton flights were reserved through the Saphir system. This high percentage clearly shows that the success of the Brussels-Luton flights did indeed depend on London European having access to the Saphir system.

(26) In the latter market, Sabena manifestly holds a dominant position as all airlines operating in Brussels (with two exceptions) are listed in the Saphir system. This means that Sabena had always given access to its system to any company which requested access. It is also a clear indication of the capital importance of such access for all companies seeking to operate competitively on the Belgian market.

The fact that two airlines operating in Brussels are not included in the Saphir system simply means that they have their own marketing policy which does not require access to the system, chiefly for reasons of cost.

(27) On the basis of the above considerations, the Commission considers that at the material time Sabena occupied a dominant position in the Belgian market for the provision of computerized reservation services.

Abuse of dominant position

(28) The question whether the behaviour of Sabena constituted one or several abuses of this dominant position may be analysed as follows:

(29) The conduct of Sabena can be viewed, first, as a means of placing indirect pressure on London European to fix a higher level of fares than, as an independent air carrier, it had planned on the basis of its costs structure and commercial strategy. As the conduct in question aimed to produce an artificial increase in fares, it is totally incompatible with a system of free competition.

(30) It should be noted that the conduct of Sabena can equally be construed as a desire to limit production, markets or technical development to the prejudice of consumers (Article 86 (b)), since Sabena's refusal could have result in London European abandoning its plan to open a route between Brussels and Luton.

(31) Finally, the two contracts, Saphir and handling, are not connected: the computer reservation contract enables travel agencies to obtain transport services for passengers as quickly and efficiently as possible. The handling contract involves ground assistance for aircraft.

One of the reasons for Sabena's refusal is thus clearly the fact that it makes the conclusion of a Saphir contract subject to the conclusion by London European of a handling contract which is not related to the subject matter of the first contract. This behaviour therefore constitutes an abusive practice expressly covered by Article 86 (d).

Effect on trade between Member States

(32) The refusal in question has an effect on the flow of trade between Member States. First, the abusive behaviour was implemented by a Belgian company against an undertaking in another Member State. Second, the behaviour was intended to produce anti-competitive effects on the Brussels-London route, since Sabena and London European did not originally enjoy the same reservation facilities. In addition, the fact that London European could not gain access to the Saphir system was liable to prevent it from operating on

the route in question. This elimiantion of London European as a competitor can thus directly and potentially affect trading conditions between Member States since, although reservations are made locally, they involve an intra-Community transaction, namely, air transport between Brussels and Luton.

(33) In any event, the case-law of the Court of Justice is very clear on the question of an undertaking in a dominant position which endeavours to eliminate a competitor. In the Zoja judgment (1) the Court ruled that Article 86 was aimed at practices which undermine a system of effective competition. It is obvious that the structure of competition on the Brussels-London route would have been different if London European had not had full access to that market.

5.3 Airport Systems as per Procedures from the European Commission and the Laws of the European Court of Justice

At this point it is necessary to specify some of the application modalities of Regulation (EC) number 2408/92. Among the objectives that define the scope and justify the creation of the EU norms, within the respect of the jurisdiction of the member States (with the limits dictated by EU norms), we can indicate: a) planning of air transportation to be achieved at European Union level, and the right of member States to establish non-discriminatory regulations for traffic allocation among airports located within the same airport system; b) regulation of traffic rights, to be compatible with safety norms and with those for environmental protection, and the general principle of non-discrimination; c) the competitiveness of the market, that imposes "*the institution of provisions to prevent unjustified economic effects on air carriers*", and also "*special provisions for public service fees, necessary to support adequate air service with domestic regions*"[8].

Essentially, articles 3 and 8 of the Regulation gave member States the main tasks for traffic allocation, forcing them to play the role of "mediator" between the interests of the various air carriers[9].

---

8 The airport regulation is a very important objective in order to control the competition among carriers and increase the infrastructures between two competitive hubs: Barrett S., *How do the demands for airport services differ between full-service Carrier and low-cost carriers?*, in *Journal of Air Transport Management*, 2004, p. 33 ff., Borenstein S., *Airline merger, airport dominance and market power*, in *American Economic Review, Papers and Proceedings,* 1990, p. 400 ff., Charlton A. *Airport regulation: Does a mature industry have mature regulation?*, in *Journal of Air Transport Management*, 2009, p. 116 ff., Dennis N.P.S., *Competition between hub airports in Europe*, paper presented at the 8th World Conference on Transport Research, 12–27 July, Antwerp, 1998.

9 See, Niemeier, H., *Regulation of Airports: The Case of Hamburg Airport – a View from the Perspective of Regional policy*, in *Journal of Air Transport Management*, 2002, p. 37 ff., Oum T.H. - Fu X., *Impacts of Airports on Airline Competition: Focus on Air-*

Object of the allocation, and consequently of the mediation, were the traffic rights, both within the individual airport and the entire airport system.

It is important to point out how Regulation 2408/92 establishes jurisdictions and modalities for the creation of new airport systems. The creation of a new airport system or the modification of an existing one depended on the decision of the State. The State would evaluate strategic, economic and commercial factors to decide whether to "group" two or more airports. In fact, it was believed that the State, through the application of the principle of subsidiarity, was best suited to define the location of the structures servicing a city or an urban agglomeration, and even to define its own urban agglomerations.

This does not mean that the European Commission did not have powers on the matter. On the contrary, in accordance with the abovementioned supervisory functions over domestic measures taken in the matter of pre-existing airport systems, the European Commission, together with the other member States, would be briefed over the domestic measures, then would verify whether they were compatible with the principles of European Union Law. In case of positive outcome, the Commission would modify attachment II of the Regulation (the part that contained the list of airport systems).

There were two types of boundaries that defined how the States were allowed to allocate traffic within an airport system (new or existing): objective and subjective. The first one subjected the State to the "*operational norms that were published and in force at the European, national and regional or local level in the matter of safety, environment protection and slot allocation*". The second one was represented by parity in treatment: domestic regulations could not discriminate against carriers because of their nationality or identification. Let's see an example of domestic provisions on traffic allocation (case 4) European Commission, 21 December 2000, Case TREN/AMA/12/00, Malpensa – Orio al Serio – Linate, in OJEU L58, 28 february 2001, p. 29):

(…)

The operative provisions of the Decree of 3 March 2000 therefore read as follows:

"Article 1
1. The provisions of this Decree on the distribution of air traffic within the airport system of Milan, following the endorsement of the requirements set out in points A, B and C of the Annex to the Prime Ministerial Decree of 13 December 1999 referred to in the preamble, shall be applicable as from 20 April 2000.

Article 2
1. Intercontinental, international, intra-Community, national and regional connections, both scheduled and non-scheduled, may be operated from the airports of Malpensa, Linate and Bergamo Orio al Serio, which belong to Milan's airport system, within the limits of those airports' individual operating capacity and in accordance with the provisions of Articles 3 and 4.

---

port Performance and Airport-Airline Vertical Relations, ITF Round Tables. International Transport Forum, 2009, p. 31 ff.

Article 3
1. Connections may be operated from Milan Malpensa taking into account the airport's operating arrangements as indicated in the preamble.

Article 4
1. From Linate, Community carriers may, using narrow-body (single-aisle) aircraft, operate point-to-point scheduled connections with other airports in the European Union identified on the basis of passenger traffic volumes, both arriving and departing, registered within Milan's airport system in the calendar year 1999, and not exceeding the limits set out below:
(a) one daily return service per carrier, using two time slots, to airport systems or individual airports with passenger traffic exceeding 350000 units and not exceeding 700000 units;
(b) two daily return services per carrier, using four time slots, to airport systems or individual airports with passenger traffic exceeding 700000 units and not exceeding 1400000 units;
(c) three daily return services per carrier, using six time slots, to airport systems or individual airports with passenger traffic exceeding 1400000 units and not exceeding 2800000 units;
(d) no limit for connections to airport systems or individual airports with passenger traffic in excess of 2800000 units.
2. From Linate, Community carriers may, with the arrangements set out in paragraph 1, operate a daily return service using two time slots to airport systems or individual airports located in 'Objective 1' regions which in the course of the calendar year 1999 registered passenger traffic of fewer than 350000 units in Milan's airport system.
3. Linate airport may be used for general aviation."

The Regulation provided for administrative procedures that, upon request by a member State or the European Commission, involved opening an investigation, requesting information from States and air carriers, and creating an advisory committee with representatives from the member States. Within a month, the Commission would conclude the investigation, declaring whether the State would be allowed to continue with the implementation of the domestic measures or not.

However, this action, granted that it was also open to challenges as per article 230 of the EC Treaty, in exceptional cases, could even be re-examined or "re-decided" by the Council: within a month of the original decision, a dissatisfied member State could defer the question to the Council. Again, within a month, the Council, with qualified majority, could modify or annul the decision by the Commission.

In order to better analyze the innovations brought to the old procedures by the new Regulation of 2008, we will follow, at least in summary, the pre-existing enforcement procedure of regulatory norms for airport systems. This way, we can verify and quantify how the recently introduced changes have truly codified the inspiring principles, or determine whether the decisions by the European Commission and the Court of Justice did not have any effect on the new measures introduced by the EU Law.

5.4 The Interchangeability of Airports for Direct Flights and the Non-discrimination Principle

As we amply described in chapter two, the "Malpensa case" came about upon notification by nine airline companies that disputed the Italian Government actions regarding traffic allotment between Malpensa and Linate airports[10].

Transportation Ministry decree, dated July, 5, 1996, identified Malpensa as the landing and departure airport for all listed connections; Ministry decree dated October 23, 1997 established the starting date of enforcement of the new system (October 25, 1998).

Linate airport, while still active for general aviation, was to be utilized for direct flights, without stops en route, that would reach a yearly volume of two million passengers or more (the only flights that would meet these requirements were the Alitalia flights to Rome).

The large number of measures taken by the Italian Government became the object of an investigation by the Regional Court of Lazio and two complaints presented to the European Commission. These litigations brought about two decisions by the European Commission, and one judgment by the Court of Justice. The most challenged point was the implementation procedure for traffic transfer and its time frame. In fact, until completion of the essential infrastructure, Alitalia was the only carrier that would benefit from the connection, since it was the only carrier that could reach the number of passengers needed to access the Linate direct flight market.

According to the European Commission, in this case, traffic allotment would not be discriminatory only if infrastructural changes were made, so that Malpensa and Linate could be considered interchangeable airports[11].

With the closing judgment, the European Court of Justice confirmed the interpretation of the Regulation as that of the principles of free provision of services, with the respect of non-discrimination and proportionality, as originally submitted by the Commission (case 5) ECJ, 18 January 2001, Case C-361/98, Italian Republic v Commission of the European Communities - Malpensa 2000, in Rep., p. I-00385):

---

[10] The study of the Malpensa case can be carried out through: Valente, *Il caso «Malpensa» dinanzi alla Corte di giustizia delle Comunità europee,* in *Giust. civ.* 2001, p. 2013 ff., Nascimbene, *Concorrenza e libera prestazione dei servizi nella regolamentazione dei sistemi aeroportuali e della ripartizione di traffico,* in *Giur. comm.*, 2003, p. 197 ff. and Masutti A., *I requisiti per l'accesso al mercato dei servizi aeroportuali: regolazione del mercato e competenze valutative*, in *Dir. trasp.*, 2002, pp. 91 ff.

[11] It is of the outmost importance to understand the relevant market of Hub airports: Dennis N.P.S., *Competition between hub airports in Europe*, paper presented at the 8th World Conference on Transport Research, 12–27 July, Antwerp, 1998.

(…)

The first plea

29 The Italian Government submits, first of all, that, within the framework of traffic distribution between the airports which make up an airport system, Article 8(1) of Regulation No 2408/92, unlike Article 9(4) and (5) thereof which grants to the Commission the power to decide whether a national measure is in any way contrary to Community law, fixes only one limit to the Member State's power, namely observance of the principle of non-discrimination on the ground of the nationality and/or identity of the air carrier. The Government claims that, by adopting the contested decision, which is based on a finding that the national measures set out in the decrees at issue are in breach of the principle of the freedom to provide services from the point of view of proportionality, the Commission has thus exceeded the limits of the power which is granted to it under Article 8(3) of that regulation.

30 The Italian Government adds that a broad interpretation of Article 8(1) of Regulation No 2408/92 is contrary to the principle of the strict legality of the Commission's power of decision for the purpose of the third and fourth indents of Article 155 of the Treaty. Furthermore, by reason of the fact that it derogates from Article 169 of the EC Treaty (now Article 226 EC), Article 8(3) of that regulation should be interpreted strictly, so that it could not be understood as authorising the Commission to use its power of decision to make assessments which are not directly related to the application of Article 8(1).

31 In that regard, as the Court has held in previous decisions, in interpreting a provision of Community law it is necessary to consider not only its wording but also the context in which it occurs and the objects of the rules of which it forms part (see, in particular, Case 337/82 St Nikolaus Brennerei [1984] ECR 1051, paragraph 10).

32 It is clear from the 1st, 2nd and 19th recitals in the preamble to Regulation No 2408/92 that the purpose of that regulation is, inter alia, to define the conditions for applying in the air transport sector the principle of the freedom to provide services which is enshrined in, inter alia, Articles 59 and 61 of the Treaty, so that all matters of market access are dealt with in the same regulation.

33 It should also be pointed out that it is settled case-law that Article 59 of the Treaty requires not only the elimination of all discrimination on grounds of nationality against providers of services who are established in another Member State but also the abolition of any restriction, even if it applies without distinction to national providers of services and to those of other Member States, which is liable to prohibit, impede or render less advantageous the activities of a provider of services established in another Member State where he lawfully provides similar services (see Case C-76/90 Säger [1991] ECR I-4221, paragraph 12; and Joined Cases C-369/96 and C-376/96 Arblade and Others [1999] ECR I-8453, paragraph 33).

34 The Court finds that the measures enacted in the decrees at issue for the purpose of governing the distribution of traffic within an airport system, within the meaning of Article 8(1) of Regulation No 2408/92, constitute restrictions on the freedom to provide services.

35 In order that such restrictions may be authorised under Regulation No 2408/92, they must be justified and, in particular, proportionate to the purpose for which they were adopted.

36 It follows that the Commission was fully entitled, within the framework of the power granted to it under Article 8(1) and (3) of Regulation No 2408/92, to examine, first, whether the national measures enacted in the decrees at issue impose restrictions which are applicable without distinction and, second, whether those restrictions are such as to achieve the objective which they envisage, without going beyond what is necessary to achieve it.

37 In those circumstances, the Italian Government's arguments based on Articles 155 and 169 of the Treaty cannot be accepted either.

38 First, as regards Article 155 of the Treaty, since the interpretation of Article 8(1) of Regulation No 2408/92 proposed by the Italian Government cannot be accepted, the criteria identified in the Court's case-law by the Commission, in the context of its examination of the legality of the decrees at issue, cannot be criticised as going beyond both the limits of its power of decision and the limits of the powers which the Council confers on it.

39 Second, as regards Article 169 of the Treaty, it is clear from paragraphs 31 to 36 above that the Commission is empowered under Article 8(1) and (3) of Regulation No 2408/92 to examine whether the national measures adopted impose restrictions which are applicable without distinction and, where appropriate, whether they are justified. The Commission is therefore not required to ensure observance of the principle of the freedom to provide services from the point of view of proportionality solely by means of the infringement proceedings provided for in Article 169 of the Treaty.

40 It follows that the Italian Republic is not justified in claiming that that provision of the Treaty was infringed.

41 The first plea must therefore be rejected.

The second plea

42 By its second plea, the Italian Government claims, in the alternative, that the Commission was wrong to consider that the decrees at issue are in breach of the principle of proportionality.

43 That plea falls into two parts.

44 First, the Italian Government disputes the reasoning on the basis of which the Commission submits that the national traffic distribution rules must observe the principle of proportionality, since that principle does not appear anywhere in Regulation No 2408/92, which is the only source of rules in the field which is the subject of the contested decision.

45 Second, the Italian Government claims that, in recital 49 in the preamble to the contested decision, the Commission erred in law. It states that the Commission there assessed whether the decrees at issue were consistent with Community law by adopting a criterion of economic interest, namely the viability of an airport system. It claims that it follows from the Court's case-law that the principle of proportionality should not be applied where a restriction is not based on an overriding reason in the general interest. According to that case-law, economic requirements cannot constitute overriding reasons in the general interest. However, in the present case, Article 8(1) of Regulation No 2408/92 allows national air traffic distribution rules on the basis of economically valid requirements, subject to observance of the principle of non-discrimination, so that it would be arbitrary to make those national rules subject to a review of proportionality.

46 As regards the first part of the second plea, it is sufficient to state that, for the reasons mentioned in paragraphs 31 to 36 above, the Commission was fully entitled, in the context of its power under Article 8(1) and (3) of Regulation No 2408/92, to examine whether the national measures enacted in the decrees at issue observed the principle of proportionality.

47 The Italian Government's argument can therefore not be accepted.

48 As regards the second part of the second plea, alleging the lack of an overriding reason in the general interest, it is common ground that aims of a purely economic nature cannot justify a barrier to the fundamental principle of freedom to provide services (see Case C-158/96 Kohll [1998] ECR I-1931, paragraph 41).

49 However, the mere fact that a Member State pursues an aim in conditions which must, in particular, be economically viable does not thereby exclude the possibility that such an aim may constitute an overriding reason in the general interest capable of justifying a barrier of that kind.

50 It should be recalled in that regard that Malpensa airport is one of the priority projects of the trans-European transport network which are listed in Annex III to Decision No 1692/96/EC and that, in accordance with Article 129c of the EC Treaty (now, after amendment, Article 155 EC), the Community's activities in the field of the establishment and development of trans-European networks are to take into account the potential economic viability of the projects.

51 Furthermore, as is apparent from the 13th recital in the preamble to Regulation No 2408/92, the distribution of traffic within an airport system makes air transport planning possible.

52 It follows that, whether or not the creation of a fully operational and viable hub is classified as an overriding reason in the general interest, a legitimate objective of that kind may justify an obstacle to the fundamental freedom to provide services only in so far as it is consistent with the principle of proportionality.

53 Accordingly, the second part of the second plea is not well founded either and that plea must therefore be rejected.

The third plea

54 By its third plea, the Italian Government challenges, in the further alternative, the application of the principle of proportionality by the Commission in the present case. In its submission, instead of focusing its examination on the legal criterion of proportionality, the Commission based the contested decision on a discretionary assessment of the merits of the action decided on by the Italian Government on the subject of Malpensa airport, so that it exceeded its powers under Article 8(3) of Regulation No 2408/92. In that regard, it claims that the assertion of a breach of that principle is based on three arguments, each of which is either immaterial or misconceived.

55 The Italian Government claims, first, that the Commission's first argument, that the volume of traffic transferred is not compatible with the current conditions of access infrastructures, is unrelated to the only criterion which is material to proportionality, that is to say whether the concentration of flights at Malpensa airport is appropriate to the Italian Government's objective. In any event, the national authorities have fully demonstrated the compatibility of the access infrastructures with the volume of traffic which will be transferred.

56 Next, the Government submits that the Commission's second argument, based on the financial structure supporting Malpensa 2000, which does not require any transfer of traffic before 31 December 2000, is manifestly not material to the assessment of the proportionality of the national decision on the transfer of traffic.

57 Finally, the Italian Government considers that the Commission's third argument, that the decision to transfer traffic from Linate airport to Malpensa airport is contrary to the intention, which was expressly stated in Decree No 46-T, of maintaining Linate airport in service in any event, is quite simply fallacious. Linate airport will remain in service anyway, even if its use is limited.

58 First of all, as regards the Italian Government's first two arguments, the Court finds that, as is clear from paragraphs 48 to 52 above, the Commission was entitled to analyse the creation of an operational and economically viable hub in relation to the principle of proportionality.

59 In the context of the examination of the proportionality of the measures enacted in the decrees at issue, the Commission was thus bound to assess whether, at the date prescribed for the transfer of air traffic to Malpensa airport, the level of access infrastructures at that airport would discourage passengers from using it. It was also bound to assess whether that transfer was necessary in order to ensure the financial viability of an operational hub.

60 It follows that there is no foundation to the Italian Government's complaints to the effect that the criteria used by the Commission, which are based, first, on the relationship between the volume of traffic transferred and the existing conditions of the access infrastructures and, second, on the financial necessity of a transfer of that traffic at a date earlier than that initially prescribed by the Italian authorities in the context of Malpensa 2000, are not material to the assessment of whether the measures adopted in the decrees at issue are proportionate to the objective pursued.

61 Second, as regards the Italian Government's challenge to the merits of the Commission's findings on the state of the infrastructures linking the city of Milan and Malpensa airport at the time of the planned transfer of air traffic, it is clear that the Government has not succeeded in establishing that those findings were incorrect.

62 Lastly, as regards the Commission's third argument in relation to maintaining Linate airport in service, it is sufficient to state that the reasoning in that respect in the contested decision is of a purely ancillary nature and that, even if the Italian Government were justified in challenging it, such a criticism cannot cast doubt on the merits of the Commission's assessment as to whether the measures adopted in the decrees at issue were, or were not, proportionate to the objective pursued by the Italian authorities.

63 In those circumstances, the third plea must be rejected.

The fourth plea

64 By its fourth plea, the Italian Government submits that the Commission's analysis in recitals 29 to 46 in the preamble to the contested decision, which is designed to establish the existence of indirect discrimination, is legally flawed for three reasons.

65 First of all, the Italian Government claims that there is no indirect discrimination in the present case because, contrary to the Commission's assertion, the national measures enacted in the decrees at issue do not produce an advantage for Alitalia and a disadvantage for the Community carriers which operate from hubs other than Rome-Fiumicino. It claims on that basis that the traffic between the cities of Milan and Rome largely consists of business

travel, most of it being daily commuting. It asserts that such traffic is thus objectively that which is best placed to be served from an urban airport such as Linate, also enabling the air route to remain competitive in relation to the rail link.

66 Next, the Italian Government submits that the Commission should have assessed the effects of the transfer of traffic to Malpensa airport on the basis of the future situation and not only the existing one. It considers that a provision can be regarded as indirectly discriminatory only if its capacity to advantage or adversely affect a person is fully demonstrated. In the new situation, when that airport will be fully turned over to intercontinental flights, the route from Linate airport to the Rome-Fiumicino hub will not, in practice, result in any competitive advantage for Alitalia.

67 Finally, the Italian Government claims that, if the Commission considered that maintaining a route between Linate airport and Rome-Fiumicino airport might bring a competitive advantage for Alitalia, it should have opted for measures against the Italian Government which were less draconian, but sufficient to ensure the Community interest in observance of the principle of non-discrimination laid down in Article 8(1) of Regulation No 2408/92.

68 First of all, as regards the first part of the fourth plea, it should be noted that none of the elements relied on by the Italian Government demonstrates that the Commission was wrong in finding that Alitalia was the only carrier in a position to access the Rome-Fiumicino hub from Linate airport, while the other Community carriers could operate their hubs only from Malpensa airport. Although it is true that Alitalia would have reduced the number of its intercontinental flights from its Rome-Fiumicino hub to the Malpensa airport hub, it is none the less true, as the Italian Government itself acknowledges, that, at the date prescribed for the transfer of air traffic from Linate airport, Rome-Fiumicino airport remained the hub for that air carrier.

69 It follows that the Commission was justified in its finding of discrimination between Alitalia and the other Community air carriers, so that the first part of the fourth plea must be rejected.

70 Next, as regards the second part of the fourth plea, concerning the alleged error of assessment which the Commission made in finding that there was indirect discrimination without taking account of the future development of Malpensa airport, it is sufficient to state that, in the present case, the Commission did not base its findings solely on information relating to the period prior to the date of the planned transfer, since it examined, as is clear from recitals 35 and 44 in the recital to the contested decision, the development prospects for Linate and Malpensa airports, and for Alitalia's hubs.

71 In the light of the foregoing, the second part of the fourth plea must be rejected.

72 Finally, as regards the third part of that plea, alleging that the contested decision is in breach of the principle of proportionality, in that it prohibits the implementation of the measures enacted in the decrees at issue, it should be recalled that, under Article 8(3) of Regulation No 2408/92, it is for the Commission merely to examine the national measure adopted by the Member State concerned and to decide, after consulting the committee referred to in Article 11 of that regulation, whether that State may continue to apply that measure.

73 In those circumstances, since the Commission was not empowered to propose an amendment to the measures enacted in the decrees at issue, it cannot be accused of infringing the principle of proportionality by having failed to suggest that the national authorities adopt less restrictive measures.

74 The fourth plea must therefore be rejected.

5.5 The Right to Serve Connecting Passengers from and to Long-range Connections

It is interesting to review the proceedings relating to the Paris airport system. Three cases (Viva Air, TAT and TAT II) were the object of large investigations by the European Commission. The claims brought forward for Malpensa were the same in the case of Paris. It was again a matter of establishing the legitimacy of Government measures relating to air traffic allotments under the alleged existence of an airport system, with consequent interchangeability of airports. The main reason for the decision reached by the European Commission was the application of the proportionality principle. The Commission found that the measures taken by Italian and French authorities - while partially justifiable - went beyond the actual steps needed for traffic planning within their respective domestic airports.

Important is the case of *"Viva Air"*, where the Commission found that the French Authorities acted in a way that was incompatible with Regulation number 2408/92 when they denied the plaintiff (*Viva Air*) permission to offer a Madrid-Paris service out of *Charles de Gaulle* airport. The same authorities offered *Viva Air* permission to operate out of *Orly* airport for the same route. The French Authorities' denial gave *Air France* the opportunity to maintain its strong position on the Madrid-Paris route out of *Charles de Gaulle*, while it deprived *Viva Air* of the benefit of serving connecting passengers from and to long-range connections, arriving at or departing from *Charles de Gaulle* (Paris international airport) on its Madrid-Paris route. According to the European Commission (case 6) European Commission, 28 May 1993, Case VII/AMA/I/93, Viva Air, in OJEU, L 140, 11 June 1993, p. 51):

(…)

The Commission considers that this provision constitutes the statement of a general principle of freedom of access for all Community air carriers to all intra-Community routes, including those within Member States, i.e. of freedom of access for all carriers in possession of an operating licence granted in accordance with the provisions of Regulation (EEC) No 2407/92.

Nevertheless, these provisions do not in themselves authorize Community air carriers to exercise traffic rights. As the French authorities maintain, authorization to exercise these rights remains the province of the Member States concerned which, if they so wish, may impose a formal authorization procedure. This is confirmed by the words, 'shall not be required to authorize', in Article 3 (2) of Regulation (EEC) No 2408/92. Nevertheless, this phrase also means that, on the contrary, under normal circumstances - i.e. where none of the restrictions or constraints provided for in Article 3 (2), Article 3 (4) or Articles 4 to 10 of Regulation (EEC) No 2408/92 is capable of applying - the Member States concerned are required to allow carriers to exercise traffic rights. Here, authorization is automatic and Member States no longer have any discretion in the matter.

The automatic granting of rights arises out of the general principle of freedom of access. It is also in line with the recitals in the preamble to Regulation (EEC) No 2408/92 which refer specifically to Article 8a of the Treaty, to the freedom to provide services in an internal market without internal frontiers and to the abolition of all restrictions regarding designation and traffic rights. It is also in line with the freedom to set fares and rates granted by Regulation (EEC) No 2409/92 since, from the economic point of view, the elimination of all rigidity on prices should also mean the elimination of all rigidity on quantities (or access to the market), if an unbalanced outcome is to be avoided.

The fact that the right to exercise traffic rights has become automatic may not, however, prevent the Member States exercising their right to apply the transitional restrictive clauses provided for in Article 3 (2), Article 3 (4) and Article 5 or the definitive restrictive clauses of Articles 4, 6, 8, 9 and 10 of Regulation (EEC) No 2408/92. Member States may therefore require carriers to lodge applications providing various items of information prior to an authorization being granted. Nevertheless, to prevent such requirements from undermining freedom of access to the market established by Regulation (EEC) No 2408/92, they must be kept to the minimum necessary to allow the Member States to operate the abovementioned restrictive clauses, where appropriate.

Also, where a Member State imposes a formal notification and authorization procedure, the deadlines for replying to airlines' applications for authorization must be kept very short for three reasons. First, the very principle of freedom of access to the market, established by Article 3 of Regulation (EEC) No 2408/92, assumes that carriers will be informed quickly of the decision on their application. Secondly, in view of the heavy investment involved in starting up a new service, particularly for small airlines, the element of uncertainty must be reduced. Thirdly, it does not take long to examine applications in the light of whether to apply the various measures restricting access to the market provided for in the Regulation.

Still with a view to reducing the amount of uncertainty for airlines and since the right to exercise the freedom is now the rule and refusal the exception, it should also be the rule that, where no reply is received by the stated deadline, authorization to operate is implicit. Further, all refusals should, on the one hand, be expressly and clearly justified in fact and in law and, on the other hand, be open to legal challenge. The Member States should therefore include appropriate provisions in their internal regulations.

On air slots, the Commission considers that air slot allocation, which is covered by Council Regulation (EEC) No 95/93 (4), is legally distinct from the question of granting of traffic rights, which is covered by Regulation (EEC) No 2408/92. Consequently, an airline's application for traffic rights may not be refused for the simple reason that the airline does not have the necessary air slots to be able to provide the service covered by the application. Knowing or not knowing whether an airline has the appropriate air slots therefore has no bearing on the matter and airlines must therefore not be asked to provide this information.

Similarly, a carrier who has, or can obtain, the slots he needs to operate a given service may not assume that this authorizes him to exercise traffic rights in respect of the service - unless, that is, the Member State concerned does not impose any special formalities in respect of obtaining such rights. Viva Air's argument that its application for a slot allocation at Paris (CDG) was equivalent to the French authorities issuing an authorization should therefore be rejected.

Finally, the Commission stresses that, contrary to the French rules which are still in force, no Member State may undermine the fundamental principle of non-discrimination on the basis of nationality by differentiating between its own licensed carriers and those licensed by other Member States in the formalities it lays down with regard to the examination of applications for traffic rights under Regulation (EEC) No 2408/92.

VII Article 8 (1) of Regulation (EEC) No 2408/92 states as follows: 'This Regulation shall not affect a Member State's right to regulate without discrimination on grounds of nationality or identity of the air carrier, the distribution of traffic between the airports within an airport system'.

When applied, these provisions could restrict the general principle of freedom of access to routes and Community airports provided for in Article 3 of the Regulation. The Commission considers that, like any exception to a general principle, any such restriction must be interpreted strictly and that the interpretation must be based on transparent and objective criteria which remain constant over a given period and are non-discriminatory. It is then the responsibility of the Member States to put forward all the relevant grounds.

The Commission also considers that the aforementioned wording of Article 8 (1) implies that rules must be laid down which are transparent and regulatory in nature, i.e. having general, and not individual, effect. This, in turn, means that the rules must be published. Only if they are published, will they meet the requirement of transparency since the reasons for, and basis of, current policy on airports will then be clear. Publication would also enable airlines to work out in advance, with a minimum of uncertainty, the airport to which they were likely to be allocated in view of their intended routes, in accordance with the freedom the Community rules sought to confer on carriers.

The fact remains that the French rules by which traffic is allocated within the Paris airport system, and particularly the rules used against Viva Air, have not been published. The Commission therefore concludes that the rules do not apply. What is more, under French law an unpublished regulatory instrument cannot be enforced against persons to whom it purports to apply. Hence, it cannot be used as a basis for an individual decision against such persons.

The fact that the decision to refuse authorization was taken on 28 December 1992, i.e. before the entry into force on 1 January 1993 of Regulation (EEC) No 2408/92, does nothing to alter the foregoing assessment since Article 9 of Council Regulation (EEC) No 2343/90 (5), which was in force prior to Regulation (EEC) No 2408/92, already included similar provisions and since the decision of 28 December 1992 continued to affect the situation after 31 December 1992.

Also, according to the information available to the Commission, as corroborated by the replies set out above which the French authorities provided on 11 March 1993, the latter have pursued a policy for the last 15 years or so - and more particularly the last five years - of promoting the expansion of Paris (CDG) Airport which is to become both the main continental European gateway and a large hub airport. It is a fact that, compared with the situation at other European airports, the physical potential for expanding this one is considerable and that, in March 1993, capacity at Paris (CDG) increased considerably when terminal 2C came into operation.

On the question of allocating traffic to airports, the policy has been gradually to transfer to Paris (CDG) all airlines formerly operating through Orly. For instance, in October 1980, once the CDG 2 terminal came into operation, the French authorities decided to transfer foreign (particularly Community) airlines from Orly-West to terminal CDG 1. It therefore has to be said that the refusal of the authorities to allow Viva Air to operate the Madrid-Paris (CDG) service runs counter to their policy on these airports so far.

The grounds given for the refusal were that the French Government operated a rule by which it did not allow airlines to run services on the same medium-haul international route from both Paris (Orly) and Paris (CDG). One wonders why this rule applies only to medium-haul international traffic and not also to domestic and to international long-haul services. The French authorities say that this differentiation is due to the type of market involved.

Turning first to long-haul services, the Commission would nevertheless note that only the French flag carrier operates an international long-haul service with departures from both Orly and CDG (Paris-New York) at frequencies comparable with those of many intra-Community airlines.

Taking the medium-haul services next, the Commission cannot accept at face value the explanations provided by the French authorities, namely that, as opposed to the situation in domestic French flights, intra-Community international flights operated by a single company may not serve both Orly and CDG because of the low level of competition with surface transport, the low level of traffic flows and the existence of several competing companies. In the first place, such a general and complete separation of national and international intra-Community flights is contrary to the very principle of a single Community market. Secondly, on several domestic French routes - and not the shortest either - there is little competition from surface transport whereas there is such competition on major intra-Community international routes departing from Paris. Thirdly, the difference in the size of traffic flows is not so great as to justify different treatment and it should be pointed out that the Paris-London[12] route is the busiest of all intra-Community routes. Lastly, domestic French flights are now also open to competition since the Community rules establishing a single internal market in civil aviation came into force on 1 January 1993.

In any case, even supposing that the rule governing traffic allocation could be regarded as justified under the provisions of Article 8 (1) of Regulation (EEC) No 2408/92, the Commission considers that, for the purposes of applying the rule, Viva Air should be regarded as separate from Iberia since Article 2 (b) of the Regulation simply defines a Community air carrier as one with a valid operating licence issued by a Member State in accordance with Regulation (EEC) No 2407/92, without any reference to the question of control. Even though both Iberia and Viva Air are incontestably members of the same group, Viva Air was founded well before the date of the contested application for traffic rights and has not only its own operating licence but also its own staff, its own commercial image and its own fleet. Furthermore, the French authorities have not alleged, nor has the Commission found, any abuse of the law or fraudulent action on the part of Viva Air or the Iberia Group.

In view of the foregoing, the Commission therefore considers that, in this case, the French authorities applied the provisions of Article 8 (1) of Regulation (EEC) No 2408/92 incorrectly. They were therefore wrong to refuse Viva Air authorization to exercise traffic rights

12 For an analysis of the English airports regulation, see Starkie D., *The airport industry in a competitive environment: A United Kingdom perspective*, in *Joint Transport Research Centre, International Transport Forum*, OECD, 2008.

on the Madrid-Paris (CDG) route from 2 January 1993. In accordance with the provisions of Article 8 (3) of Regulation (EEC) No 2408/92, the decision must therefore be that the French authorities may not continue to apply this measure, without any need to examine whether or not the other points submitted by Viva Air are well founded, that is to say those based on the discriminatory nature of the measure as shown in particular by the fact that Euralair - which operates a direct flight from Madrid to Paris (Orly) - is in fact part of the Air France group which itself operates the Madrid-Paris (CDG) route,

5.6 The Liberalization of Cabotage and Infrastructures Saturation

Equally important is the decision dated April 27, 1994, number 94/291, by the European Commission, where another French measure was found discriminatory and disproportionate. French Authorities, in distributing air traffic between Paris *Orly* and Paris *Charles de Gaulle*, restricted free circulation of services by other member States' carriers by reserving *Orly* strictly for domestic connections (with the exception of certain flights to Spain, Greece and Portugal), and *Charles de Gaulle* for international traffic[13].

This way, member States' carriers (including *TAT European Airlines*, that wanted to operate a service between London and Paris *Orly*) could not operate via *Orly*, which was more easily accessible from the city and where French cabotage traffic would flow, thanks to higher demand for transit traffic on intra-Community connections offered by the involved carriers. Therefore

(…)

the Commission considers it necessary to use those powers to decide whether France may continue to apply the measure refusing Community carriers and TAT in particular, traffic rights on the scheduled routes between Paris(Orly)-Marseille and Paris(Orly)-Toulouse on the grounds that operation of the Paris-Marseille and Paris-Toulouse routes is only authorized from and to CDG airport, as the French authorities have applied Article 5 of the Regulation in question to the same two routes to and from Orly.

As stated before, the European Commission based its decision on the application of the principle of proportionality, judging insufficient the justifications presented by the French Authorities. In fact, according to the European Commission,

(…)

---

13 The market of international traffic of passengers should be analyzed taking into consideration the differences between the ordinary airlines and the low cost companies; see Francis G. – Humprheys I. – Ison S., *Airports' perspectives on the growth of low- cost airlines and the remodeling of the airport-airline relationship*, in *Tourism Management*, 2004, p. 507 ff. and Franke M., *Competition between network carriers and low-cost carriers – retreat battle or breakthrough to a new level of efficiency?*, in *AirTransport Management,* 2004, p. 15 ff.) They are, in fact, two different products.

In reply to the aforementioned correspondence, France's Permanent Representative to the European Communities sent to the Commission the French authorities' observations on the substance of the complaint by TAT, in a letter dated 21 December 1993 which was formally recorded by the Commission's Secretariat-General on 23 December. With reference to the application of Article 5 of Regulation (EEC) No 2408/92, the French authorities first stated that, with the exception of the Paris-Nice route, the abovementioned agreement of 30 October 1990 only laid down multiple designation status for certain French domestic routes to or from CDG. They further pointed out that the Paris(Orly)-Marseille and Paris(Orly)-Toulouse routes met the criteria laid down for application of the said Article 5, inasmuch as they were domestic routes, Air Inter had been granted an exclusive concession in a clearly identified legal instrument referring explicitly to the routes in question and, lastly, no other forms of transport capable of providing an adequate and uninterrupted service were available on those routes. It should be pointed out here that the French authorities made no reference to Article 8 of Regulation (EEC) No 2408/92 at this stage.

The European Commission viewed investment issues and infrastructure saturation as objectives deserving consideration and protection, being general overriding reasons. In fact, infrastructure saturation and the pursuit of a policy for airport traffic can be considered overriding requirements of general interest, and as such they can justify traffic allocation measures that might involve access restrictions to Orly airport. However, the Commission felt that the French Government did not adequately substantiate the reasons based on the saturation of Orly airport. French Authorities did not produce specific elements that would show how Orly airport is truly more congested than CDG. On the contrary, they admit that during peak times both airports report difficulty with the traffic.

Having considered overriding reasons of general interest as theoretically appropriate to limit freedom of access to a specific airport, thus giving legitimacy to measures for traffic allocation by a State's Authorities, the Commission went on to apply the principle of proportionality from the specifically approved provision. Overriding requirements of this kind must result into measures that respect the principle of proportionality. The Commission deemed that this case does not meet said condition. Within this evaluation, as expected, the Commission felt that the measures taken by the French Government were radical and excessive in relation to *Orly'*s saturation issue, which, in any case, had not been fully justified. Indeed the Commission found that the scope of the measures was disproportionate in relation to the objectives pursued by the French Authorities as presented in their relation: the short-term objective of limiting infrastructure saturation, and the long-term objective of promoting CDG airport as a large European hub, while developing Orly for its closeness to the Parisian agglomerate. The measure in question, actually, was quite radical and causes substantial restrictions to freedom of access to the market within the Community.

We must add that the French provision has also undermined the EU Community's introduction of cabotage operations. Consequently, even with the mitigating factor of cabotage opportunities offered at Orly to the advantage of Greek, Spanish and Portuguese carriers only, the restriction introduced by article 4 of the decree dated December 6, 1993 in France tended to nullify most of the effects of the introduction of cabotage, specifically wanted and approved by the European Council as of January 10, 1993.

It should be noted that, while evaluating the level of proportionality of the traffic allocation measures, usually the authority that takes the measure has the ability to prove that the objective could not be reached by any other mean that would be less invasive in terms of freedom to market access. Indeed, French authorities did not demonstrate nor even invoked the fact that the desired results could not be achieved through means that were less restrictive and less prejudicial to trade between member States.

On the contrary, the fact that the French Government had already adopted a policy for the development of *Orly*, was interpreted as indication of the fact that there was no need to limit traffic to that airport. It is clear that the French Authorities' intent, as in the case of the Italian Authorities with regards to Malpensa (see part 1), was to re-launch *Air France*, reserving for it a large quota of traffic. As we can see below, the European Commission thought that also in this case the French decree on traffic allotment constituted illegitimate restrictions to the freedom of access to market, because it was unjustified by the proportionality with the declared objectives of general interest (case 7) European Commission, 27 April 1994, Case VII/AMA/IV/93, TAT, in OJEU L127, 19 may 1994, p. 32):

(…)

With particular regard to the principle of non-discrimination, a distinction must be drawn between discrimination on grounds of the carrier's nationality and discrimination on grounds of the carrier's identity.

The prohibition of any form of discrimination based on the carrier's nationality, embodied in Regulation (EEC) No 2408/92, is laid down by Article 6 of the Treaty establishing the European Community. It has given rise to many decisions of the Court of Justice.

In adopting Regulation (EEC) No 2408/92, however, the Council considered that the absence of discrimination on grounds of the carrier's nationality was not sufficient, in view of the structure of air transport in the Community, to ensure the satisfactory working of the internal market in civil air transport and to ensure compliance with the principle of free access to the market laid down in Article 3 (1) of that Regulation. Consequently, it added the principle of non-discrimination on the basis of the air carrier's identity.

The Commission considers that the principle of non-discrimination on grounds of the air carrier's identity prevents a Member State, without objective grounds, from withholding from one or more carriers, whether already operating on a route or applying to do so, the traffic rights granted to a limited number of other carriers who are or can be precisely identified to operate the same service on comparable terms; or, conversely, from granting to one or more carriers traffic rights a limited number of other carriers who are or can be precisely identified to operate the same service on comparable terms. The limited number and identity of Community carriers who benefit from, or, conversely, are penalized by, the discriminatory measure may emerge directly from that measure or may be ascertained indirectly from the de facto circumstances.

These considerations should be taken into account in examining the measure by which the French authorities continue to refuse Community carriers in general, and in particular TAT, traffic rights on the Paris(Orly)-Marseille and Paris(Orly)-Toulouse routes.

First, it has to be said that this measure breaches the principle of non-discrimination on grounds of the carrier's identity as specified above. The French authorities have stated that the operation of scheduled services by Community airlines between Paris and Marseille and between Paris and Toulouse was fully authorized for flights from and to CDG airport in accordance with the provisions of Article 3 (1) of Regulation (EEC) No 2408/92. TAT does in fact operate scheduled services on the Paris(CDG)-Toulouse and Paris(CDG)-Marseille routes, as does Air Inter. However, the French authorities maintain an exclusive concession of Air Inter on the same routes to and from Orly airport under Article 5 of the same Regulation. In doing so they refuse to allow any Community airline other than Air Inter to serve Orly airport as part of its operation of scheduled air services between the Paris airport system and Toulouse or Marseille. This is clearly a case of discrimination to the advantage of Air Inter alone in the allocation of traffic between the airports within the Paris airport system.

Another question to be examined is whether France could legally derogate from the non-discrimination principle laid down by Article 8 (1) of Regulation (EEC) No 2408/92 by applying the provisions of Article 5 of the same Regulation. On this point, the Commission considers that the correct application of Article 5 of the Regulation could not possibly lead to discrimination on the grounds of the carrier's identity as prohibited by Article 8. As will be demonstrated below, maintaining the exclusive concession in question is in fact a roundabout means of allocating traffic within the Paris airport system through the incorrect application of Article 5 of Regulation (EEC) No 2408/92.

According to Article 5 of Regulation (EEC) No 2408/92: 'On domestic routes for which at the time of entry into force of this Regulation an exclusive concession has been granted by law or contract, and where other forms of transport cannot ensure an adequate and uninterrupted service, such a concession may continue until its expiry date or for three years, whichever comes first'.

In the Commission's opinion, by allowing certain scheduled routes that had previously been operated on an exclusive basis a period of grace in which to adjust to market forces, this Article is designed to ensure the survival of adequate transport services between two points (cities or regions) within the same Member State. The other forms of transport referred to in Article 5 therefore take into account all other facilities for transport between two cities, including intermodal means - that is, mainly transport by train or by bus. It may also include transport by plane in the case of indirect flights or where an alternative airport is available. Here it should be noted that in the wording of Article 5 the expression 'forms of transport' is used rather than 'modes of transport'. In other words, exclusive rights may only be maintained under Article 5 where there is no other way of travelling from one city to another by an adequate and uninterrupted means. In the case of an airport system serving a single town or region, therefore, exclusive rights to a route terminating in that airport system would only serve their purpose where such rights applied to all the airports in the system. They cannot therefore be maintained under Article 5 unless they expressly refer to an entire airport system and not just to a single airport.

In this particular case, moreover, the Agreement of 5 July 1985 by which the French State granted concessions to Air Inter on certain routes, including the two concerned here, itself defines these routes as point-to-point rather than airport-to-airport routes and includes no reference to the different airports of the Paris airport system.

By authorizing TAT to operate on the Paris-Marseille and Paris-Toulouse routes to and from CDG airport with effect from 1 March 1992 and, more recently, by raising no objection to other Community airlines' operating on the same routes, therefore, the French authorities have put an end to the exclusive rights that Air Inter might otherwise have enjoyed between Paris and Marseille or Toulouse. In effect, the measure used against TAT, based on Article 5 which does not apply in this case, appears to be simply a rule governing the allocation of traffic between Orly and CDG airports.

Furthermore, the Commission considers that Article 5 of Regulation (EEC) No 2408/92 is not applicable in this case since, on 1 January 1993 - the date of entry into force of the Regulation - Air Inter did not hold an exclusive concession for the Paris-Marseille and Paris-Toulouse routes from either airport in the Paris airport system. Firstly, in the case of the Paris-Marseille route, the abovementioned Agreement of 5 July 1985 gave express permission to UTA and Air Afrique to operate the selfsame route at the same time as Air Inter, thereby eliminating the exclusive nature of the concession held by that airline. Secondly, as regards the Paris-Toulouse route, and also by extension, Paris-Marseille, the consequence of the provisions of point 1.1.1 of the Agreement of 30 October 1990 referred to in section II, which makes no reference to airport allocations, is that Air Inter's exclusive concession to operate the route ended on 1 March 1992 at the latest.

In view of all the foregoing, the Commission considers that the French authorities have carried out the allocation of traffic rights in the Paris airport system in a discriminatory manner and have therefore infringed the provisions of Article 8 (1) of Regulation (EEC) No 2408/92 by misapplying Article 5 of the Regulation in question and that they have maintained an exclusive concession for Air Inter on the Paris-Marseille and Paris-Toulouse routes to and from Orly airport alone.

It should also be noted here that, even if the concept of 'route' in Article 5 were to be interpreted differently, the conclusion would be the same. Given that an exclusive concession could be properly defined within the meaning of Article 5 on the scheduled air services between Orly and Marseille or Toulouse - an approach rejected by the Commission - there are other forms of transport besides airlines which could ensure an adequate and uninterrupted service between Paris and Marseille and between Paris and Toulouse: the existing direct air services between Paris (CDG) and Marseille and between Paris (CDG) and Toulouse, each of which includes five daily return flights, fulfil the 'adequate and uninterrupted' criteria. This fact, which precludes the use of Article 5 in the case of departures or arrivals at Orly alone on the two routes concerned, also demonstrates that it is impossible to apply Article 5 in respect of these routes except to the entire Paris airport system.

It should finally be stressed that the effects of the discrimination at issue here are considerable. Orly airport is the travellers' choice and accounts for between 85 % and 90 % of all French domestic traffic to and from Paris. The split of domestic traffic between Orly and CDG has been stable for several years at approximately 85 % and 82 % in Orly's favour on the Paris-Marseille and Paris-Toulouse routes respectively. With a regular annual flow of some two million passengers each, these routes are amongst the busiest in the Community. It is also more expensive to operate them from CDG airport than from Orly, partly for geographical reasons.

To sum up, the Commission considers that the French authorities incorrectly applied Article 8 (1) of Regulation (EEC) No 2408/92 by refusing to allow Community carriers to exercise traffic rights on the Paris-Marseille and Paris-Toulouse routes to and from Orly airport. Consequently it must be decided, in accordance with Article 8 (3) of Regulation (EEC) No 2408/92, that the French authorities may not continue to apply the measure concerned for allocating traffic between Orly and CDG airports. This Decision is not, however, intended in principle to prevent the continuation of an exclusive concession for Air Inter on routes fulfilling the conditions laid down in Article 5, as these are made clear above. It is also important to reiterate that the provisions of Regulation (EEC) No 2408/92, and Article 4 on public service obligations in particular, are a way of ensuring continuity of services throughout the domestic route networks in the Member States, and of serving the objectives of regional development policy. However, since in the particular circumstances of this case this Decision may have major repercussions on the structure and organization of the routes in question, the Commission considers it advisable to allow a delay for adjustment, expiring on 27 October 1994.

5.7 Traffic Allocation of International Flights According to the Proportionality Principle

The TAT II case, also decided by the European Commission on April 27, 1994, involved denial by French Authorities to allow TAT Airways to operate transportation services between Paris *Orly* and London *Gatwick*. Upon specific request by the British company, the general director of the French Civil Aviation communicated to TAT European Airlines that their request could not be accepted because of provisions of article 8 of the Regulation (EEC) number 2408/92, which allows member States to regulate traffic allotment between airports within the same airport system, without discrimination based on the nationality or identification of the air carrier[14]. On the subject, the general director of civil aviation declared that, within the policy of traffic allotment between airports in the Paris area, scheduled international passenger services to most European Countries, and specifically to Great Britain, have been authorized exclusively from Charles de Gaulle airport.

Following extensive correspondence and discussions, the French Government decided to reserve international traffic for *Charles de Gaulle* airport by approving a decree by the ministry of Transportation, dated December 6, 1993. Articles 4 and 5 of said decree state:

Article 4 – International intra-Community air services will be offered from Charles de Gaulle airport.

Article 5 – Notwithstanding the provisions from article 4, the following air services may be offered from Orly airport: scheduled air services from or to Spain, Greece and Portugal, with a weekly frequency of three or more return flights for the duration of at least one

[14] This situation had some legal issues in common with the German market that can be analyzed in Malina R., *Competition in the German Airport Market: an empirical investigation*, in Forsyth P. - Gillen D. (ed.), *Airport competition: the European experience*, Burlington, 2010, p. 239 ff., while a complete analysis of European Countries can be seen in Marques R. - Brochado A., *Airport regulation in Europe: Is there need for a European Observatory?*, in *Transport Policy Journal*, 2004, p.163 ff. For a comparison with thee UK market, see Starkie D., *Reforming UK airport regulation*, in *Journal of Transport Economics and Policy*, 2001, p. 119 ff.

IATA season; non-scheduled international air services from or to intra-Community airports, operated by carriers whose main operational center is located at Orly airport, for seasonal flights for a duration of less than four months per year, or for a series of flights whose frequency will not exceed three return flights per week; scheduled international air services from or to intra-Community airports, operated by non-EU carriers, as per the applicable international agreements, under condition that this situation does not harm the trade with member States.

The European Commission censured this provision as well. Among the reasons presented by the European Commission, one that considerably stands out is the fact that national borders may not be used as a criterion for apportionment. The measure resulted to be neither objective nor constant in time. Indeed, It was based exclusively on the national borders of the member States, without properly established criteria to justify the choice of national borders.

Therefore, after having stated that denial of authorization to TAT was a discriminatory measure, the European Commission maintained that, even supposing that there was no discrimination, allocation measures could be regularly enforced only after a reasonable period of time between their publication and their entry into effect. Such period of time must be sufficient to allow companies to adapt to possible restrictions and avoid discriminatory effects due to the carrier nationality or identification.

Even in the case of TAT II the European Commission found that the requirement of proportionality was unsatisfied in relation to the objective of avoiding saturation at *Orly* airport (case 8) European Commission, 27 April 1994, Case VII/AMA/II/93, TAT II, in OJEU, L127, 19 may 1994, p. 22):

(…)

Firstly, Articles 3, 4 and 5 (first and second indents) of the abovementioned Decree of 6 December 1993 draw a distinction between air services to or from airports in metropolitan France and French overseas departments, which may be operated concurrently at Orly and CDG airports, on the one hand, and, on the other hand, intra-Community international air services other than scheduled air services to or from Spain, Greece and Portugal, which may only be operated at CDG airport. Article 4 lays down a general prohibition on the operation of intra-Community international air services at Orly airport. Article 5 of the Decree lays down three exceptions to this general prohibition, including scheduled air services to or from Spain, Greece and Portugal. Consequently, Community carriers may not perform consecutive cabotage services between Orly and the French provinces when they are an extension of or preliminary to services between Orly and Member States other than France, Portugal, Spain and Greece.

Orly against takes the bulk of traffic between Paris and the French provinces. In economic terms, too, extension of intra-Community services by consecutive-cabotage services within France provides Community carriers other than those established in France, and particularly those from northern Europe, with a favourite means of penetrating the French domestic market. This is particularly so where the cabotage service is an extension of or preliminary to a service from or to the State of registration of the carrier. The reason is, firstly, that operation of French domestic routes by consecutive-cabotage services implies little investment by these carriers, secondly, that the main French domestic routes serve destinations in the southern half of France from Orly. In these circumstances, the Decree in question must be regarded as introducing, in practice, discrimination against Community carriers other than those established in France, and, to a lesser extent, other than Greek, Portuguese and Spanish carriers as regards the operation of French domestic routes terminating at Paris.

Furthermore, Article 3 (2) of Regulation (EEC) No 2408/92 provides that cabotage within Member States may be restricted until 1 April 1997 to services which are an extension of a service originating in the State of registration of the carrier or preliminary to a service to that State. France has made use of this restriction. In conjunction with this, the Decree of 6 December 1993 has the result of restricting consecutive-cabotage services on French domestic routes to departures or arrivals at CDG airport only, except where these services are extensions of or preliminaries to a service from or to Spain, Greece or Portugal. Ultimately, only French, Greek, Spanish and Portuguese carriers are actually able, until 1 April 1997, to operate scheduled air services between Orly airport and airports in the French provinces.

It results from the foregoing that the abovementioned provisions of the Decree of 6 December 1993 disregard the principle of lack of discrimination based on the nationality of the air carrier laid down in Article 8 (1) of Regulation (EEC) No 2408/92.

Secondly, the measure is apparently neither objective nor consistent. It is, first of all, based solely on Member States' national frontiers and not based on duly established criteria which could warrant this choice of national frontiers as its basis. The reason: since 1 January 1993 national frontiers as such are no longer among the objective criteria for deciding the distribution of intra-Community traffic within an airport system, because Regulation (EEC) No 2408/92 aims specifically to establish an internal market as 'an area without internal frontiers'. Admittedly, the French authorities in their explanatory memorandum made the point, at least implicity, that the amount of transfer traffic was substantially greater on intra-Community international routes terminating at Paris than on French domestic routes serving Paris. The French authorities, however, have failed to provide data to justify this argument which, if soundly based for each route in isolation, could justify the choice of national frontiers as the criterion.

The allocation of most intra-Community international air services to CDG airport alone appears all the less objective because not only French domestic routes but also many extra-Community international services, including medium-haul services, are operated concurrently at Orly and CDG airports by French or by non-Community airlines. A total of 27 destinations outside the Community, seven of them medium-haul destinations, are served both from and to Orly and CDG airports.

Although routes between Paris and Mediterranean destinations are chiefly assigned to Orly, routes to and from Italy, for no apparent reason, may be served only at CDG.

In their explanatory memorandum of the Decree, the French authorities also state their intention of progressively opening up Orly to high-density intra-Community international routes. It emerges from Decision 93/347/EEC on the Viva Air case, however, that in the absence of clearly established, published rules, the only rule applicable up to 10 December 1993, the date on which the Decree of 6 December 1993 was published, was the rule of freedom of access pursuant to Article 3 (1) of Regulation (EEC) No 2408/92 and affecting both CDG and Orly airports. The principles of objectivity and consistency run counter to the French authorities' powers under Article 4 of the Decree of 6 December 1993 to suspend freedom of access to Orly airport in this way for a few months before progressively reintroducing it thereafter.

This applies particularly to the Paris (Orly)-London route, which is the subject of the complaint from TAT, for the authorization of which the French authorities intend to revise the Decree in question not later than 31 March 1994, as provided in

Article 7

of the Decree. It is important to point out in this connection that restrictions which would apply to operating licences on this route, even assuming them to be non-discriminatory, objective and consistent, would not in any event be legal until a reasonable period of time had elapsed between their date of publication and their date of entry into force. Such a period of time would be intended to enable airlines to adapt to any such restrictions, and thus avoid any risk of discriminatory effects depending on the nationality or identity of carriers.

X Furthermore, the Commission is of the opinion that the correctness of the restrictions imposed pursuant to Article 8 (1) of Regulation (EEC) No 2408/92 must also be examined on the basis of the principles governing the freedom to provide services as spelled out by decisions of the Court of Justice (3).

In its judgment on Parliament v. Council (4), the Court held that the obligations laid upon the Council by Article 75 (1) (a) and (b) of the Treaty included that of instituting freedom to provide services in the transport field and that the scope of that obligation was clearly defined by the Treaty itself, in Articles 59 and 60 in particular. Also according to the Court, the Council has no discretionary power on this point; since the desired outcome is laid down by Articles 59, 60, 61 and 75 (1) (a) and (b) in conjunction, only the detailed rules for bringing about this outcome may provide an occasion for the exercise of a degree of discretion.

In connection with air transport, the same line of argument must be followed. In providing for the Community to adopt measures with the aim of progressively establishing the internal market before 31 December 1992, Article 7a of the Treaty expressly cites Article 84. And Article 84 (2) makes a direct reference to the procedural provisions of Article 75. In air transport particularly, freedom to provide services within the Community was achieved, within the framework of the common transport policy, with the adoption of the third package, which has been in force since 1 January 1993. Regulation (EEC) No 2408/92 is entirely of a piece with the common transport policy and constitutes a measure fully harmonizing access for Community air carriers to intra-Community air routes. In adopting that Regulation, therefore, the Council determined, on the basis of Article 84 (2), the detailed rules for applying the principles laid down by Articles 59 and 62. As a result, on the subject of freedom of access to the market for Community air carriers, it is henceforth necessary to refer directly to those principles (5), on which the Commission recently issued an imperative communication (6).

Here, the Commission would point out that measures restricting the free movement of services include measures affecting the ability of the service-provider to provide the service and measures preventing potential customers from availing themselves of such services as they wish. Furthermore, the concept of a restriction on the free movement of services goes beyond the prohibition of discrimination. Even where they apply without distinction to national service-providers and those from other Member States, barriers to the freedom to provide services are unacceptable if they are not warranted for objective and overriding grounds in the common interest or if the same result can be obtained by means of less-binding rules (the proportionality principle).

It is apparent, firstly, that the distinction made by Articles 3, 4 and 5 of the Decree of 6 December 1993 is a measure restricting the freedom to provide scheduled air services between the Paris airport system and airports in Member States other than Spain, Greece and Portugal. If affects both the ability of carriers to provide those services at Orly and users wishing to travel within the Community from or to Orly airport. The restriction is an important one, moreover, because customers prefer to use Orly airport, which is closer to the city centre. With about 25 million passengers in 1992, substantially equal to CDG's traffic level, Orly is also among the world's 15 leading airports. Besides this, in the explanatory memorandum introducing the Decree in question, quoted in paragraph V, the French authorities make clear that Orly is both the 'gateway to Paris' and the 'hub of the domestic network'. The measure thus erects barriers to freedom of trade not only between Paris and most of the Member States, but also between those Member States and the French provinces via the Orly hub.

In view of the discrimination on the grounds of carriers' nationality considered in section IX, these obstacles are incompatible with the freedom to provide services. Even aside from this discrimination, however, the Commission is of the opinon that the other requirements set out in the decisions of the Court are not fulfilled in this case.

In their explanatory memorandum, cited in section V, the French authorities pointed to the need to take account of the present situation and of prior investment by the airlines as justification for the provisions of the Decree of 6 December 1993. In the competitive environment for intra-Community air transport prevailing since 1 January 1993, however, it is for the economic operators alone to decide the optimum allocation of their resources, according in particular to the needs and wishes of their customers. And the liberalization measures which entered into force on 1 January 1993 were preceded by several successive stages from 1987 onwards - including the first and second air-transport packages, when Member States had time to make the necessary adjustments.

The French authorities have also put forward the saturation of facilities, the importance of CDG airport as a hub for transfers (connecting flights), and the long-term objectives of their airport policy. The Commission does not dispute these general objectives, nor the right of the French authorities to operate an airport policy in order to fulfil them. Saturation of facilities, and the pursuit of an airport policy, may be regarded as general overriding requirements such as may warrant traffic allocation measures including, where necessary, a restriction of access to Orly airport. The French authorities, however, did not provide any specific evidence to show that Orly airport was much more congested than CDG. On the contrary, they acknowledge that congestion problems occur at peak hours at both airports. Furthermore, overriding requirements of this kind must be reflected in measures which abide by the principle of porportionality. The Commission does not consider it to be so in this case.

The scope of the measure exceeds what is necessary to attain the objectives put forward by the French authorities in their explanatory memorandum, namely to limit saturation of facilities in the short term and, in the longer term, to promote CDG as a great European transit forum whilst developing Orly as the close-in airport for the Paris conurbation. The restriction in question is indeed drastic and, as pointed out earlier, imposes an important restriction on freedom of access to the market within the Community. About 85 % of French domestic traffic originating or terminating at Paris is concentrated at Orly airport, compared with only 15 % at CDG. Thus, even allowing for the cabotage opportunities available at Orly to Spanish, Greek and Portuguese carriers (only), the restriction imposed by Article 4 of the Decree of 6 December 1993 nullifies, in France, much of the practical effect of the introduction of the cabotage expressly desired and decided upon by the Council from 1 January 1993 towards.

The French authorities have not established, nor even alleged, that the outcome which they seek cannot be obtained by less binding measures and ones less harmful to intra-Community trade. The stated intention of the French authorities of progressively opening up Orly airport to high-density intra-Community international services tends, indeed, to show the opposite. Here, the Commission must take into consideration the continuation of charter services at Orly airport under Article 5 of the Decree of 6 December 1993, or again the continuation at Orly of many extra-Community international services - intercontinental services in particular - operated by airlines from non-Community countries or even by Air France. The Commission would also point out that French domestic services may also be operated without restriction by Air Inter from or to Orly airport, which in any case is far from being permanently saturated.

Having regard to all of the foregoing, the Commission is of the opinion that the French authorities have misapplied Article 8 (1) of Regulation (EEC) No 2408/92 by assigning intra-Community international air services to CDG airport alone, by the Decree of 6 December 1993. Consequently, they were wrong in refusing and continuing to refuse Community carriers, in particular TAT, traffic rights on the Paris (Orly)-London route. It is therefore appropriate to decide, pursuant to Article 8 (3) of Regulation (EEC) No 2408/92 that the French authorities may not continue to apply this measure regarding traffic allocation between Orly and CDG airports, as far as the Paris-London route is concerned. This Decision, however, in no way calls into question the rights of the French authorities to pursue an active airport policy, provided that policy complies with the principles of Community law as set out above.

The abovementioned decisions make us reflect on some important issues for the purpose of this study. They are all inspired by a single logic, directed to ascertain that traffic rights allotment measures are not discriminatory, or, in case of discrimination, that they do not go beyond what deemed strictly necessary to pursue national transport planning (proportionality principle). From the examined rulings, we see that the discriminating measures adopted by the French Authorities did not meet the proportionality requirements, because for the air carriers it was not an equal condition to operate out of *Charles de Gaulle* rather than *Orly*. Inevitably, we have to consider the profit deriving from "collecting" transit passengers. In fact, being forced to operate in a "destination only" airport, would force carriers to loose the abovementioned profits. It is also clear that such loss would not come into being if adequate infrastructure had been in place between *Charles de Gaulle* and *Orly*, so that transit passengers arriving at *Charles de Gaulle* could reach *Orly* within a negligible amount of time, from the perspective of an entire international trip.

We can conclude that, in all cases examined above, the major difficulties in the interpretation of Regulation 2408/92 regarded the concept of interchangeability of airports, or rather the conditions that make a traffic allotment measure non-discriminatory.

But the member States' measures have to be analyzed also according to the State aids rules contained in article107 TFEU which allows public intervention in the companies only according to the private investor principle. In an important decision on the agreementbetween the Charleleroi airport and Ryanair[15], the Court of First Instance carried out specific reasoning (case 9) Court of First Instance 17 December 2008, Case T-196/04, Ryanair Ltd v Commission of the European Communities, in Rep., p. II-03643):

(...)

Preliminary Observations

36 For a measure to be classified as aid within the meaning of Article 87(1) EC, all the conditions set out in that provision must be fulfilled. First, there must be an intervention by the State or through State resources. Second, the intervention must be likely to affect trade between Member States. Third, it must confer an advantage on the recipient by favouring certain undertakings or the production of certain goods. Fourth, it must distort or threaten to distort competition (see Case T-34/02 *Le Levant 001 and Others* v *Commission* [2006] ECR II-267, paragraph 110 and case-law cited).

37 In the present case, it is clear that the only condition disputed by the applicant is whether there is an advantage.

38 In that regard, it is clear from the case-law that the expression 'aid', for the purposes of that provision, necessarily designates advantages granted directly or indirectly through State resources or constituting an additional charge for the State or for bodies designated or established by the State for that purpose (Joined Cases C-52/97 to C-54/97 *Viscido and Others* [1998] ECR I-2629, paragraph 13, and Case C-53/00 *Ferring* [2001] ECR I-9067, paragraph 16).

39 The Court of Justice has held, in particular, that in order to determine whether a State measure constitutes aid it is necessary to establish whether the recipient undertaking receives an economic advantage which it would not have obtained under normal market conditions (Case C-39/94 *SFEI and Others* [1996] ECR I-3547, paragraph 60, and Case C-342/96 *Spain* v *Commission* [1999] ECR I-2459, paragraph 41).

---

15 An analysis of the agreement of the Charleroi airport with Ryanaair and its implications concerning the state aids policy, see: Barbot C., *Low-cost airlines, secondary airports, and state aid: An economic assessment of the Ryanair–Charleroi Airport agreement*, in *Journal of Air Transport Management*, 2006, p. 197 ff. and De Beys J., *Aides d'État: annulation de la décision Ryanair par le Tribunal de première instance*, in *Journal des tribunaux / droit européen*, 2009, p.74 ff., Gunther J.P. - Tayar D. - Ababou D., *Affaire Ryanair: le TPICE censure la Commission dans son analyse du critère de l'investisseur privé, Revue Lamy de la Concurrence*, in *droit, économie, régulation*, p.43 ff., Tetzlaff T., *Transparency, Unbundling, and Goal-definition - Consequences of the Ryanair-decision for Airlines, Airports, and States*, in *Zeitschrift für Luft- und Weltraumrecht*, 2005 p.1 ff., Bruyninckx T.B., *Het arrest Ryanair: staatssteunverlenende overheden als "economische eenheid"*, in *Nederlands tijdschrift voor Europees recht*, 2009 p.172 ff., Rando, G., *Attività economica e principio dell'investitore privato: il Tribunale annulla la decisione della Commissione nel caso Ryanair-Charleroi*, in *Diritto pubblico comparato ed europeo*, 2009 p.900 ff. and García Heredia A., *Jurisprudencia del Tribunal de Justicia de las Comunidades Europeas*, in *Revista española de Derecho Financiero*, 2009 p.883 ff.

40 Finally, it must be noted that since aid, as defined in the Treaty, is a legal concept and must be interpreted on the basis of objective factors, the Community judicature must, as a general rule, having regard both to the specific features of the case before them and to the technical or complex nature of the Commission's assessments, carry out a comprehensive review as to whether a measure falls within the scope of Article 87(1) EC (Case C-83/98 P *France* v *Ladbroke Racing and Commission* [2000] ECR I-3271, paragraph 25, and Case T-98/00 *Linde* v *Commission* [2002] ECR II-3961, paragraph 40).

41 On the other hand, it must be remembered that the assessment by the Commission of whether an investment satisfies the private investor test involves a complex economic appraisal. When the Commission adopts a measure involving such an appraisal, it consequently enjoys a wide discretion and judicial review is limited to verifying whether the Commission complied with the relevant rules governing procedure and the statement of reasons, whether there was any error of law, whether the facts on which the contested finding was based have been accurately stated and whether there has been any manifest error of assessment of those facts or any misuse of powers. In particular, the Court is not entitled to substitute its own economic assessment for that of the author of the decision (see, to that effect, order in Case C-323/00 P *DSG* v *Commission* [2002] ECR I-3919, paragraph 43, and Case T-152/99 *HAMSA* v *Commission* [2002] ECR II-3049, paragraph 127 and case-law cited).

42 It is by reference to those principles that the arguments of the parties must be examined: first, whether the private investor principle applies to the measures adopted by the Walloon Region.

Whether the private investor principle applies to the measures adopted by the Walloon Region

43 The applicant essentially claims that BSCA and the Walloon Region were one single economic entity. Accordingly, the private investor principle should have been applied to them both together. According to the applicant, the agreements at issue were envisaged by the parties as one single package of financial measures. The Commission should have considered the related measures to be part of one single package when examining whether they constitute State aid.

44 The applicant further maintains that, if the reason for the dual approach adopted by the Commission was that the private investor principle could not be applied to the Walloon Region, the Commission was wrong to conclude, in order to exclude application of that principle, that the Walloon Region did not act in the present case as an economic operator but as a regulatory authority.

45 The Court will first examine whether the Walloon Region and BSCA ought to have been regarded as one single economic entity when the measures at issue were considered and, as necessary, examine whether, notwithstanding the interests of the Walloon Region and BSCA being identical, the Commission could correctly exclude application of the private investor principle to the advantages granted by the Walloon Region by taking the view that its action, in the present case, was within the ambit of its public authority powers.

The existence of a single legal entity: 'Walloon Region – BSCA'

(…)

53 As is clear from the file, BSCA is a public undertaking controlled by the Walloon Region. Its share capital largely consists of public capital. More specifically, and as identified by the Commission itself, at the material time the Walloon Region owned, directly or

indirectly, 96.28% of BSCA shares. On 2 November 2001, a contract was entered into by BSCA and Ryanair which imposed reciprocal obligations.

54 The Walloon Region is, for its part, the owner of the Charleroi airport infrastructure. On 6 November 2001 it entered into an agreement with Ryanair, whereby it undertook to grant to Ryanair, first, a reduction in landing charges and, second, an indemnity in the event of losses which that company might suffer following any change, as a result of legislation or regulation, in the airport charges or opening hours of Charleroi airport. It must be noted that, as the Commission moreover stated in paragraph 21 of the letter inviting interested parties to submit their comments on the measures at issue (see paragraph 11 above), that agreement solely contains undertakings given by the Walloon Region to Ryanair.

55 The Commission acknowledged, both in the decision to initiate the procedure and in the contested decision, the economic and legal links binding the Walloon Region to BSCA and in particular the fact that BSCA was an entity economically dependent on the Walloon Region.

56 The Commission stated, in paragraph 80 of the letter inviting interested parties to submit their comments on the measures at issue (see paragraph 11 above), in relation to whether the private investor principle was applicable to the present case, that 'the roles of the [Walloon] Region as a public authority and of BSCA as an airport management company had been greatly confused, which made the application of that principle very difficult'. The Commission also stated in paragraph 101 of that letter that 'the dominant influence of the Walloon Region on BSCA was visible first of all in the structure of the share capital' and that 'BSCA's form of organisation, according to its articles of association of June 2001, reserve[d] control of the company to category A shareholders, namely the [Walloon] Region and its specialised companies'. Lastly, the Commission stressed the fact that 'the Walloon Region's dominant influence on BSCA [was] undeniable when account is taken of how the public authorities have designed its overall environment since its creation in 1991'.

57 The conclusion that the Walloon Region and BSCA are closely linked is also clear in the contested decision. The Commission thus stated that the financial structure of BSCA was closely connected to that of the Walloon Region (see in particular recitals 161 to 166 and recital 237 of the contested decision), in particular as regards responsibility, under the concession, for the costs of fire and maintenance services (see recitals 208 to 216 of the contested decision). The Commission also observed, in the section dealing with whether in the present case there was a transfer of State resources, that 'BSCA [was] a public undertaking over which the Walloon Region exercise[d] both control and a dominant influence, and those measures [were] attributable to it' (see recital 246 of the contested decision).

58 Notwithstanding those various observations, the Commission considered the measures in question separately according to whether they had been granted by the Walloon Region or by BSCA.

59 It is however necessary, when applying the private investor test, to envisage the commercial transaction as a whole in order to determine whether the public entity and the entity which is controlled by it, taken together, have acted as rational operators in a market economy. The Commission must, when assessing the measures at issue, examine all the relevant features of the measures and their context (see, to that effect, Joined Cases T-228/99 and T-233/99 *Westdeutsche Landesbank Girozentrale and Land Nordrhein-Westfalen* v *Commission* [2003] ECR II-435, paragraph 270), including those relating to the situation of the authority or authorities responsible for granting the measures at issue.

60 Accordingly, contrary to what is stated by the Commission, the financial links binding the Walloon Region to BSCA are not irrelevant, since it cannot a priori be excluded that the Walloon Region not only took part in the activity carried out by BSCA (see, by analogy, Case C-222/04 *Cassa di Risparmio di Firenze and Others* [2006] ECR I-289, paragraph 112), but also obtained financial consideration for granting the measures at issue.

61 In the present case, it must therefore be concluded that the Walloon Region and BSCA ought to have been regarded as one single entity for the purposes of application of the private investor principle. There remains the question whether the Commission was correct to refuse to apply the private investor principle to the measures adopted by the Walloon Region because of the role specifically played by the region, namely its alleged regulatory role.

Treatment of the Walloon Region as a legislative or regulatory authority and non-application of the private investor principle to the measures adopted by it

(...)

81 The agreement entered into by the Walloon Region and Ryanair provides for, first, a discount on landing charges and, second, an indemnity in the event of any change in the airport opening hours or the level of airport 'taxes'.

82 The Commission states in recital 160 of the contested decision the following:

'The Commission ... concludes that the principle of private investor in a market economy is not applicable to the action of the Walloon Region, and that the reduction in airport charges and the compensation guarantee constitute an advantage within the meaning of Article 87(1) [EC]. These advantages allow Ryanair to reduce its operating costs.'

83 In reaching that conclusion, the Commission took account of the following factors:
- the fixing of airport taxes falls within the legislative and regulatory competence of the Walloon Region (recital 144 of the contested decision);
- by fixing the level of airport taxes payable by users for the use of the Walloon airports, the Walloon Region was regulating an economic activity, but was not acting as a company (recitals 145 and 158 of the contested decision);
- the 'airport charges' fixed by the Walloon Region allowed the financing of a specified transfer of resources: 65% was allotted to the airport concession holder (BSCA) and 35% to an environment fund (recitals 146 to 150 of the contested decision);
- the Walloon Region infringed the relevant national regulations by granting a reduction to Ryanair by means of a contract under private law and thereby placed itself in a situation of 'confusion of powers' (recitals 151 to 153 of the contested decision);
- the applicant's assertion that the contested decision amounts to discrimination between 'private airports' and 'public airports' is unfounded, in light of the various methods of fixing charges in Europe (recitals 154 to 159 of the contested decision).

84 Before examining the merits of those grounds, the Court notes that, for the purposes of determining whether a measure of State aid constitutes an advantage within the meaning of Article 87(1) EC, a distinction must be drawn between the obligations which the State must assume as an undertaking exercising an economic activity and its obligations as a public authority (see, to that effect, as regards the distinction which must be made between the situation where the authority granting the aid acts as a shareholder in a company and the situation in which it acts as a public authority, Joined Cases C-278/92 to C-280/92 *Spain* v

Commission [1994] ECR I-4103, paragraph 22, and Case C-334/99 *Germany* v *Commission* [2003] ECR I-1139, paragraph 134).

85 While it is clearly necessary, when the State acts as an undertaking operating as a private investor, to analyse its conduct by reference to the private investor principle, application of that principle must be excluded in the event that the State acts as a public authority. In the latter event, the conduct of the State can never be compared to that of an operator or private investor in a market economy.

86 The Court must therefore determine whether or not the activities concerned in the present case are economic activities.

87 It is clear from the case-law that any activity consisting in offering goods and services on a given market is an economic activity (Case 118/85 *Commission* v *Italy* [1987] ECR 2599, paragraph 7, and *Aéroports de Paris* v *Commission*, paragraph 66 above, paragraph 107).

88 Contrary to what is stated by the Commission in recital 145 of the contested decision, it must be held that the actions of the Walloon Region were economic activities. The fixing of the amount of landing charges and the accompanying indemnity is an activity directly connected with the management of airport infrastructure, which is an economic activity (see, to that effect, *Aéroports de Paris* v *Commission*, paragraph 66 supra, paragraphs 107 to 109, 121, 122 and 125).

89 On that point, the airport charges fixed by the Walloon Region must be regarded as remuneration for the provision of services within Charleroi airport, notwithstanding the fact, mentioned by the Commission in recital 147 of the contested decision, that a clear and direct link between the level of charges and the service rendered to users is weak.

90 Unlike the situation in *Freskot*, paragraph 63 above, the airport charges must be regarded as the consideration obtained for services rendered by the airport owner or concession holder. The Commission itself admits, in recitals 147 to 149 of the contested decision, that, both in the present case and in its practice in previous decisions, it was appropriate to regard those charges as 'fees' and not as 'taxes'

91 Accordingly, the provision of airport facilities by a public authority to airlines, and the management of those facilities, in return for payment of a fee the amount of which is freely fixed by that authority, can be described as economic activities, although such activities are carried out in the public sector, they cannot, for that reason alone, be categorised as the exercise of public authority powers. Those activities are not, by reason of their nature, their purpose or the rules to which they are subject, connected with the exercise of powers which are typically those of a public authority (see, a contrario, Case C-364/92 *SAT Fluggesellschaft* [1994] ECR I-43, paragraph 30).

92 The fact that the Walloon Region is a public authority and that it is the owner of airport facilities in public ownership does not therefore in itself mean that it cannot, in the present case, be regarded as an entity exercising an economic activity (see, to that effect, *Aéroports de Paris* v *Commission*, paragraph 66 supra, paragraph 109).

93 In that regard, the Commission acknowledged, at the hearing, that the owner of a public airport may act both as a regulator and as a private investor. In addition, the Commission stated that if BSCA had not acted as an intermediary between the Walloon Region, as owner of Charleroi airport, and Ryanair, as a customer of that airport, it would have been possible to regard the Walloon Region as a private investor in a market economy. The

Commission however maintains that in the present case the Walloon Region acted only as a regulatory authority in using its regulatory and fiscal powers. The Commission points out, inter alia, that at the material time the powers of the Walloon Region in relation to setting airport charges, including aircraft landing charges, others being irrelevant to the present case, were laid down by the decree of the Walloon Government of 16 July 1998 on the fixing of fees to be levied for the use of airports in the Walloon Region (*Moniteur belge* of 15 September 1998, p. 29 491), as amended by a decree of the Walloon Government of 22 March 2001 (*Moniteur belge* of 10 April 2001, p. 11 845). Under Article 8 of that decree, a consultative committee of users, composed of a representative of the ministry responsible for transport, two representatives of the airport concession holder, a representative of the Transport Directorate General within the Ministry of Infrastructure and Transport and a representative of the airport users, was required to give an opinion on proposed changes to the system of fees. The Commission submits that those factors indicated the exercise of the powers of a public authority.

94 The Court considers, however, that that argument cannot be accepted, since it does not affect the fact that the activity concerned in the present case, namely the setting of airport charges, is closely connected with the use and operation of Charleroi airport, which must be described as an economic activity.

95 In that regard, the Commission stated, in recital 156 of the contested decision, the following:

'An airport always fulfils a public function, which explains its general submission to certain types of regulation, even if it belongs to and/or is managed by a private company. Private airport managers can be subject to this regulation and their fee-fixing powers are often contained within the framework of national regulators' instructions because of their monopolistic position. The airports' position of strength in relation to their users can thus be controlled by the national regulators who fix fee levels that must not be exceeded ("price caps"). Asserting that a private airport is free to fix its fees without being subject to certain forms of regulation is in any case inaccurate.'

96 Accordingly, the Commission itself, while refusing to apply the private investor principle to the measures adopted by the Walloon Region because of the regulatory nature of the powers available to it, pointed out that an airport was generally subject to some form of regulation, and moreover 'even if it belongs to and/or is managed by a private company'. Consequently, the argument that there are various methods of setting airport charges is not, by itself, capable of excluding application of the private investor principle to the advantages granted by the Walloon Region.

97 Nor, moreover, can the Court accept the argument that the Walloon Region infringed the relevant national regulations in granting a discount to Ryanair by means of a contract under private law, and thus placed itself in a situation of 'confusion of powers' (recitals 151 to 153 of the contested decision).

98 When examining the measures at issue, the Commission should have differentiated between the economic activities and those activities which fell strictly under public authority powers. In addition, whether the conduct of an authority granting aid complies with national law is not a factor which should be taken into account in order to decide whether that authority acted in accordance with the private investor principle or granted an economic advantage in contravention of Article 87(1) EC. It does not follow from the fact that an activity represents in legal terms an exemption from a tariff scale laid down in a regulation that that activity must be described as non-economic.

99 The Commission's approach in the contested decision finds no support in its guidelines on the application of Articles 87 EC and 88 EC and Article 61 of the EEA agreement to State aid in the aviation sector. Those guidelines do no more than provide that 'the construction of infrastructure projects represents a general measure of economic policy which cannot be controlled by the Commission under the Treaty rules on State aid' while stating that 'the Commission may evaluate activities carried out inside airports which could directly or indirectly benefit airlines'. Far from supporting the Commission's position, those guidelines note that the operation of airports, and the setting of associated charges, even by public bodies, constitutes an economic activity for the purposes of the application of competition law.

100 In addition, the Commission itself, by stating that 'the Walloon Region could ... have decided that the onus was on BSCA to fix a fee in exchange for services rendered to users, provided certain principles and conditions were complied with' (see recital 157 of the contested decision), or by admitting that a system of promotional reductions in airport charges was not in itself contrary to Community law (recital 159 of the contested decision), recognises that the granting of a reduction in airport charges and an indemnity of the kind at issue in this case cannot be connected with public authority powers.

101 The mere fact that, in the present case, the Walloon Region has regulatory powers in relation to fixing airport charges does not mean that a scheme reducing those charges ought not to be examined by reference to the private investor principle, since such a scheme could have been put in place by a private operator.

102 In light of all of the foregoing, it must be concluded that the Commission's refusal to examine together the advantages granted by the Walloon Region and by BSCA and to apply the private investor principle to the measures adopted by the Walloon Region in spite of the economic links binding those two entities is vitiated by an error in law.

103 Since the examination together of the measures at issue required the application of the private investor principle, not only to the measures adopted by BSCA but also to the measures adopted by the Walloon Region, it is unnecessary to consider the last part of the plea in law, namely that there was an incorrect application of the private investor principle to BSCA. It cannot be excluded that the application of that principle to the single body made up of the Walloon Region and BSCA might have led to a different conclusion.

104 The Commission's argument that a re-assessment of all of the measures at issue by reference to the private investor principle would have led to a conclusion even more unfavourable to the applicant cannot be accepted. As the applicant stated, separate examination of the measures at issue, according to whether they were granted by the Walloon Region or by BSCA, substantially affected the Commission's analysis in so far as the Commission was able to classify as State aid the measures adopted by the Walloon Region without recourse to the private investor principle. It is clear from the case-law cited in paragraph 41 above that application of the private investor principle to the overall transaction involves a complex economic examination and assessment which it is not for the Court to carry out. In that regard, it must be remembered that, in an action for annulment, the Court adjudicates on the legality of the assessments made by the Commission in the contested decision. It is not for the Court, in such an action, to reassess the wisdom of the investment and to rule on whether a private investor would have made the proposed investment at the time when the contested decision was adopted (see, to that effect, Case T-296/97 *Alitalia* v *Commission* [2000] ECR II-3871, paragraph 170 and case-law cited).

105 Consequently, in light of the Commission's error of law, the claims of the applicant must be upheld and the contested decision must be annulled; there is no need to examine the arguments in support of the first plea in law.

5.8 Modifications Brought About by Regulation Number 1008/2008

The recent approval of Regulation (EC) number 1008/2008 specifies the scope of application of the notion of "airport system".

The matter is covered by article 19 of the Regulation. The first thing we can notice is the elimination of the term "airport system". However, after a more in depth analysis, we can see that, even though "airport systems" no longer formally exist, they are still present as a concept in the wording of the provision. Moreover, we can see that the concept is specified and modified with the clear purpose of dispelling the interpretation doubts that were so powerfully introduced in the leading cases examined above.

Regarding any justification for regulatory intervention, on the basis of the principle of subsidiarity, the Regulation states that a more uniform application of EU Law in the matter of aviation internal market may not be adequately reached by individual member States, due to the international nature of air transportation. This goal can more easily be reached at the Community level. Regarding airport systems, at point 23, it is stated that, *"it is appropriate to clarify and simplify the current rules regarding traffic distribution between airports that cater to the same city or conurbation"*. It then examines the particularly confusing situation deriving from the application of article 8 of Regulation (EEC) 2408/92, that never supplied clear and certain parameters to identify an "airport system", to justify the traffic allotment measures adopted by member States.

We must first note that member States maintain the right to distribute air traffic between airports at their own discretion, within certain, well-defined limits. In fact, *"one member State, after consultation with all parties involved (including air carriers and airports), without any discrimination towards Community destinations, or on the basis of nationality or identification of the carrier, may regulate air traffic distribution between airports that meet"* some specific conditions regarding connections between the airports involved. The article also lists the conditions for allowing States to distribute air traffic between airports that: *"a) serve the same city or conurbation; b) are served by adequate transportation infrastructure for, possibly, direct connection, allowing passengers to reach the other airport in less than ninety minutes, even across borders; c) are connected to each other and to the city or conurbation they serve by frequent, reliable and efficient public transportation; d) offer the necessary services to air carriers without prejudice to commercial opportunities"*.

Even at a first look we can detect the higher precision of terms used in defining the elements that make up the notion of "airport system". Also, the objective conditions that must be met to justify a State's intervention in the distribution of air traffic are consolidated in specific norms.

On the other hand, Regulation (EEC) number 2408/92 simply sanctioned *"the right of member States to regulate, without discrimination based on the nationality or identification of the air carrier, traffic allocation between airports belonging to the same airport system"*, where *"airports are grouped as airports serving the same city or conurbation."* This latter concept was further specified and interpreted by the European Commission and by the European Court of Justice. These two entities eventually developed a notion of "airport system" based on the actual interchangeability of the airports that serve the same urban conglomerate. Interchangeability must be evaluated on the basis of the difference it makes to the passengers reaching one airport rather than the other; in other words, we must consider the efficiency of the ground infrastructure that connects the airports involved.

All this was transposed into a new regulation that goes even further, stating that all airports involved must be reachable within a maximum of ninety minutes and must be connected to one another and to the city or urban conglomerate they serve through frequent, reliable and efficient public transportation.

Basically, we see innovation in the provision for a defined time frame for connection between the airports. Even though this parameter may appear too restrictive, we must consider that, after the introduction of high-speed rails, a ninety-minute connection time has become a reasonable expectation in the case, for example, of airports in Northern Italy. In the *Malpensa* case, the airports involved, Malpensa, Linate, Orio al Serio, were poorly connected. However, with increased infrastructure efficiency, it is now possible to reach any of the three airports from the Milan urban conglomerate within ninety minutes. The same would apply to the airports serving the Paris urban conglomerate.

Substantially, the new Regulation, without mentioning airport systems, confirms the importance of such concept, bringing to the legislative level the interpretations given by the European Commission and the European Court of Justice.

In fact, article 19 specifies that, *"Every regulatory decision for air traffic allotment between the involved airports will respect proportionality principles and will be based on objective criteria"*. In fact, we already saw how the European Commission based its examination of traffic allotment measures on the respect of proportionality and transparency principles, with the expressed purpose of avoiding discrimination towards air carriers. Even this aspect, that was clearly inferable from the norms of the treaty, has been specifically defined with reference to the distribution of traffic rights. All this offers effective evaluation parameters to the European Commission.

One last thought must be given to the changes made to the evaluation procedure to establish the legitimacy of traffic allotment measures taken by member States. Regulation number 2408/92 gave a time frame of one month to update the list of airport systems, as per attachment II of the same Regulation. Now, the term has been increased to six months, giving the European Commission time to decide whether the traffic allocation measures meet the conditions required by article 19, or not.

While member States can now count on a clearer and more predictable body of norms, the new procedure presents some aspects that are not too favorable to the member States. The six-month term may prolong approval times, becoming a deterrent for potential new air traffic distribution measures by member States. There is no longer a provision for deferment of a question to the European Council, while, in the past, the Council, in the case of exceptional circumstances, had the power to decide differently from the European Commission.

We can say that the scope of the innovation brought about by Regulation (EC) number 1008/2008 is due to the increased level of clarity and predictability of the body of norms. However, the new regulation has also limited the remediation and dialogue instruments that were available under the previous regulation.

This consideration should not make us judge the new regulations as a negative development. In fact, putting aside actual evaluation for future procedure, the clarity of the body of norms can potentially create a different legal environment that progressively streamlines procedures, and may justify the lower degree of protection given to the member States.

Bibliography

Barbot C., *Low-cost airlines, secondary airports, and state aid: An economic assessment of the Ryanair–Charleroi Airport agreement*, in *Journal of Air Transport Management*, 2006, p. 197 ff.

Bhadra, D. - Texter, P., *Airline networks: an econometric framework to analyze domestic U.S. air travel*, in *Journal of Transportation and Statistics,* 2004, p. 87 ff.

Baldwin R. - Cave, *Understanding regulation: Theory, strategy and practice*, Oxford, 1999.

Bain J.S., *Barriers to new competition.* Cambridge, 1956.

Barrett S., *Airport competition in the deregulated European aviation market*, in *Journal of Air Transport Management*, 2000, p. 13 ff.

Barrett S., *How do the demands for airport services differ between full-service Carrier and low-cost carriers?*, in *Journal of Air Transport Management*, 2004, p. 33 ff.

Borenstein S., *Airline merger, airport dominance and market power*, in *American Economic Review, Papers and Proceedings,* 1990, p. 400 ff.

Bruyninckx T.B., *Het arrest Ryanair: staatssteunverlenende overheden als "economische eenheid"*, in *Nederlands tijdschrift voor Europees recht*, 2009 p.172 ff.

Carbone S.M. – Munari F., *L'attuazione nell'ordinamento comunitario della direttiva sul libero accesso al mercato dei servizi aeroportuali*, in *Dir. Comm. Int.*, 2000, p. 95 ff.

Charlton A. *Airport regulation: Does a mature industry have mature regulation?*, in *Journal of Air Transport Management*, 2009, p. 116 ff.

De Beys J., *Aides d'État: annulation de la décision Ryanair par le Tribunal de première instance*, in *Journal des tribunaux / droit européen*, 2009, p.74 ff.

Dennis N.P.S., *Competition between hub airports in Europe*, paper presented at the 8th World Conference on Transport Research, 12–27 July, Antwerp, 1998.

Forsyth P., *Locational and monopoly rents at airports: creating them and shifting them*, in *Journal of Air Transport Management*, 2004, p. 51 ff.

Forsyth P., *Airport competition: A perspective and synthesis*, in Forsyth P. - Gillen D. (ed.), *Airport competition: the European experience*. Burlington, 2010.

Forsyth P., 2006. *Airport Competition: Regulatory Issues and Policy Implications*, in Lee D. (ed), *Advances in Airline Economics, Vol 1 Competition Policy and Antitrust*, Amsterdam, 2006, p. 343 ff.

Francis G. – Humprheys I. – Ison S., *Airports' perspectives on the growth of low-cost airlines and the remodeling of the airport-airline relationship*, in *Tourism Management*, 2004, p. 507 ff.

Franke M., 2004: Competition between network carriers and low-cost carriers – retreat battle or breakthrough to a new level of efficiency?, in *AirTransport Management,* 2004, p. 15 ff.

Frenke K. - Van Terwisgam S. -Verburg T. - Burghouwt G., *Airline competition at European airports*, in *Tijdschrift voor Economische en Sociale Geografie,* 2004, p. 233 ff.

García Heredia A., *Jurisprudencia del Tribunal de Justicia de las Comunidades Europeas*, in *Revista española de Derecho Financiero*, 2009 p. 883 ff.

Graham, A., *Managing Airports – an international perspective*, Amsterdam, 2005.

Gunther J.P. - Tayar D. - Ababou D., *Affaire Ryanair: le TPICE censure la Commission dans son analyse du critère de l'investisseur privé, Revue Lamy de la Concurrence*, in *droit, économie, régulation*, p. 43 ff.

Kunz, M., *Airport regulation: The policy framework*, in Pfähler, W. - Niemeier H.M.- Mayer O. (ed.), *Airports and air traffic – regulation, privatisation and competition*, Frankfurt, 1999.

Malina R., *Competition in the German Airport Market: an empirical investigation*, in Forsyth P. - Gillen D. (ed.), *Airport competition: the European experience*, Burlington, 2010, p. 239 ff.

Marques R. - Brochado A., *Airport regulation in Europe: Is there need for a European Observatory?*, in *Transport Policy Journal*, 2004, p. 163 ff.

Masutti A., *I requisiti per l'accesso al mercato dei servizi aeroportuali: regolazione del mercato e competenze valutative*, in *Dir. trasp.*, 2002, p. 91 ff.

Munari F., *La liberalizzazione del trasporto aereo nell'Unione europea tra lotta alle discriminazioni e compressione delle competenze statali*, in *Dir. Un. Eur.*, 1999, p. 207 ff.

Müller-Rostin C., *Airport Entry and Exit: An European Analysis*, in Forsyth P. - Gillen D. (ed.), *Airport competition: the European experience*, Burlington, 2010, p. 31 ff.

Nascimbene, *Concorrenza e libera prestazione dei servizi nella regolamentazione dei sistemi aeroportuali e della ripartizione di traffico,* in *Giur. comm.*, 2003, p. 197 ff.

Niemeier, H., *Regulation of Airports: The Case of Hamburg Airport – a View from the Perspective of Regional policy*, in *Journal of Air Transport Management*, 2002, p. 37 ff.

Oum T.H. - Fu X., *Impacts of Airports on Airline Competition: Focus on Airport Performance and Airport-Airline Vertical Relations, ITF Round Tables. International Transport Forum*, 2009, p. 31 ff.

Rando, G., *Attività economica e principio dell'investitore privato: il Tribunale annulla la decisione della Commissione nel caso Ryanair-Charleroi*, in *Diritto pubblico comparato ed europeo*, 2009 p. 900 ff.

Starkie D., *The airport industry in a competitive environment: A United Kingdom perspective*, in *Joint Transport Research Centre, International Transport Forum*, OECD, 2008.

Starkie D., *Reforming UK airport regulation*, in *Journal of Transport Economics and Policy*, 2001, p. 119 ff.

Tetzlaff T., *Transparency, Unbundling, and Goal-definition - Consequences of the Ryanair-decision for Airlines, Airports, and States*, in *Zeitschrift für Luft- und Weltraumrecht*, 2005 p.1 ff.

Tuo C., *Il trasporto aereo nell'Unione Europea tra diritti fondamentali e relazioni esterne,* Torino, 2008.

Valente, *Il caso «Malpensa» dinanzi alla Corte di giustizia delle Comunità europee,* in *Giust. civ.* 2001, p. 2013 ff.

MIX
Papier aus verantwortungsvollen Quellen
Paper from responsible sources
FSC® C105338
FSC
www.fsc.org

If you have any concerns about our products,
you can contact us on
ProductSafety@springernature.com

In case Publisher is established outside the EU,
the EU authorized representative is:
Springer Nature Customer Service Center GmbH
Europaplatz 3, 69115 Heidelberg, Germany

Printed by Libri Plureos GmbH
in Hamburg, Germany